Developing Professional Practice 7–14

Developing Professional Practice series

The *Developing Professional Practice* series provides a thoroughly comprehensive and cutting edge guide to developing the necessary knowledge, skills and understanding for working within the 0–7, 7–14 or 14–19 age ranges. Each of the three titles offers a genuinely accessible and engaging introduction to supporting the education of babies to young adults. Discussion of current developments in theory, policy and research is combined with guidance on the practicalities of working with each age group. Numerous examples of real practice are included throughout each text.

The *Developing Professional Practice* titles each provide a complete resource for developing professional understanding and practice that will be invaluable for all those involved with the education of children from birth to 19 years.

Titles in the series:

Blandford and Knowles, *Developing Professional Practice 0–7*

Wilson and Kendall-Seatter, *Developing Professional Practice 7–14*

Armitage, Donovan, Flanagan and Poma, *Developing Professional Practice 14–19*

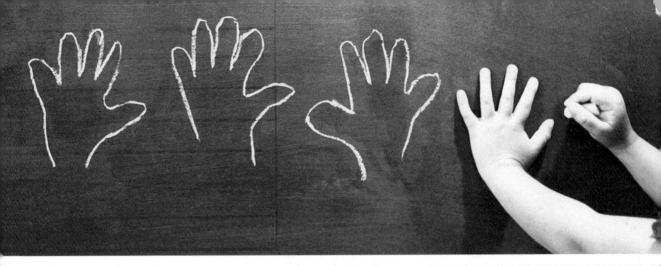

Developing
Professional
Practice 7–14

Viv Wilson and Sue Kendall-Seatter
Canterbury Christ Church University

Longman
is an imprint of

PEARSON

Harlow, England · London · New York · Boston · San Francisco · Toronto · Sydney · Singapore · Hong Kong
Tokyo · Seoul · Taipei · New Delhi · Cape Town · Madrid · Mexico City · Amsterdam · Munich · Paris · Milan

Pearson Education Limited
Edinburgh Gate
Harlow
Essex CM20 2JE
England

and Associated Companies throughout the world

Visit us on the World Wide Web at:
www.pearsoned.co.uk

First published 2010

ISBN: 978-1-4058-4115-3

British Library Cataloguing-in-Publication Data
A catalogue record for this book is available from the British Library

Library of Congress Cataloging-in-Publication Data
Wilson, Viv.
  Developing professional practice, 7–14 / Viv Wilson and Sue Kendall-Seatter.
    p. cm. – (Developing professional practice series)
  ISBN 978-1-4058-4115-3 (pbk.)
  1. Teachers–Training of–Great Britain. 2. Teachers–Professional relationships–
Great Britain. 3. Effective teaching–Great Britain. I. Kendall-Seatter, Sue. II. Title.
  LB1725.G6W55 2010
  370.71'55–dc22
                                                                        2010013480

10 9 8 7 6 5 4 3 2 1
14 13 12 11 10

Typeset in 9.75/12pt Giovanni Book by 35
Printed by Ashford Colour Press Ltd., Gosport

Brief Contents

Contents

Part 3 – Enhancing Teaching for Learning

Supporting resources

Visit **www.pearsoned.co.uk/7-14** to find valuable online resources

Companion Website for students

- Interactive chapter tutorials
- Podcast interviews with students and practitioners
- Self-study questions to test and extend your knowledge
- Extra case studies
- Online glossary defining key terms

For instructors

- Downloadable PowerPoint slides for use in presentations

Also: The Companion Website provides the following features:

- Search tool to help locate specific items of content
- E-mail results and profile tools to send results of quizzes to instructors
- Online help and support to assist with website usage and troubleshooting

For more information please contact your local Pearson Education sales representative or visit **www.pearsoned.co.uk/7-14**

Guided Tour

Each chapter begins with a list of **Learning objectives**, providing a quick overview of what will be covered and clearly setting out the key learning goals.

Case Study boxes present vignettes that give an insight into real practice. The short questions posed in the **Thinking it Through** boxes provide regular opportunities to stop and reflect on what you've learnt.

Research briefings explore classic and contemporary research studies, and examine their applications in the classroom.

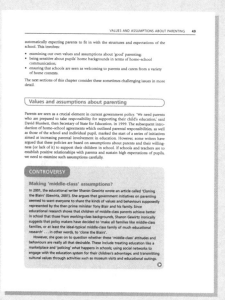

Controversy boxes tackle the more divisive topics, encouraging you to examine both sides of the argument and helping you to form your own point of view.

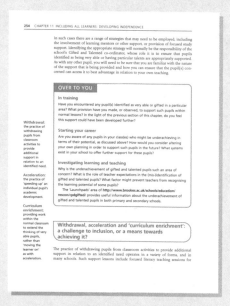

The **Over to you** feature includes questions and activities that encourage you to interrogate core issues, and reflect on their influence on your attitudes and your practice. Throughout the book you'll find clear, concise definitions of the relevant **Key terms** in the margin.

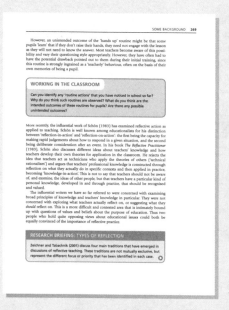

The **Working in the Classroom** feature helps you to make direct connections between the chapter content and your own classroom experience.

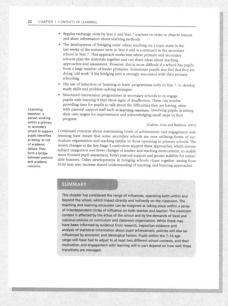

End of chapter **Summary** boxes pull together the key topics covered in the chapter, to help consolidate your understanding.

Guided Tour continued

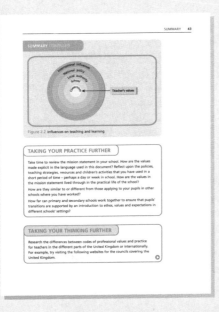

The **Taking your thinking further** and **Taking your practice further** boxes provide a starting point for exploring the themes of the chapter in more depth, both in your reading and research, and in your practice.

The **Find out more** feature directs you to related additional reading, useful websites and Teachers' TV programmes. At the end of each chapter a **Glossary** is provided with clear definitions of all the key terms introduced in the chapter.

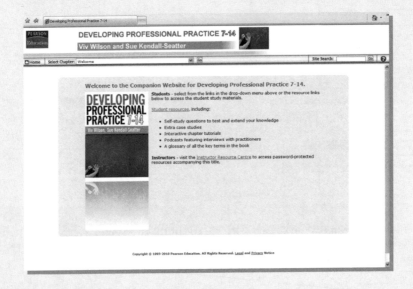

> Learning does not consist only of knowing what we must or we can do, but also of knowing what we could do and perhaps should not do.
>
> (Umberto Eco: *In the Name of the Rose*)

What kind of a teacher do you intend to be?

Will you be someone who only does what they *must* do?

Will you be someone who settles for what they *can* do?

Or will you be someone who wants to know what they *could* do – and someone who recognises what they should *not* do?

If you answered yes to the last question, then we hope that *Developing Professional Practice 7–14* will help you to become the kind of teacher you want to be.

We believe that pupils learn best with teachers who never stop learning themselves. This book is intended to stimulate you to develop your practice through trying out ideas in your classroom, asking yourself questions about teaching and learning and finding out more about how to answer them.

The purpose of this book

This book is part of a series aimed at developing professional understanding and practice for all those involved with the education of children from birth to 19 years. In addition to offering support to trainee teachers, this book aims to engage teachers working with pupils between the ages of 7 and 14 in reflecting upon and examining their practice in the early stages of their career. The current *Professional Standards for Teachers*, including the *Standards for the Award of Qualified Teacher Status* (TDA, 2007), establish a clear expectation that teachers should engage in personal professional development, involving reflecting on and improving their practice, identifying areas for further professional development and maintaining a constructively critical approach towards innovation (Q7 and Q8, C7 and C8, TDA, 2007). Although these Standards apply only to teachers in England, similar expectations are common to all four countries of the UK. This book supports this process through the use of features such as case studies, research summaries and questions to support reflection and further development. A companion website will provide further links and supporting materials.

Additionally, recent developments in postgraduate Initial Teacher Training in England have introduced opportunities for trainee teachers to gain Master's degree credits as part of their initial training, and the Children's Plan (DCSF, 2007) outlines the present government's intention to make teaching in England a Master's level profession (ibid., para 4.24, p. 91). Where appropriate, links are made to current research articles and material that could support Master's level work.

Why 7–14?

The *Developing Professional Practice* series has been designed to focus on three significant phases of the education of children and young people, in line with developing policy and practice in schools: 0–7, 7–14 and 14–19. Just as children's educational experiences in the early years lay the foundations for their future engagement with learning, the 'middle years' of schooling need to sustain this engagement through a period of personal and educational transition. Although a pattern of transfer to secondary education at the age of 11 is widely established throughout the UK, the need for both primary and secondary teachers to have a broader understanding of pupils' learning and development is vital in order to support learners as individuals.

A number of current developments support the need to move away from a separation of primary- and secondary-focused knowledge and expertise. Many more pupils now enter adolescence while in primary school than was the case even 20 years ago, with consequent effects on academic, social and emotional learning. Recognition of the 'dip' in pupils' achievement and engagement on moving from primary to secondary schooling has led to a number of initiatives aimed at easing this transition, bringing primary and secondary schools into closer contact. In some secondary schools, this has resulted in the revision of curriculum approaches to create a learning environment with greater similarities to the primary classroom. Other teachers are now regularly moving between primary and secondary phases as specialists in areas such as Music, Modern Languages and Physical Education. There are already schools where all pupils from the ages of 4 to 19 are educated within the same school structure, resulting in the blurring of the distinction between primary and secondary settings. More developments of this kind seem likely. Although standardised testing of pupils at the age of 11 is still current policy in England, early discussions are taking place about possible changes linked to 'stage not age', and such developments would continue to break down barriers between the primary and secondary phases. Last, but not least, the development of communities of schools, linked by the *Every Child Matters* agenda (DfES, 2004), will also facilitate such developments.

It is with this changing educational climate in mind that *Developing Professional Practice 7–14* has been written.

The structure of this book

This book is divided into four themed parts.

Part 1: Influences on Teaching and Learning offers an overview of the range of factors affecting both learner and teacher in the classroom. The first chapter considers some of the ways in which local and national contexts impact on teaching and learning and on the role of the teacher. It also discusses some implications of transition between phases of schooling for pupils in the 7–14 age range. The following chapters then explore how the values held by teachers and the relationship between the school and its community can significantly affect the nature and quality of the learning encounter. Teaching and learning are also influenced by the developmental and individual contexts of the pupils. The final chapters in this part review developmental aspects for pupils in the 7–14 age range in relation to learning, and discuss the combination of factors which can affect the pupil's sense of identity and self-esteem and which can impact on their educational achievement.

Part 2: Teaching for Learning looks at six fundamental aspects of teaching and discusses how these contribute to engagement and learning for pupils in the 7–14 age range. This part begins by examining the different kinds of knowledge that teachers need in order to support pupils' learning, and also begins to ask questions about the kinds of knowledge that teachers will need in the future. The following chapter considers the different elements which make up the 'learning environment' and discusses how these can interact to promote or hinder learning. As learning technologies (such as digital technologies, Interactive White Boards etc.) are such a significant aspect of most classroom environments, part of this chapter also examines their potential to support learning and considers how they can be utilised to best effect. Chapter 8 considers issues around the topic of pupils' learning styles, and takes a critical look at some popular ideas about learning that may not be supported by research evidence. The following two chapters examine ways in which teachers can support pupils in developing and sustaining classroom behaviour that promotes learning, and how the use of formative assessment strategies can help pupils become more self-aware and independent as learners. Finally, Chapter 11 considers the challenging topic of inclusion: how an inclusive ethos might be developed and how all pupils can be supported towards being more independent as learners.

Part 3: Enhancing Teaching for Learning builds on the previous part by considering four further areas of professional practice that are regarded as having a positive impact on pupils' learning. The first two chapters in this part consider how teacher reflection can improve learning and teaching and how classroom-based investigation into learning and teaching can help teachers develop a better understanding of their pupils' needs as learners and of their own effectiveness as teachers. Chapter 14 reviews the ways in which different forms of collaboration contribute to enhanced learning, and Chapter 15 examines current developments in the area of pupil participation in schools, often called 'pupil voice', in order to discuss how greater consultation with pupils can make a positive difference to the learning atmosphere and ethos of the classroom and the school.

Part 4: Learning Futures considers some current developments that are likely to affect learning and teaching in the near future. We consider the importance of different partnerships between schools and other organisations within and beyond the immediate community, and how they can enhance learning. In Chapter 17 we discuss the development of 'global citizenship' within the curriculum and consider the ways in which learning from international experience can make a difference to both teachers and pupils in schools. Chapters 18 and 19 draw some of the threads from earlier chapters together, to reflect on the ways in which changing learning environments and technologies are likely to impact on approaches to teaching and learning, and what this might mean for reviewing the role of the teacher over the next few years. Changing environments and educational contexts will mean changes in teacher–pupil relationships, and we end the book by suggesting that these will lie at the heart of all our learning futures.

We believe that this is an exciting time to be entering the teaching profession, and that some of the traditional barriers between primary and secondary schools are in the process of being lowered, or even dissolved. We hope that you will find this book helpful for your own professional development, and that it will support you in your early experience of a changing and developing education context.

References

DCSF (2007) *The Children's Plan*. Available at: **http://www.dcsf.gov.uk/publications/childrensplan**.

DfES (2004) *Every Child Matters: Change for Children*. Available at: **http://www.everychildmatters.gov.uk/publications**.

TDA: Training and Development Agency for Schools (2007) *Professional Standards for Teachers*. Available at: **http://www.tda.gov.uk/teachers/ professionalstandards**.

Words and phrases in **bold blue text** have brief definitions or explanations in the margin of the page, and also appear in the full glossary at the back of the book.

Questions and activities within the text

This book is aimed at both trainee teachers and those in the early stages of their teaching career. In most cases the suggested questions and activities are relevant for readers in both categories and can be interpreted on the basis of your current experience.

However, at certain points within the text, depending on the topic of the chapter, questions and activities have been categorised under three headings:

In training, *Starting your career* and *Investigating learning and teaching*.

In training

Questions or activities identified under this heading are likely to apply to readers who are currently following a teacher training programme (undergraduate, PGCE or Graduate Teacher). It is assumed that all readers at this stage will have had some experience of being in a school setting, since this is a prerequisite for entry to a training programme. However, this experience may have been mainly limited to classroom observation, rather than teaching, depending on your stage in your training programme. These questions and activities require reflection on practice observed in schools, which should therefore be accessible to all readers. More experienced trainees could also consider some questions and activities under the following heading.

Elements of the section at the end of each chapter, 'Taking your practice further', could apply at any stage of training. The section at the end of each chapter, 'Taking your thinking further' [is specifically aimed at readers in this category] could also be helpful for trainee teachers on undergraduate routes into teaching, particularly towards the end of their training.

Starting your career

Questions and activities under this heading assume some teaching experience, although this will not necessarily be extensive. They would be relevant to all trainees approaching or completing a final teaching placement, to Newly Qualified Teachers or those in the early years of teaching.

The section at the end of each chapter, 'Taking your practice further', is also relevant for readers in this category. The section at the end of each chapter, 'Taking your thinking further', is aimed at readers who want to reflect more deeply on some of the issues covered in the chapter.

Investigating learning and teaching

Questions and activities under this heading are intended to support critical reflection and discussion of aspects of teaching and learning, which could be developed further through academic reading and writing. This includes current opportunities for Master's level work already offered in many PGCE programmes and the proposed Master's in Teaching and Learning programme aimed at teachers in the early stages of their career. Readers engaging in academic reading and writing, including at Master's level, might therefore be at any stage of training, and wherever possible these questions and activities do not assume extensive teaching experience.

The section at the end of each chapter, 'Taking your thinking further', is specifically aimed at readers in this category, but could also be helpful for trainee teachers on undergraduate routes into teaching, particularly towards the end of their training.

Further activities and recommended reading

At the end of each chapter there are suggestions for *Taking your practice further* and *Taking your thinking further*, which are described above.

There are also suggestions for additional reading, useful websites and Teachers' TV programmes under *Find out more*, and there is a brief outline of the content of each resource.

Acknowledgements

The publishers would like to thank the panel of reviewers. This includes:

Lori Altendorff, University of Sussex

Professor Martin Ashley, Edge Hill University

Sara Bubb, Institute of Education

Dr Trevor Davies, Director, International Centre for Studies in Education and Training, Institute of Education, University of Reading

Dr Lesley-Anne Pearson, Secondary ITE Course Director, University of Huddersfield

Penny Sweasey, Manchester Metropolitan University

Elizabeth Taylor, Senior Lecturer in Education, Liverpool John Moores University

Jo Tregenza, University of Sussex

Publisher's acknowledgements

We are grateful to the following for permission to reproduce copyright material:

Figures

Figure 10.2 from *The Assessment for Learning Strategy*, Department for Children, Schools and Families (ref: DCSF-00341-2008 2008) p. 5, © Crown copyright 2008; Figure 13.1 from *A Teacher's Guide to Classroom Research*, 3rd edition, Open University Press, Buckingham (Hopkins, D. 2002) (based on Kemmis and McTaggart 1988:14), Reproduced with the kind permission of Open University Press. All rights reserved; Figure 15.1 from *Pupil voice is here to stay!*, QCA Futures (Professor Jean Rudduck) http://www.qcda.gov.uk/libraryAssets/media/11478_rudduck_pupil_voice_is_here_to_stay.pdf, copyright © Qualifications and Curriculum Authority; Figure 5.2 from *Motivation and Personality*, 3rd Edition (Maslow, A.H., Frager, R.D. and Fadiman, J.) copy-

right (c) 1987, Adapted by permission of Pearson Education, Inc., Upper Saddle River, NJ.; Figure 5.3 from *Possibly Ethnicity and Education: The Evidence on Minority Ethnic Pupils aged 5-16*, Department of Education and Skills (ref: 0208-2006DOM-EN, 2006) p. 23, © Crown copyright 2006; Figure 8.1 from *Cognitive Styles and Learning Strategies: Understanding Style Differences in Learning and Behaviour* David Fulton Publishers (Riding, R. and Raynor, S. 1998) copyright (c) Cengage Learning Services Ltd; Figure 9.1 from 'A systematic review of how theories explain learning behaviour in school contexts', *Research Evidence in Education Library* (Powell, S. and Tod, J. 2004), London: EPPI-Centre, Social Science Research Unit, Institute of Education.

Tables

Table 14.1 from QTS Standards Guidance, www.tda.gov.uk/teachers/professionalstandards/ Professional Standards for Teachers, copyright © TDA; Table on page 419 from Standards for new teachers, 2008, http://www.tda.gov.uk/teachers/ professionalstandards.aspx, copyright © TDA; Table 4.1 from 'Erikson's Stages' from *Psychology*, 5th ed., Allyn & Bacon (Lefton 1994) copyright (c) 1994 Allyn & Bacon. Reproduced by permission of Pearson Education, Inc.; Table 5.2 from *Ethnicity and Education: The Evidence on Minority Ethnic Pupils aged 5–16 Research Topic Paper: 2006 edition*, Department for Education and Skills (ref: 0208-2006DOM-EN, 2006) p. 28, © Crown copyright 2006; Table 6.1 adapted from Effective components of CPD, www.teachernet.gov.uk, © Crown copyright 2010; Table on pages 149–150 from *Harnessing Technology Review 2008: The role of technology and its impact on education, Summary report*, Becta (2008) copyright © Becta 2008.

Text

Extract on page 11 from *International Trends in Primary Education. INCA Thematic Study No. 9* (Joanna Le Métais 2003) copyright © London: Qualifications and Curriculum Authority; Extract on page 21 from The Annual Report of Her Majesty's Chief Inspector of Education, Children's Services and Skills 2006/07, www.ofsted.gov.uk/publications/ annualreport0607, Crown Copyright material is reproduced with permission under the terms of the Click-Use Licence; Extract on pages 4–5 from 'National Curriculum for England Key Stages 1 and 2 Values, aims and purposes' The content relates to the 1999 programmes of study and attainment targets, http://curriculum.qcda.gov.uk/key-stages-1-and-2/Values-aims-and-purposes/index.aspx copyright © Qualifications and Curriculum Authority; Extract on page 217 from 'Beware the Consequences of Assessment!', *Assessment in Education: Principles, Policy & Practice*, Vol. 9 (3), pp. 285–288 (Broadfoot, P. 2002), Copyright © 2002 Routledge; Extract on pages 225–226 adapted from 'Assessment for Learning has fallen prey to gimmicks, says critic', *Times Educational Supplement*, 17/10/2008 (Ward, H.), www.tes.co.uk, copyright (c) Times Eduational Supplement; Extract on page 235 from *Evaluating Educational Inclusion: Guidance for inspectors and schools*, Ofsted (Ref HMI 235, 2001) p. 4, © Crown copyright 2001, © Crown Copyright; Extract on page 238 from *The Salamanca Statement and Framework for Action on Special Needs Education*, United Nations Educational, Scientific and Cultural Organization and Ministry of Education and Science Spain (Salamanca, Spain, 7–10 June 1994) pp. viii–ix, http://www.unesco.org/education/pdf/SALAMA_ E.PDF, copyright © United Nations, 1994. Reproduced with permission; Extract on page 242 from *Special Educational Needs and Disability: Towards Inclusive Schools*, Ofsted (HMI 2276, 2004) p. 16, 17, © Crown copyright 2004, © Crown Copyright; Extract on page 248 from Statutory inclusion statement, December 2009, http://curriculum.qcda.gov.uk/key-stages-3-and-4/organising-your-curriculum/inclusion/ statutory_inclusion_statement/index.aspx, copyright © Qualifications and Curriculum Authority; Extract on page 248 from Education Act 1996, Chapter 56, Section 312 (c) Crown Copyright; Extract on

pages 256–257 adapted from 'Bethan Marshall: Why should the gifted and talented be favoured?', *The Independent*, 10/08/2006, copyright (c) The Independent; Extract on page 289 adapted from Synopsis of the Presidential address to the British Educational Research Assocation 29 September 1991, Nottingham, published as 'Creating Education through Research', *British Educational Research Journal*, Vol. 18 (1), pp. 3–16 (Bassey, M. 1992), Taylor & Francis, copyright © 1992 Routledge; Extract on page 296 from http://nationalstrategies.standards. dcsf.gov.uk; Extract on page 297 from *A Teacher's Guide to Classroom Research* 3rd edition, Open University Press, Buckingham (Hopkins, D. 2002) pp. 52–53, Reproduced with the kind permission of Open University Press. All rights reserved; Extract on page 301 from *A Teacher's Guide to Classroom Research*, 3rd edition, Open University Press, Buckingham (Hopkins, D. 2002) pp. 106–107, Reproduced with the kind permission of Open University Press. All rights reserved; Extract on page 290,295 from TDA Core Standards, C8, http://www. tda.gov.uk/teachers/professionalstandards.aspx, copyright © TDA; Extract on page 314 after 'Core offer' 2010, http://www.teachernet.gov.uk/ wholeschool/extendedschools/teachernetgovuk coreoffer/ (c) Crown Copyright 2010; Case Study on page 314 from 'School becomes a centre for the community for education, leisure, information, advice and support' Whitefield School, London, http:// www.teachernet.gov.uk/casestudies/search.cfm; Case Study on page 314 from 'North Solihull are working in a cluster to provide extended services', http://www.teachernet.gov.uk/casestudies/ casestudy.cfm?id=456; Extract on page 318 from *Personalising learning – 5, Mentoring & coaching, and workforce development*, Specialist Schools and Academies Trust (Hargreaves, D. 2005) p. 7, copyright © Specialist Schools and Academies Trust, 2005; Extract on page 318 from 'Mentoring and Coaching CPD Capacity Building Project, National Framework for Mentoring and Coaching' p. 3, http://www.curee-paccts.com/files/publication/1219925968/National-framework-for-mentoring-and-coaching.pdf, © Copyright CUREE Limited; Extract on page 319 from Learning Mentors, http://www.cwdcouncil.org.uk/ learning-mentors/; Case Study on page 320 from 'Use of Transition Learning Mentors in Nottingham

City' Fairham School, North East, http://www. teachernet.gov.uk/casestudies/casestudy.cfm?id=80 (c) Crown copyright 2010; Extract on page 332 from Convention on the Rights of the Child, General Assembly resolution 44/25 of 20 November 1989. Article 12, http://www2.ohchr.org/english/law/ crc.htm#art12, copyright © United Nations, 1989. Reproduced with permission; Extract on page 334 from 'How about "teacher voice" for a change?', *Times Educational Supplement*, 11/04/2008 (Kent, M.), www.tes.co.uk, copyright (c) Times Eduational Supplement; Extract on page 343 from The Primary National Strategy, 2005, http://nationalstrategies. standards.dcsf.gov.uk/ (c) Crown Copyright 2005; Extract on page 332,337 from *Pupil voice is here to stay!*, QCA Futures (Professor Jean Rudduck) http:// www.qcda.gov.uk/libraryAssets/media/11478_ rudduck_pupil_voice_is_here_to_stay.pdf, copyright © Qualifications and Curriculum Authority; Extract on pages 335–336 from 'Pupil voice? It's bad for discipline', *Times Educational Supplement*, 4/04/2008 (Bloom, A.), www.tes.co.uk, copyright (c) Times Eduational Supplement; Extract on pages 341–342 adapted from 'Pupil voice: comfortable and uncomfortable learnings for teachers', *Research Papers in Education*, Vol. 20 (2), pp. 149–168 (McIntyre, D., Pedder, D., and Rudduck, J. 2005), Taylor & Francis, copyright © 2005 Routledge; Extract on page 350 from Our aim and objectives https://www.ssatrust. org.uk/whatwedo/Pages/aimandobjectives.aspx; Extract on page 354 from *Government Response to Paul Roberts' Report on Nurturing Creativity in Young People*, Department for Culture Media and Sport (2006) p. 4, http://www.culture.gov.uk/images/ publications/Govt_response_creativity.pdf © Crown Copyright 2006; Extract on page 361 from *Community Cohesion: Seven Steps, A Practitioner's Toolkit*, Cohesion and Faiths Unit (2005) p. 2, http:// www.communities.gov.uk/archived/publications/ communities/sevensteptool. (c) Crown Copyright 2005; Extract on page 368 from *A big picture of the curriculum*, Qualifications and Curriculum Authority (2008) http://www.qcda.gov.uk/libraryAssets/media/ Big_Picture_2008.pdf, copyright © Qualifications and Curriculum Authority; Extract on page 373 from DCSF, www.teachernet.gov.uk/sustainableschools (c) Crown Copyright 2009; Extract on page 374 from National Framework, http://www.teachernet.gov.uk/ sustainableschools/framework/ (c) Crown Copyright 2009; Case Study on page 377 from Widening participation through Comenius, http://www. britishcouncil.org/comenius-case-studies copyright (c) British Council; Extract on page 383 from *Curriculum Review Diversity & Citizenship*, Department for Education and Skills (ref: 00045-2007DOM-EN 2006) p. 30, http://publications. teachernet.gov.uk/eOrderingDownload/DfES_ Diversity_&_Citizenship.pdf, © Crown Copyright 2007; Extract on page 367, 371 from *Putting the World into World-Class Education, An international strategy for education, skills and children's services*, Department for Education and Skills (ref: DfES/1077/2004, 2004) pp. 3, 6, http://publications. teachernet.gov.uk/eOrderingDownload/1077-2004GIF-EN-01.pdf, © Crown copyright 2004; Extract on pages 383–384 from YouGov 2008 poll of teacher views for teaching 'British values', commmissioned by Teachers' TV copyright (c) YouGov; Extract on page 396 from *The Shape of Things to Come: personalised learning through collaboration*, Department for Education and Skills (Leadbeater, C. 2005) p. 4, ref: DfES-1574-2005, http://www. innovation-unit.co.uk/images/stories/files/pdf/ TheShapeofThingstoCome.pdf, © Crown Copyright 2005; Extract on page 401 adapted from *Classrooms of the future*, The Innovation Unit, Department of Education and Skills p. 9, http://www.innovation-unit. co.uk/images/stories/classrooms_of_the_future.pdf (c) Crown Copyright 2009; Extract on page 402 from *2020 and beyond, Future scenarios for education in the age of new technologies* Futurelab (Hans Daanen and Keri Facer 2007) p. 4, http://www. futurelab.org.uk/resources/documents/opening_ education/2020_and_beyond.pdf, copyright © Futurelab 2007; Extract on page 404 from 'Social websites harm children's brains: Chilling warning to parents from top neuroscientist', *The Daily Mail*, 24/02/2009 (Derbyshire, D.), copyright © Solo Syndication 2009; Extract on pages 393–395 adapted from *2020 Vision, Report of the Teaching and Learning in 2020 Review Group*, Department for Education and Skills (ref: 04255-2006DOM-EN, 2006) pp. 9, 10, http://publications.teachernet.gov.uk/ eOrderingDownload/6856-DfES-Teaching%20and% 20Learning.pdf (c) Crown Copyright 2006; Extract on page 401,405 from *Curriculum and teaching innovation, Transforming classroom practice and personalisation*, Futurelab (Ben Williamson and Sarah Payton 2009) pp. 33, 4, http://www.futurelab.org.uk/resources/documents/handbooks/curriculum_and_teaching_innovation2.pdf, copyright © Futurelab 2007; Extract on pages 414–415 from *Be prepared . . . Future trends*, VisionMapper (2009) http://www.visionmapper.org.uk/ideas/beprepared.php (c) Copyright Futurelab 2009; Extract on page 37 from 'Non-Statutory Framework for Religious Education' 2005, www.qcda.org.uk, copyright © Qualifications and Curriculum Authority; Extract on page 38 adapted from 'Some Practical Ideas for confronting curricular bias, Seven Forms of Bias in Instructional Materials', http://www.sadker.org/curricularbias.html, copyright (c) David M. Sadker, Ed. D.; Extract on page 40 from 'QTS standards guidance' Q2, 2007, http://www.tda.gov.uk/teachers/professionalstandards, copyright (c) TDA; Extract on page 40 from 'Supporting the induction process: TDA guidance for newly qualified teachers' C2, 2007, http://www.tda.gov.uk/teachers/professionalstandards, copyright (c) TDA; Case Study on pages 36–37 from Education Reform Act 1988, Chapter 40, 8(3), Crown Copyright material is reproduced with permission under the terms of the Click-Use Licence; Extract on pages 40–41 from *Handbook for the Inspection of Initial Teacher Training For the Award of Qualified Teacher Status 2005–2011*, Ofsted (Reference no: 070191 2007) p. 58, © Crown Copyright 2007; Extract on page 48 from *Materials for Schools Involving Parents, Raising Achievement* (Professor Bastiani, J. edited by White, S. 2003) p. 3, © Crown Copyright 2003; Extract on page 59 from *Extended schools: a report on early developments*, Ofsted (Ref HMI 2453, 2005) p. 3, © Crown Copyright 2005; Extract on page 59 from *Extended services in schools and children's centres*, Ofsted (Ref HMI 2609, 2006) p. 6, © Crown Copyright 2006; Extract on pages 52–53 adapted from Based on Teaching and Learning Research Programme Project 13 published by TLRP, Reproduced with permission of TLRP and Professor RM Hughes, copyright (c) Teaching and Learning Research Programme; Extract on page 100 adapted from 'Pursuit of happiness is personal', *The Australian*, 7/08/2008 (Furedi, F.), copyright (c) Frank Furedi; Extract on page 110 adapted from 'Respect for all ethos', www.qcda.org.uk, copyright ©

Qualifications and Curriculum Authority; Extract on page 133 from *2020 Vision: The Report of the Teaching and Learning in 2020 Review Group*, Department of Education and Skills (ref: 04255-2006DOM-EN, 2006) p. 10 (c) Crown Copyright 2006; Case Study on pages 124–125 adapted from 'Terry's Learning: some limitations of Shulman's pedagogical content knowledg', *Cambridge Journal of Education*, Vol. 25 (2), pp. 175–187 (Anne Meredith 1995), Taylor & Francis, copyright © 1995 Routledge; Extract on page 139 from *Report on the School Environment Survey 2007 results*, Teacher Support Network and the British Council for School Environments p. 2, copyright (c) Teacher Support Network; Extract on page 143 adapted from 'On display: wall-to-wall learning', *Curriculum Briefing*, Vol. 5(2) (Andrew-Power, K. and Gormley, C.), copyright (c) Optimus Education, www.optimus-education.com; Extract on page 147 from Education Outside the Classroom Manifesto, Department for Education and Skills, 2006, www.lotc.org.uk (c) Crown copyright 2006; Extract on pages 157, 158–159 from *Interactive whiteboards in the classroom*, Futurelab (Rudd, T.) p. 7, www.futurelab.org.uk/events/listing/whiteboards/report, copyright © Futurelab 2007; Extract on page 169 from *The Manual of Learning Styles* (Peter Honey and Alan Mumford 1985) copyright (c) Peter Honey Publications Ltd; Extract on page 181 adapted from *Pedagogy and Personalisation*, Department for Education and Skills (Ref: 00126-2007DOM-EN, 2007) p. 4, © Crown Copyright 2007; Extract on pages 172–173 from *Neuroscience and Education: Issues and Opportunities*, TLRP (2006) pp. 11, 15–16, www.tlrp.org, Reproduced with permission from TLRP and Paul Howard-Jones, copyright (c) Teaching and Learning Research Programme; Extract on page 190 from *Professional Standards for Teachers, Qualified Teacher Status*, TDA (2007) p. 12, http://www.tda.gov.uk/upload/resources/pdf/s/standards_qts.pdf, copyright (c) TDA 2007; Extract on page 195 from *Learning Behaviour: Lessons Learned. A review of behaviour standards and practices in our schools* (Sir Alan Steer, ref: DCSF-00453-2009,) p. 78, © Crown Copyright 2009; Case Study on page 201 adapted from *Behaviour for Learning: Proactive Approaches to Behaviour Management*, David Fulton Publishers (Ellis, S. & Todd, J. 2009) copyright (c) Cengage

Learning Services Ltd; Extract on page 207 from *Managing challenging behaviour*, Ofsted (HMI 2363, 2005) p. 4, © Crown Copyright 2005.

In some instances we have been unable to trace the owners of copyright material, and we would appreciate any information that would enable us to do so.

Picture Credits

The publisher would like to thank the following for their kind permission to reproduce their photographs:

(Key: b-bottom; c-centre; l-left; r-right; t-top)

Alamy Images: Dan Sullivan 203tc/9.2; **Getty Images:** 51tc/3.1; **Pearson Education Ltd:** 219tc (Numbered photo 10.1), Ann Cromack. Ikat Design 130c (Numbered photo 6.2), 155tr (Numbered photo 7.2), 181c (Numbered photo 8.2), Clark Wiseman 19tc (Numbered photo 1.2), digital stock 392bc (Numbered photo 18.1), Ian Wedgewood 56tl (Numbered photo 3.2), 61tc (Numbered Photo 3.3), 111t (Numbered photo 5.2), 146tl (Numbered photo 7.1), 194bc (Numbered photo 9.1), 241bc (Numbered photo 11.1), 274c (Numbered photo 12.1), 278bc (Numbered photo 12.2), 298bc (Numbered photo 13.1), 300c (Numbered photo 13.2), 313c (Numbered photo 14.1), 318bl (Numbered photo 14.2), 353t (Numbered photo 16.1), 355t (Numbered photo 16.2), Jules Selmes 340bc (Numbered photo 15.2), 403tc (Numbered photo 18.2), Naki Kouyioumtzis 416tc (Numbered photo 19.1), Photodisc 97c (Numbered photo 5.1), Photodisc. Lawrence M. Sawyer 251bc (Numbered photo 11.2), Phovoir. Imagestate 1tc (Unnumbered photo Part 1), 420c (Numbered photo 19.2), Rob Judges 69tr (Numbered Photo 4.1), 117t (Unnumbered photo Part 2), 177cr (Numbered photo 8.1), 224cl (Numbered photo 10.2), Rob van Petten 29c (Numbered Photo 2.1), Studio 8. Clark Wiseman 265t (Unnumbered photo Part 4), 336bc (Numbered photo 15.1); **Pearson Education Ltd:** Ian Wedgewood 347t; **Education Photos Ltd:** 8tc; **Report Digital:** (Numbered photo 6.1), 371c (Numbered photo 17.1), Janina Struk 373tc (M17NP17.2), Stefano Cagnoni 33tc.

All other images © Pearson Education

Every effort has been made to trace the copyright holders and we apologise in advance for any unintentional omissions. We would be pleased to insert the appropriate acknowledgement in any subsequent edition of this publication.

"The raised expectations regarding personal professional development reflected in the National Standards for both trainee and qualified teachers make this a timely publication. Not only does it encourage and support practitioners' engagement with current research making creative links between theory and practice, it provides a far-sighted perspective of how current developments in learning and teaching will extrapolate in the future.

Having a strong personal interest in the 'middle-years' and the on-going tensions that surround the whole process of cross-phase transition, I am also delighted that there is now a publication that contextualises itself within this area encouraging intellectual engagement and reflective practice rather than simple 'tips for teachers'. This book will certainly be included on our recommended course reading lists and our trainee teachers actively encouraged to draw upon its content in both their academic work and professional development."

Philip Stephenson, University of Cambridge

Pearson Education Ltd/Phovoir. Imagestate

PART 1 Influences on Teaching and Learning

As teachers, the most important aspect of our role is our day-to-day contact with learners in classrooms. However, this contact does not take place in some kind of bubble, but is affected by a whole range of influences: those that both we and our pupils bring with us from our own daily lives and backgrounds, and also those relating to social, political, local, national and even international influences. On top of this, each of our pupils is experiencing their own growth and development differently, and trying to make sense of who they are as individuals. Many of these significant developments take place between the ages of 7 and 14, including the transition between primary and secondary education. Making sense of our classrooms, and the learning that takes place within them, means making sense of some of these influences as well.

The chapters in this part consider some of these influences.

CHAPTER 1

Contexts of Learning

In this chapter you will:

- Reflect on your own beliefs about the aims and purposes of education
- Begin to consider the social and political influences which affect teaching and learning
- Begin to consider the ways in which schools develop a distinctive ethos
- Begin to identify the ways in which different learning contexts can impact on individual learners
- Apply this understanding to pupils' experiences of transition between phases of education

Introduction

However much we might sometimes wish it to be the case, life in the classroom cannot be isolated from a range of other influences. The policies and practices of the school, its local community, and educational policies in the local authority as well as national policies all impact on teaching and learning every day (see Figure 1.1). The contexts *of* learning directly affect the ways the classroom operates as the context *for* learning.

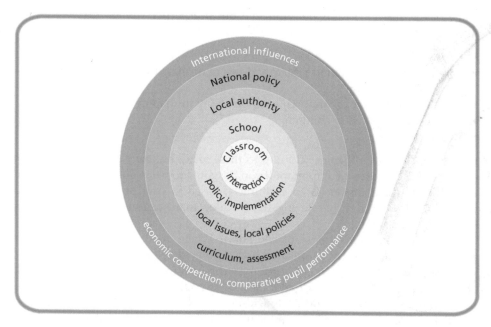

Figure 1.1
Influences on teaching and learning

This chapter examines some of these influences as a start in considering the ways in which different learning contexts can impact on individual learners. We will focus mainly on three areas:

- national policies for education, and some of the influences that affect how policy is developed;
- school ethos and how this can affect the experience of individual learners;
- transition between primary and secondary education, as this is a significant event in the educational lives of pupils within the 7–14 age range, and how well this process is managed can have a significant effect on their future educational achievement.

What is education for?

We start by considering some 'big questions': what do you think is the purpose of education? and why have you chosen to teach? While this book will not provide a definitive answer to the first question, and only you can provide an answer to the second, we think it is important for teachers to keep asking these questions in order to remind themselves why they want to teach and what kind of teacher they want to be.

Why did you decide you wanted to teach?

Some of the answers to this question that our prospective student teachers give at interview are as follows:

- I want to make a difference to children's lives.
- I am really interested in my subject and I want to share this, and encourage my pupils to feel the same.
- I think teachers have an important responsibility in shaping the future.
- I am really interested in children.
- Your own answer...?

Individuals will give different priorities to these ideas, but we would like to suggest that *all* these responses are important if you are going to be an effective teacher. What underpins all these answers is an enthusiasm based in your personal interests and values, but also the idea that having an education matters, and that education is an intrinsically good thing.

So what *is* the main purpose of education? Where do the key ideas about why education is important come from, and how do they shape education policy?

Socialisation: a term used by sociologists to define the process of learning to live within one's particular culture.

Although educational practices may appear different in different parts of the world, one of the fundamental aims of education in any society, formal or informal, is to equip learners to function effectively within a particular cultural context. This is a significant aspect of socialisation and is inextricably linked to the values and beliefs operating within a particular culture, although these links are not always explicitly stated. These values and beliefs are promoted through the content of the curriculum and its organisation, and also through the ways in which teaching and learning take place in the classroom.

THINKING IT THROUGH: FORMS OF EDUCATION

EXAMPLE 1

The film *Cave of the Yellow Dog* tells the story of a young girl living a nomadic existence in Mongolia. The film was shot on location, using a genuine Mongolian family as the main characters, not professional actors. In one sequence, the girl watches her mother making cheese and dried sausage for sale in a market and in another she rides out with her father to see the herds. These episodes are examples of her education as a member of her tribe.

THINKING IT THROUGH: *CONTINUED*

EXAMPLE 2

Foremost is a belief in education, at home and at school, as a route to the spiritual, moral, social, cultural, physical and mental development, and thus the well-being, of the individual. Education is also a route to equality of opportunity for all, a healthy and just democracy, a productive economy, and sustainable development. Education should reflect the enduring values that contribute to these ends. These include valuing ourselves, our families and other relationships, the wider groups to which we belong, the diversity in our society and the environment in which we live. Education should also reaffirm our commitment to the virtues of truth, justice, honesty, trust and a sense of duty.

At the same time, education must enable us to respond positively to the opportunities and challenges of the rapidly changing world in which we live and work. In particular, we need to be prepared to engage as individuals, parents, workers and citizens with economic, social and cultural change, including the continued globalisation of the economy and society, with new work and leisure patterns and with the rapid expansion of communication technologies.

Thinking it through

Are these two examples fundamentally different? Both are underpinned by beliefs about what is important for members of a particular society to learn.

The second example is taken from the statement of values and purposes in the National Curriculum for England. It contains a number of statements which it assumes are widely shared within our own society.

- Using a highlighter pen, or underlining, indicate examples of these key themes from this statement: personal, social, and economic values or purposes.

  (If you don't want to mark this book download this from **www.qcda.org.uk** and follow links to 'National Curriculum'. The values statement is available in both Key Stage 1 and 2 and Key Stage 3 and 4 areas.)

- Do you agree with all these purposes for education? What do *you* consider to be the most important aims and purposes of education?

  You might like to compare this statement with that of the revised Scottish National Curriculum: *Curriculum for Excellence* (**www.curriculumforexcellencescotland.gov.uk**). What similarities and differences can you identify?

Influences on the curriculum

All countries with national education systems have some form of statement outlining the values or principles on which their system is based. The curriculum of any country is not value-neutral, but reflects that country's culture and beliefs as expressed in public policy (Figure 1.2). International comparisons of primary education systems indicate that there are apparent similarities between countries in terms of the *names* given to subjects within the curriculum, but the names used do not indicate the *content* of the subject curriculum, nor the pedagogical approaches which are commonly used to teach these subject areas (Hall and Øzerk, 2008).

In recent years there have been changes to curriculum content in many countries, including the UK, that reflect changing social and political priorities (Shuayb and O'Donell, 2008). Many Western countries, including those within the UK, are now placing a greater emphasis on thinking skills or 'learning how to learn'. This is to respond to a need for people with more flexible learning skills in order to respond to changing technologies as these economies move away from industrial production towards the so-called **'knowledge economy'**. As a result of increasing diversity in the populations of many Western countries there is also an increasing emphasis on citizenship or civics education, although this is currently non-statutory in English primary schools. *2020 Vision: The Report of the Teaching and Learning Review Group* (DfES, 2006) indicates ways in which the curriculum may need to be developed further in order to provide children currently entering education with the skills and understanding they are likely to need as adults in the rest of the twenty-first century.

Knowledge economy: this is a term used to identify the use of 'intangibles' such as knowledge, skills and innovative ideas in the 'information age' as resources to bring about economic advantages for countries.

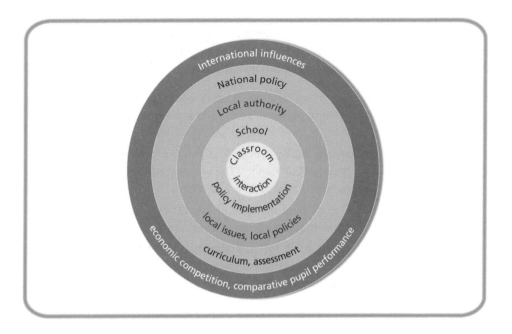

Figure 1.2
Influences on teaching and learning

CASE STUDY

'We don't do that here'

Angela is a black pupil in a secondary school in a small seaside town in southern England with a largely white population. Her family emigrated from East Africa several years ago and she has apparently settled well into the English system and is seen as a high achiever. However, when she asked her head of History why the school did not celebrate Black History Month (held every October; see **www.black-history-month.co.uk**), she was disturbed to be told 'We don't do that here – there isn't any need.'

Angela campaigned among her classmates, all of whom are white, and wrote letters to the head of year and the head teacher arguing for the importance of pupils in *all* schools being aware of black history issues. As a result she was invited to talk to the whole school, in an assembly, about her views. Whether the school will celebrate Black History Month in future remains to be seen. . . .

Inevitably, the content of the curriculum will be a selection from the full range of cultural activities or knowledge existing within any given society. So, for example, some books are chosen rather than others; some events in history do not appear on the curriculum; some areas of the world are not studied in Geography. It is, of course, impossible for the school curriculum to contain everything, but there are certainly debates to be had about why some elements of content are chosen rather than others. The fact that the content of the curriculum has to be a selection from all the possible options available may result in some pupils feeling marginalised or rejected by an education system which does not appear to value their own cultural interests and experiences.

The tension between recognising cultural diversity and maintaining curriculum cohesion within a national education system presents a challenge, but the National Curriculum for England maintains an expectation that *all* schools will prepare pupils for life in a culturally diverse society. In some other countries in Europe cultural diversity is given a lower priority in national curriculum statements, and there is correspondingly less recognition of cultural diversity within their curriculum content. In England, the values statement in relation to diversity directly affects the curriculum and thus the teaching and learning context of the classroom.

OVER TO YOU

Look back at your list of examples of personal, social and economic values from the values and purposes statement from the National Curriculum.

Drawing on your knowledge of the curriculum and your observations or experience in schools so far, what examples can you find to show how each of these is reflected in practice?

Influences on assessment

Photo 1.1
Primary pupils in England experience more 'high stakes' testing than in many other countries

Source: Education Photos Ltd

The formal assessment systems we use in schools also tell us a lot about the values underpinning our education system.

RESEARCH BRIEFING

What is and what is not assessed, the nature of assessment and how it takes place, as well as the purposes and effects of assessment all provide insights into what knowledge and skills are valued by a society.

(Hall and Øzerk, 2008: 13)

Accountability: being publicly responsible for outcomes, including taking responsibility if pupils fail to perform as expected.

Kathy Hall and Kamil Øzerk have undertaken a comparative study of the differences between the curriculum and assessment systems in the four countries of the UK, France, Norway and Japan. This study is part of the much larger Cambridge Primary Review which has been examining all aspects of primary education in England (see **www.primaryreview.org.uk**).

Hall and Øzerk found that the assessment systems in England place a much higher emphasis on accountability compared with other countries. There has been more frequent external testing, in more subjects and from a younger age than elsewhere. The outcomes of external tests are also 'high

RESEARCH BRIEFING: *CONTINUED*

stakes' for both pupils and schools, through the publication of 'league tables' which can have a significant effect on how schools are viewed within the local community.

Hall and Øzerk outline the features of the assessment system in English primary schools which distinguish it from those of the other countries in their study:

- The detailed attainment targets in the National Curriculum make it possible to design statutory tests linked to these criteria.
- Statutory testing takes place at least twice during the primary years of schooling (although this situation is changing).
- Schools have to predict pupils' expected results and then report on the actual results of the tests *and* the difference between these and their predictions.
- Results are then compared with nationally expected standards and also with the actual results of other schools in similar catchment areas.

All these factors mean that parents are more likely to believe that the results of statutory assessment provide an accurate picture of schools, and to use them to decide where they wish their children to be educated.

OVER TO YOU

What information about schools might be missing from statutory test results?

Why do you think some other countries have fewer (or no) statutory tests for primary pupils?

Does the level of testing and public accountability within the English education system tell us anything about how *teachers* are regarded?

This particularly strong emphasis on standards and accountability in England is not shared to the same extent either by other countries in the UK or elsewhere. Hall and Øzerk (2008: 15) argue that this emphasis dates back to the origins of the National Curriculum in the late 1980s, developed within a political climate of concern about international competitiveness and a belief in market forces as an indicator of success or failure. During this period a link between educational achievement and national economic success was created in the minds of the public, and this link has continued to exist. Since there was a strong belief in the power of the market – the idea that customers would decide which ideas or products were successful on the basis of which ones they bought – this concept was also applied to education. Parents were positioned as 'consumers' of education who needed clear information about the performance of individual schools in order to make the best choices for their children. Although attitudes towards parents within education policy have changed since the 1980s, the effects of these beliefs remained influential in terms of statutory assessment until very recently.

Influences on government policies for education

While government policy has a significant impact on the national educational context and reflects national concerns, these policies themselves are also influenced by external factors. We may need to look beyond national boundaries in order to make sense of some of the initiatives that affect the daily lives of pupils and teachers in primary and secondary schools. Thus global developments, national events, and national and international research evidence all play a part in determining policy directions.

One major national initiative in England that has brought several developing policy strands together is *Every Child Matters: Change for Children* (DfES, 2004), further developed in *The Children's Plan* (DCSF, 2007). Figure 1.3 illustrates the range of influences

Figure 1.3
Influences affecting education policy development

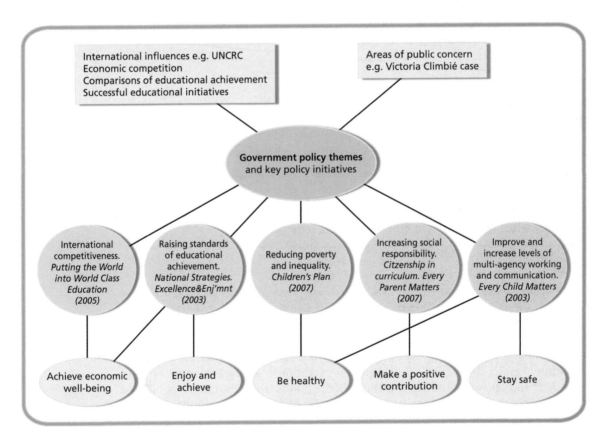

which can affect education policy development, and therefore the learning contexts for teachers and pupils. Each of these influences is briefly discussed below.

Public concerns: The Victoria Climbié Inquiry

One of the catalysts that precipitated the publication of *Every Child Matters* (ECM) was the report of an investigation into the death of a young child as the result of continued abuse (*The Laming Inquiry*, HMSO, 2003). This report emphasised the fragmented nature of children's services – Victoria was twice admitted to different hospitals with injuries possibly caused by abuse, but these concerns apparently did not reach the appropriate social workers. Her aunt with whom she was living moved from one local authority area to another and contact with Victoria was lost for a period. Social workers received information that Victoria was not attending school, but did not know about her hospital visits. They were repeatedly unable to gain access to the flat where she and her aunt were living and believed that they might have left the country. On the same day that social workers closed the case file, Victoria died in yet another hospital. Inadequate monitoring systems meant that the line of responsibility for following up concerns about the child's welfare was unclear, and as a result her case had 'slipped through the net', with tragic results. There was a huge public outcry when these facts became known.

'New Labour' policy directions

In 1997 the New Labour government of Tony Blair had come to power with a mani-festo based on a number of key principles, referred to by Blair as the 'Third Way' (Blair, 1998). These principles included a strong commitment to principles of increasing opportunities in society or **social justice**, alongside an equal belief that individuals needed to be responsible citizens in order to improve the conditions of their lives and those of their families. Raising standards of achievement through education was presented as the main route for social improvement and national economic growth and competitiveness in a global market.

International influences

The relationship between education and the economic well-being of a country is recognised by all countries. As a result, close attention is paid to international com-parative data about pupils' achievement. A study on international trends in primary education, commissioned by the **Qualifications and Curriculum Development Agency (QCDA)**, notes:

> There is an increasing tendency to refer to performance in international surveys (such as the Third International Mathematics and Science Study (TIMSS) and the OECD Programme for International Student Assessment (PISA)) to explain or justify national policy changes.
>
> *(Le Metais, 2003)*

(The TIMSS and PISA surveys involve the administration of tests to pupils in a number of countries. TIMSS looks at the maths and science knowledge of pupils around 9–10

Social justice: the belief that every individual should have the chances and opportunities to make the most of their lives and use their talents to the full.

Qualifications and Curriculum Development Agency (QCDA): the official body responsible for all aspects of curriculum development and statutory assessment in England.

and 15–16 years in over 60 countries on a four-year cycle. PISA looks at levels of reading, mathematical and scientific understanding, and problem-solving skills in 15 year olds every three years. The number of countries participating in PISA has risen from 43 in 2000 to 67 in 2009.)

The QCA study, mentioned above, comments: 'In some cases, dissatisfaction with performance in international surveys has led to specific programmes, especially in mathematics.' The introduction of the National Numeracy Strategy in 1999, now part of the National Primary Strategy, was in part influenced by the findings of the first TIMSS survey held in 1994–5. Subsequent governments continue to keep a close eye on the performance of UK pupils in these surveys.

National Strategies (Primary and Secondary): these are professional development programmes for primary and secondary teachers. They provide resources to support teaching, and suggested frameworks for the curriculum.

The New Labour government was also looking at evidence from other countries about educational developments that seemed to be raising standards, and seeking ways to include some of these ideas in educational policy in England. One such development was that of 'Extended Schools' which will be discussed more fully in Chapter 3.

The United Nations Convention on the Rights of the Child (UNCRC) had established its principles in 1989: these include rights to survival and development, rights to protection and rights to participation in society (**www.unicef.org/crc**). The UK signed the majority of the Convention in 1991, and is now required to make regular reports to the UN on progress towards achieving the agreed outcomes for children, which include opportunities for young people to express their views and to be heard, and a reduction in the impact of poverty on children's lives. In 2005 the government appointed the first Children's Commissioner to ensure that children and young people are consulted about policy developments that directly affect them.

The influence of research on policy

Both national and international research evidence also plays a part in policy development (Figure 1.4), although there are different views as to how far research evidence influences policy initiatives, practice in schools, or what *kind* of research is seen as being influential. There are often references to research evidence within policy documents of various kinds. However, depending on the intended audience, these references may not be particularly detailed or explicit, which can make it harder to determine whether policy is being influenced by research evidence; whether research is being selected to support a particular initiative; or whether only certain aspects of a research study are being selected as being useful for policy development. It is likely, of course, that all three things happen at different times and in different contexts; however, research evidence is always unlikely to be the only influence on policy development, for the reasons we have already considered.

The following few examples indicate where research evidence has explicitly influenced policy and practice in schools:

- The introduction of 'assessment for learning' strategies, following research evidence which suggested that pupil achievement was measurably increased

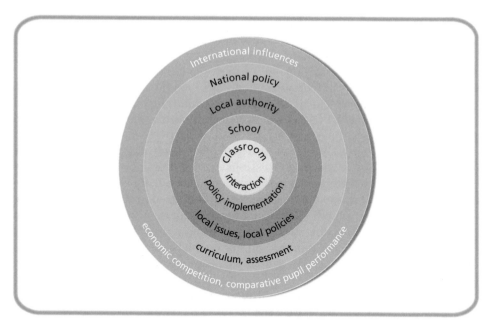

Figure 1.4
Influences on teaching and learning

where teachers gave pupils specifically focused feedback about how to improve their work in relation to clear learning objectives (see also Chapter 8).

- The development of the Scottish *Curriculum for Excellence*, which has been informed by reviews of research in each of the seven main areas of the revised curriculum. These research reviews have identified key findings, such as the evidence about factors that improve progress in scientific understanding in the transition between primary and secondary schools (Review of research literature: science education, available at: **www.curriculumforexcellencescotland.gov.uk**).

- Government support for involving parents more closely with their children's education at home, following a research report indicating that parental involvement had a more significant effect on pupil achievement than the quality of schools (Desforges, 2003).

OVER TO YOU

Based on your own knowledge of a subject that particularly interests you, how far do you think the research evidence has contributed to practice in schools?

Are you aware of other research evidence which might question aspects of currently recommended practice in your subject?

The relationship between research and professional practice in the classroom will be considered more fully in Chapter 12.

Influences on the school

Government policy is obviously one of the most significant influences on the school context: the curriculum and its assessment, pedagogical approaches, and school organisation and management are all affected by a wide range of existing policies and will continue to be subject to change in the future as new policies are introduced (Figure 1.5).

Local authority policies also have an effect on individual schools, and thus the experiences of the pupils and teachers within them. For example, the experiences of pupils and teachers will be very different in areas where there is selective secondary education, based on local testing of 11 year olds, compared to those areas with comprehensive secondary education. The amounts of funding available for different educational developments also vary from area to area, according to local authority priorities. If you have an opportunity to do so, you might compare the similarities and differences in the local education system where you grew up with someone from another part of the country.

Moving from the local authority to the more immediate context of the school itself, the local community will also have a significant effect on the learning context within the school. The physical extent of each school's local community may vary considerably, with some secondary pupils travelling further away to attend a specific specialist or selective school, but in general terms primary schools and most secondary schools draw their pupils from the immediate neighbourhood. This means that your understanding of local conditions, in terms of housing, employment and social issues, will be helpful in terms of considering the learning context of a given school. However, while it is certainly the case that there are links between levels of family income and

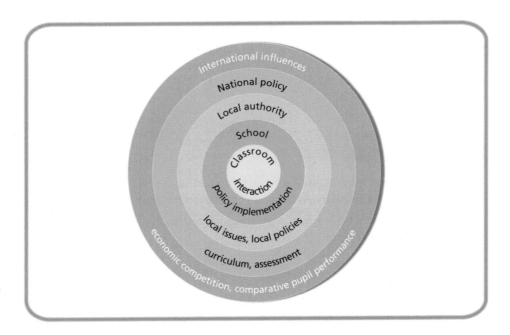

Figure 1.5
Influences on
teaching and
learning

educational achievement, the way in which the school responds to local circumstances will still be significant in terms of pupils' achievement and well-being. This issue will be considered further in Chapter 3.

School ethos as a context for learning

Each school develops its own unique culture, more commonly termed its 'ethos'. The concept of a school ethos operates on at least two levels: that of a formalised public statement, often called a 'mission statement', and that of everyday practice. Evidence suggests that schools are more effective in improving pupil achievement when the publicly expressed aims for the school are supported by consistent practice on a whole-school basis (Sammons, Hillman and Mortimore, 1995). On an everyday basis, ethos is expressed as a combination of values, norms and customs, or 'the way we do things here'. Expectations about pupils' learning behaviour and the ways staff and pupils interact are fundamental to the development of school ethos, and are reflected in school rules, policies, and approaches to the curriculum and pedagogy.

Ethos: derived from Greek, meaning 'to be accustomed to', this has come to mean the distinctive character and fundamental values of a particular social grouping.

OVER TO YOU

Once upon a time . . .

'At the girls' grammar school that I attended in the 1960s we were expected to stand behind our chairs at the start of every lesson until we were told we could sit. If another teacher entered the room during a lesson, we had to stand up immediately, and in silence, regardless of what we were doing. Each year, prizes were given for achievement in different subjects (always a book), and also for 'deportment', by which the school meant the way a pupil behaved herself in lessons and around the school. My memory suggests that winners of the deportment prize were girls who got on with their work quietly, were well behaved and did not ask questions in class. I was told off more than once for asking questions – not about things I did not understand, but because I wanted to know more. This seemed to be seen as being impertinent, and no – I never won a deportment prize, although I do still have my copies of some of the others!'

(Personal recollection)

This true story provides some examples of both explicit and implicit norms and customs (sometimes described as 'rituals'). Standing behind chairs or standing up on the entry of a teacher were *explicit* customs – when pupils arrived at the school these customs were formally explained to them.

What *implicit* messages were being given to the girls in this school about how they should behave towards teachers and how they should think of themselves?

Although these events took place more than 40 years ago, and society's expectations of the role of women and of the relationships between teachers and pupils have changed a great deal, schools do still convey messages to their pupils through the ways in which their ethos is communicated. In many instances, the values, norms and customs that make up the ethos of the school operate implicitly, which can have both positive and less positive effects on learners, depending on how well the norms and values of the school match with those which pupils bring from outside the school. Where differences exist, the resulting tensions experienced by the pupil may not always be easy to resolve. For example, a pupil who has been encouraged to 'stand up for himself' at home may be described by the school as a bully or a troublemaker.

Children from single-parent families may find themselves being presented with images of 'traditional' families as a social norm, so that their own home circumstances are implicitly devalued.

THINKING IT THROUGH

What expectations might you have about schools with the following mission statements?

School A: 'Educating the individual: working as an efficient and effective team within a caring environment, we aim to achieve a standard of excellence appropriate to each individual, enriching, encouraging and equipping each child for their future education.'

School B: 'Achieving Excellence Together: a thriving community school committed to developing successful citizens for the future.'

How might these expectations be different?

Differentiation: the adjustment of the teaching process according to the learning needs of pupils.

For example, school A might have a stronger emphasis on differentiation and might set or group by ability, whereas school B might place more emphasis on collaboration, and might teach pupils in mixed-ability groups or classes.

Can you think of other ways in which the schools might be different? For example, consider the use of phrases such as 'standard of excellence' or 'community school'.

The role of the teacher in creating the school and classroom ethos

The role of school leadership is critical in establishing and maintaining consistency between public statements and actual practice (Figure 1.6), but leadership should not be seen as being confined to those in senior management positions. School ethos can also be reinforced or undermined by teachers' behaviours, and an emphasis on

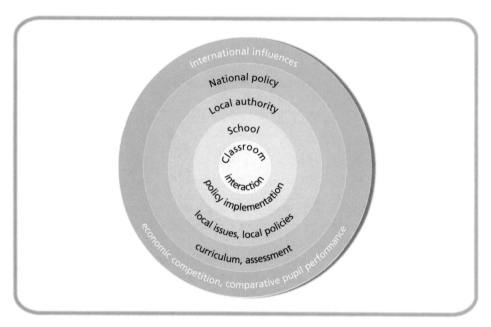

Figure 1.6
Influences on
teaching and
learning

becoming self-aware, and on recognising the value stances implicit in the ways you relate to pupils and demonstrate your expectations, is a repeated theme within this book.

Teachers also take responsibility for the management of other adults and for maintaining a consistent ethos within their own classrooms. The Teachers' TV programme *Primary Management – Attainment and Inclusion – Lessons Learnt* (**http://www.teachers.tv/ video/2588**) provides an example of how one school sought to change its learning culture. The head teacher, Maggie Buttress, explains: 'There was a growing culture of "not doing" things, of put-downs from other children and of not contributing in class.' In order to change this culture, teachers, teaching assistants, parents and children all needed to adopt different attitudes and to believe that 'we can, if . . .'. As a result, the school now has a much more inclusive ethos.

This programme emphasises that the ethos of a school rests on the bedrock of values held by its staff, and school leaders play a significant role in seeking to ensure that these values are understood, and shared as much as possible by the staff as a whole.

The ethos or atmosphere of the school and classroom is conveyed by all aspects of the learning environment:

- Visual environment: for example, what messages are conveyed by classroom displays?
- Physical environment: for example, what messages are conveyed by furniture arrangements in the classroom?
- Shared principles for teaching and learning: for example, what the school policies on assessment or homework imply about the school ethos.
- Consistent expectations for learning behaviour and social interaction amongst pupils: are these applied in all classes?
- Teachers' attitudes towards pupils: for example, how teachers express their expectations of individual pupils in terms of behaviour or achievement.

- The extent to which pupils have opportunities to participate in the life of the school: for example, how involved pupils feel with the discussions and decisions of the school council.

All of the areas above are also considered in later chapters within this book.

OVER TO YOU

In training

Select a school (or subject department) with which you are familiar and identify the ways in which an ethos or atmosphere is created by considering the factors listed above.

Note that all the factors can be either positive or negative – the fact that shared principles or consistent expectations exist does not necessarily mean that the effect on pupil learning will be positive.

Are there other factors which you feel are also important in the establishment of a school ethos? For example, religious or denominational affiliation? Single-sex secondary schools, or co-educational schools?

Starting your career

Can you identify particular customs (or rituals) that are significant within your school or department? You may have had to adjust to these yourself, on first arriving in your present or previous school(s).

These might include the ways in which achievement is (or is not) publicly acknowledged; the types of achievement that seem to be valued; and/or the use of language which is highly context specific and would probably not be understood by an outsider to the school or department.

In what ways might these factors impact on the learning of individual pupils? What might this imply for your practice?

Investigating learning and teaching

Research indicates that school ethos has a powerful effect on pupil learning (Sammons, Hillman and Mortimore, 1995). However, there is no single recipe for the development of a positive school ethos. The Scottish education website Learning and Teaching Scotland has links to a page on school ethos (**www.ltscotland.org.uk/healthpromotingschools/practitioners/schoolethos**). From here you can access materials and case studies from the Scottish Schools Ethos Network which examine how individual schools developed a more positive ethos in respect of improving attainment, improving behaviour and tackling bullying.

Transition: a significant issue for pupils in the 7–14 age range

Photo 1.2
Effective communication between primary and secondary schools can ease anxieties and get pupils off to a good start in Year 7

Source: Pearson Education Ltd. Clark Wiseman

So far, this chapter has taken a general look at the factors which impact on learners and teachers, and create a context for learning. A significant area particularly affecting pupils in the 7–14 age range, in addition to the areas of curriculum and assessment, is the management of transition between primary and secondary school. Research evidence indicates that the impact of changes in pedagogy and ethos in the two phases can have an adverse effect on the personal and academic well-being of some pupils (Galton *et al.*, 1999). Although pupils need to become accustomed to a different routine and classroom ethos each year as they progress through primary school, these smaller-scale transitions occur within a familiar overall context. The opportunities for effective communication about personal and academic issues between teachers are also greater within the smaller school setting.

Pupils within the 7–14 age group will have moved schools at least once, and in many cases twice, by the time they are 14. In each case they will need to adjust to a range of factors:

- a new physical environment, which may be confusing or intimidating both inside and outside the school buildings;
- a different school culture and ethos, with different expectations for behaviour and relationships with teachers and other adults;
- different approaches to curriculum and pedagogy, with more subject-based teaching;

- 'micro-cultures' associated with different subject-based teaching approaches in secondary schools, for example the different safety rules in laboratories and practical work areas, or expectations about how written work is set out in different subjects.

While many pupils look forward to their new school and the sense of 'being grown-up' associated with transfer, they also experience anxieties associated with how they will be treated by older pupils and by new teachers. Fears about bullying are particularly strong for more vulnerable pupils transferring to secondary school, but they are also experienced by those who are more confident and academically secure.

Most junior and secondary schools have effective induction systems focusing on pastoral support, which involve visits by key staff to feeder infant or primary schools and opportunities for Year 2 or 6 pupils to spend a 'taster day' at their future school. 'Buddy mentoring' schemes involving older pupils who have a specific responsibility for explaining school routines and practices to new pupils have become established within many schools.

In some cases, pastoral staff or teaching assistants designated as 'transition mentors' for vulnerable pupils entering Year 7 also help to ease anxieties and enable pupils to establish new social relationships. Transition mentors in primary schools may assist parents with school choices for primary pupils, support Year 6 children on visits to their new schools once their places have been confirmed and visit children in their secondary schools during their first term to follow up on any transition issues, such as liaising with pastoral and support staff. For a short case study about the work of one transition mentor go to **www.teachernet.gov.uk/casestudies** and follow links to 'Pupil support' and 'Transition'.

CASE STUDY

Two approaches to managing transition

Teachers' TV also provides useful case studies of effective pastoral systems to support transition.

Secondary Pastoral Care – Transition from Primary traces the work of the head of Year 7 in one secondary school as she visits local primary schools and organises familiarisation visits for Year 6 pupils to the secondary school during the summer term prior to their arrival. Former pupils of the primary schools who attend the local secondary also return to talk to Year 6 pupils about their experiences and what has helped them make the adjustment to secondary school life. The programme focuses particularly on a group of pupils who have been identified as being likely to find transition stressful, owing to social and learning difficulties. Special activities are provided to support them in preparing for their first visit to the school, and for starting the new term in September.

School Matters – Hi Tech Transition looks at two schools that use ICT to support the process of transition, alongside strategies such as preliminary visits by Year 6 pupils. In one example, video conferencing is used to introduce pupils to new teaching and learning approaches, and in the other a website and portal has been created specifically for Year 7 pupils. After visiting the school for two days, new pupils are encouraged to log on to the portal from home, for virtual tours of classrooms and an introduction to the curriculum.

For the majority of pupils, arrangements such as these appear to be helpful, although Ofsted (2002) found that very few schools undertook any evaluation of their induction programmes or transfer arrangements by seeking pupils' views on their experiences, or fed back to feeder primary schools on the subsequent progress of pupils in Year 7. It would appear that where pupils are identified as needing additional support at transition, for example those with recognised Special Educational Needs (SEN), this is usually forthcoming. However, other pupils who have not been specifically identified for support also continue to feel vulnerable, and could lose momentum and engagement with learning as a result. Year 7 pupils interviewed by Ofsted in 2002 said that although they were generally satisfied with transition and induction arrangements, they would have liked better supervision at lunchtimes and more personal support from teachers.

The Key Stage 3 'dip'

While the pastoral aspect of transition is often well managed, the evidence concerning continuity in terms of academic progress is much more mixed. Research evidence, and evidence from school inspections, clearly indicates the adverse effects of transition on pupil progress. Galton *et al.* (1999) found that up to 40% of pupils either slowed down or made no progress during the year after transfer. In 2003 a similar situation applied: approximately 30% of pupils made no progress in mathematics between Year 6 and Year 7, and the figure jumped to approximately 50% in English and science (DCSF, 2008: 3).

According to a report in 2002, although both primary and secondary schools recognised the importance of good communication and transfer of information between them, they did not give this a high priority. This was especially true in terms of providing detailed assessment information about pupils and some Year 7 pupils reported that they were repeating work they had already covered in English and mathematics lessons in Year 6 (Ofsted, 2002).

This situation had not altered very much in 2006/7, according to the *Annual Report of Her Majesty's Chief Inspector* (Ofsted, 2007), which reported:

> Where practice is best, primary schools ensure that teachers' assessments of Year 6 pupils are passed to their secondary schools in the term before they transfer, identifying those in need of additional support. In other cases, however, detailed records of pupils' progress in primary school are not passed to their new schools. Secondary school staff do not always know about the approaches to teaching and learning in use in their partner primary schools. As a result, teachers in one phase do not know enough about the practice of colleagues in the other to ensure continuity for pupils entering Year 7.

Thus continuity in learning not only involves curriculum content, but approaches to teaching and learning as well. Several strategies are in use to try to address problems of continuity:

Ofsted: the Office for Standards in Education is the government department responsible for inspecting schools and local authorities.

Special Educational Needs (SEN): the legal definition is that a child has learning difficulties or disabilities that make it harder for them to learn than most children of the same age.

- Regular exchange visits by Year 6 and Year 7 teachers in order to observe lessons and share information about teaching methods.

- The development of 'bridging units' where teaching on a topic starts in the last weeks of the summer term in Year 6 and is continued in the secondary school in Year 7. This approach works best where primary and secondary schools plan the materials together and can share ideas about teaching approaches and assessment. However, this is more difficult if a school has pupils from a large number of feeder primaries. Sometimes pupils also feel that they are doing 'old work' if the bridging unit is strongly associated with their primary schooling.

- The use of induction or 'learning to learn' programmes early in Year 7, to develop study skills and problem-solving strategies.

- Structured intervention programmes in secondary schools to re-engage pupils with learning if they show signs of disaffection. These can involve providing time for pupils to talk about the difficulties they are having, often with pastoral support staff such as **learning mentors**, involving pupils in setting their own targets for improvement and acknowledging small steps in their progress.

(Galton, Gray and Ruddock, 2003)

Learning mentor: a person working within a primary or secondary school to support pupils identified as being 'at risk' of academic failure. They form a bridge between pastoral and academic concerns.

Continued concerns about maintaining levels of achievement and engagement with learning have meant that some secondary schools are now utilising forms of curriculum organisation and teaching similar to those operating in primary schools. The recent changes to the Key Stage 3 curriculum support these approaches, which involve subject integration and fewer changes of teacher and teaching environment, to enable more focused pupil assessment, better pastoral support and greater stability for vulnerable learners. Other developments in bringing schools closer together arising from ECM may also increase shared understanding of teaching and learning approaches.

SUMMARY

This chapter has considered the range of influences, operating both within and beyond the school, which impact directly and indirectly on the classroom. The teaching and learning encounter can be imagined as taking place within a series of interdependent circles of influence on both teacher and learner. The classroom context is affected by the ethos of the school and by the demands of local and national policies on curriculum and classroom organisation. While these may have been informed by evidence from research, inspection evidence and analysis of statistical information about pupil achievement, policies will also be influenced by economic and ideological factors. Pupils within the 7–14 age range will have had to adjust to at least two different school contexts, and their motivation and engagement with learning will in part depend on how well these transitions are managed.

TAKING YOUR PRACTICE FURTHER

How much do you know about the systems in place in your school to ensure effective transitions between Key Stages 1 and 2 and/or Key Stages 2 and 3?

What information do you feel is, or would be, most helpful to you in supporting pupils' learning in a new school context, whether this involves movement between year groups or phases of education? How might you gain this information most effectively? What arrangements could you make to observe teaching in another Key Stage?

What strategies do you use, or have you observed, that are designed to help pupils adjust to the learning ethos in your classroom?

TAKING YOUR THINKING FURTHER

Consider a policy initiative which relates to your subject interest, or a particular aspect of education. Why do you think this policy has been introduced?

How does it relate to the aims and purposes of the National Curriculum (or equivalent document elsewhere in the UK)?

How far do you feel the initiative has been influenced by factors such as economic competitiveness or international developments?

How has it impacted on your local authority, local school and classroom context?

Find out more

If you are interested in the nature and purpose of the curriculum, you may wish to read:

White, J. (ed) (2004) *Re-thinking the School Curriculum; Values, Aims and Purposes.* **London: Routledge.**
This edited text considers how far different subjects are presently meeting the statement on Values and Purposes in the National Curriculum, discussed at the start of this chapter, and what changes to the curriculum is each area need to be made.

If you want to find out about international comparative data on pupil performance, this can be accessed as follows:

TIMSS (Trends in International Mathematics and Science). Available at: **http://timss.bc.edu**.

Surveys were conducted with primary and secondary pupils in 1995, 1999, 2003 and 2007.

PIRLS (Progress in International Reading Literacy Study). Surveys conducted with primary aged pupils in 2001 and 2006. Also at: **http://timss.bc.edu/**.

PISA (OECD Programme for International Student Assessment) surveys literacy, mathematics and science with 15 year olds. The latest survey was in 2006. Available at: **www.pisa.oecd.org**.

If you are interested in understanding more about educational policy:

Scott, D. (2000) *Reading Educational Research and Policy.* **London: RoutledgeFalmer.**

Chapter 2 in this book provides a framework for making sense of the ways policy documents are constructed.

White, J. (2008) *Aims as Policy in English Primary Education (Primary Review Research Survey 1/1).* **Cambridge: University of Cambridge Faculty of Education.**
This review looks at how the aims of primary education have been expressed at various points in the past, and how this has been reflected in policy.

If you want to find out more about issues relating to transition:

The Primary Review published this report on May 2008, available online at **www.primaryreview.org.uk**:

Blatchford, P., Hallam, S., Ireson, J. and Kutnick, P., with Creech, A. (2008) 'Classes, Groups and Transitions: structures for teaching and learning' (*Primary Review Research Survey 9/2***). Cambridge: University of Cambridge Faculty of Education.**

Alongside discussion of grouping in primary schools, and the effect of class size on learning, this review looks at the evidence about managing transition between Key Stages.

www.teachers.tv offers a number of programmes focusing on issues related to transition between primary and secondary phases, including subject-specific topics as well as pastoral issues, two of which are briefly described in this chapter.

Case studies on transition are also available at: **http://www.teachernet.gov.uk/casestudies/SubCatHome. cfm?id=55&sid=54**.

If you want to know more about new approaches to the curriclum at Key Stage 3, examples of three schools that have adopted these approaches can be seen at **www.teachers.tv** (search on 'KS3 New Visions'). The schools have very different catchment areas, but all have adopted cross-curricular ways of working that have had a positive impact on pupils' engagement with schooling and willingness to learn.

Glossary

Accountability: being publicly responsible for outcomes, including taking responsibility if pupils fail to perform as expected.

Differentiation: the adjustment of the teaching process according to the learning needs of pupils.

Ethos: derived from Greek, meaning 'to be accustomed to', this has come to mean the distinctive character and fundamental values of a particular social grouping.

Knowledge economy: this is a term used to identify the use of 'intangibles' such as knowledge, skills and innovative ideas in the 'information age' as resources to bring about economic advantages for countries. This is in contrast to economies based on the industrial production of 'tangible' products. For further information see **http://www.esrcsocietytoday.ac.uk/ ESRCInfoCentre/facts/index4.aspx**.

Learning mentor: a person working within a primary or secondary school to support pupils identified as being 'at risk' of academic failure. They form a bridge between pastoral and academic concerns.

National Strategies (Primary and Secondary): these are professional development programmes for primary and secondary teachers They provide resources to support teaching, and suggested frameworks for the curriculum.

They are widely used in schools, but are non-statutory. See **www.nationalstrategies.standards.dcsf.gov.uk/**.

Ofsted: the Office for Standards in Education is the government department responsible for inspecting schools and local authorities. It publishes reports on a wide range of topics, using evidence from inspections.

Qualifications and Curriculum Development Agency (QCDA): the official body responsible for all aspects of curriculum development and statutory assessment in England. It is sponsored by the Department for Children, Schools and Families (DCSF).

Socialisation: a term used by sociologists to define the process of learning to live within one's particular culture. This process of inducting individuals into values and assumptions about social roles enables social and cultural continuity to be maintained, but can also result in the continuation of stereotypical views about gender, ethnicity etc.

Social justice: the belief that every individual should have the chances and opportunities to make the most of their lives and use their talents to the full.

Special Educational Needs (SEN): the legal definition is that a child has learning difficulties or disabilities that make it harder for them to learn than most children of the same age.

References

Blair, T. (1998) *The Third Way*. Full article originally at **www.BritainUSA.com**; excerpts at **http://history.hanover.edu/courses/excerpts/111blair**.

DCSF (2007) *The Children's Plan*. Available at: **www.standards.dcsf.gov.uk**.

DCSF (2008) *Strengthening Transfers and Transitions: Partnership for Progress*. Available at: **www.standards.dcsf.gov.uk** or **www.teachernet.gov.uk/publications**.

Desforges, C. with Abouchaar, A. (2003) *The Impact of Parental Involvement, Parental Support and Family Education on Pupil Achievement and Adjustment*. DfES Research Report RR433. London: DfES.

DfES (2003) *Excellence and Enjoyment: A Strategy for Primary Schools*. Nottingham: DfES.

DfES (2004) *Every Child Matters: Change for Children*. Available at: **www.teachernet.gov.uk/publications**.

DfES (2006) *2020 Vision: The Report of the Teaching and Learning Review Group*. Available at: **www.teachernet.gov.uk/publications**.

Galton, M., Gray, J., Ruddock, J., *et al*. (1999) *The Impact of School Transitions and Transfers on Pupil Progress and Attainment*. Research Report RR131. Nottingham: DfEE.

Galton, M., Gray, J. and Ruddock, J. (2003) *Transfer and Transitions in the Middle Years of Schooling (7–14). Continuities and Discontinuities in Learning*. Research Report RR443. Nottingham: DfES.

Hall, K. and Øzerk, K. (2008) *Primary Curriculum and Assessment: England and Other Countries (Primary Review Research Survey 3/1)*. Cambridge: University of Cambridge Faculty of Education.

HMSO (2003) *The Victoria Climbié Inquiry: Report of an Inquiry by Lord Laming*. London: HMSO.

Le Metais, J. (2003) *International Trends in Primary Education. INCA Thematic Study No. 9*. London: QCA.

Ofsted (2002) *Changing Schools: An Evaluation of the Effectiveness of Transfer Arrangements at Age 11*. Available at: **www.ofsted.gov.uk**.

Ofsted (2007) *Annual Report of Her Majesty's Chief Inspector*. Available at: **www.ofsted.gov.uk**.

Sammons, P., Hillman, J. and Mortimore, P. (1995) *Key Characteristics of Effective Schools: A Review of School Effectiveness Research*. London: Institute of Education.

Shuayb, M. and O'Donnell, S. (2008) *Aims and Values in Primary Education: England and Other Countries (Primary Review Research Survey 1/2)*. Cambridge: University of Cambridge Faculty of Education.

CHAPTER 2

Values to Promote Learning

Because a significant portion of the practice in education[al administration] requires rejecting some courses of action in favour of a preferred one, values are generally acknowledged to be central to the field.

(Willower, 1992)

In this chapter you will:

- Reflect on your own values as an educator and explore their roots and genesis
- Consider recent social, political and cultural influences upon educational values
- Evaluate how values are manifest in the classroom – curriculum, school organisation and relationships

The central aim of this chapter is to realise that 'values are an integral part of teaching, reflected in what is taught and also how teachers teach and interact with pupils. Pupils spend the greatest amount of their daily time with teachers, who have significant opportunities to influence them' (Arthur, Davison and Lewis, 2005: 6). In exploring this aim, it will become apparent that the values underpinning classroom work are both explicit and implicit in the minute-by-minute operational as well as strategic decision making. Classrooms are a microcosm of society, and thus reflect the bigger debates and issues that society is seeking to address. The teacher's role is pivotal and hence it is of utmost importance that teachers reflect on the professional imperative that is their duty.

Introduction

The point of transition from primary to secondary education is arguably one of the most important rites of passage in the pupil's learning journey. Throughout this book, we highlight the conflicting experiences through this transition, but in exploring values in education we have the opportunity to evaluate the strands that could support the move between the phases.

In considering values in education, it is appropriate to search for a working definition of 'values' to serve as a reference point in the discussion. However, as we begin this exploration it is worth remembering that 'values is not a technical term. In talking about values we are talking about something which is part of the experience of everyone' (Haydon, 2007: 6). Values are experienced by all, though they may be challenging to define and vary in the way individuals regard and respond to them. The disciplines of sociology and moral and ethical philosophy contribute to this search for a definition.

J. Mark Halstead, an influential writer in the field of education and values, provides an accessible starting point in the following definition, which, interestingly, is the one subscribed to by the Values Education Council for the United Kingdom (the VEC is an important organisation in the promotion of education and values; **www.ve1. valueseducation.org.uk/**).

> Values are principles, fundamental convictions, ideals, standards or life
> stances which act as general guides to behaviour or as points of reference in
> decision-making or the evaluation of beliefs or actions and which are closely
> connected to personal integrity and personal identity.
>
> *(Halstead and Taylor, 1996: 5)*

While he is clear that values are about personhood, it is perhaps more explicit in other definitions that values motivate actions, and that a person's or community's values are made explicit in the actions they choose to pursue or reject. Clyde Kluckhohn, an eminent anthropologist and theorist in this area, takes us further by stating that the values lived out through chosen desirable actions are what characterises a group or an individual (Kluckhohn, 1951). This motivational or 'drive' quality begins to lift our conception of values from what might be thought of as a passive set of beliefs or principles to attributes which give meaning and purpose to our ways of living.

The values to which we subscribe actively inform choices we make. One might argue that, when applying values in decisions about right or wrong, we are displaying moral or ethical values. In the classroom setting, clearly the teacher will be making moral value judgements throughout the working day. Pre-planned classroom routines such as furniture layout and the grouping of pupils through to immediate behaviour management decisions will all call on the teacher to deploy his or her values to make a decision about who might be seated where or encouraged to work with whom. This might illustrate the teacher's values about inclusion, the ways in which he or she supports positive relationships or what work is of most importance. While this might hint at values being fixed and decisions somehow being 'black or white', sociologists such as Milton Rokeach suggest that 'a value system is an enduring organization of beliefs concerning desirable modes of conduct or end-states of existence along a continuum of relative importance' (1973: 54). In other words, a value system has, at its core, a set of outcomes which are considered preferable, and decisions which have these goals in mind are made along the way.

On reflection, it is apparent that teachers are working in a values-driven environment and are constantly being called upon to execute values-informed decisions. The National Curriculum Council, the predecessor to the **Qualifications and Curriculum Development Agency**, went so far as to say that:

> Values are inherent in teaching. Teachers are by the nature of their profession 'moral agents' who imply values by the way they address pupils and each other, the way they dress, the language they use and the efforts they put into their work.
>
> *(NCC, 1993)*

The NCC recommendations have been incorporated into the Training and Development Agency for Schools' (TDA) Standards for the award of **Qualified Teacher Status (QTS)** and the General Teaching Council for England (GTCE) make it clear that there is a cluster of attributes and behaviours that they label 'professional values' which a competent teacher is expected to display. A further consideration of professional values will be made later in this chapter.

Qualifications and Curriculum Development Agency (QCDA): the official body responsible for all aspects of curriculum development, and statutory assessment in England.

Qualified Teacher Status (QTS): Professional Standards are the current government's requirements that all teachers need to meet in order to be recognised as qualified teachers in England. They are organised in a progressive framework starting with *Qualified Teacher Status* and moving on to the *Core Standards* by the end of the first year of teaching.

WORKING IN THE CLASSROOM

The following quote is from the General Teaching Council for England (GTCE) Statement of Professional Values and Principles. Reflect on the passage and highlight the 'values' words. Can you think of examples, for each word, where you have been in a classroom and had to make a decision which has been influenced by the value?

> *Teachers treat young people fairly and with respect, take their knowledge, views, opinions and feelings seriously, and value diversity and individuality. They model the characteristics they are trying to inspire in young people, including enthusiasm for learning, a spirit of intellectual enquiry, honesty, tolerance, social responsibility, patience, and a genuine concern for other people.*
>
> **(http://www.gtce.org.uk/standards/professional/sopv)**

How does this statement relate to Halstead's definition above?

Where do your values come from?

Having explored some definitions of values, and glimpsed how these relate to the role of the professional teacher, it is appropriate to pause and consider where values come from and how they are formed. Educational philosopher Richard Bailey summarises the issues in stating that:

> Whilst we might like to think that we generate our views through raw intelligence and reason alone, the reality is that our beliefs often reflect our upbringing, previous experiences and social background.
>
> *(2006: 170)*

Photo 2.1 Values and beliefs are strongly influenced by family, social and cultural experiences

Source: Pearson Education Ltd. Rob van Petten

It is imperative that as teachers we are open to considering where our values are coming from and how they influence our operations in the classroom. Making this process explicit to ourselves ought to support the consistent and fair deployment of values-informed actions. According to Swatos, a sociologist of religion, it is the cognitive or 'thought-through' element that serves to distinguish values from subjective feelings and emotions (Swatos, 1998). Educational philosopher Graham Haydon suggests that we need to reflect on the origins of our values in order that we are best placed to meet values that are different from our own, or deal with values we feel less comfortable with in ourselves (Haydon, 2007). Indeed, Linda Rice, expert in group work, would go so far as to say that this engagement will 'necessitate change' (2005: 55) and therefore our values do not remain fixed.

Christopher Hodgkinson, expert in education leadership, offers a model for thinking about the influences and sources of people's values. He does this by encouraging us to consider the justification for our values. He divides these sources into three categories which have a sense of hierarchy and become progressively more sophisticated.

1. Subrational – values based in preference. This would include a range of values which are purely personal preference, where no moral imperative is at risk. An example might be a liking for a particular flavour of food or colour scheme.

2. Rational – values based in either consensus or consequences. Consensus values would include those which are generally shared by a group, community or society. An example here might be a consensus view that people should queue in an orderly fashion when waiting for a bus.

   Values based in consequence give consideration to the outcome of the decision. Following the above example, expecting a line of people at the bus stop gives consideration to the consequence of people using buses safely and avoiding accident.

3. Transrational – values with no rational basis which are called fundamental principles. This set of values is grounded in ethical thinking and might include aspects such as liberty, equality and justice. An example here could be the commitment to the inclusion of all learners in the classroom.

(Adapted from Hodgkinson, 1991)

THINKING IT THROUGH

Consider a lesson you have taught; perhaps go back to your evaluations to prompt you. In your mind, move through the lesson chronologically, listing any decisions or actions for which you were responsible that illustrate the subrational, rational (including consensus or consequence) and transrational.

Bailey (2006) points out the immediate and obvious shaping factors (family, friends, communities); we might call these consensus rational or even transrational if we are using the above model. The factors are opened out manifold if we consider the impact of global perspectives brought to us through the media and travel. By way of illustration, consider a recent news bulletin showing footage of children, in some impoverished communities in Europe, being used as street beggars and robbers. The children were shown taking money from bags, asking for food in café restaurants and then being beaten if they did not 'earn' enough for their families. We might be confronted by values which challenge our consensus views (begging is not desirable) or consequential factors (being beaten or caught). Our transrational values might be challenged by seeing children used in this way or by the act of theft. However, the commentary accompanying the images challenges us further in a different way by asking fundamental questions about human poverty and society's provision for those less well off.

The Kluckhohn Center for the Study of Values in the United States has been instrumental in motivating a wealth of study in the area of culture and values. They pioneered the development of the Values Orientation Model (VOM) which is a tool used to identify differences in core values between and across cultures. The variations are evidenced in the way people respond to questions around the five core human concerns. Table 2.1 is an adapted version.

Table 2.1 An adapted version of the VOM

Core human concerns/ orientations	Possible responses		
Human nature: What is the basic nature of people?	**Evil.** Most people can't be trusted. People are basically bad and need to be controlled.	**Mixed.** There are both evil people and good people in the world, and you have to check people out to find out which they are. People can be changed with the right guidance.	**Good.** Most people are basically pretty good at heart; they are born good.
Man–nature relationship: What is the appropriate relationship to nature?	**Subordinate to nature.** People really can't change Nature. Life is largely determined by external forces, such as fate and genetics. What happens was meant to happen.	**Harmony with nature.** Man should, in every way, live in harmony with nature.	**Dominant over nature.** It the great human challenge to conquer and control nature. Everything from air conditioning to the 'green revolution' has resulted from having met this challenge.
Time sense: How should we best think about time?	**Past.** People should learn from history, draw the values they live by from history, and strive to continue past traditions into the future.	**Present.** The present moment is everything. Let's make the most of it. Don't worry about tomorrow: enjoy today.	**Future.** Planning and goal setting make it possible for people to accomplish miracles, to change and grow. A little sacrifice today will bring a better tomorrow.
Activity: What is the best mode of activity?	**Being.** It's enough to just 'be'. It's not necessary to accomplish great things in life to feel your life has been worthwhile.	**Becoming.** The main purpose for being placed on this earth is for one's own inner development.	**Doing.** If people work hard and apply themselves fully, their efforts will be rewarded. What a person accomplishes is a measure of his or her worth.
Social relations: What is the best form of social organisation?	**Hierarchical.** There is a natural order to relations, some people are born to lead, others are followers. Decisions should be made by those in charge.	**Collateral.** The best way to be organised is as a group, where everyone shares in the decision process. It is important not to make important decisions alone.	**Individual.** All people should have equal rights, and each should have complete control over one's own destiny. When we have to make a decision as a group it should be 'one person, one vote.'

Source: Kohls (1981) reproduced in Gallagher (2001)

> ### WORKING IN THE CLASSROOM
>
> It is interesting to apply these to our own lives as individuals and then see how far they match up with our immediate circle of family and friends. Take some time to consider Table 2.1 and reflect upon how these core human concerns are evidenced in a school setting with which you are familiar.

Professional Development: the ongoing training, development and education that is available to a person working in a profession such as teaching.

Enculturation: the process of acceptance of another culture: the gradual acceptance by a person or group of the standards and practices of another person or culture.

Acculturation: might be considered a change in the cultural behaviour and thinking of a person or group of people through contact with another culture.

Assimilation: the process by which individuals or groups are absorbed into and adopt the culture of another society or group.

There appear to be two ways of utilising a model such as the VOM. First, one might use it as a tool to raise awareness amongst teachers as to the cultural differences they might encounter and to support their abilities to manage these in the classroom. This seems a valuable tool to support teachers' professional development and encourage reflection on their practice.

On the other hand, is it justifiable to use this as a matrix to support a programme of planned enculturation or acculturation for learners? Are teachers required to 'enculturate' or encourage their pupils into following the rules of the dominant society, so supporting the establishment agenda? Or is a teacher's professional duty to support acculturation and assimilation of a range of communities and groups?

CONTROVERSY

I think display work is very important, and I wanted to mark the celebration of my pupils' religious festivals with displays at the appropriate time in the entrance hall. I asked my mentor if I could do this with the help of some of my pupils. My mentor said the head wouldn't allow it. The head wasn't keen on religion – thought it was the cause of much of the world's problems – and would say that it would be divisive, leaving out those pupils who didn't have a religion.

(A student teacher quoted on **www.multiverse.ac.uk**)

If enculturation is about acquiring the expected values and norms of the dominant culture which surrounds you, and acculturation is about learning from different cultures at first hand, what do you think about:

- The head teacher's policy and practice in this school?
- The approach the student wished to take?

While we are all aware of different achievement patterns across cultural groups, with underperformance reported in Afro-Caribbean boys, Pakistani and Traveller pupils (see **http://www.ttrb.ac.uk/ViewArticle2.aspx?ContentId=10341** for a good summary), how far do we have a responsibility to include different value preferences in the teaching and curriculum, or should we be maintaining the dominant values and

Photo 2.2 Communal school gatherings and festivals are an important way to celebrate the diversity of beliefs and values of the pupils

Source: Report Digital

provide access programmes for learners to adapt their values base in order to succeed?

Lifelong learning expert Michael Kazanjian provides a powerful conclusion to this dilemma. He argues that traditional schooling, through its resistance to cultural changes, might be considered 'static and inert' and therefore does not have the capacity to generate that which is new or relevant to the contemporary world. He argues that this renders society at risk of falling into 'a backward state of chaos and dehumanization' (2002: 99). In a global society, schools must necessarily involve engaging with new and different value sets. This has implications for the professional values expectations required of teachers, and will be revisited in the last section of this chapter.

What is education for?

The previous discussion began to hint at the purposes of education. How a society conceives of its schools, the curriculum and the education workforce are all manifestations of the values in action. In Chapter 1 we considered briefly the aims and purposes of curricula, and made some introductory remarks as to the values underpinning them. In this section we will be taking this further by exploring the values threads as traced through from legislation to policy and into practice. At the point of writing, the English curriculum is poised at what is probably the most significant cusp

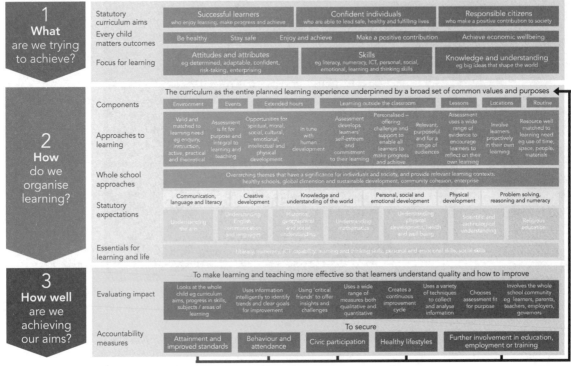

Figure 2.1
A big picture of the curriculum

Source:
http://www.qcda.org.uk/library/Assets/media/BigPicture_2008.pdf

of change since the introduction of a national curriculum 20 years ago. The government's Qualifications and Curriculum Development Agency (QCDA) has been leading a review of the secondary curriculum which has resulted in the revision of the Key Stage 3 curriculum and the principles enshrined in the 'big picture' (Figure 2.1). This is an attempt at providing an overview of all aspects of pupils' work in school, which slot together to provide a coherent learning experience.

These principles are now being used to inform a 'root and branch' (DCSF, 2007: 17) review of the primary curriculum.

THINKING IT THROUGH

Use the 'big picture' diagram in Figure 2.1 or download a copy of it. Taking a highlighter, select all the words which relate to values. Reflect on your highlights against Kohls' (Table 2.1). How far can you map the values onto the cultural differences? Does there appear to be a dominant set of values emerging?

As highlighted in Chapter 1, a key driver for current education policy is the *Every Child Matters* agenda (DfES, 2003a), which provides a focus on the child's individual needs. Sitting alongside this is the imperative to raise standards which is documented in several government publications, such as *Excellence and Enjoyment* (DfES, 2003b) which relates to the primary ages. Maya Shuayb and Sharon O'Donnell, writing for the Primary Review (**www.primaryreview.org.uk**), highlight the tensions in the way the curriculum is developing, with it being expected to respond to and reflect societal and government agendas. They refer to this as an example of a 'hybrid' approach to values and aims in the [primary] curriculum which are 'economically driven, learner-centred, and society-influenced which can . . . sometimes appear contradictory' (2008: 2.4): An illustration here might be the possible clash of values around including all learners as set against the pressure to achieve and publish a good set of academic results in exam or league tables.

It is interesting to explore how we have arrived at this eclectic mix of values. Bailey (2006) charts the influence of key educational thinkers, namely Plato, Rousseau and Dewey, and explores how their influences can be seen in the curriculum. While he is writing about the primary curriculum, his views can equally be applied across the phases of education.

Plato was a classical Greek philosopher. In summary, his thinking might be evidenced in education that is community based, where a person needs to be aware of the hierarchy and their position within it. This might lead to a system which values different educational input and priorities for different people, so leading to practices such as streaming or selection. Rousseau, an eighteenth-century philosopher, focused on the individualism of learners and the notion that this should be a core value in schooling. This would lead to a system which promoted education through planned learning experiences appropriate to the child's stage of development. John Dewey was a philosopher and educational reformer. His work, developing on from Rousseau, focused on an education which allowed children to develop through problem-solving activities closely matched to their own interests.

Education in post-war Britain has grappled with its expression of the values and aims of education. This journey is articulated very effectively in some of the findings of the current independent Primary Review (http://www.primaryreview.org.uk/). This major series of studies, directed by Sir Robin Alexander of Cambridge University, is reporting on all aspects of primary education, including the curriculum. The findings will be relevant across all key stages. One of the key dichotomies of the past 60 years is the divide between child-centred, progressive education and the socio-economic and political drivers which advocated a more centralised curriculum focusing on content and process.

Child-centred education was considered progressive in that all learning was constructed from and around the needs and interests of the individual child. At its extreme, this might be seen in a child being given complete freedom to choose what he or she chose to do at school and when.

The economic and political drivers for education might be considered to be the skills and knowledge which learners will ultimately need to contribute to the prosperity of society. For example, the current focus on raising interest and achievement in science and technology is considered vital if the country is to compete in the world economy.

There is much written about the fact that in the development of the current National Curriculum, little attention was paid to underpinning aims and values until

Child-centred education/ pedagogy: an approach to teaching which focuses on the learning needs of the children in the class, rather than on following a pre-set curriculum with objectives determined by the teacher or adminstrators.

after the content had been published. In 2008, John White, also writing for the Primary Review, is critical of the fact that aims and values appeared to have been added as an afterthought and even then went largely ignored.

Nonetheless, in commenting upon the list of aims and values that were eventually included in the National Curriculum, White summarises the tensions discussed in the previous paragraphs. He notes that the aims and values are fit 'for a tolerant, liberal democratic society concerned with its economic well-being and aware of its global responsibilities' (2008: 7–8) (**http://curriculum.qca.org.uk/uploads/Statement-of-values_tcm8-12166.pdf**).

Having considered the historical factors influencing the values underpinning the curriculum, how does this impact upon the curriculum content and how it is addressed in schools? The curriculum, as it is currently conceived, sees pupils learning a series of discrete subjects. White (2008) argues that the subjects have driven the aims of the curriculum until relatively recently. The introduction of the new Key Stage 3 curriculum from September 2008, the proposed extension of early principles for integrated cross-curricular learning and the possible phased introduction of foundation subjects in the primary sector seem to suggest that the 'power house' that is the domain of the subjects is perhaps being shifted. An increased emphasis upon the skills and processes in the curriculum, rather than content is further evidence that the values in education are being conceived around the ability of the learner to engage with, manipulate and problem-solve, rather than being a passive recipient of, a body of knowledge.

Nonetheless, it must be acknowledged that there has been, and still is, a body of knowledge within each domain of the curriculum which is considered worthy of study.

CASE STUDY

Religious Education

While not part of the National Curriculum, RE has a statutory status on the curriculum in schools and must be taught to all pupils in stated schools. Legislation in 1944 (Education Act) and 1988 (Education Reform Act) enshrined the unique status of RE, the content of which is to be determined by representative groups to reflect the local communities. A period of considerable diversity and variation in local interpretation ensued after 1988, but all under the banner of legislation which prescribed that syllabi 'shall reflect the fact that the religious

traditions in Great Britain are in the main Christian whilst taking account of the teaching and practices of the other principal religions represented in Great Britain' (Education Reform Act; DES, 1988: Chapter 40, 8(3)).

Debates ranged from those which focused on which religions should be studied, in which key stage, through to which pedagogical strategies were most effective (see Grimmitt, 2000) and whether a teacher needed a faith or not.

In 2005, heavily influenced by Ofsted reports on the variation in standards in RE, the QCA published a Non-statutory Framework for

Religious Education (QCA, 2005). The Steering Group was made up of representatives from 27 faith, professional and political associations. The introductory rationale for the publication is as follows:

> The framework was developed by QCA in partnership with the DfES and a wide range of faith and belief communities and professional RE associations. The framework sets out standards for learning and attainment and exemplifies the contribution of religious education to the school curriculum. The framework highlights the significant contribution religious education makes to pupils' spiritual, moral, social and cultural development and its important role in preparing pupils for life in a diverse society.
>
> The guidance is designed to benefit all pupils by improving the quality of teaching and learning in religious education.
>
> (QCA, 2005)

THINKING IT THROUGH

In reflecting on this case study, consider the following questions

- Which religions should be included in the curriculum? Why?
- Should teachers be expected to teach a faith that is not their own?
- What is the place of RE in the wider curriculum and society?

Reflect on your answers to these questions having had a discussion with your peers. Can you identify a values base to your answers and deliberations? Where do you agree and what points do you find are most contentious?

Michael Grimmitt, an influential religious education theorist, explores the values base underpinning the teaching of RE through his discussion of the social and political journey of the subject. This provides an excellent example of how the education curriculum, not only RE, 'has become the victim of ideological agendas' (2000: 7) Grimmitt's work traces the social, cultural and political influences that have shaped, buffeted and restricted the content and the teaching strategies for the subject. These influences include immigration, multi-culturalism and the perceived status of the Church of England as the national religion.

Once the content of the curriculum has been decided, teachers then have to to make decisions about how they teach the syllabus and the resources they use to support the learning. Once again, values are used as a reference point for these decisions. Looking back to Table 2.1, with particular attention to the row on social relationships, it is possible to see how the teacher's values will significantly influence the pedagogical choices adopted. If, for example, the teacher has values tendencies which support hierarchical as opposed to collateral views of social relationships, then he or she is likely to use more didactic, teacher-directed teaching methods. Of course, this

Didactic: teaching through direct instruction or demonstration with little pupil involvement.

necessarily has implications for the choice of resources. Textbooks and visual and technological resources all convey sets of values. This is illustrated by David Sadker, an American equality expert, who provides a useful model for the detection of bias in educational materials. In summary, he urges that we seek out 'seven forms of bias' evident in:

- Invisibility – the partial or complete exclusion of a group of society in the text.
- Stereotyping – the application of a set of characteristics to a group. For example, women portrayed as homemakers.
- Imbalance and selectivity – the presentation of a selected set of views and the omission of others. For example, texts chosen for an English course are from white male authors.
- Unreality – sometimes the 'glossing' over of unpleasant events. For example, the ignoring of events or facts from history.
- Fragmentation and isolation – the separation of one group in a text or they are shown not interacting with others in society. For example, a section dedicated to black scientists.
- Linguistic bias – language is used to convey bias about a group in society. For example, chairman, mankind.
- Cosmetic bias – the cover of a resource presents a multi-cultural image but the contents focus on work by one group in society.

(Sadker, accessed 28 May 2008)

While Sadker acknowledges the significant progress in this area, he is clear that vigilance is still needed in order to avoid unintended stereotyping or marginalising of certain groups within the classroom.

Texts on leadership in education (for example, Haydon, 2007) suggest that teachers and pupils need to work in an environment where there is a clear and jointly owned sense of values underpinning the **ethos** of the institution. This leaves the teacher with a clearer reference point for decision making.

Ethos: derived from Greek, meaning 'to be accustomed to', this has come to mean the distinctive character and fundamental values of a particular social grouping.

It could be argued that the government recognised the need to support the explicit teaching of values to pupils in the classroom by the introduction of Citizenship as a curriculum area in 2004. This explicitly promotes a view that pupils should be pro-active individuals who explore social justice and moral responsibility, and consider the impact of their decisions on others. This explicit and often discrete teaching of values is supported by a significant proliferation of classroom resources. This centralisation and standardisation, while following the same pattern as other aspects of UK and other government education policies, at best may have at its core the laudable aim of making pupils articulate and reflective in relation to the motivating factors behind their behaviours. However, one might question the motives around increased central control and direction in the content and delivery of the curriculum. Maha Shuayb and Sharon O'Donnell, in reporting for the Primary Review, provide a comprehensive précis of education policies which have been subject to increasing central control (Shuayb and O'Donnell, 2008).

THINKING IT THROUGH

The following is a list of concepts and values which underpin citizenship education:

a) equality and diversity;
b) law and human rights;
c) the common good;
d) rights and responsibilities;
e) power and authority;
f) freedom and order;
g) conflict and co-operation;
h) individuals and society;
i) democracy;
j) the rule of law and justice.

Refer back to the previous discussion on 'acculturation' and 'enculturation' in relation to values in the classroom. How far does the Citizenship curriculum provide space for acculturation, or is it in fact the Establishment's way of supporting a programme of enculturation?

Teachers: professional values

In order to be qualified to work in the United Kingdom, teachers need to be registered with their relevant professional body. Membership of bodies such as the General Teaching Council of England (GTCE) is dependent upon passing a set of standards at the initial and induction stages of their career. As noted earlier, this requires 'sign-up' to a code of conduct which includes professional values. Since their original inception, the standards for Qualified Teacher Status (QTS) have passed through several iterations. The early version, first published as a set of competences in 1992, was the first attempt to define criteria for entry into the profession. These served to define teachers as content experts capable of operating in a school organised around subject delivery. It was only in 2002, and following considerable representation from the GTCE, that the Standards included a section on professional values. Professor of Education James Arthur and colleagues explore the complexities and tensions in supporting the importance of the values base to the profession, yet at the same time wishing to avoid the 'forensic detail' (Arthur *et al.*, 2005: viii) and emphasis upon outcomes that come with a Standards-driven model. The values base provides a reference point and rationale for the inclusion of the many individual Standards which teachers must demonstrate.

The latest version, titled '**Professional Standards for Teachers**', came into effect in 2007 and the context for its development is very illuminating. Recent government

Professional Standards: the current government requirements that all teachers need to meet in order to be recognised as qualified teachers in England.

policy initiatives, inspired by the *Every Child Matters* agenda (DfES, 2003a) and *The Children's Plan* (DCSF, 2007), sit within the larger review of the education workforce. For the first time there is an attempt to lay out the progression opportunities and pathways for a range of professionals working with children. For teachers, this starts with the Qualifying (Q) Standards as part of initial training and continues into early professional development Core (C) Standards. There is then the expectation that teachers will continue in their careers through Post-threshold (P), to Excellent teacher (E) and finally Advanced skills teacher (A). There are similar pathway maps for support workers and leaders in schools. In this context it is useful to look at the values-related standards for teachers.

At the initial training stage, teachers are expected to 'demonstrate the positive values, attitudes and behaviours they expect from children and young people' (TDA, 2007: Q2) and then, once in their early career, there is an expectation that teachers 'hold positive values and attitudes and adopt high standards of behaviour in their professional role' (TDA, 2007: C2). Moving on up the Standards levels, it could be considered alarming that all discrete mention of 'values' disappears from the Standards for post-threshold, excellent and advanced skills teachers! Even if one is more subtle in the trawl by searching for embedded values in language around relationships and respect, it is disappointing to note that these too are similarly lacking in the advanced stages of career development. This seems to contradict the need for an explicit articulation of values at leadership level as proposed by researchers such as Haydon (2007).

The Standards, being measures of output, necessarily require a process of summative assessment. Institutions invest significantly in these assessment and moderation procedures to ensure consistency of judgement. In recognition of the fact that an atomistic approach to assessment of performance in the classroom is not always helpful, recent trends have been to work to a holistic approach. The following extract is but one example of this methodology. It comes from the *Handbook for the Inspection of Initial Teacher Training* (Ofsted, 2007).

THINKING IT THROUGH

Read the following 'characteristics of a satisfactory trainee, grade 3'. Highlight the words or phrases which are indicative of the teacher's values in action in the classroom. There is the potential for this candidate to move to grade 2 (good) and grade 1 (outstanding). In discussion with a colleague, consider what this trainee might need to do to move to the higher grades.

Trainees expect pupils to learn and aim to raise pupils' achievement appropriately as a result of their teaching. They evaluate their teaching in order to improve it, but some may need the additional help of more experienced teachers to assess its impact on pupils' learning. Trainees contribute usefully to the corporate life of the school and relate to pupils well, respecting their backgrounds and interests.

THINKING IT THROUGH: *CONTINUED*

Trainees have sound knowledge and understanding in the subjects or areas of learning they are trained to teach and are proficient in their use of ICT. They are able to describe and communicate relevant concepts and skills to pupils. They know and understand, as appropriate, national curriculum and national strategy frameworks, guidance and statutory requirements and use them to support their planning.

Trainees set clear objectives for their lessons, but not always with the appropriate, specific detail, and this means that the match of activities and resources to intended outcomes is not always fully worked out. They take account of the needs of different groups of pupils and are able to differentiate their teaching accordingly with guidance from an experienced teacher. Trainees are aware of the potential range of teaching strategies, but do not use them all with equal confidence in their own teaching. They organise and manage time and resources to support their learning objectives. They establish a clear framework for classroom discipline, in line with the school's expectations. Relationships with pupils are sound, enabling pupils to learn effectively.

Trainees use a range of assessment strategies and, with the help of more experienced teachers, are able to identify pupils' individual needs. They are able to use the school's performance data to place the performance of the pupils they teach into context. They mark pupils' work constructively, provide helpful feedback and record and report achievement, guided by the school's practice.

Source: Ofsted (2007) p. 58

In general terms it is to be welcomed that policy and practice in relation to teacher development are recognising the intrinsic worth of a values base to the profession. In reality, this shift in emphasis is not without issue or tension. This is to be expected through any change process. It is worth highlighting the strong (re)emergence of the desirability of reflection in the teacher's list of skills and attributes. Work sponsored by researchers such as Donald Schön in the 1980s and beyond promoted the view that a teacher as professional will need to be engaged in 'reflection-in-action'. Increasingly, this view is being given credence in policy documents. The TDA QTS Standards (2007) require a new teacher to be able to 'reflect on and improve their practice' (Q7a) and Ofsted (2007) are required to look for evidence of teachers' evaluations being used to improve their teaching. There is a need for caution here, as it is most often the case that, when teachers are asked to reflect, they tend to focus on technical aspects of their practice such as behaviour and resource management, and leave aside exploration of values and aims, the implication being that the current criteria for assessing teachers do not provide a structured incentive to reflect on the values underpinning their practice.

It could be suggested that what is required is an explicit framework to serve as a reference point for reflecting on values. Teachers might then feel supported to reflect on those areas of their practice, such as values, which are more about the affective or human aspects of teaching and learning.

WORKING IN THE CLASSROOM

In conclusion, take time to review the Values Orientation Model (Table 2.1) in relation to the classroom incident below. What values are evident in the pupil's and teacher's behaviours? If this scenario happened to a colleague, what advice would you give them?

A Year 7 class has arrived at their lesson in a south London secondary school in an agitated and lively manner. One boy of Afro-Caribbean heritage is seen to trip up a fellow pupil deliberately. The white female teacher in her mid-twenties, having seen the incident, asks to speak with him. She knows that there is a history of disruptive behaviour on the part of this pupil. While talking to him outside the classroom, his head remains lowered to the floor. The teacher becomes agitated because he will not lift his head to make eye contact as she speaks to him.

On reflection, the teacher was becoming increasingly anxious because she 'cannot get through to him about his behaviour. He just will not look at me!'

Schön argues that 'reflection-in-action is central to the art through which practitioners sometimes cope with the troublesome "divergent" situations of practice' (2002: 7). Using the VOM might help the teacher articulate her values in relation to authority and compliance, while at the same time exploring the cultural differences which might mean one shows respect by keeping a head bowed to a teacher.

SUMMARY

This chapter has provided the space for you to reflect upon your own values as an individual and as an educator. Values are the underpinning reference points for decision making, whether it be subconscious or explicit, for the teacher in the classroom or the policy maker in central government (see Figure 2.2). This complex network of values is informed and directed by cultural, social and political factors. Pupils transferring from primary to secondary school will see values expressed in different ways as they make the journey of transition. The curriculum and ethos need to provide a space where they can explore and articulate their understandings of underpinning values. It is at this time that teachers need to be finely in tune with the subtle variations in expression of values to support their pupils.

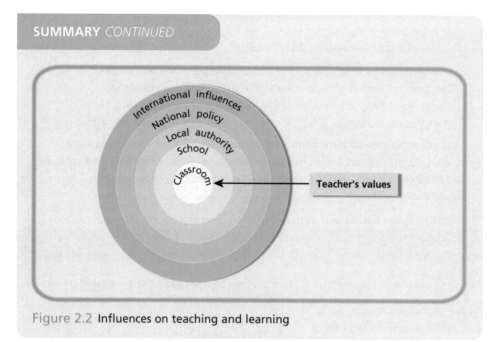

Figure 2.2 Influences on teaching and learning

TAKING YOUR PRACTICE FURTHER

Take time to review the mission statement in your school. How are the values made explicit in the language used in this document? Reflect upon the policies, teaching strategies, resources and children's activities that you have used in a short period of time – perhaps a day or week in school. How are the values in the mission statement lived through in the practical life of the school?

How are they similar to or different from those applying to your pupils in other schools where you have worked?

How far can primary and secondary schools work together to ensure that pupils' transitions are supported by an introduction to ethos, values and expectations in different schools' settings?

TAKING YOUR THINKING FURTHER

Research the differences between codes of professional values and practice for teachers in the different parts of the United Kingdom or internationally. For example, try visiting the following websites for the councils covering the United Kingdom.

> **TAKING YOUR THINKING FURTHER** *CONTINUED*
>
> The General Teaching Council for Scotland **http://www.gtcs.org.uk/**
> The General Teaching Council for Wales **http://www.gtcw.org.uk/**
> The General Teaching Council for England **http://www.gtce.org.uk/**
> The General Teaching Council for Northern Ireland **http://www.gtcni.org.uk/**
>
> Consider their mission statements and other publications. How far are they similar? Do they reflect local or cultural variations? How might they impact upon you differently if you were to teach in the different countries?

Find out more

If you are interested in finding out more about cultural variation in values you may wish to look into the work of the Kluckhohn Center for the Study of Values. There are various papers available online, best located using a search engine, which explore the application of the Values Orientation Model. The following two papers provide a good outline of the model and attempt to explore practical applications: **http://www.joe.org/joe/2001december/tt1.php** and **www.spokanecounty.org/.../Values%20Orientation%20Method.doc.**

If you wish to explore different types of values, it is worth reading further on the Rokeach Value System (RVS). A copy of this survey can be found at **http://www.cbe.wwu.edu/kristityran/MGMT313/Rokeach%20Value%20Survey.DOC.**

There are several journals focusing on values in education, many of which are available online. The *Journal of Values in Education* is a Scottish publication which can be accessed through the website **www.valueseducation.co.uk**. The *Journal of Beliefs and Values* (available at **www.informaworld.com**) and the *Journal of Moral Education* (available at **www.tandf.co.uk**) are highly respected publications which explore values education in relation to religious and moral perspectives.

Glossary

Acculturation: might be considered a change in the cultural behaviour and thinking of a person or group of people through contact with another culture. In this chapter this is conceived of as a two-way process.

Assimilation: the process by which individuals or groups are absorbed into and adopt the culture of another society or group.

Child-centred education/pedagogy: an approach to teaching which focuses on the learning needs of the children in the class, rather than on following a pre-set curriculum with objectives determined by the teacher or adminstrators. It is closely linked to, but not identical to, differentiation, which can also be employed in the context of a predetermined curriculum.

Didactic: teaching through direct instruction or demonstration with little pupil involvement.

Enculturation: the process of acceptance of another culture: the gradual acceptance by a person or group of the standards and practices of another person or culture.

Ethos: derived from Greek, meaning 'to be accustomed to', this has come to mean the distinctive character and fundamental values of a particular social grouping.

Professional Development: the ongoing training, development and education that is available to a person working in a profession such as teaching.

Professional Standards: the current government requirements that all teachers need to meet in order to be recognised as qualified teachers in England. They are organised in a progressive framework starting with those for *Qualified Teacher Status (QTS)* and moving on to the *Core Standards* by the end of the first year of teaching.

Qualifications and Curriculum Development Agency (QCDA): the official body responsible for all aspects of curriculum development, and statutory assessment in England. It is sponsored by the Department for Children, Schools and Families (DCSF).

References

Arthur, J., Davison, J. and Lewis, M. (2005) *Professional Values and Practice. Achieving the Standards for QTS.* London: RoutledgeFalmer.

Bailey, R. (2006) The aims of primary education, in Arthur, J. Grainger, T. and Wray. D. (eds) *Learning to Teach in the Primary School.* London: Routledge.

DCSF (2007) *The Children's Plan.* Available at: **http://www.dcsf.gov.uk/publications/childrensplan.**

DES (1988) *Education Reform Act.* London: HMSO. Available at: **http://www.opsi.gov.uk/Acts/acts1988/Ukpga_19880040_en_1.htm.**

DfES (2003a) *Every Child Matters.* London: DfES.

DfES (2003b) *Excellence and Enjoyment: A Strategy for Primary Schools.* Available at: **http://www.standards.dfes.gov.uk/.**

DfES (2004) *Every Child Matters: Change for Children.* Available at: **www.everychildmatters.gov.uk.**

Grimmitt, M. (2000) *Pedagogies of Religious Education: Case Studies in the Research and Development of Good Pedagogic Practice in RE.* Great Wakering: McCrimmons.

Halstead, J. and Taylor, M. (eds) (1996) *Values in Education and Education in Values.* London: Falmer Press.

Haydon, G. (2007) *Values for Educational Leadership.* London: Sage.

Hodgkinson, C. (1991) *Educational Leadership: The Moral Art.* New York: State University of New York.

Kazanjian, M. (2002) *Learning Values Lifelong.* New York: Rodopi.

Kluckhohn, C. (1951) Values and values-orientations in the theory of action, in Parsons, T. and Shils, E. (eds) *Towards a General Theory of Action.* Cambridge, MA: Harvard University Press.

Kohls, L. (1981) *Developing Intercultural Awareness.* Washington, DC: Sietar Press; reproduced in Gallagher, T.

(2001) The values orientation method: a tool to help understand cultural differences, *Journal of Extension, vol. 39, No. 6* (accessed 29 May 2008 at **www.joe.org**).

National Curriculum Council (1993) *Spiritual and Moral Development.* London: HMSO.

Ofsted (2007) *Handbook for the Inspection of Initial Teacher Training.* Available at: **www.ofsted.gov.uk.**

QCA (2005) *Non-statutory Framework for Religious Education.* Available at: **www.qcda.org.uk.**

Rice, L. (2005) *Professional Values And Practice: Meeting The Standards.* London: Routledge.

Rokeach, M. (1973) *The Nature of Human Values.* New York: Free Press.

Sadker, D. (accessed 28 May 2008) *Some Practical Ideas for Confronting Curricular Bias.* Available at: **www.sadker.org/curricularbias.htm.**

Schön, D. (2002) Reflection in Action, in Pollard, A. (ed.) *Readings for Reflective Teaching.* London: Continuum.

Shuayb, M. and O'Donnell, S. (2008) *Aims and Values in Primary Education: England and other countries (Primary Review Research Survey 1/2).* Cambridge: University of Cambridge Faculty of Education. Available at: **www.primaryreview.org.uk.**

Swatos, W. (1998) *Encyclopedia of Religion and Society.* Available at: **http://hirr.hartsem.edu/ency/values.htm** (accessed 25 June 2008).

TDA: Training and Development Agency for Schools (2007) *Professional Standards for Teachers.* Available at: **http://www.tda.gov.uk/teachers/professionalstandards.**

White, J. (2008) *Aims as Policy in English Primary Education (Primary Review Research Survey 1/1).* Cambridge: University of Cambridge Faculty of Education. Available at: **www.primaryreview.org.uk.**

Willower, D. (1992) Educational administration: intellectual trends, *in Encyclopedia of Educational Research.* Toronto: Macmillan.

3 Communities of Learners

In this chapter you will:

- Consider the potential learning communities with which schools and teachers engage
- Consider ways in which effective communication between the home and school can be developed and maintained
- Begin to understand the relationship between schools and their communities in terms of the duty to promote community cohesion
- Develop your understanding of the range of Continuing Professional Development opportunities that exist within and beyond schools

Pearson Education Ltd/Phovoir. Imagestate

What do all these examples have in common?

- Schools in Manchester where some 8–11 year old pupils and their families have up to 10 hours per week mentoring and family support in areas where gang membership and gun crime rates are high. The mentors are mainly 16–18 year olds from the local area who work with younger pupils to encourage them to engage in sports or arts activities.

- A group of primary schools whose teachers worked together for a year, supported by local university lecturers, on a shared project to develop children's writing skills.

- Clubs run in schools around Milton Keynes where parents can develop their IT skills, while at the same time researching local history topics to produce websites for school and community use.

Introduction

This chapter looks at the ways in which schools can operate as part of a community of learners, which includes parents and members of the local community as well as pupils and teachers (see Figure 3.1). The examples given above provide very different views of how such learning communities might operate. During this chapter you will be encouraged to recognise the ways in which learning communities exist within the schools with which you are familiar, and also to think about how you can contribute to the development of a positive learning community as a new teacher.

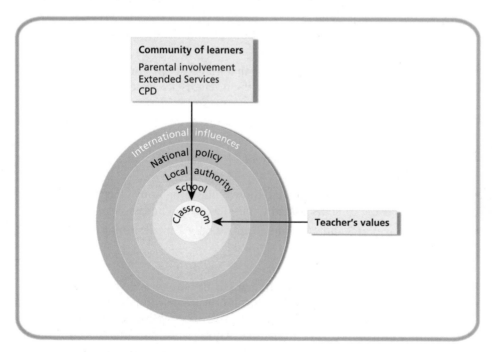

Figure 3.1
Influences on teaching and learning

The term 'learning community' can be used in a variety of contexts, but as a starting point for this chapter we are using it to mean a school that values and actively supports learning for everyone who is connected with it in some way. It also means that there is an ethos within the school of valuing continuing learning for all staff, whatever their role. Later in the book, we will consider the importance of collaborative learning as a significant aspect of developing a full 'community of learners'.

Schools and their communities – parents as partners

Whatever your stage of professional development, your appreciation of the role of parents in their children's education will be very important, both to you as a teacher and to the children in your class(es). Government policy guidelines and research evidence agree in placing a high value on the role of parents in supporting pupils' learning.

John Bastiani's booklet *Involving Parents, Raising Achievement* (Bastiani, 2003) was published by the Department for Educational and Skills (DfES) to support this message. The booklet identifies evidence from research which indicates the powerful effects of parental involvement on pupils' achievement between the ages of 5 and 16.

Key findings on parental involvement in education

- Children of parents who take an active interest in their schooling, and show high levels of interest, progress 15% more in maths and reading between 11 and 16 years than other children.
- Gains in pupil achievement that stem from parental involvement programmes and activities tend to be permanent.
- In schools with matched intakes, those that do best have, among other things, strong links with parents and families; the reverse is also true.
- Family influences have a much more powerful effect upon children's attitudes and achievements than either school or neighbourhood factors – even when these are added together.
- Much of the variation in achievement of 14 year olds in English, maths and science is due to home factors.
- When similar schools are compared, those with strong home–school links have consistently fewer problems related to pupil work and behaviour.
- Between the ages of 5 and 16, children spend only a small proportion (15%) of their lives in school.

(Bastiani, 2003: 3)

These findings indicate that parental influence is the strongest determinant of educational success with the 7–16 age group. It is thus extremely important that schools as institutions, and teachers as individuals, are able to establish genuine and positive relationships with parents. This means that schools and individual teachers should look for ways of relating to the various cultures of their local community, rather than automatically expecting parents to fit in with the structures and expectations of the school. This involves:

- examining our own values and assumptions about 'good' parenting;
- being sensitive about pupils' home backgrounds in terms of home–school communication;
- ensuring that schools are seen as welcoming to parents and carers from a variety of home contexts.

The next sections of this chapter consider these sometimes challenging issues in more detail.

Values and assumptions about parenting

Parents are seen as a crucial element in current government policy. 'We need parents who are prepared to take responsibility for supporting their child's education,' said David Blunkett, then Secretary of State for Education, in 1999. The subsequent introduction of home–school agreements which outlined parental responsibilities, as well as those of the school and individual pupil, marked the start of a series of initiatives aimed at increasing parental involvement in education. However, some writers have argued that these policies are based on assumptions about parents and their willingness (or lack of it) to support their children in school. If schools and teachers are to establish positive relationships with parents and sustain high expectations of pupils, we need to examine such assumptions carefully.

CONTROVERSY

Making 'middle-class' assumptions?

In 2001, the educational writer Sharon Gewirtz wrote an article called 'Cloning the Blairs' (Gewirtz, 2001). She argues that government initiatives on parenting seemed to want everyone to share the kinds of values and behaviours supposedly represented by the then prime minister Tony Blair and his family. Since educational research shows that children of middle-class parents achieve better in school that those from working-class backgrounds, Sharon Gewirtz ironically suggests that policy makers have decided to 'make all families like middle-class families, or at least the ideal-typical middle-class family of much educational research' . . . in other words, to 'clone the Blairs'.

However, she goes on to question whether these 'middle-class' attitudes and behaviours are really all that desirable. These include treating education like a marketplace and 'policing' what happens in schools; using social networks to engage with the education system for their children's advantage; and transmitting cultural values through activities such as museum visits and educational outings.

What Gewirtz questions is not the principle of seeking ways to combat poverty and inequality, which is also part of the government agenda, but the assumptions about working-class parents and families that are implicit within some of the initiatives. She is not opposed to opportunities for children to have educational opportunities outside school, but she is concerned that those who are unable to provide such opportunities will somehow be seen as less effective parents:

Finally, there are barely disguised moral authoritarian overtones to these . . . policies which are based upon, and may well serve to perpetuate, a deficit model of working-class parents who are blamed for the under-attainment of their children.

(Gewirtz, 2001: 375)

THINKING IT THROUGH

How far do you agree with the arguments in this summary? Do you think the points made by Sharon Gewirtz are valid today? Have attitudes to parents and parenting changed, and if so in what ways?

You might wish to read *Every Parent Matters* (2007), available at **http://www.teachernet.gov.uk/docbank/index.cfm?id=11184**, for a recent view of government thinking.

Do you think that certain assumptions are made about 'good' parenting that might prejudice some teachers against parents who do not conform to these expectations?

Do you think that legislation, such as parenting orders, should be used to enforce minimum levels of parental involvement with education?

Effective home–school links depend on a good, non-judgemental understanding of the cultures and lifestyles of parents. Gill Crozier, who has worked with parents from a range of social backgrounds and ethnic groups, also suggests that many black and working-class parents feel excluded by the 'middle-class' norms of current models of parental involvement (Crozier, 2000; Crozier and Reay, 2005). Understanding these issues can take time to develop where teachers are new to an area, which is perhaps unlike the one where they grew up or where they live. Initial Teacher Training courses aim to provide as much opportunity as possible for experiences of different social and cultural school contexts, but depending on where the course is based, this experience can sometimes be quite limited. You are very likely to find yourself facing unfamiliar family backgrounds and circumstances as you start your career, where you will need to keep an open mind and try not to make assumptions about individual pupils and their families.

Involving parents in education

Photo 3.1 Many opportunities exist for out-of-school learning in children's everyday lives. What are the potential learning activities in this situation, and how can teachers build on these experiences?

Source: Getty Images

One area where misunderstanding can arise is where different groups (such as teachers and parents) use the same language to mean slightly different things. For example, a survey commissioned by the DfES in 2004 showed an increase in the percentage of parents who felt 'very involved' in their children's education, compared to 2001 (Moon and Ivins, 2004). This result would seem to be encouraging, but on closer examination it became clear that the conception of what 'involvement' meant varied according to socio-economic background.

Parents in professional, clerical and skilled occupations were more likely to define this as:

- being involved in parent–teacher associations;
- taking their children on visits to museums, or on other educational visits;
- playing sport with their children;
- feeling confident helping with homework.

Parents in semi-skilled or unskilled occupations tended to regard parental involvement as being limited to going on school trips and helping with dinner duties. Despite this, they were *more* likely to say they knew all they needed to know about their children's education than the parents from professional and skilled occupations. These different definitions of parental involvement could inadvertently contribute to misunderstandings between schools and parents, where parents felt they were 'very involved' and schools felt they were not!

The reasons for these different responses from parents in less skilled occupations could be any (or all) of the following:

- lack of confidence about understanding information from school;
- reluctance to be involved with school because of poor previous experiences of education;
- lack of knowledge about the ways in which they could become more involved, assuming time and other resources were available;
- lack of confidence to actively support children's learning out of school, whether homework or in less formal situations;
- not recognising the different forms of learning that take place within the home.

The last point indicates another area where assumptions can prevent the development of stronger relationships between home and school: the assumption that learning in school is more important than the learning that takes place informally at home. A research study carried out with a group of primary schools indicated that much of the traffic between home and school was one-way – that is, from school to home (Burke *et al.*, 2004). At the start of the project, the information that teachers asked for from home tended to be narrow and closely related to the school curriculum. Although the teachers said they valued home–school partnership, they gave little recognition to the range of out-of-school learning in which pupils engaged. Parents seemed to feel less involved in partnership with the schools, and wanted more detailed information about the work being undertaken by their children rather than a termly newsletter. They particularly regretted the additional loss of contact between schools and home once pupils entered secondary school.

Following from this initial study, the research team, which included teacher-researchers as well as university lecturers, developed several projects to develop closer links between schools and parents, focusing on out-of-school learning and supporting transition between primary and secondary schools.

RESEARCH BRIEFING: HOME–SCHOOL KNOWLEDGE EXCHANGE PROJECTS

Home to school: out-of-school learning in primary mathematics and literacy

Using disposable cameras, pupils took photographs to show examples of mathematical activities which took place out of school, such as reading a timetable or setting the video. These were then discussed in class and captions were written to explain how mathematics was used in each activity.

Pupils also took photographs related to class themes, such as living things or the local environment, which were then used to support writing activities in school. With support from the teachers involved, parents identified other literacy- and mathematics-based opportunities at home, such as writing shopping lists, reading labels and calculating change.

RESEARCH BRIEFING: *CONTINUED*

Home to school: shoeboxes

Pupils brought significant objects from home into school inside a shoebox. These were then used to support literacy activities, but also provided teachers with valuable insights about children's home lives.

School to home: video material to support transition to secondary school

Videos were made for Year 6 pupils and their parents about life in secondary school. These included a Year 7 pupil unpacking her school bag to show the items she needed to remember to bring into school each day, and one of the school cooks explaining the lunch options and system of lunch passes for pupils with free school meals. Other Year 7 pupils talked about their own concerns when they started at the school and how these were resolved.

The parents and teachers of Year 6 pupils watched the videos and were then able to discuss the issues in a group setting.

Home to school: supporting secondary transition

During the summer holidays Year 6 pupils took photographs of their out-of-school lives, These were taken into their new schools and shared with teachers and other students. In one school these were used to discuss different kinds of learning and made into a display that parents were invited to visit.

More information and publications about these projects can be found at **www.tlrp.org.uk**.

Source: Based on the work of the Teaching and Learning Research Programme Project 13 **www.home-school-learning.org.uk**

How can schools and teachers build meaningful relationships with parents?

- Through recognition of the difficulties many parents or carers have in attending meetings in school owing to different working hours, and/or complex child-care arrangements, and seeking ways to address this, for example through home visits or flexible school visiting times.

- Through recognition of the variety of religious and/or cultural backgrounds of parents and carers, and ensuring effective communication through, for example, bilingual/multilingual newsletters and the appointment of bilingual staff in positions such as the school front office.

- Through recognition of the fact that newly arrived families (whether from overseas or elsewhere in the UK) may have particular difficulties in establishing a relationship with the school staff and other parents, and providing support through, for example, a 'hot line' telephone link to a single member of staff who is able to develop a personal relationship with the family.

- Through recognition of the fact that some parents/carers feel unable to support their children owing to their own educational background, and providing non-threatening opportunities to improve their understanding of the curriculum. Examples could include 'help with homework' workshops, or through Family Literacy sessions. These sessions can show parents how to improve their children's communication skills and also improve the literacy levels of the parents themselves, and of other members of the family.

- Through consulting with parents/carers on school matters using both formal and informal methods, to meet the varying needs of individuals. Formal methods include school meetings, surveys and parents' evenings, whereas more informal methods could include drop-in sessions, discussions held at the end or start of the school day and telephone calls to home, by agreement.

- Regular contact with the parents/carers of 'at-risk' pupils, including at times when things are going well, not just when difficulties arise.

- Giving status to learning activities which take place out of school, through actively seeking information about family events and activities.

- Being sensitive to the nature of homework tasks in terms of the resources that might be required, or the need that individual pupils may have for support when completing the homework.

- Through recognition of a range of ways that parents/carers can be involved with the school, apart from attending meetings or accompanying pupils on school trips. These include providing opportunities for parents to evaluate and comment on aspects of school life: in addition to paper-based questionnaires, the internet provides opportunities for parents to engage with electronic surveys and to participate in web-based discussions such as online question and answer sessions with teachers that can build into a library of 'frequently asked questions'.

All of the above suggestions are based on an assumption that parents and carers *are* interested in their children's educational progress and want to support them, although perhaps they may not feel confident in doing so. This is a values-based position, which suggests that schools need to continue to look for explanations for lack of communication with parents or carers, rather than to assume lack of interest. While this position can sometimes be difficult for schools and individual teachers to maintain, it can help to sustain a positive attitude towards the pupils involved, which is very important when home–school communication is difficult. In some cases, persistence in looking for explanations can result in the development of new understandings between different teachers and groups of parents. For example, in some cultures parents do not expect to be involved with the education of their children, as this might be seen as disrespectful to teachers. Once this perspective is appreciated, what appeared to be lack of involvement is reinterpreted and discussions take place on a different basis.

OVER TO YOU

In training

In what easily recognisable ways do the schools with which you are familiar ensure they are 'parent friendly'?

Some strategies may be less obvious, particularly in large secondary schools. Whichever age phase you are primarily involved with, find out which member(s) of staff are responsible for this aspect of the school's work and try to arrange a discussion.

Starting your career

What do you consider to be some of the barriers that parents might encounter when seeking to become more involved with their children's education?

In what ways do the school(s) with which you are familiar take these into account?

How many of the ideas listed in this chapter have you identified in your response?

Although not all of these ideas can be implemented by individual teachers, are there any aspects of your own practice you could reconsider as a result of reading these suggestions?

Investigating learning and teaching

A review of the research literature on the impact of parental involvement in education (Desforges, 2003) suggests that parent–child interaction in the home is more significant in terms of raising achievement than the involvement of parents with the school. However, schools can support parents by helping to develop confidence in holding learning conversations at home. What strategies do you think could help with this approach?

You will find it useful to access a commentary on the research report and some related case studies at **http://www.gtce.org.uk/teachers/rft/parents_feb06/**.

Parents' evenings and informal opportunities for contact with parents and carers

Even if you are not yet in a position to influence broader school policies, you will still be able to develop positive relationships with parents and carers through both formal and informal contact during the school year.

Photo 3.2
Taking the
time to talk
to parents in
a relaxed
environment
can help to
build good
relationships
with a positive
effect on pupil
learning

Source: Pearson
Education Ltd.
Ian Wedgewood

Teachers of primary-aged pupils may have more informal opportunities to talk with parents at the beginning and end of the school day than their secondary colleagues, but these can often be very busy times with little chance of genuine 'quality time' in which to develop a real dialogue. Such limited opportunities are no substitute for a planned, extended discussion about a pupil's learning, during which time the teacher listens as much as they talk! However, these brief, informal opportunities can be critical in enabling individual parents or carers to feel able to share family information as it arises, and to feel welcomed in the school, and should be valued accordingly.

If a meeting is formal, i.e. a planned parent–teacher meeting or an arranged appointment, try to ensure that there is sufficient time to establish a real dialogue, and give some consideration to the physical context in which you meet parents and carers to ensure that this will be comfortable and conducive to the discussion. You should be prepared with some ideas for achievable targets, and evidence to support the discussion. This might take the form of a selection of the pupil's work, a home–school work record and a recent report, if available. Before launching into a discussion about future targets, however, take time to review what has been achieved, looking for the positive elements in the pupil's academic work and behaviour so that targets are seen to build on existing progress. Aim to end with a joint agreement on targets which will also take the views of the pupil into account. Ideally this should clarify how the parent or carer can support the learner in reaching their targets, and when and how these will be reviewed.

WORKING IN THE CLASSROOM

Evidence suggests that few targets identified in such meetings are systematically reviewed or monitored (Bastiani, 2003). How could you ensure that both parents/carers and pupils are aware that you value the support provided within the home, and that you monitor and review targets so that they form the basis of future discussions?

Extended services: supporting learning in the community

Extended services (often known as 'extended schools') usually operate in two dimensions: they aim to provide additional facilities for the community, in addition to traditional educational provision, and they usually extend the time the school is open for its pupils, in order to provide further support for learning (see Figure 3.2). Although it might sometimes be assumed that the idea of extended services arose from the *Every Child Matters* (ECM, DfES, 2003) agenda, in fact there have been versions of

Extended services (extended schools): by 2010 all schools are expected to offer 'extended services' to pupils and the local community.

Figure 3.2 Extended Services – factfile

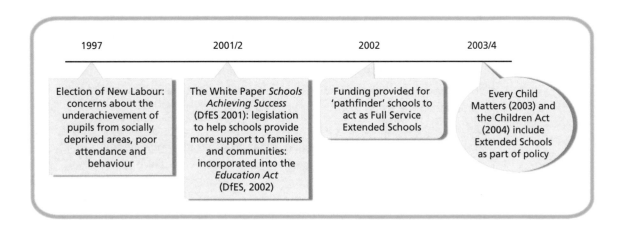

1997	2001/2	2002	2003/4
Election of New Labour: concerns about the underachievement of pupils from socially deprived areas, poor attendance and behaviour	The White Paper *Schools Achieving Success* (DfES 2001): legislation to help schools provide more support to families and communities: incorporated into the *Education Act* (DfES, 2002)	Funding provided for 'pathfinder' schools to act as Full Service Extended Schools	Every Child Matters (2003) and the Children Act (2004) include Extended Schools as part of policy

extended schools in operation in the UK for many years (Ball, 1998). These schools were usually called community schools or community colleges and extended their facilities for community use after school hours and at weekends. Some community colleges operated inter-agency provision through regular liaison meetings with agencies such as social services, community police officers and educational psychologists (Brett, 1987).

In developing the concept of the 'extended school', policy makers in England drew on the experience of these community schools, and also on initiatives from other countries. In the USA, for example, versions of 'extended service' schools (also generally known as community schools) have been in operation for over 20 years and the evidence has suggested that these schools are successful in improving attendance, behaviour, and community involvement and cohesion. In Scotland the 'New Community Schools' development (Scottish Office, 1998) has also aimed to link education, health and social services provision in deprived areas, and has similarly drawn inspiration from the American experience (Sammons *et al.*, 2000). An evaluation of the first three years of a pilot project for New Community Schools (Sammons *et al.*, 2003) indicates improvements in provision and support for vulnerable children and families as a result of the initiative. There is evidence of increased parental and community engagement and also more opportunities for out-of-school care or learning, particularly for vulnerable pupils. Although the evaluation stressed that three years is a relatively short time for significant results to be shown, the responses to the evaluation were generally very positive.

Ofsted evaluated the effectiveness of 17 of the pilot 'Full Service Extended Schools' (FSES) (Ofsted, 2005) and, in a separate survey, 20 other settings which had not been part of the pilot project but offered similar services. Full Service Extended Schools were schools offering additional activities and access to other services such as health and social services. The Extended Service settings included 12 schools (four secondary and eight primary or junior schools) (Ofsted, 2006). The findings from both surveys are very similar (Table 3.1).

WORKING IN THE CLASSROOM

If you are not already familiar with this information, find out the ways in which your school is implementing the ECM proposals for Extended Services. These will vary depending on your local context.

How far can you link the findings of the Ofsted surveys (Table 3.1) with the situation in the school(s) with which you are familiar?

Ofsted also found that few schools were evaluating the impact of extended services on pupils' learning. What do you think would be the most important indicators of success for the school(s) with which you are familiar?

Table 3.1 Findings of Ofsted surveys		
Main themes	Full Service Extended Schools (Ofsted, 2005)	Extended Service Settings (Ofsted, 2006)
Benefits to pupils	Well-targeted interventions are improving behaviour, motivation and attendance for some identified pupils, but it is not possible to attribute these improvements to FSES alone. Pupils are motivated by the additional activities in school and this can improve their learning.	The major benefits to children, young people and adults were enhanced self-confidence, improved relationships, raised aspirations and better attitudes to learning.
Importance of leadership	Inspirational and committed leadership from head teachers and good management have been crucial to the development of FSES.	Strongly committed leaders and managers were key factors in successful provision. They had a clear understanding of the features of extended provision and how it would work in their contexts.
Parents and community involvement	Parents are very enthusiastic about the benefits of FSES and the provision has been transformational for some. In particular, they have benefited from access to relevant courses and to support services based in schools.	The most successful providers shaped the provision gradually to reflect their community's needs and wants in collaboration with other agencies. They gave sufficient time to gather information on local requirements before setting up any provision. There was no single blueprint for success.
Multi-agency provision	FSES enable multi-agency teams to deliver services directly from the school and this improves access for children, families and the community.	Regular consultation by services was vital. Successful services fulfilled the community's needs, were of high quality and maintained interest.
Collaboration between services	Services work well together to support children when they collaborate on agreed protocols for working practices.	Agencies worked together most effectively when there was a lead co-ordinator in the setting and agreed protocols for working practices.
Role of local authorities	The impact of FSES is greatest where LEAs provide early support for schools in planning and developing provision.	The role of local authorities was important in establishing effective, well-coordinated plans and support structures.

Extended services appear to be most effective when they make strong connections with their local community and respond to local needs, linking with local voluntary organisations and other agencies such as Children's Centres and family health services in order to do so. The messages here appear to be similar to those concerned with building effective parent–teacher relationships: taking time to develop understanding, respecting the views of others and listening to suggestions rather than assuming superior knowledge.

Community cohesion

Since September 2007 schools have had a legal duty to promote 'community cohesion'. This concept goes beyond the ECM offer for Extended Schools, although it is closely related, and is specifically identified within *The Children's Plan* (DCSF, 2007a).

> Schools can and should play a lead role in creating greater cohesion. The values our children learn will shape the country Britain becomes. We are a nation built from and by people from other countries. We should celebrate our history and how it has created today's diversity, recognising the role played by immigrants in our success.
>
> *(Alan Johnson, Secretary of State for Education, The Guardian, 26 January 2007)*

The three areas where schools are asked to review their practice are those of teaching and curriculum, equity and excellence, and engagement and ethos (DCSF, 2007b).

The important role of schools in helping to prepare pupils for life in a culturally diverse society is emphasised in a number of current and recent curriculum initiatives. The revisions to the Key Stage 3 curriculum and the introduction of cross-curricular themes place a greater emphasis on developing the skills and understandings which help pupils recognise and appreciate the contribution of different communities to life in Britain. This aspect of the curriculum will be considered in more detail later in this book.

The area of 'equity and excellence' focuses on ensuring that similar life opportunities are available to all, which is a key concept underpinning community cohesion. In this respect, schools should monitor the educational performance of pupils closely in relation to the variety of factors which can affect attainment, some of which are considered in Chapter 5. Schools should also monitor disciplinary incidents involving bullying, harassment, prejudice or discrimination to ensure that everything possible is done to reduce these events.

Finally, 'engagement and ethos' brings us back to the role of the Extended Services and the ECM core offer, which is required to be in place by 2010. As we have already indicated above, the services provided through Extended Services need to reflect the needs of the local community through consultation with parents, local community groups and pupils. The importance of 'pupil voice' in contributing to the future of schools in a variety of ways will be discussed in Chapter 15.

A community of learners within the school

Photo 3.3 Working collaboratively towards an agreed outcome can contribute to the development of a learning community. This is strengthened where the focus of the activity is chosen by the teachers themselves, rather than imposed from outside

Source: Pearson Education Ltd. Ian Wedgewood

So far within this chapter we have discussed the ways in which a school reaches out to its local community, but the school itself also forms a community of learners. Active and effective learners benefit from teachers and other members of the school community who are also active and effective learners and it is a normal expectation that teachers and other members of the school workforce will engage in Continuing Professional Development (CPD) activity throughout their careers. The current Professional Standards for teachers in England (**www.tda.gov.uk/teachers/professionalstandards**) identify a commitment to improving one's own practice through appropriate professional development as a Core Standard, which should be demonstrated by every teacher (Core Standard C7). This commitment is expected to begin during initial training, where trainees should take responsibility for identifying their professional needs through reflection on their practice, and also identify priorities for early professional development in their induction year (QTS Standard Q7). The topic of reflection on practice is discussed further in Chapter 12.

CPD takes many forms, including:

- specific training targeted at new policy initiatives for individual schools;
- training related to national priorities provided on a local area basis;
- informal events such as collaborative planning and *ad hoc* discussions;
- formal structures of coaching, mentoring and peer observation within schools;
- small-scale investigations into improving teaching and learning undertaken by teachers in a single school;

- larger-scale projects planned by school or subject networks;
- attendance at one-day courses and conferences;
- involvement in Post-graduate Professional Development leading to nationally recognised awards.

Although the majority of items on the above list could be described as formal CPD opportunities, that is, those that have been deliberately planned, there is also evidence to suggest that informal learning also plays a large part in professional development. By its very nature, informal learning is hard to define. The term encompasses all learning outside formal educational contexts, and in school-based terms this would include staff-room conversations, planning meetings (which might be formal occasions, but may not be specifically targeted as CPD activity), *ad hoc* opportunities to observe other teachers in action, or opportunities to visit other classrooms or other schools. Informal learning also includes learning about the norms and values of the workplace (Eraut, 2000: 19) and acquiring an understanding of 'how things are done here'.

THINKING IT THROUGH

How far do you consider the more informal discussion and activities surrounding planning and teaching to be part of CPD? Can you identify an informal occasion that has made you consciously re-evaluate an aspect of your practice?

Make a list of your own CPD experience(s) to date and identify which of these have been 'informal' and which 'formal' experiences.

Schools are now increasingly likely to be part of 'learning communities' of various kinds. These will include teachers and other members of the school workforce, and may also include members of other services, such as Local Authority Behaviour Support Services and National Strategy Consultants. University researchers may also work with individual schools or groups of schools to collaborate in different learning opportunities, which might involve recognised programmes of study such as Master's degree work and other school-based research investigations.

Many schools were part of the Networked Learning Communities initiative, which ran from 2002 to 2006. The project was supported by the National College for School Leadership (NCSL), the General Teaching Council for England (GTCE) and the Department for Education and Skills (DES). Its purpose was to develop partnerships between schools in order to share knowledge, expertise and good practice. In many cases, the connections established between schools during this period have been sustained beyond the end of the formal initiative. ECM has also provided opportunities for groups of schools in local communities to work together with shared agendas, so that opportunities for learning within individual schools are increased.

Even where such wider networks do not exist, teachers can be involved in collaborative learning within a single school or subject department, on a sustained basis.

Some forms of collaborative learning operate through peer mentoring or coaching activities, which are discussed in more detail in Chapter 14, along with other forms of collaborative CPD. Groups of teachers can also work together to investigate specific aspects of learning and teaching through small-scale research projects (Cordingley *et al.*, 2003). More information about ways to investigate practice is provided in Chapter 12.

OVER TO YOU

In training

Connections between other schools, groups of teachers, or members of the school workforce may not be obvious if you are following a teacher training programme, and spend a relatively limited time in one school. How does your own practice, and understanding of educational issues, benefit from discussions with trainees who have experience in different schools from yourself? What might be the benefits of continuing similar discussions into your NQT year, and beyond?

Starting your career

List the learning communities of which you consider yourself to be a member. Do any of these involve people outside your immediate workplace? Are there opportunities for you to engage in learning with colleagues from other schools or professional contexts?

Investigating learning and teaching

Different opportunities will exist for you to investigate the processes of your own learning throughout your initial training and your NQT year, through the use of reflective learning journals and/or written assignments which ask you to consider your own developing understanding. You may also choose to develop your study at Master's level where some courses also involve the use of learning journals.

Depending on your stage of professional development, review one or more of your learning journals to identify examples of professional learning arising from independent reading or reflection, and those where your learning took place as a result of interaction with other peers or colleagues. Were these examples based in formal or informal learning situations? Which do you feel have been most influential in your career so far? How might you ensure that you engage with both independent and collaborative learning opportunities in your future career?

SUMMARY

This chapter has considered the range of communities of learners with which schools and teachers may engage. It has examined the significant impact of parental involvement on pupil attainment, and discussed the ways in which schools can seek to engage with parents and the local community in a positive and non-judgemental way. We have argued for the recognition of the relationship between home learning and school learning, and discussed ways in which effective home–school communication can be fostered. The role of the Extended School within the wider community has been considered, alongside the importance of promoting community cohesion within the curriculum and also within the wider community. Finally, we have discussed the importance of the school as a community of learners for all its members, where both formal and informal learning should be recognised and valued, along with the range of different learning communities which may exist within and beyond the school.

These interlinking dimensions are further factors which can affect the learning encounter within the classroom (see Figure 3.3).

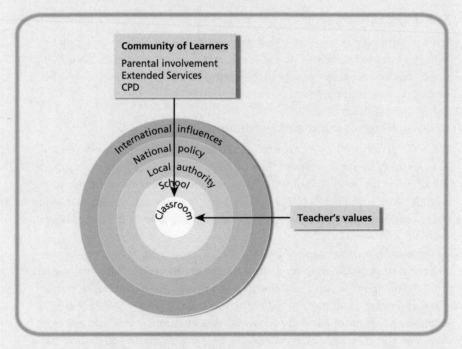

Figure 3.3 Influences on teaching and learning

TAKING YOUR PRACTICE FURTHER

Follow up your review of the ways in which you (and your school if appropriate) work to establish relationships with parents and carers, to identify any areas for improvement.

Consider establishing a system for following up targets agreed during parent–teacher meetings.

How will parents and pupils be informed of progress against these targets?

This chapter has outlined the benefits of collaborative CPD activity. Review your own list of CPD involvement to date.

Are there areas where you could increase your opportunities to learn through collaboration with others in your school?

Have you had opportunities to develop your practice through learning from/with others outside your school context?

You may wish to discuss these with your induction mentor or during your performance management meeting, depending on your stage of professional development.

TAKING YOUR THINKING FURTHER

Research into the impact of CPD on learning indicates that it is difficult to make direct connections between involvement in CPD and improvements in pupils' learning and/or motivation (Cordingley *et al.*, 2003). The TDA suggest that CPD co-ordinators ask how any planned CPD activities will impact on pupils' achievement (**http://www.tda.gov.uk/teachers/ continuingprofessionaldevelopment/cpdleadership/**).

What kinds of evidence would *you* look for, how would you record it and how would you evaluate it?

Find out more

If you are interested in the changing relationship between schools and families, you may wish to read:

Muschamp, Y., Wikeley, F., Ridge, T. and Balarin, M. (2007) *Parenting, Caring and Educating (Primary Review Research Survey 7/1)*. **Cambridge: University of Cambridge Faculty of Education. Available at: www.primaryreview.org.uk.**

This review article applies more widely than the primary phase and would be useful reading for anyone involved with secondary pupils. The article identifies the complex arrangements which now often characterise family life and considers the research on the relationship between parents, schools and children's attainment. It looks at recent policy developments in relation to parents and schools, and argues that a 'one size fits all' approach is unlikely to be effective.

This article is also reviewed by the TTRB, **www.ttrb.ac.uk** article ID 14194.

Crozier, G. (1996) Black parents and school relationships: a case study, *Educational Review*, **Vol. 48, No. 3: pp. 253–267.**
This paper outlines the views of a group of black parents about their relationships with their children's schools. It helps to identify the constraints on developing effective home–school relationships experienced by some members of the black community.

Gill Crozier has also written two books on home–school relationships:

Crozier, G. (2000) *Parents and Schools: Partners or Protagonists*? **Stoke on Trent: Trentham Books.**

Crozier, G. and Reay, D. (eds) (2005) *Activating Participation: Parents and Teachers Working Towards Partnership*. **Stoke on Trent: Trentham Books.**

www.teachernet.gov.uk has a section on Parenting Support, which includes a downloadable document on 'Parenting Support Know-How'.

If you are interested in the Home–School Knowledge Exchange project, further information is available at: **www.tlrp.org.uk/projects**.

Teachers' TV has a series of programmes on *Working with Parents*.

If you are interested in projects where schools or groups of teachers have worked together, a number of these can be located via **www.teachernet.gov.uk** or via the NCSL site on Networked Learning Communities **http://www.ncsl.org.uk/networked-index.**

Teachers' TV offers programmes which consider collaborative activity, for example:

Primary CPD: Teamwork and Collaboration – how collaborative practice 'turned one school around' and how this work is being shared through a local network.

School Matters: Action Research – three case studies, two of which involve teachers working collaboratively to improve an aspect of practice in their school.

If you want to know more about how extended schools have made effective links with their local community:

www.teachernet.gov.uk has a large section devoted to information, and case studies on extended schools including links to Ofsted evaluations, videos and other information.

The DCSF booklet *Extended Schools: Building on Experience* (DCSF, 2007) contains a number of case studies of extended schools and can be downloaded from **www.everychildmatters.gov.uk/ childrensworkforcestrategy/** or **www.teachernet.gov.uk/publications**.

www.teachernet.gov.uk also has an area devoted to community cohesion. There are case studies on each of the three main aspects outlined in the chapter.

Teachers, TV has a programme on small schools/community schools in the *Lessons from America* sequence.

QiSS (Quality in Study Support) provides a national recognition for schools that meet the DCSF Study Support Code of Practice. Information about how schools can seek recognition is available at: **www.canterbury.ac.uk/education/quality-in-study-support.**

Glossary

Extended services (extended schools): by 2010 all schools are expected to offer 'extended services' to pupils and the local community. These services can be offered by schools working together, rather than independently. The services depend on local demand, but typically involve extended opening hours for childcare, after school clubs, sports and other facilities, such as ICT rooms available to the local community, parent support activities and access to specialist services such as speech therapy, youth workers, police, careers advice etc.

References

Ball, M. (1998) *School Inclusion: The School, the Family and the Community*. York: Joseph Rowntree Foundation.

Bastiani, J. (2003) *Involving Parents: Raising Achievement* (edited by Sheila White for the DfES). London: Department For Education and Skills.

Blunkett, D. (1999) Excellence for the many not just the few: raising standards and extending opportunities in our schools. *The CBI Presidents Reception Address*, 19 July.

Brett, M. (1987) Pastoral care – an inter-agency approach – one school's experience', *Pastoral Care*, November: pp. 200–203.

Burke, S., Scanlan, M., Salway, L. and Stinchcombe, V. (2004) Exchanging knowledge between home and school to raise achievement, *Research Summary for National Teacher Research Panel*. Available at: **www.standards/dfes.gov.uk/ntrp** or via TTRB review no. 13023 at **www.ttrb.ac.uk**.

Cordingley, P., Bell, M., Rundell, B. and Evans, D. (2003) The impact of collaborative CPD on classroom teaching and learning, in *Research Evidence in Education Library*. London: EPPI-Centre, Social Science Research Unit, Institute of Education, University of London.

Crozier, G. (2000) *Parents and Schools: Partners or Protagonists?* Stoke-on-Trent: Trentham Books.

Crozier, G. and Reay, D. (2005) *Activating Participation: Parents and Teachers Working towards Partnership*. Stoke-on-Trent: Trentham Books.

DCSF (2007a) *The Children's Plan*. London: DSCGF.

DCSF (2007b) *Guidance on the Duty to Promote Community Cohesion*. London: DCSF.

Desforges, C. with Abouchaar, A. (2003) *The Impact of Parental Involvement, Parental Support and Family Education on Pupil Achievement and Adjustment*. DfES Research Report RR433. London: DfES.

DfES (2001) *White Paper: Schools Achieving Success*. London, DfES.

DfES (2002) *Education Act*. London, DfES. Summary available at: **http://www.teachernet.gov.uk/educationoverview/briefing/educationact/summary/**.

DfES (2003) *Every Child Matters*. London: DfES.

DfES (2004) *The Children Act*. London: HMSO.

Eraut, M. (2000) Non-formal learning, implicit learning and tacit knowledge in professional work, in F. Coffield (ed) *The Necessity of Informal Learning*. Bristol, The Policy Press.

Gewirtz, S. (2001) Cloning the Blairs: New Labour's programme for the re-socialization of working class parents, *Journal of Education Policy*, Vol. 16, No. 4: pp. 365–378.

Moon, N. and Ivins, C. (2004) *Parental Involvement in Children's Education*. London: DfES.

Ofsted (2005) *Extended Schools: A Report on Early Developments*. Available at: **wwww.ofsted.gov.uk.**

Ofsted (2006) *Extended Services in Schools and Children's Centres*. Available at: **wwww.ofsted.gov.uk.**

Sammons, P., Power, S., Elliot, K., Robertson, P., Campbell, C. and Whitty, G. (2003) *New Community Schools in Scotland. Final Report. National Evaluation of the Pilot Phase*. London: Institute of Education. Available at: **http://www.scotland.gov.uk/Resource/Doc/933/0007611.pdf.**

Sammons, P., Power, S., Robertson, P., Campbell, C., Elliot, K. and Whitty, G. (2000) Evaluating the New Community Schools Initiative in Scotland. *Paper presented at the European Conference on Educational Research,* Edinburgh, 20–23 September.

Scottish Office (1998) *New Community Schools Prospectus*. Available at **http://www.scotland.gov.uk/library/documents-w3ncsp-00.htm** (accessed 23 January 2003).

Development and Learning

CHAPTER 4

In this chapter you will:

- Consider the different aspects of development which may affect pupils' learning in the 7–14 age range
- Develop your understanding of a range of models which can be applied to the cognitive, social and emotional development of pupils in the 7–14 age group
- Reflect on strategies you use, or you have seen in action, which take developmental issues into account

Pearson Education Ltd/Phovoir. Imagestate

In an imaginary Year 6 or Year 7 classroom

Photo 4.1
What are these pupils thinking? Their stages of physical, cognitive, social and emotional development may be having a significant impact on their engagement with learning

Source: Pearson Education Ltd
Rob Judges

- Amber is miserable because Jane, her best friend, didn't want to play with her at lunchtime.
- Jason and Andrew are play-fighting with rulers. Andrew is six inches or more taller than Jason, who is small for his age.
- Gemma is the tallest person in the class, and also academically successful. She feels that everyone thinks she is a freak.
- Jane knows that Amber is upset, but she doesn't care because she is far more interested in thinking about 14 year old Tom.

All these statements are connected to different stages of pupils' physical, cognitive, social and emotional development.

How can the teacher cater for all these different stages?

Introduction

There are obviously substantial differences between most 7 and 14 year olds in terms of their physical, cognitive, social and emotional development, and many approaches to teaching and learning which are generally appropriate for 7–8 year olds are inappropriate for 13–14 year olds, and vice versa (see Figure 4.1). However, any class with pupils aged between 10 and 13 years will contain pupils who are entering puberty learning alongside those who are still at earlier stages of development. It is also the

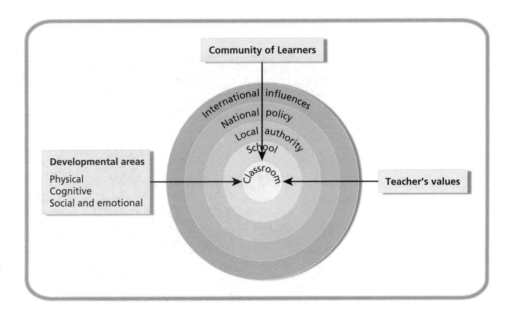

Figure 4.1
Influences on
teaching and
learning

case that some aspects of social and emotional development may not be primarily
age-related. As the pupils from the imaginary classroom suggest, both primary and
secondary teachers need to be aware of the continuum of developmental factors and
how these can influence learning.

Making sense of the ways in which the different areas of physical, cognitive, social
and emotional development interact can be difficult to unravel. In the first place, opinions differ as to how far there are 'stages' in each area of development through which
all children pass, which can be labelled and described in terms of their main features.
It might be more helpful to think of 'development' as the result of a combination of
all these processes operating together.

Although this chapter will discuss ideas derived from stage models for different aspects
of development, no one theoretical model will be promoted. Bronfenbrenner, an
influential American psychologist, developed his 'eco-systems' theory (Bronfenbrenner,
1979), which suggests that different systems interact to affect the development of
the individual. These different systems are both external, including the school, community and the family context, and internal, including the cognitive, emotional and
biological systems (Paquette and Ryan, 2001) Thus, while this chapter considers
different aspects of development in relation to their influence on learning, it is very
important to remember that each of these developmental areas affects, and is affected
by, the others.

How far stages in development really exist is an area of controversy amongst developmental psychologists which this chapter cannot examine in depth. The suggestions
for further reading at the end of this chapter will provide you with an opportunity to
pursue this question in more detail.

OVER TO YOU

Based on your present knowledge of developmental issues, what are the areas you feel are *most* significant for the pupils you teach?

- Physical development – such as relative height, or the development of sexual characteristics?
- Cognitive development – such as the ability to think logically or give reasons for events?
- Social and emotional development – such as pupils' abilities to be 'good losers' or to maintain friendships?

Do you think the emphasis would be different for different age groups within the 7–14 range?

Physical development and learning

While we know that nutrition is a significant factor in the development of infants and young children, tracing the connections between the different factors affecting physical growth gets harder as children grow older. Environmental factors, such as family size and location in urban or rural communities, appear to have some effect on children's physical development. For example, children from larger families may be below average height, and those from rural backgrounds may also be shorter and lighter than those raised in urban contexts. These are not absolute rules, however, and it is likely that you will be able to find exceptions from your own experience.

Socio-economic class is probably the largest determinant of physical size and rate of development (Tanner, 1990). Although this might be translated into an association between diet and physical growth, a close correlation between these two factors would be difficult to prove, given the range of variables, including genetic factors, which would need to be taken into account for individuals. It also assumes that pupils from less affluent homes have a poorer diet, which may not always be the case. Nevertheless, the provision of free school meals and the development of breakfast clubs are associated particularly with areas of socio-economic deprivation, as attempts to ensure that pupils receive sufficient nutrition to enable them to remain physically healthy and to learn effectively. Eating breakfast prior to attending lessons is claimed to aid concentration and increase creative and problem-solving abilities (Shemilt *et al.*, 2004) as well as contribute to the total range of nutrients necessary for growth and development. Research into the nutrient intake of pupils attending breakfast clubs suggests that these may play a recognisable role in enhancing the dietary intake of some pupils (Simpson *et al.*, 2003).

Gender differences in physical development

During most of the primary school years there is little overall difference between boys and girls in terms of mean height and weight – although there are considerable differences between individuals. By the age of 7 years, most children have developed good hand and eye co-ordination, and both boys and girls are physically active, with bodily control increasing during the next two to three years. An interest in team games often develops in children around the age of 9 or 10, which is also associated with increasing social interests and co-operative play, and also a stronger awareness of fairness and the significance of rules. Boys do seem to engage in more 'rough play' than girls, although it is difficult to separate elements of physical development from the effect of cultural expectations in terms of gendered behaviour. Research into gender differences in children's play in the 8–12 age phase suggests that peer group expectations are significant within the age group (Lever, 1998). Boys are more likely to play outside and in larger groups than girls, who are more likely to prefer to play indoors, usually with one other person. Here again we can see the interaction of different aspects of the child's 'eco-system'.

Physical development and puberty

Between the ages of 10 and 11 the mean height and weight of girls begin to exceed those of boys, as girls experience a growth spurt associated with early puberty. This spurt occurs later in boys, who 'catch up' with girls in terms of height and weight about two years later. By the age of 14 boys are generally taller and heavier than girls – again using the mean figure for measurements taken from a large population sample (Whitehead, 1991). However, between the ages of 10 and 14 the differences between boys and girls, and between individuals within both sexes, are at their greatest, with girls on average manifesting the signs of puberty about two years earlier than boys. These differences are not only physical, but also cognitive and emotional, so that individuals within the same educational setting can have widely differing responses to the same activity. This has considerable implications for teachers working with this age range, in both primary and secondary schools.

Back in the imaginary classroom

The teacher has been reading the novel *Goodnight Mister Tom* by Michelle Magorian with the class. In this book the central character experiences the death of his baby sister as a result of his mother's extreme religious beliefs. During the reading of this chapter in the book, and in the subsequent discussion, the teacher is aware of the following responses:

• Jason and Andrew have been engaged with other events in the story, but seem unmoved by the description of the death of the child.

- Some pupils of both genders, including Amber and Jane, fail to make the connection between the mother's behaviour and the child's death.
- Some pupils, including Gemma, are able to empathise with the emotions of the central character.
- Only one pupil is able to offer a suggestion as to why the mother may have behaved as she did.

The teacher accepts that these differing responses are due to pupils being at varying stage of cognitive, social and emotional development, and tries to target questions to pupils accordingly.

WORKING IN THE CLASSROOM

How far do you feel that the curriculum for your age group or subject accommodates the differing maturation rates of boys and girls?

Do you think that teachers should take gender issues into account when planning work or selecting teaching strategies?

If so, what strategies do you use, or have you observed in practice, which might support these differing needs?

The differing maturation rates of girls and boys mean that stresses about appearance, sexuality and social relationships manifest themselves differently in mixed groups of similar aged pupils. Coleman and Hendry (1990) found that adolescent boys appeared to cope with these stresses in sequence, rather than simultaneously. Eleven year olds are generally more concerned with issues of heterosexuality, whereas 14 year olds are more concerned about being rejected by their peer group. Boys who mature early appear to enjoy social advantages within their peer group, amongst both boys and girls, compared with those who mature later. Early maturing boys may appear more 'grown-up' to their peers. They often take on leadership roles and thus enjoy greater self-confidence. However, girls have a more mixed experience, since although early maturity can also lead to greater self-confidence, it may also result in un-popularity with the peer group if they are visibly physically different (taller, more developed) than the rest of their group (Woolfolk, Hughes and Walkup, 2008: 80).

The involvement of girls in physical education and sporting activities decreases in adolescence: a situation which is now causing concern for health-related reasons. One reason for the decrease in activity is ascribed to self-consciousness amongst girls as they enter puberty. School sports wear and swimwear tend to be revealing, and expose girls to the 'gaze' of others at the stage of social and emotional development when they are most sensitive to other people's opinions. Early adolescence is a time when pupils are examining their gender identity and many sporting activities may also be perceived as unfeminine. The following chapter will consider issues of gender as they may affect individual learners, but it is important to recognise the interrelationship here between physical development, social and emotional development and engagement with the curriculum.

Puberty and the brain

It is not only the body that is changing with the onset of puberty. Recent developments in neuroscience suggest that physical changes are also taking place in the brain, which may have an influence on both cognition and emotional development, and thus on learning.

Synapse: the tiny space between neurons. Chemical messages cross this gap between the fibres of different neurons and allow the neurons to form interconnected circuits.

Neuron: a nerve cell in the brain that stores and transfers information. Neurons have long and short fibres through which connection to other cells takes place, across the **synapses**.

RESEARCH BRIEFING: THE ADOLESCENT BRAIN

If you thought that the brain stops developing in early childhood, and that we have developed all the 'brain cells' we will ever need at that stage, then think again. It is now known that the brain continues to develop much later than was previously believed, and that an especially important period occurs during adolescence.

In order to understand this process, we need to look at how information is transmitted within the brain. From early infancy, the brain develops connections (synapses) between neurons, creating the pathways through which the information is transmitted. The infant brain develops more connections than will finally be used by the developing individual, however, and studies of the brain have recently shown that periods when there is a proliferation of connections are followed by periods of 'synaptic pruning' where some connections are reinforced and others, which are used less, are effectively lost (Blakemore and Frith, 2005: 23–31).

Early adolescence is a 'sensitive period' in brain development where some reorganisation of networks within the brain is taking place. Just as in infancy, at the onset of puberty the number of synapses in the brain increases, particularly in the frontal cortex of the brain. This area is responsible for functions such as holding information, planning, selecting actions, and being able to do two things at once. Neuroscientists now believe that this growth spurt in brain connections has an adverse effect on some of these functions.

In an experiment, a large group of children aged 10–17 years were given a computer-based task in which they had to match pictures of facial expressions to the word describing the appropriate emotion, such as 'happy', 'sad', 'angry', as quickly as possible. The researchers found that 11–12 year olds were 15% slower on this task than 10–11 year olds, and while performance improved again with 13–14 year olds, the levels of the youngest group were only matched by the 16 year olds. This experiment suggested that the onset of puberty, around 11–12, results in a dip in performance in this type of task, which involved holding two ideas at once and planning and selecting actions. It is assumed that this 'dip' occurs as a result of the growth spurt of brain connections.

RESEARCH BRIEFING: *CONTINUED*

During early adolescence, some of these connections are 'fine tuned' or 'pruned', which would explain why performance in the matching task improved again.

It is possible that the excess of synapses at puberty, which have not yet been incorporated into specialised functional systems, result in poorer cognitive performance for a while. Only later, after puberty, are excess synapses pruned into specialized efficient networks.

(Blakemore and Frith, 2005: 120)

Two important ideas follow on from this research:

1 The 'dip' in performance approximately coincides with the transition between primary and secondary schooling.
2 Since brain development is still taking place during secondary schooling (and possibly even later), education has a significant part to play in helping the establishment of efficient neural networks.

Cognitive development and learning

Neuroscience examines changes in the brain, and is beginning to tell us what occurs as the *results* of learning, through the creation of synaptic connections. However, it does not help us understand the *process*, or ways by which we learn. So to gain a better understanding of the development of the ways children and young people think (known as cognitive development), we need to turn to the work of cognitive psychologists.

Two of the most influential cognitive psychologists, who have had a strong influence on the curriculum and pedagogical approaches commonly used in the UK, are Jean Piaget (1896–1980) and Lev Vygotsky (1896–1934). This chapter will look only briefly at the key ideas of each psychologist, but there are suggestions for further reading about their work at the end of the chapter.

Piaget was a Swiss psychologist, who proposed a developmental sequence of cognitive skills, underpinning the individual child's readiness for new learning (Piaget, 1954) His view established the concept of 'stage' theory, which is the idea that all children move through a series of predetermined stages in cognitive development.

In Piaget's system, there are four main stages of cognitive development, three of which occur by the time the child is around 7 years of age:

- the *sensori-motor* stage between approximately 0 and 2 years, where the infant begins to remember things and to engage in deliberate, rather than reflex, actions;
- the *pre-operational* stage, between approximately 2 and 7 years, where the young child develops language and can operate logically in some contexts, but has difficulty seeing another person's point of view;

- the *concrete operations* stage, between the approximate ages of 7 and 11, where the child can solve problems logically in a hands-on (concrete) context. During this stage children can classify objects according to more than one criterion (such as colour and shape, rather than by one or the other), and are able to recognise the principle of conservation (for example, that the amount of modelling clay remains the same whether it is rolled into a ball or into a long sausage shape).

Most significant for the 7–14 age range is the shift from what Piaget called the *concrete operations* stage to the *formal operations* stage: a shift from patterns of thinking that are largely located in direct experience to the ability to generalise, using deductive logic, and to hypothesise. This is often called 'abstract thinking', although within the 11–14 age range this is still developing (see the Case study later in this chapter). Although Piaget felt that not everyone reached this stage, even in adulthood, the earliest age at which this was likely to begin was around 11–12. As this is also the age of transition between primary and secondary schooling in most parts of the UK, the implications of Piaget's theory are significant for teachers in both primary and secondary schools.

Another important aspect of Piaget's thinking concerns the ways in which he believed children develop their knowledge and understanding of the world. He suggested that humans (among other species) have an inherent tendency to organise their experiences into systems or categories, which he called *schemes*. Schemes can refer to both large categories, such as recognising something as an animal rather than a plant, and smaller ones, such as identifying an animal as a cat rather than a dog. People's learning develops through the process of refining their schemes to adjust to their environment, a process which Piaget called *adaptation*.

New experiences are *assimilated* into existing schemes of knowledge if they fit in with what is already understood. Sometimes this can result in *misconceptions*, where the child provides an explanation for an event based on his or her limited previous experience: for example, young children have difficulty recognising that there is a relationship between water and ice, because one is hard and the other is not. Thus they may believe that ice on a puddle has been added to it, in the same way that ice is added to drinks at home. These misconceptions can sometimes be quite difficult to change, because they seem to make sense to the child. However, where the new information cannot be fitted into any existing schemes the learner *accommodates* the new information by altering their existing schemes or developing new ones and reaches a state of *equilibration*, where there is no longer a conflict between the old and new knowledge. Learning thus develops through the continual process of organising information and then reaching equilibration through assimilation or accommodation.

What is important to teachers about Piaget's ideas is his view that learners actively construct their understanding, and are not the passive recipients of information provided by others. This means that learning should be supported by practical experiences, related to contexts that make sense to the learner. The concept of the learner as a constructor of their own knowledge has led to all theories drawing on this idea being called constructivist theories. These theories are highly influential in current educational thinking throughout the primary and secondary phases of schooling.

Constructivism: a view of learning that emphasises the active role of the learner in building understanding, and making sense of information from experience.

Socio-cultural group: people with shared attitudes and values (culture) living within a particular society.

Zone of proximal development: this is generally described as the difference between what learners can do by themselves and what they can do with the help of a more knowledgeable adult or peer.

Scaffolding: the process whereby an adult or more experienced peer supports the learner to acquire new skills or understanding that are currently beyond their ability.

Although Piaget's theories have been challenged, especially in relation to the thinking of young children at the *pre-operational stage* (Donaldson, 1978), his ideas have remained very influential. Most cognitive psychologists today agree that children's thinking does develop along the lines identified by Piaget, but they question the existence of four separate stages. Whereas Piaget believed these stages to be sequential and age related, the work of other psychologists and educational researchers has called these assumptions into question.

Probably the most influential of these is Vygotsky, a Russian psychologist who was born in the same year as Piaget, but who died young of tuberculosis. In his relatively short life, Vygotsky produced a large body of work, but it was banned in Stalin's Russia for political reasons. Thus Piaget would not have been aware of Vygotsky's ideas, as his work was not available for translation in the West until the 1960s.

Vygotsky argued that social experience plays a major part in cognitive development, with the interaction of the child with more experienced members of his or her socio-cultural group as a central factor (Vygotsky, 1962). Cognitive development is thus more dependent on social experience than on age, and language is an important part of this process. Vygotsky explored the role of language in supporting the development of learning about the world in several forms, not all of which can be covered here. Woolfolk *et al.* (2008) provide a more detailed overview of his key ideas. For teachers the most influential of Vygotsky's theories is that of the zone of proximal development (usually known as the ZPD). This theory suggests that each learner has the potential to move beyond what he or she already knows, and is capable of understanding unaided, if he or she receives support from an adult or more experienced peer. This form of support has since become known as scaffolding, and underpins ideas about differentiation. Vygotsky's work has become known as social constructivism, to emphasise the important role of social interaction in the learner's construction of knowledge and understanding.

A number of other cognitive psychologists have built on the work of Piaget and Vygotsky in different ways, including Jerome Bruner (1996, 1983) who based his 'theory of instruction' on a combination of both their ideas. Bruner coined the term 'scaffolding' to apply to the role of the adult or experienced peer who supports learners to extend their understanding within their ZPD, and then withdraws support as it becomes unnecessary. Bruner also coined the term 'spiral curriculum' to designate a form of curriculum design where key concepts are revisited at increasing levels of complexity. This approach to the curriculum informs most areas of the primary and secondary national curriculum documents in the countries of the UK.

Another example where the ideas of Piaget and Vygotsky have been brought together is in the area of cognitive acceleration which has been studied by researchers at King College, London University for more than 20 years. Work in science and mathematics education (Shayer and Adey, 2002) appears to show that learners who are encouraged to reflect on their own learning are able to enhance their learning potential beyond that previously expected for their chronological age. This form of reflection is known as meta-cognition, roughly translated as 'thinking about how we think'. Robin Alexander, a well-known educationalist, also suggests that the use of the 'dialogic' teaching approach supports the development of logical thinking and generalisation in primary-aged pupils (Alexander, 2006). This approach involves encouraging pupils to build on each others' ideas, and is explored further in Chapter 8.

Differentiation: the adjustment of the teaching process according to the learning needs of pupils.

Social constructivism: the theory that learning is constructed through active participation with others within the contexts of the **socio-cultural group**.

Cognitive acceleration: a teaching approach which claims to develop pupils' general thinking abilities, involving the social construction of knowledge and the development of meta-cognition.

Meta-cognition: being aware of how we think and behave in learning situations.

Constructivist learning: key principles and implications

(Based on Wray and Lewis, 1997)

You should be able to identify the ideas of the key theories outlined above in these principles:

- Learning is a process of interaction between what is known and what is to be learnt.
- Learning is a social process.
- Learning is a situated process (it is specific to the situation in which it is learnt).
- Learning is a meta-cognitive process.

From these principles, the suggested implications for teaching are:

- Learners need sufficient previous knowledge and experience to help them make sense of new things. They need help to make the links between previous and new knowledge explicit (to themselves as well as to others).
- Discussion and social interaction are an important aspect of learning – both with and without the teacher.
- Meaningful contexts for learning are important, to enable the transfer of understanding from one situation to another (for example, being able to add or subtract numbers, and being able to give and receive change in shops) – but contexts that are meaningful to the teacher may not be meaningful to the child, so careful thought is needed.
- Learners need to be supported to be aware of their own thought processes, and to reflect on them as appropriate.

OVER TO YOU

In training

Reflect on a lesson you have observed, or one you have taught. Can you identify examples of the key principles outlined above within the lesson? Do you think constructivist approaches are suitable for all learning contexts?

Starting your career

Reflect on several lessons you have taught, to identify how often you draw on constructivist principles in your teaching. If you do not use them in some lessons, why do you think this is?

If all the above ideas are familiar to you, you might wish to ask your mentor or another colleague to observe you teaching a lesson and to comment on your use of the key principles to support pupils' learning.

If some of these ideas are less familiar, how will you begin to include these in your teaching?

Investigating learning and teaching

The theories outlined above are only some of the theories which inform our understanding of teaching and learning. The texts identified at the end of the chapter will introduce you to further theories, such as behaviourism, Information Processing Theory, and the development of long-term memory. What are the roles of these theories in understanding learning and how might they impact on your practice?

Some broad indicators of cognitive development in the 7–14 age range

Bearing the above discussion in mind, the next section outlines some generally accepted 'milestones' in terms of cognitive development, with the idea that 'stage not age' is the important consideration.

- Most 7 year old children are able to simultaneously identify more than one dimension of a situation: they will be aware that the same amount of modelling clay can be made into a round ball or a long snake (an example of Piaget's concept of conservation discussed above). Thus they will recognise that *amount* or *weight* and *shape* are different aspects of the modelling clay, both operating at the same time.

- By 7, children also exhibit some understanding of other people's points of view, and are increasingly able to take turns in games or conversations without being reminded of the need to do so. This developing social awareness enables co-operative learning to take place more easily. It also supports the development of concepts of fairness and right and wrong, which become more complex through the primary years as logical thinking also develops.

- By the age of 9 most pupils have increased their attention span and are developing distinctive personal interests. They have fairly well-established concepts of space and time, and understand cause and effect. Their ability to share and to work co-operatively increases, as does their sense of moral responsibility. As we have seen, this accompanies a stronger sense of 'fairness' and the importance of rules which extends beyond physical activities into other aspects of their school and social lives. This can affect their relationships with friends, and also with adults, as they have a clearer sense of both obligation and entitlement, as anyone who has failed to honour a carelessly made promise to a 9–11 year old can confirm. As pupils increase in independence, they may also become less compliant!

RESEARCH BRIEFING

The capacity for abstract thinking enables us to think hypothetically and to assess multiple outcomes. While this capacity develops during adolescence, many pupils in its early stages are still thinking mainly in more concrete terms. An interesting examples of these types of thinking can be seen in the example shown in Figure 4.2, drawn from a medical context.

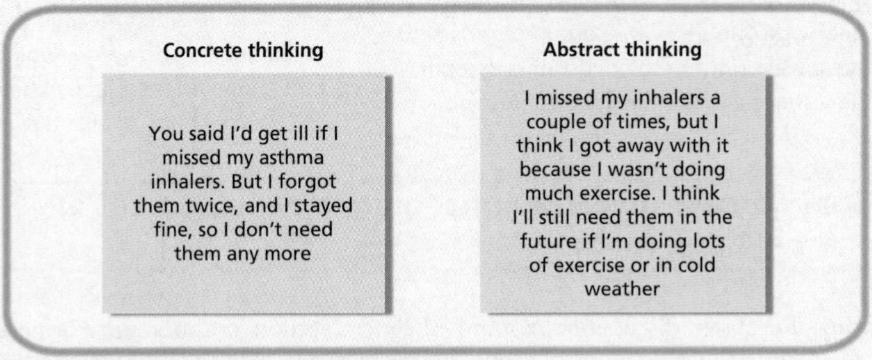

Concrete thinking	Abstract thinking
You said I'd get ill if I missed my asthma inhalers. But I forgot them twice, and I stayed fine, so I don't need them any more	I missed my inhalers a couple of times, but I think I got away with it because I wasn't doing much exercise. I think I'll still need them in the future if I'm doing lots of exercise or in cold weather

Figure 4.2 **Concrete and abstract thinking**
Source: Christie, D. and Viner, R. (2005) Clinical review: ABC of adolescence, *BMJ*, Vol. 330 (5 February): pp. 301–304

Similarly, pupils were set the task of imagining the creation of a new society and asked 'What is the purpose of laws?' Younger adolescents tended to respond in more concrete terms: 'If we had no laws people could go round killing people', whereas older pupils gave replies such as 'To ensure safety and enforce the government' and 'They are basically guidelines for people' (Adelson, 1971, cited in Coleman and Hendry, 1990: 42).

As younger adolescents develop more independent reasoning, you may find that they demonstrate certain characteristics, which can be interpreted as confrontational, but may actually be a normal part of cognitive developmental processes. These include attempts to argue for the sake of arguing, and a tendency to jump to conclusions. In domestic situations these may also manifest as constantly finding fault with parents' or other adults' viewpoints, and while direct confrontation of this kind is less common in the school environment, it may translate into 'over-dramatic' responses to criticism or reprimand.

CASE STUDY

Two 'pen portraits'

Anna is always bright and alert and dresses smartly. She is, however, not always on time for classes and thinks she can deflect attention from this with humour and charm.

She puts a huge amount of effort into her work. She sits with a group of girls who are always right in the midst of classroom discussions and are always offering opinions. She is motivated by success and has been very upset when an assignment receives a lower grade than the one she was expecting.

She is very argumentative and holds her views strongly. With the encouragement of those around her she does not hesitate to engage in discussions on any topic and is remarkably inflexible in her views. She has once or twice stuck to her views so vociferously in the face of contrary text-based evidence that I have had to ask her to stop holding the class up with her immovable point of view.

Tom is a healthy and apparently happy pupil. He arrives on time for classes and is always alert and well dressed.

Early in his first term with me he enjoyed trying to use very long words in class and assignments, with the professed aim of catching me out. He didn't manage to do this and I marked him down on two occasions because the big word he used had been used incorrectly.

He enjoys the company of a small group of other boys, all of whom are quiet in class. He has become increasingly quiet in class as well. I would say that his peer group are a negative influence and they are not the sort of boys who respect academic success as much as they will respect a little quiet rebellion and attempts to avoid learning. When left to their own devices they do as little as possible and have not responded well to attempts to give them some independence of learning.

With thanks to Damien Scott-Masson

THINKING IT THROUGH

These descriptions of Anna and Tom (both 13 year olds) were written by a teacher at an early career stage. How far do you feel they are 'typical' of young adolescents? As you read on, consider how models such as that of Levin (below) could be applied to their behaviours as described here.

Social and emotional development and learning

The psychoanalyst Erik Erikson (1980) suggests that there are eight stages of psychosocial development through which individuals pass, although the last two are

Psychosocial: the combination of psychological and social factors affecting mental health or social and emotional development.

seen as those of middle and late adulthood. Erikson's theory is based on the idea that we develop our sense of social identity, or 'self-concept' through our relationships with others, which can be experienced positively or negatively. Thus each stage is presented as being made up of two possible forms of experience. Erikson also links transitions from one stage to another with a 'crisis' or important conflict which the individual needs to resolve if they are to proceed to the next stage positively.

As with Piaget's stage theory, applications of Erikson's work have been criticised for being too rigidly applied, but as we shall see, his ideas are helpful in considering some of the challenges faced by adolescents and how these impact on the context for learning.

For the 7–14 age ranges, Erikson's stages are as follows:

Table 4.1 Erikson's stages for the 7–14 age range

Stage	Approximate age	Important event	Description
Industry versus inferiority	6–12	School	The child must deal with the demands of learning new skills or risk a sense of inferiority, failure and incompetence
Identity versus role confusion	Adolescence*	Peer relationships	The teenager must achieve identity in occupation, gender roles, politics and religion

From: Lefton (1994) *Psychology*, (5th edition). Boston MA, Allyn and Bacon. Reproduced in Wolfolk *et al.* (2008 p. 86).

* Erikson's concept of adolescence extends for approximately the 6 years from 12–18.

Pam Levin (1988) also proposes a series of stages of social and emotional development, from birth to maturity, with a series of 'tasks' to be learned during each stage. Levin's theory, based on the study of children and young people in a range of cultures, suggests that individuals need to have opportunities to complete the developmental tasks most appropriate to their age. For example, she suggests that younger children, between the ages of 3 and 6 years, need to learn (among other things) that they are individuals with the power to affect others and the feelings of others, and to understand the difference between fantasy and reality. Adults can support children in this learning through the use of 'affirmations': positive statements or behaviours which can help to structure support for the individual in achieving the developmental tasks appropriate for their age or stage. These positive statements or behaviours enable the learner to feel secure in developing their new understanding, and to feel able to make mistakes or to express emotion.

Within the age group of 6–12 years, some of the developmental tasks suggested by Levin include:

- being able to learn from mistakes
- developing internal control
- learning the relevance of social rules and experiencing the consequences of breaking them
- learning to listen in order to collect information and to learn
- understanding individuals can disagree with others, but still be wanted
- developing the capacity to co-operate

Many of these tasks continue in to adolescence, where young people also need to develop increasing independence and personal interests.

Positive 'affirmations' by adults could involve demonstrating to the child that they are still valued when they make mistakes, or making it clear that while independence is important, it is still all right to ask for help, or showing that the child is still loved and valued, even when we disagree with what they say or do. These principles also underpin approaches to developing behaviour for learning, as we will see in Chapter 9.

Where these tasks are completed satisfactorily, the individual develops emotional stability, but unfinished tasks remain as needs which may be re-visited later, and which may emerge at particular transition stages – such as secondary transfer for example, but also where family breakdown or other strong emotional experiences occur. At such times, pupils may 'regress' and demonstrate behaviours that appear to be inappropriate for their chronological age.

CASE STUDY

Andrea is coming to the end of her time in Year 6. Her class teacher is concerned about how she will cope at secondary school as she still seems to be very immature in some respects. She becomes very upset when faced with tasks she finds difficult, but refuses to accept help. On occasions she has torn up her work or thrown it on the floor. However, she generally completes her work to a good standard and her test results indicate that she is slightly above average ability in both English and mathematics. Andrea also argues with other pupils in the class, and will not back down from the position she has taken. As a result she is sometimes isolated, which she also finds very upsetting.

Applying Levin's ideas to Andrea's behaviour, it could be argued that she has not fully completed the developmental 'tasks' for her stage of social and emotional development. She needs support in developing internal control; in accepting that one can accept help without compromising independence and in recognising that she can accept the views of others without feeling her own value as a person is diminished. Possibly Andrea may still need to learn that she is not the centre of the universe – a task that Levin suggests belongs to the younger 3–6 year group. However, as we will see, many adolescents are also very conscious of the opinions of others, and this may also be affecting Andrea's behaviour.

Photo 4.2
Some children become easily discouraged when they cannot complete a task, and may become reliant on adult assistance. How can teachers support children to overcome this 'learned helplessness'?

Source: Pearson Education Ltd/Rob Judges

There is overlap between Levin's framework and Erikson's developmental stages, although the underpinning theory is different. Erikson also identifies the stage between 7–11 as a period when children need to learn more formal skills, such as playing by the rules and engaging in team work. As Erikson believed each stage contained an essential conflict, he saw this period as opposing 'industry' with 'inferiority'. Children at this stage experience satisfaction when they persevere to complete a task effectively; in other words they are rewarded by 'industry'. If a child experiences constant failure, either through an inability to complete tasks, or by being compared to others, they will develop feelings of inferiority. The 'conflict' characteristic of this stage is that children need to risk failure in order to learn, but at the same time they need to learn that failure is part of growing up. Erikson sees self concept being developed, positively or negatively through interaction with others, and Levin's ideas suggest ways in which adults can provide positive support during this process.

Between the ages of 7 and 9 children increasingly engage in single sex group play and the division between girls and boys is usually fairly distinct by the end of this period.

The concept of 'friendship' becomes well developed during this period, and by the age of 9 or 10 many children have established close relationships with a 'best friend' or with a selected group, which can be all-engrossing. If such relationships break down, either temporarily or more permanently, many children experience significant emotional distress at being excluded. This may be another time when adult affirmation may be needed to help the child come to terms with rejection and to develop new relationships.

Social cognition – recognising the existence of the separate thoughts and feelings of others, is part of cognitive development, as well as a vital aspect of social competence. This is sometimes called 'theory of mind' (Blakemore and Frith 2005) and we recognise its importance particularly when we encounter those individuals who appear to lack this ability, such as those with forms of autism such as Asperger Syndrome. People with forms of autism often find it difficult to recognise that other people may have intentions or wishes that are different from theirs. For example, they may not respond to a statement such as 'I'd like to stop walking for a moment' as meaning that the speaker actually wishes to stop, and might well carry on walking, apparently ignoring what the first speaker thought was a request. Teachers working with pupils who have forms of autism need to be aware of this tendency to take statements literally, and of the feelings of distress and confusion which autistic pupils can experience in trying to make sense of commonly used phrases, such as 'Give me your attention'.

Although children in the 7+ age group are able to recognise that other people may have a different social perspective from their own, the ability to appreciate reciprocal perspectives develops more slowly. This is the ability not just to recognise the existence of another perspective, but to take it into account in social interaction, by anticipating that another person might be pleased or distressed by our actions on the basis of how we would feel ourselves.

By the age of 9 or 10 the majority of children are capable of empathising with others to some extent. However, they are often highly competitive and may argue over issues of fairness, even when they are technically in the wrong. As both Levin and Erikson suggest, children in this age group are beginning to accept failure as sometimes inevitable, although it is often hard for them to admit their mistakes and to take responsibility for them. They appear to have a more independent sense of right and wrong than younger children, but sometimes have difficulty admitting guilt themselves.

Pupils in the 10–14 age range (early adolescence) are aware that others have different perspectives, but may also believe that other people are formulating opinions about them and become highly pre-occupied with the imagined opinions of other people. This is often referred to as adolescent ego-centrism, and is one of a range of social and emotional dimensions of adolescence that we will consider in the next section, as well as another aspect of social cognition.

Ego-centrism: the assumption that other people view the world in the same way as yourself.

THINKING IT THROUGH

Look back at the first descriptions of the pupils in the imaginary classroom at the start of this chapter.

Drawing on the information in this section of the chapter, how would you describe Amber, Jane, Jason, Andrew and Gemma in terms of their social and emotional development.

Adolescence – social and emotional development

CONTROVERSY

Are schools helpful for adolescents?

'Many adolescents are trying to "find their feet", develop a new identity and develop new relationships with adults, especially parents. At the same time, the academic pressures of school demand that pupils make far-reaching choices about careers. . . .

'Schools have a vital part to play in this developmental period. They exist unequivocally to further the development of pupils and must try to provide the environment in which personal autonomy can grow. At the same time, and to cope with several hundred young people in a confined space, schools must provide a disciplined context not just for the healthy growth of the individual, but for everyone. Having many young people all together means that these conditions are not necessarily compatible with those for the emergence of the autonomous individual.'

Source: Jepson and Turner (2005)

OVER TO YOU

Although perhaps older primary and younger secondary aged pupils do not yet experience pressures about careers and subject choices, their need to begin to assert their own individuality is very much present.

Jessop and Turner imply that the school environment may be counter-productive for this development.

In what ways do schools with which you are familiar seek to create an 'environment in which personal autonomy can grow'?

The term adolescence is used both in a technical sense and in more common usage. Often, the concept of the adolescent and that of the 'teenager' are seen as being the same. However, the World Health Authority defines adolescence as being the age range between 10 and 19. This is in line with the onset of puberty, as we have seen, but extends well beyond the time when most young people reach sexual maturity, to encompass continuing issues relating to psychological development.

School pupils in the 9–13 age group are defined as being in the 'early adolescent stage', which is seen as having its own distinctive features (American Psychological Association, 2002). These include a strong commitment to their peer groups, usually of the same sex, accompanied by a lessening of commitment to adults such as parents and teachers (Constanzo and Shaw, 1966). In some cases, the influence of the peer group has been shown to shift during early adolescence, from a point where peer influence is likely to be positive in terms of social behaviour, for example in continuing to encourage effective work habits and positive attitudes to school, towards a stronger tendency for antisocial behaviour in 14–15 year olds (Berndt, 1979). This might involve experimentation with drugs or alcohol, or involvement in forms of vandalism or crime.

As a result of cognitive development, younger adolescents are also beginning to recognise their personal uniqueness and are seeking their own identity, but have usually not yet made a firm commitment to the kind of person they wish to be. According to the American Psychological Association (2002), identity is made up of two components:

- **Self-concept**: the set of beliefs about oneself, including attributes, roles, goals, interests, values and religious or political beliefs.
- **Self-esteem**: how one feels about one's self-concept.

In early adolescence, self-concept is still fluid and strongly influenced by the views and norms of others, although the influence of the family group may lessen or even be rejected. Young people in this age range often adopt 'celebrities' of various kinds as role models, and also become much more aware of their own physical appearance. Younger adolescents are often highly self-conscious as a result of the physical changes following puberty and feel themselves to be under constant scrutiny by an imaginary audience. When adolescents were asked what they did and did not like about themselves, those in early adolescence were much more likely to describe themselves in terms of their physical appearance (usually negatively) as opposed to intellectual or social aspects of personality (Coleman and Hendry, 1990). This feeling may affect their behaviour in social situations, including that of the classroom, where some pupils may avoid calling attention to themselves by not answering questions, or be reluctant to come out to the front of the class to use the Interactive White Board (IWB) as part of the lesson.

Many younger adolescents enter a second 'egocentric' stage (the first stage being in early childhood). They hold the view that their own thoughts and feelings are unique, and not shared by others, and they may even come to believe that they are abnormal in some way. Although this belief diminishes around the age of 15 or 16, it can often lead to conflict with parents and other authority figures such as teachers, who are seen as lacking in 'understanding'. Perhaps also associated with this belief in their uniqueness are feelings of invulnerability, where young adolescents engage in risk-taking behaviours. Carried to extremes, these may include substance abuse and sexual experimentation as well as physically dangerous or antisocial activities, but risk taking is also part of normal experimentation in developing identity and trying out new decision-making skills and independence.

Another area of development in adolescence is an increased social awareness and sense of responsibility, which is often characterised by the development of strong political opinions, for example about animal rights, ecological issues etc. However, although older primary pupils and younger adolescents do have strong opinions on these issues, research suggests that these tend to be absolutist, expressed in straightforward terms as right or wrong, whereas older pupils of 14 or above are more likely to recognise multiple perspectives.

THINKING IT THROUGH

If there are significant developmental differences between individuals of the same chronological age leading to differences in achievement, should we be organising our education system on an age-related basis?

The practice of setting or grouping by ability is an attempt to cater for these differences, but how far does setting take developmental factors other than cognitive ability into account? Although ability grouping is recommended in current policy documents (DfES, 2006a, 2006b) research indicates that it does not necessarily improve performance, and may lower self-esteem in some pupils.

For a commentary on current policy and links to research evidence see 'Are we really grouping pupils for success?'
www.ttrb.ac.uk/ViewArticle2.aspx?ContentId=12855.

Would mixed ability teaching provide a better solution, or would this exacerbate developmental differences within a class group?

Are you aware of any current developments which seek to respond to these challenging questions?

SUMMARY

This chapter has discussed a range of developmental issues affecting the learning behaviours of pupils in the 7–14 age range. We have emphasised that 'stage' should not be confused with 'age' (Wong and Bradshaw, 2004), and while there are broad indicators of physical, cognitive, social and emotional development associated with age groups, pupils should be considered in terms of their individual characteristics when we are planning for effective learning experiences.

We have briefly considered ideas from some key theorists in cognitive psychology and in the field of personal, social and emotional development, and indicated how an understanding of these theories can be helpful to teachers on a day-to-day basis in the classroom. There are many other theories which we have not considered, which you may also find helpful, and some suggestions for further reading are given below.

TAKING YOUR PRACTICE FURTHER

Have you ever made assumptions about pupils' capabilities mainly on the basis of their age? What other evidence would you need to support your judgement?

Do you consciously attempt to develop pupils' meta-cognitive understanding of their learning (see also Chapters 8 and 10)?

> ### TAKING YOUR PRACTICE FURTHER *CONTINUED*
>
> Are there pupils in your class(es) whom you consider to be at a different developmental stage from their peers in terms of social and emotional development (apart from those identified by the school as having Social and Emotional Behavioural Difficulties, who may require different approaches)? What strategies might you use to support them to engage in learning, based on the models provided in this chapter? (See also Chapter 11.)

> ### TAKING YOUR THINKING FURTHER
>
> This chapter has suggested that social and emotional development is related to a developing sense of personal identity, which in turn impacts on learning. The work of Carol Dweck (1999) indicates that the use of frequent praise for achieving low-level tasks, which is sometimes seen as a way of building pupils' self-esteem, does *not* build confidence in learning. Guy Claxton (2002) argues that 'resilience' – the ability to tolerate a degree of strangeness or challenge – is a crucial learning disposition. Resilience as a disposition has a relationship with how we view ourselves as learners and how we expect learning to take place. How do you support pupils to develop 'resilience' in overcoming difficulties in learning, and to recognise that they can learn from their mistakes?

Find out more

If you are interested in finding out more about brain development and learning, the following texts provide a good introduction:

Blakemore, S. and Frith, U. (2005) *The Learning Brain; Lessons for Education.* **London: Blackwell.**
This book provides a basic introduction to the ways in which neuroscientists investigate the brain, and outlines the state of knowledge about how the brain operates in relation to educational topics such as learning to read and acquiring mathematical understanding, as well as adolescent brain development. The book also discusses some disorders such as autism and ADHD in terms of what neuroscience can tell us.

Neuroscience and Education: Issues and Opportunities. **A commentary by the Teaching and Learning Research Programme. Available at: www.tlrp.org.**

This downloadable resource briefly outlines the contribution that neuroscience can make to educational understanding. It also examines some of the popular trends in schools, such as 'Brain Gym', in the light of scientific evidence.

The General Teaching Council for England has published a summary of a lengthy international review on neuroscience, drawing on a number of research projects. The summary contains several case studies of linked research showing educational relevance and also addresses a number of 'neuromyths' – such as the idea that we only use 10% of our brains, or that learners can be regarded as 'left brained' or 'right brained'. Available at: **www.gtce.org.uk/teachers/rft/neuroscience/**.

If you are interested in finding out more about cognitive development, there are a number of excellent texts available, including:

Child, D. (2007) *Psychology and the Teacher*. New York: Continuum.

Pritchard, A. (2005) *Ways of Learning*. London: Fulton.

Wood, D. (1998) *How Children Think and Learn: The Social Contexts of Cognitive Development*, 2nd edn. Oxford: Blackwell.

Woolfolk, A., Hughes, M. and Walkup, V. (2008) *Psychology in Education*. Harlow: Pearson.

All of these texts contain chapters on theories of cognitive development, and how these can help to inform the work of teachers.

Woolfolk *et al.* is an authoritative text which covers many aspects of cognitive development and constructivist learning theory. It provides a number of concrete examples applied to teaching, and summaries of the ideas of Piaget and Vygotsky.

If you are interested in finding out more about social and emotional development and its effects on learning:

Head, J. (1997) *Working with Adolescents: Constructing Identity*. London: Falmer.

This text looks at gender differences in development and sexual behaviour, the development of identity, beliefs and values, and current issues in schooling. Activity boxes are provided to support the reader's understanding.

Woolfolk, A., Hughes, M. and Walkup, V. (2008) *Psychology in Education*. Harlow: Pearson. Chapter 3.

Again, this is an authoritative text which covers many developmental aspects. It provides a number of concrete examples applied to teaching, and summaries of the ideas of a number of significant theorists such as Freud and Erikson.

Glossary

Cognitive acceleration: a teaching approach which claims to develop pupils' general thinking abilities, involving the social construction of knowledge and the development of meta-cognition. See: http://www.kcl.ac.uk/schools/sspp/education/research/projects/cognitive.html

Constructivism: a view of learning that emphasises the active role of the learner in building understanding, and making sense of information from experience.

Differentiation: the adjustment of the teaching process according to the learning needs of pupils.

Ego-centrism: the assumption that other people view the world in the same way as yourself.

Meta-cognition: being aware of how we think and behave in learning situations. Ultimately this implies active control over the process of thinking; for example: planning the way to approach a learning task, monitoring comprehension, and evaluating progress towards the completion of a task.

Neuron: a nerve cell in the brain that stores and transfers information. Neurons have long and short fibres through which connection to other cells takes place, across the **synapses**.

Psychosocial: the combination of psychological and social factors affecting mental health or social and emotional development.

Scaffolding: the process whereby an adult or more experienced peer supports the learner to acquire new skills or understanding that are currently beyond their ability. Different techniques may be used, such as breaking the task down into smaller sections, questioning, cueing or modelling, but the important thing is that the pupil completes as much of the task as possible, and only receives support in those aspects that they cannot master at present. Once they have mastered the task or demonstrated the necessary understanding, the teacher or peer withdraws support, or 'removes the scaffolding'.

Social constructivism: the theory that learning is constructed through active participation with others within the contexts of the **socio-cultural group**.

Socio-cultural group: people with shared attitudes and values (culture) living within a particular society. The terms culture and society are often used interchangeably, but this combined term is used to indicate that larger social groups, whether nations or local communities, are composed of smaller groups of people with distinct attitudes and values. Thus one child's learning in terms of social constructivism may be very different from another's, even when they live in the same area.

Synapse: the tiny space between neurons. Chemical messages cross this gap between the fibres of different neurons and allow the neurons to form interconnected circuits.

Zone of proximal development: this is generally described as the difference between what learners can do by themselves and what they can do with the help of a more knowledgeable adult or peer. See **scaffolding**, above. The ZPD is constantly changing as the learner increases their understanding, so that ongoing assessment is an essential part of this process.

References

Alexander, R. (2006) *Towards Dialogic Teaching: Rethinking Classroom Talk*, 3rd edn. York: Dialogos.

American Psychological Association (2002) *Developing Adolescents: A Reference for Professionals*. Washington, DC: American Psychological Association.

Berndt, T.J. (1979) Developmental changes in conformity to peers and parents, *Developmental Psychology*, Vol. 15, No. 6: pp. 606–616.

Blakemore, S. and Frith, U. (2005) *The Learning Brain; Lessons for Education*. London: Blackwell.

Bronfenbrenner, U. (1979) *The Ecology of Human Development*. Cambridge, MA: Harvard University Press.

Bruner, J.S. (1966) *Towards a Theory of Instruction*. New York: W.W. Norton.

Bruner, J.S. (1983) *Child's Talk: Learning to Use Language*. Oxford: OUP.

Children's Workforce Development Council (CWDC) (2007) *Induction Training Programme Module 2: Understanding Children and Young People's Development*. Leeds: CWDC.

Claxton, G. (2002) *Building Learning Power: Helping Young People Become Better Learners*. Bristol: TLO.

Coleman, J.C. and Hendry, L. (1990) *The Nature of Adolescence*, 2nd edn. London: Routledge.

Constanzo, P.R. and Shaw, M.E. (1966) Conformity as a function of age level, *Child Development*, Vol. 37, pp. 967–975.

DfES (2006a) *Pupil Grouping Strategies and Practices at Key Stage 2 and 3: Case Studies of 24 Schools in England*. London: DfES. Available at: **http://www.dfes.gov.uk/research/data/uploadfiles/RR796.pdf**.

DfES (2006b) *Grouping Pupils for Success*. London: DfES. Available at: **http://www.standards.dfes.gov.uk/primary/publications/literacy/group_pup_succ/ns_grp_succ_0394506.pdf**.

Donaldson, M. (1978) *Children's Minds*. London: Fontana/Collins.

Dweck, C. (1999) *Self Theories: Their Role in Personality, Motivation and Development*. Hove: Psychology Press.

Erikson, E.H. (1980) *Identity and the Life Cycle*. New York: W.W. Norton.

Jepson, M. and Turner, T. (2005) Growth development and diet, in Capel, S., Leask, M. and Turner, T. (eds) *Learning to Teach in the Secondary School*, 4th edn. London: Routledge.

Lever, J. (1998) Sex differences in the games children play, in Myers, K., Anderson, C. and Risman, B. (eds) *Feminist Foundations*. Thousand Oaks, CA: Sage.

Levin, P. (1988) *Cycles of Power: A Guidebook for the Seven Seasons of Life*. Dearfield Beach, FL: Health Communications. *Florida Health Communications*.

Paquette, D. and Ryan, J. (2001) *Bronfenbrenner's Ecological Systems Theory*. National-Louis University. Available at: **http://pt3.nl.edu/paquetteryanwebquest.pdf**.

Piaget, J. (1954) *The Construction of Reality in the Child*. New York: Basic Books.

Shayer, M. and Adey, P. (eds) (2002) *Learning Intelligence: Cognitive Acceleration across the Curriculum from 5–15*. Buckingham: Open University.

Shemilt, I., Harvey, I., Shepstone, L., Swift, L., Reading, R., Mugford, M., Belderson, P., Norris, N., Thoburn, J. and Robinson, J. (2004) A national evaluation of school breakfast clubs: evidence from a randomized controlled trail and an observational analysis, *Child Care Health and Development*, Vol. 30, No. 5: pp. 413–427.

Simpson, D., Summerbell, C., Crow, R. and Wattis L. (2003) School breakfast clubs, social background and nutritional status. *Practical Research for Education*, NFER, Spring 2003, Issue 29. Available at: **www.ttrb.ac.uk/ViewArticle2.aspx?ContentId=13827**.

Tanner, J.M. (1990) *Foetus into Man*. Cambridge, MA: Harvard University Press.

Vygotsky, L.S. (1962) *Thought and Language*. Cambridge, MA: MIT Press.

Whitehead, R.G. (1991) *Report on Health and Social Subjects No. 41*. London: HMSO.

Wong, G. and Bradshaw, E. (2004) It doesn't matter what age you are – It's what stage you are at that counts, in Barrow, G. and Newton, T. (eds) *Walking the Talk: How Transactional Analysis is Improving Behaviour and Raising Self-Esteem*. London: David Fulton.

Woolfolk, A., Hughes, M. and Walkup, V. (2008) *Psychology in Education*. Harlow: Pearson.

Wray, D. and Lewis, M. (1997) *Extending Literacy*. London: Routledge.

5 Learners as Individuals

In this chapter you will:

- Consider a further range of influences on teaching and learning which can affect individual learners
- Examine your personal beliefs about the relationship between gender, ethnicity and achievement
- Reflect further on factors which can affect self-identity, self-esteem and motivation
- Begin to consider how schools and teachers can seek to reduce some barriers to learning and achievement

Who are you?

- Are you female or male? What is your sexual orientation?
- How would you describe your ethnic and cultural background: as 'working-class', 'middle-class' or perhaps something in between?
- Do you consider yourself to be a member of a religious or faith group?
- When you are asked to identify your ethnic origin, do you identify yourself within a specific category (such as Asian or White British) or do you withhold this information?
- What position do you hold in your family? Are you an only child, or the oldest/youngest/middle child in the family? Perhaps this is a question that is difficult to answer if you have become separated from your family for some reason.

Your response to these questions will indicate some of the ways in which your own sense of self-identity may have been shaped. These areas were chosen to indicate major influences on pupils' learning and achievement as individuals, apart from the developmental features discussed in the previous chapter.

Introduction

We all recognise that each learner is unique – but while this is easy to say, and obviously true, it is much more challenging to consider all the factors that can affect an individual pupil's motivation to learn, and to try to take these into account in our teaching.

In the last chapter we looked at the ways that physical, cognitive, social and emotional development affect learning. Although these factors alone have a considerable effect on the experience of each learner, they are not the only influences we need to consider in reflecting on the needs of learners as individuals. Family background and cultural values within local communities will also play a large part in forming pupils' attitudes towards schooling and education, which is why the relationships with parents and the local community discussed in Chapter 3 are so important. Attitudes about gender also play a part in influencing the ways in which boys and girls engage with learning. We know from government statistics that socio-economic status (SES) has an effect on pupil achievement, as measured through end of Key Stage tests. Each individual pupil responds differently to these multiple influences of family background, socio-economic status, ethnicity, gender and developmental issues.

In this chapter we will look at some of the personal contexts of individual learners, and begin to reflect on how effectively, or otherwise, these influences support learning and the development of self-concept or self-identity (see Figure 5.1).

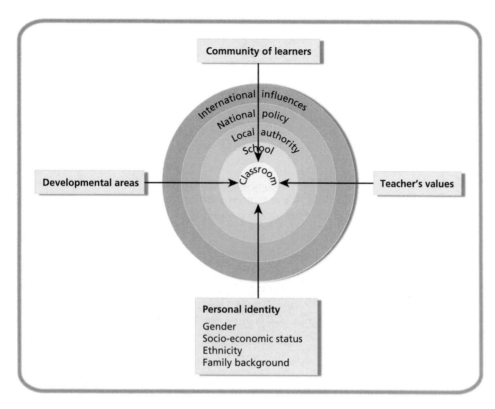

Figure 5.1
Influences on teaching and learning

Motivation, self-concept and self-esteem

Psychologists have identified three key aspects of motivation that contribute to the incentive to start a task and carry it through:

Direction – which activities do people choose to start?
Persistence – how far do people carry on with a task?
Intensity – how much effort will they put in?

The factors that influence pupils' motivation to learn are highly complex, but **self-concept** and **self-esteem** are certainly significant. Self-concept is influenced by factors such as gender, ethnicity, home culture and teacher expectations: all or any of these can influence the individual pupil's belief in their ability to succeed in a given area, and their motivation to do so. Individuals whose self-concept includes the belief that they are unlikely to succeed in certain areas, whether they are academic, creative or sporting areas, are less likely to persist in the face of difficulties, or to recover from the experience of failure. Such beliefs can be based on expectations derived from their home culture and background, but also from their experiences in schools. Theories about motivation incorporate consideration of the teacher's values, as well as those of the pupil, and your general beliefs about learners and learning will influence the ways in which you approach the design of learning experiences for pupils. Additionally, any

Self-concept: the set of beliefs about oneself, including attributes, roles, goals, interests, values and religious or political beliefs.

Self-esteem: how one feels about one's self-concept.

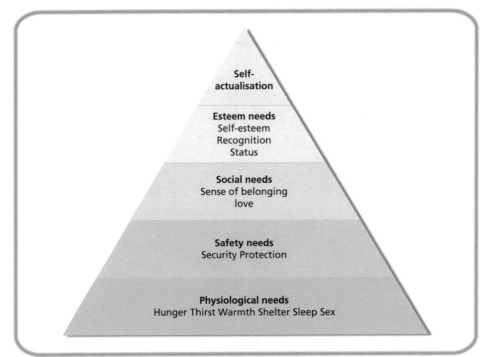

Figure 5.2
Maslow's hierarchy of needs

Source: Maslow, A. (1970) *Motivation and Personality*, 2nd edn. New York: Harper and Row. Reprinted by permission of Ann Kaplan

assumptions you hold about gender and/or ethnicity in relation to learning and achievement will influence aspects of your teaching.

Abraham Maslow (1908–1970) was an American psychologist who studied a number of 'exemplary' people, including Eleanor Roosevelt and Albert Einstein. On the basis of his observations, he developed his well-known 'hierarchy of needs' (Maslow, 1970) which identifies self-esteem as a basic human need, without which no-one can achieve 'self-actualisation' or a sense of personal fulfilment (see Figure 5.2).

Maslow's theory suggests that, if the experience of schooling denies pupils a sense of self-esteem, they are more likely to become demotivated or actively disaffected. As a result, they may seek other sources of self-esteem through peer recognition and 'alternative' cultures. Schools can deny self-esteem through failing to recognise pupils as individuals, or by failing to ascribe value to their home background, religion or culture. The evidence shows that pupils from certain sectors of the population are more 'at risk' than others in terms of under-achievement, either in all aspects of education or in some subject areas. These include boys from lower SES groups, and pupils identified as belonging to certain ethnic groups: Black or White and Black Caribbean, Bangladeshi and Traveller/Roma pupils. Many families in these ethnic groups also live in areas identified as having greater levels of poverty (DfES, 2006), so that the multiple factors of gender, ethnicity and SES interact to place Black Caribbean boys within one of the lowest-attaining groups in terms of results at GCSE.

In considering the development of self-concept and its effect on learning, the areas of gender and ethnicity will be considered in turn. However, just as with the different developmental aspects discussed in Chapter 4, it is the interrelationship of these influences, alongside others, that influences the development of individual self-concept.

The importance of the individual's self-concept for learning

Chapter 4 outlined the ways in which young adolescents increasingly turn to their peer group for support, and the consequent influence of the peer group on the individual sometimes outweighs that of the family. These influences are not always negative: as we saw, peer groups can reinforce positive attitudes to learning, particularly in the upper primary years (Berndt and Keefe, 1995), as well as promoting alternative values that might be less in tune with school cultures.

Photo 5.1
The peer group expectations about 'normal' behaviour and appearance are a powerful influence on young adolescents

Source: Pearson Education Ltd/Photodisc

Children and young people also begin to develop their sense of self-concept or self-identity through social interaction with their peers, as well as through the influence of their family and the local community. The individual's sense of self develops in line with other aspects of cognitive development, as outlined in the previous chapter, moving from the general assumption that other people think in similar ways to one-self towards an appreciation that other people may think about things very differently. The previous chapter identified some of the challenges posed for pupils in the 7–14 age group as they increasingly recognise their own individuality. Individual conceptions relating to gender, ethnicity and educational achievement also have a powerful effect upon the development of individual pupils' self-concept, and are affected by the community and school environments and their interrelationship, as discussed in Chapter 3 (see Table 5.1).

Table 5.1 Some factors influencing an individual's self-concept

Dimension	Key questions	Significant factors influencing self-concept
Physical appearance	*What do I look like?*	Age, gender, ethnicity, physical disability, peer group expectations
Social relationships	*Do people like me? Do I 'fit in'?*	Gender, home culture, ethnicity, physical disability, academic ability/difficulty, emotional, social and behavioural difficulty
Beliefs about success in academic, sports and creative areas	*How good am I?*	Home culture, peer expectations, teacher expectations, school culture and ethos

These components are frequently interrelated, as indicated by peer group labelling. For example, terms such as 'geek', 'anorak', 'goth' or 'chav' carry with them associations of physical appearance as well as assumptions about academic ability or the ability to make social relationships.

The expectations of others are also powerful in terms of belief about success in different areas of achievement, and can be limiting as well as empowering. Although schools are nowadays more aware of challenging embedded assumptions about gender and ethnicity, research in the past indicated implicitly held teacher beliefs about girls and science learning, or about pupils of African-Caribbean descent and success in sports rather than academic subjects. As we will see later in this chapter, it is possible that some strategies aimed at challenging gender stereotyping may actually be continuing to reinforce some beliefs about boys' and girls' learning and achievement. Such assumptions can directly impact on the individual's self-concept and self-esteem.

Self-esteem, although closely related to self-concept, is concerned with the value *we* place on our characteristics and abilities. Children and younger adolescents derive most of their values from their immediate community, which includes the school, but also those of their family and peers. These also include the values promoted by the forms of popular media that are preferred by their friends, such as magazines and favourite television programmes. If the values of the school and those of other components of the individual's personal life are significantly at odds with each other, this can result in lowered self-esteem in the educational context, and potentially in disaffection. Position in the family, lack of stability in family relationships, or the absence of family can all also influence an individual's self-esteem to varying extents. While the links between self-esteem, motivation and educational achievement are well established, it is also worth noting that high self-esteem may not always be a positive attribute where it leads to insensitivity towards others or to avoidance of criticism or challenging tasks (Woolfolk Hughes and Walkup, 2008: 110).

This chapter concentrates particularly on gender and ethnicity as important aspects of self-identity, which are also related to academic achievement. However, it is important to remember that the measures of academic achievement, in terms of A–C grades at GCSE used in policy documents, need not be the only indicators of individual success or of self-actualisation for pupils. The values and ethos of the school, and of individual teachers, can have a significant effect on how pupils perceive themselves, as we discussed in Chapter 1. There are many ways in which teachers, and schools as communities, can celebrate the individuality and successes of pupils, apart from through examination results.

CASE STUDY

In one primary school classroom we know, every pupil is depicted by a life-sized 'self-portrait', based on an outline of the actual pupil which has been drawn around, painted and then cut out. Each pupil has then labelled their image with statements about the things they are 'good at' – both in and out of school.

OVER TO YOU

In training

Based on your observations in schools, and in discussion with colleagues, how many examples of similar 'esteem-boosting' strategies can you list?

Starting your career

What strategies do you use in your own teaching? What strategies have you observed in use by other teachers?

Are there pupils in your own class(es) for whom you feel further 'esteem-boosting' strategies could be helpful?

Investigating learning and teaching

Criticisms have been levelled at what is perceived as a 'self-esteem industry'. Some writers argue that too much attention to boosting self-esteem can lead to a lack of resilience and autonomy in pupils. How would you respond to the comments by Frank Furedi in the box below? Do they apply to all pupils in all circumstances?

You might also want to read an article by Katherine Ecclestone, 'Learning or therapy? The demoralization of education' (Ecclestone, 2004).

CONTROVERSY

Frank Furedi is a Professor of Sociology at the University of Kent. He is well known for expressing critical views about various aspects of life in Britain today. Below are some comments he has made about what he terms the 'therapy culture' in schools. By this he means a range of activities such as 'Circle Time' which are intended to increase pupils' 'emotional literacy'.

Perversely, the ascendancy of self-esteem education in the classroom has been paralleled by an apparent increase in mental health problems among children. The relation between the two is not accidental. Children are highly suggestible and the more they are required to participate in wellbeing classes, the more they will feel the need for professional support.

The teaching of emotional literacy and happiness should also be viewed as a cop-out from tackling the fundamental problems confronting schools. When many schools find it difficult to engage children's interest in core subjects such as reading, science and maths, it is tempting to look for non-academic solutions and therapies.

Many educators find it more comfortable to hold forth about the importance of making children feel good about themselves than to teach them how to read and count. At the very least this therapeutic orientation serves to distract pupils and teachers from getting on with the job of gaining a real education.

Teachers, of course, have always hoped their work would inspire their students and make them feel good about learning and life. But until recently happiness was not seen as an end in itself or something that could be promoted on its own terms. Everyday experience suggests that not everything that has to be learned can be taught. How to feel well is not a suitable subject for classroom teaching. Why? Because genuine happiness is experienced through the interaction of the individual with the challenges thrown up by life.

Source: First published by *The Australian*, 7 August 2008. Full article available at: **http://www.frankfuredi.com/index.php/site/article/233/**

Gender

Socialisation: a term used by sociologists to define the process of learning to live within one's particular culture.

Gender identity (identifying oneself as male or female) carries with it varying expectations in terms of gender behaviours, which may affect both learning and behaviour in school. Most children establish gendered play preferences while in the infant school, which in turn is more likely to lead to play partners of the same sex. Thus although same-sex groupings in the 7–11+ age range are commonly identified as a developmental stage, as in Chapter 4, they are also the product of socialisation. Skelton and Hall (2001), who have conducted extensive research into gender and education, found that children entering schooling at age 4–5 held remarkably rigid views about sex roles in terms of toys, behaviour and likely future careers. Although these rigid views relax to some extent as children grow older, views about male occupations tend to remain more stereotypical.

RESEARCH BRIEFING: WHAT DOES IT MEAN TO BE
A BOY OR GIRL?

Researchers from the University of Roehampton were commissioned by the Equal Opportunities Commission to investigate the area of gender and achievement in schools. In their report they review a wide range of research literature on gender in education, and examine the statistics on achievement.

They found that 'learning' what it means to be a boy or girl varies according to situation, such as whether they are in primary or secondary school, and according to social class and ethnicity. However, the constant feature in all these contexts is that being a boy (or girl) means acting and behaving in ways that are the opposite to the ways that girls (or boys!) are seen as behaving.

Peer groups in schools also play an important part: 'the ethos and practices of individual schools, and the peer groups that exist in these, influence what kind of being "a boy" or "a girl" is seen as appropriate in that setting' (Skelton, Francis and Valkanova, 2007: vi). Since pupils usually sit in same-gender groups and friendship groups tend to be composed of pupils of the same gender, the influence of peers is central. The researchers found that: 'Both primary and secondary pupils respectively "police" the gendered behaviour of their peers, and punish failure to conform to traditional gender norms' (Skelton *et al.*, 2007: vi). The research report does not go into detail about how this takes place, but this is likely to involve exclusion from the group, or even bullying, in response to 'non-standard behaviour' according to the gender norms of the group. For example, in 'laddish' cultures this tends to involve 'having a laugh', not working hard, disrupting lessons and adopting views of women as objects.

Research evidence indicates that schooling, too, plays its part in contributing to gender behaviours and gendered self-concept in both male and female pupils. The school context can perpetuate gender stereotypes, and many research investigations have shown how constructions of masculinity and femininity are perpetuated: for example, mis-behaving girls are described as 'spiteful' or 'scheming little madams' while boys displaying similar behaviour are just 'mucking about' (Reay, 2001). Research also indicates that boys have more interactions with teachers than girls, in both primary and secondary classrooms (for example: Jones and Dindia, 2004). While these interactions are not necessarily all positive, the result is that boys occupy a disproportionate amount of teachers' attention. Teachers are also more likely to ask questions of boys and to give more feedback, as a means of ensuring attention and appropriate learning behaviour (Younger, Warrington and Williams, 1999), with the result that girls initiate fewer interactions as they move through secondary schooling.

CASE STUDY

'Benwood' Primary School

Christine Skelton (2001) is a well-known researcher in the area of gender and education. In her book *Schooling the Boys* (Skelton, 2001) she provides a vivid case study of 'Benwood' Primary School, situated in an economically deprived area, with a local tradition of tough masculinity or 'hard men'. The strategies used by the teachers to communicate with pupils, particularly male pupils, and to maintain discipline appeared to draw upon the same strategies employed by the pupils' parents, as they felt these were the only strategies which would be effective:

> although the intention was to distinguish between what the school expected and what was expected of children 'outside', the perpetuation of stereotypical images of 'good quiet girls' and 'tough naughty boys' could be seen in assemblies, wall displays, stories and the attitudes of some teachers.
>
> (Skelton, 2001: 94)

Examples of the ways in which these stereotypes were perpetuated included having male teachers called upon (by the female acting head teacher) to move equipment, lead singing or take other authority roles; through stories in assemblies which appeared to praise girls' desirable behaviours, while also apparently accepting the antisocial behaviour of boys; and through publicly expressed expectations about boys that effectively condoned their conduct.

(Skelton, 2001: 92)

While 'Benwood' Primary School may appear to be an extreme example of the ways in which schools construct and perpetuate gender stereotypes, the differences between boys' and girls' attitudes to education become more marked as they progress into secondary schools.

These differences have been particularly noticeable in secondary mathematics and science classes, where girls have tended to perform less well than boys in the past, although this gap is now narrowing. Some co-educational secondary schools have decided to operate single-sex teaching in these subjects in an attempt to address this difference. However, research indicates that single-sex teaching is insufficient in itself to have a significant effect on achievement, and other factors such as the subject knowledge of the teacher, pupils' attitudes towards the subject and the teacher's classroom management skills are more important. Single-sex teaching also works best where there has been careful preparation by the school, including consultation with pupils and staff, and care has been taken to try to avoid gender stereotypical attitudes or approaches. This might involve additional staff training and/or collaborative planning and discussion about teaching approaches (Warrington and Younger, 2003).

Gender and ability

There is no clear evidence as to whether differences in male and female brains have a direct effect on achievement, and it seems likely that social conditioning is a more powerful force than physiology. Recent neuroscientific research has identified some consistent differences in the sizes of certain areas of the brain in both men and women, and in brain activation measured through magnetic resonance imaging (Blakemore and Frith, 2005: 63). These differences may support other research findings which suggest that women outperform men on verbal tasks, while men tend to be better at spatial tasks. However, it is extremely important to emphasise that 'there are brain differences between genders, but even bigger differences between individuals' (Blakemore and Frith, 2005: 63).

Thirty years ago, boys were generally out-performing girls in mathematics at secondary school in most countries where data was available, but this gap has now halved. This would suggest that previously assumed gender differences in ability were largely socially induced. Nevertheless, high-achieving boys do still tend to perform better in mathematics than high-achieving girls, and possibly there may also be an element related to sex differences in the brain, although this is far from certain (Blakemore and Frith, 2005: 62). However, in terms of attitudes and motivation towards different school subjects, the evidence suggests that differences between male and female pupils are more strongly based in pupils' self-identity in relation to gender, rather than as a result of cognitive or neurological differences (Pajares and Valiente, 2001).

As you may already be aware, there is currently a high level of concern about boys' underachievement, especially in the area of literacy. One suggested explanation for this is that English may be perceived by boys as a 'feminine' curriculum area. This phenomenon is not confined to the UK, however, and the gap may be narrower than in a number of other countries. Differences in achievement between boys and girls also vary according to subject area, although overall girls out-perform boys in terms of A*–C GCSE grades. It would appear to be the case that girls are now more willing to engage with traditionally 'masculine' subjects such as science, mathematics, technology and ICT, whereas boys are still reluctant to involve themselves in subjects such as modern languages, humanities or RE. However, it is important not to generalise or to over-simplify the notion of boys' underachievement by applying it across all subjects, although competence in literacy can, of course, influence successful learning in many curriculum areas.

Controversies about boys' and girls' learning

WORKING IN THE CLASSROOM

Do boys and girls *learn* differently? Some popular practical classroom guides suggest that many boys tend to be kinaesthetic learners, who require shorter activity periods, more active learning and less open-ended tasks than many girls. Girls are characterised as being more able to sustain attention and more willing to engage with open-ended tasks, such as those associated with response to literature where there may not be a single 'right' answer.

What is your experience?

Kinaesthetic: applied to education, this term means being actively involved in learning through doing, rather than by listening or watching.

It has also been suggested that primary-aged girls are better at learning mathematics through co-operative activities rather than competitively. Would employing different teaching approaches for boys and girls reduce or reinforce gendered identities? Do such *generalisations* about gendered learning preferences run the risk of disadvantaging those boys who are not kinaesthetic learners, and those girls who do not prefer group work? Skelton *et al.* argue:

> One reason why schools that have adopted some of the strategies to raise boys' achievement have had such disappointing results is that they have encouraged teachers and pupils to view boys and girls as gender stereotypes. Other aspects of identity, such as ethnicity, also have a strong impact on pupils' curriculum preferences. Teaching practices based on assumptions of different preferences and abilities due to gender inevitably build on stereotypes and can exacerbate differences, channelling pupils down different routes of learning.
>
> *(Skelton et al., 2007: ix–x)*

So how can schools attempt to challenge gender stereotypes, without inadvertently reinforcing them? Skelton *et al.*'s report for the Equal Opportunities Commission (Skelton *et al.*, 2007) makes some suggestions which are broadly summarised below:

- To reduce gender stereotyping schools should consider paying *less* attention to issues of gender in terms of specific pedagogical strategies, rather than more. For example, some guidance suggests using different approaches for boys and girls in the same class (group work for girls; more tightly structured tasks for boys).

- Teachers need to reflect carefully on their own responses to male and female pupils in terms of expectations of behaviour and achievement, the relative amounts of attention or praise given to each group and differences in response – for example, being more 'robust' with boys and 'gentler' with girls. This is not easy – research in the 1980s suggests that even when teachers thought they were consciously controlling the amount of time they spent on boys as opposed to girls, boys still received more attention!

- Schools need to take a whole-school approach, especially in the secondary phase when gender identities are more entrenched and are also being reinforced by peers who are more influential than adults at this stage, as we have seen. As with many other aspects of successful school leadership and management, the commitment of the senior staff is crucial, as is the involvement of all school staff through consultation, discussion and agreed actions. These would include active responses to derogatory remarks or behaviour rooted in gender, and challenging stereotypical assumptions about future careers.

- Teachers should look for legitimate opportunities to discuss gendered attitudes and to encourage reflection on social assumptions by their pupils, in order to promote the idea that there are many constructions of masculine or feminine identity. These discussions need to take place within the local context of the school and community, and be based on some knowledge of pupils' experiences outside school. The appendices to the Equal Opportunities Commission report (Skelton *et al.*, 2007) provide some useful examples of questions and teaching approaches, although as the writers acknowledge, this is an under-resourced area in terms of helpful material for teachers.

For example, areas it could be useful to consider are those of popular media and sport. With primary pupils, discussion around favourite television programmes or films could stimulate reflection on how boys and girls are portrayed and how far this reflects the real world. What other ways of being a 'proper' boy or girl can they think of?

Secondary pupils might reflect on the ways in which the media and popular magazines portray males and females and consider how far these are stereotypes, or which sports are most often presented on television. Why are there not more televised sporting events involving women?

Pupils in both Key Stage 2 and Key Stage 3 could identify the kinds of work and other roles undertaken by members of their families, friends and by men and women in their local communities. Are there different ways of being male and female in the community? Are these the same elsewhere in the country or elsewhere in the world?

Sexual orientation

While many pupils within the 7–14 age group will not be sexually active, or consciously focused on their own sexual orientation, many assumptions about sexuality are established during this phase of pupils' schooling, including those about 'normal' heterosexual behaviours, such as expressing interest in members of the opposite sex. As we have seen, peer groups can 'police' members in respect of gendered appearance and behaviour:

CASE STUDY

'I don't like wearing dresses or having long hair and I am into sports and rather hang around with other girls than with boys. They started to call me a lesbian and are getting really nasty. I don't even know whether I am and we are not talking about these issues in PSHE at all so how am I supposed to know?'

'But I feel left out because I don't seem to be like others.' (Year 7 girl)

Source: CWDC Learning Mentor Training Module 2 (2005)

OVER TO YOU

In the case above, the pupil does not yet have a clear sense of her own sexual orientation (which may or may not be lesbian), and although she has a clear self-identity in terms of her own preferences for appearance and behaviour, the homophobic language used by her peers is highly likely to affect her sense of self-esteem.

How seriously should her school take this incident?

Ethnicity

The term 'ethnicity' refers to cultural identity, but is sometimes taken to apply to all those originating from a particular area of the world, For example, government statistics are gathered on pupils according to categories such as 'Black African' or 'Indian'. In order for the statistical information to be useful, it is necessary for information to be gathered on reasonably large numbers of pupils, and these categories do provide valuable information, as we shall see. However, they can also be misleading, and can contribute to stereotypical assumptions about pupils' background and heritage when applied to individual pupils.

Members of the same ethnic group will share all or some of the following features: language, food, music and other art forms, social customs and religion. However, the differences between those members of the population whose origin is in south India, as opposed to those from the north, and between those whose origin is from West Africa and those from Somalia or East Africa, may be greater than the similarities. It is therefore important for us to be aware of, and to try to learn more about, the distinctive home cultures of pupils from different ethnic groups.

Cultural diversity within the UK

The UK is becoming increasingly culturally diverse, with 21% of primary pupils and 17% of secondary pupils in England classified as belonging to an ethnic minority group (DfES, 2006). However, these pupils are not evenly distributed throughout the country, but are heavily concentrated in certain areas (see Table 5.2). It is also important to note that the numbers of pupils identified as belonging to specified

Table 5.2 Distribution of minority ethnic pupils across Government Office Regions as of January 2006 (provisional) (DfES, 2006)

	Primary (%)	Secondary (%)
North East	1.4	1.3
North West	9.1	7.9
Yorkshire and the Humber	7.9	7.6
East Midlands	5.9	6.4
West Midlands	12.9	13.2
East of England	7.2	7.9
Inner London	19.3	17.2
Outer London	23.2	25.1
South East	9.8	10.2
South West	3.3	3.2
TOTAL	**100.0**	**100.0**

groups vary by area and over time. Numbers of Black Caribbean and Irish pupils have decreased compared with 2004, while numbers for Asian and African pupils have increased (DfES, 2006).

As we have already seen, the statistical evidence based on pupils gaining five A*–C grades at GCSE indicates generally lower achievement amongst Black, Pakistani, Bangladeshi and Roma/Traveller pupils, with boys achieving lower than girls in all groups. Seventy per cent of Bangladeshi pupils and almost 60% of Pakistani and Black African pupils live in the 20% most deprived postcode areas (defined by the Index of Multiple Deprivation), as compared to less than 20% of White British pupils (DfES, 2006: 19).

While the most significant contributory factor to the underachievement of pupils from both White British and ethnic minority groups is SES, factors such as school culture and teacher expectation remain as important in respect of pupils from ethnic minority groups as they are in respect of gender. Gillborn and Gipps (1996) report that many parents of black pupils believe that schools are less tolerant of black pupils, and it would seem likely that where these views are held within the family, pupils' expectations of success in school are likely to be lowered. Other research into school exclusion (Wright, Weekes and McGlaughlin, 2000) suggests that some black pupils may be excluded on the basis of their response to racist behaviour. In other words, their reaction is seen as unacceptable – not the original racist action that precipitated it. Where such incidents occur, it is understandable that pupils might regard this as discriminatory behaviour on the part of the school, and be less willing to conform to its perceived values.

RESEARCH BRIEFING: TEACHERS' (MIS)PERCEPTIONS OF MIXED HERITAGE PUPILS

A study by Haynes, Tikly and Caballero (2006) used quantitative and qualitative data techniques in order to identify the barriers to achievement for minority ethnic pupils. The authors found no evidence to support claims that underachievement is a feature of all Mixed minority ethnic groups (e.g. White/Black Caribbean pupils may be underachieving, but White/Asian are doing well in relation to other groups). They discovered that White/Black Caribbean pupils experienced similar challenges to those of Black Caribbean pupils and that these were related to a combination of factors. Firstly, they were from a low socio-economic position. Secondly, their teachers had low expectations of them because they misunderstood Mixed White/Black Caribbean identities and backgrounds. For example, the majority of teachers in this study thought their pupils experienced 'identity problems' and were disadvantaged because they were from single-mother (White) homes where the (Black) father was absent or a poor role model. However, the teachers had no statistical evidence to support the view that households were constituted in this way. Interviews with pupils indicated that they had a positive sense of identity but were frustrated by how teachers saw them as having identity problems, and while some did come from single-parent homes, not all did.

Teacher attitudes do not have to be negative in order to affect self-identity, as we have seen in relation to gender: 'If you expect most Asian girls to be quiet and passive and good at written work, then that is not only what they do, but also perhaps all they do' (Noyes and Turner, 2005). Such attitudes, even though they appear to be positive on the surface, are effectively prejudiced in terms of their stereotypical assumptions, and limit teachers' expectations. If these kinds of expectations can have an adverse effect on pupils' self-identities as learners, 'colour blindness' is also counter-productive. Although an ethos which says that 'we don't see colour (or gender) here' may appear to be positive, the evidence is that this may actually disadvantage the pupils concerned. Between 2003 and 2005 the DfES funded an 'African Caribbean Achievement Project' involving 30 schools, with the aim of raising the attainment of African Caribbean pupils. Evaluation of the project showed that where schools had a 'colour blind' ethos, staff were less willing to focus on the specific needs of African Caribbean pupils, despite the fact that these pupils were achieving below expectations (DfES, 2006: 95).

In contrast with many White British pupils, religious belief and its effect on pupils' way of life is important to a substantial majority of pupils from minority ethnic backgrounds (see Figure 5.3). Forty-two per cent of White British pupils and 37% of those of mixed heritage say they have no religious affiliation and two-thirds of White British pupils said that religion was not important or not very important to their way of life, compared to only 13% of Black Caribbean pupils and 1% of Pakistani and Bangladeshi pupils (DfES, 2006: 23). See Figure 5.3.

Asian girls, particularly those from Muslim backgrounds, are typically perceived as passive and strongly influenced by family expectations. However, a recent report for the Equal Opportunities Commission suggests that their self-concept may be different from this typical perception. While the majority of Pakistani and Bangladeshi girls

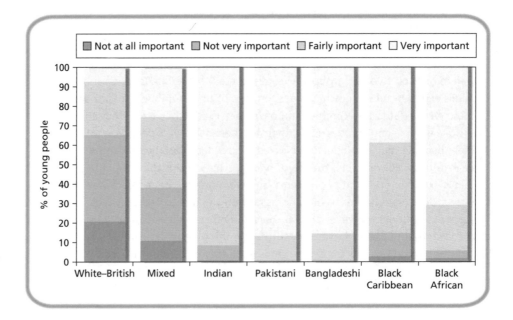

Figure 5.3
Importance of religion to a young person's way of life

Source: DfES (2006: 23)

said their parents had a big say in their future careers (64% and 55% respectively), only 43% of Pakistani girls and 35% of Bangladeshi girls said they were happy to follow their advice. Additionally, they were 10% more likely to describe themselves as confident than any other group of girls within the survey (White British, Black Caribbean or Indian) (Bhavnani, 2006).

RESEARCH BRIEFING: TEACHER ASSUMPTIONS AND HIDDEN CULTURAL CONFLICTS

A comparative study of Indian and English pupils aged between 7 and 9 years suggested that Indian pupils sometimes experienced more conflicts between the values of home and school than teachers realised. These could lead to forms of depression and lack of concentration in school, although they did not usually manifest themselves in forms of visibly disruptive behaviour. Apparently positive statements such as 'The Indian children are the best behaved in our class' suggested that teachers were unaware that some pupils found difficulty in managing the different expectations of home and school in terms of the behaviour expected of children in the two different contexts.

Interestingly, this study also found that Indian pupils whose home background retained a strong sense of cultural identity, including the use of the native language, appeared to experience greater well-being and to exhibit fewer examples of problem behaviour than Indian pupils from more Westernised home backgrounds. While it should be acknowledged that these pupils were living in predominantly Asian communities, there are implications for strengthening the place of home languages, and these pupils' sense of self-identity and self-esteem, within the school context (Naama, Pike and Barrett, 2004).

OVER TO YOU

What other stereotypical assumptions do you feel exist about pupils from different ethnic groups, such as Chinese, Indian, Afro-Caribbean or Black African pupils?

In what ways might these assumptions affect teachers' expectations and implicit behaviours?

What are the possible effects on pupils within these groups, and also on those from other ethnic groups, including White British, in respect of these assumptions?

Anti-racist teaching

Just as it is important for teachers to recognise legitimate opportunities to challenge stereotypical attitudes to issues of gender or ethnicity within their teaching, it is also very important that all teachers respond directly and immediately to any use of racist language or behaviour by pupils. In Chapter 3 we discussed the role of schools in promoting community cohesion, and there are several curriculum initiatives specifically aimed at improving inter-cultural respect and understanding and preparing pupils for life in a diverse society. The QCDA website area *Respect for All* (**www.qcda.org.uk**) provides links to a number of resources, and Chapter 18 also discusses the concept of global citizenship in more detail.

Racist behaviour can be a difficult area to confront, particularly where pupils have limited contact with members of other cultures, and suggestions as to how misperceptions about certain groups, such as refugees, can be challenged are provided in the resources linked to Chapter 18. While there are some forms of language and behaviour whose content is incontrovertibly racist, there may be temptations to find partial excuses for other less explicit behaviours, such as not involving pupils from minority ethnic groups in play activities. Where there are isolated pupils from specific minority ethnic backgrounds in schools they may be particularly vulnerable to forms of social exclusion by other pupils – regardless of whether these pupils are White British or from other minority ethnic groups. It is important for schools and teachers to maintain awareness of these possibilities and to identify ways to address these issues both within and outside the classroom.

QCDA provide a series of questions for teachers to ask themselves, to ensure they are prepared to address issues of racism and diversity in the classroom. Some of these also relate to other current initiatives such as elements of the Social and Emotional Aspects of Learning (SEAL) programmes in the National Strategies, and specific units within the Citizenship curriculum in secondary schools:

- How confident am I about introducing new topics or conveying key messages? Do I need to do more research or preparation?
- How comfortable am I discussing this topic? Should I talk through some of the issues with a colleague or friend so that I am better prepared?
- If some pupils express offensive or provocative views, am I confident that I know how to respond? Do I need to rehearse or role-play my responses?
- Will all pupils in the group feel comfortable with this topic? What steps can I take to ensure that the discussions and activities will feel safe for all concerned?
- Are some pupils likely to resist or strongly identify with particular messages? What reactions do I anticipate and how should I handle them?
- What preparatory work will I need to do with the class, for example agreeing the boundaries, learning aims, definitions or key terms?
- What ground rules could I suggest, for example about coping with angry feelings, respecting differences or learning from conflicting viewpoints?

Photo 5.2
Pupils from minority ethnic groups that are not otherwise established in the local community can be vulnerable to social exclusion, even in culturally diverse areas. What strategies might be used to help this pupil feel part of the school community?

Source: Pearson Education Ltd/ Ian Wedgewood

 **CASE STUDY**

Boys will be boys?

A student teacher of Chinese background struggled to develop a relationship with her primary class of Year 5 pupils. She observed one boy pulling his eyelids outwards to create 'slanty-eyes' on several occasions when he thought she was not looking, and sought support from a senior member of the school staff. She expressed the view that this was racially prejudiced behaviour, and asked for some action to be taken by the school. The response of the member of staff was that this was an over-reaction to normal childish misbehaviour, and that to draw attention to it would exacerbate the situation.

OVER TO YOU

Do you feel this was racist behaviour on the part of the pupil?

Do you agree with the response of the school?

What would you have done in the student teacher's situation?

SUMMARY

In the chapter we have suggested that an individual pupil's engagement with education will depend on their self-concept and levels of self-esteem. Although there are criticisms of some developments in education in relation to esteem building, there does appear to be considerable evidence to suggest that on *an individual level*, pupils' self-esteem is a significant factor in their educational achievement.

In addition to developmental areas discussed in the previous chapter, gender and ethnicity are individually significant factors that affect achievement and engagement with education in different ways for all pupils, but it is when these are combined with low SES that the impact on achievement is most marked. While individual schools and teachers cannot directly address issues such as unemployment or poor housing, they may be able to make some difference in relation to assumptions based on gender and ethnic background. Thus the extent to which these factors influence outcomes for pupils may partly depend on the attitudes and awareness of teachers, and the ethos of the schools they attend, as well as the broader issues of cultural background and social expectations.

TAKING YOUR PRACTICE FURTHER

This chapter has discussed a range of issues affecting the learning of individual pupils in terms of their self-identities as learners. It has focused particularly on gender and ethnicity as two of the major influences on pupil achievement within the 7–14 age group, after socio-economic status.

- Monitor your interactions with male and female pupils during one of your lessons and attempt to categorise these. You could do this by leaving a tape recorder running unobtrusively, or by asking your mentor or another teacher with whom you have a peer coaching relationship to observe and record each incident.

   What patterns emerge, and what do you think the impact on individual pupils' learning might be?

   What types of behaviour are being encouraged or repressed?

   Might you consider seeking to alter some aspects of your teaching as a result?

(Possibly this could be combined with an activity suggested at the end of Chapter 9, although you should try to separate out your use of the information to be considered for different reflective purposes).

- What opportunities can you find within your curriculum for involving your pupils in discussion of gendered attitudes?

- Are you aware of stereotypical assumptions of any kind about pupils from minority ethnic groups which might be affecting the learning of pupils in your class(es)? How might you alter your expectations of these pupils in order to challenge these stereotypes?

- In what ways could you incorporate positive references to other cultures into your everyday curriculum, as a matter of course rather than as a special event?

- If you have pupils in your class(es) whose home language is not English, what opportunities could be created for pupils to use their home language in school?

TAKING YOUR THINKING FURTHER

This chapter has considered three areas that research indicates have an effect on educational achievement in both Key Stage 2 and Key Stage 3: the importance of self-esteem, gender and ethnicity. It has also identified social-economic status as being more significant than either gender or ethnicity in relation to achievement, although these factors are interrelated.

Research by Gazeley and Dunne, available at **www.multiverse.ac.uk** Article id **11862**, indicated that teachers were uncomfortable talking about social class issues, but they they also held stereotypical views about working-class pupils and their parents which meant that they viewed the causes of underachievement as being rooted in the home rather than the classroom.

What parallels do you see between this research and evidence about teachers' assumptions around gender and ethnicity?

In what ways can such assumptions be addressed, and how might they be identified in schools?

Find out more

If you are interested in issues relating to gender and achievement, the following report offers an analysis of the data on gender and achievement, located within a comprehensive review of research literature:

Skelton, C., Francis, B. and Valkanova, Y. (2007) *Breaking Down the Stereotypes: Gender and Achievement in Schools*. **Manchester: Equal Opportunities Commission. Available at: www.eoc.org.uk/research.**
It also contains useful appendices of case studies and examples of teaching approaches designed to reduce gender stereotyping.

DfES (2007) *Gender and Education: The Evidence on Pupils in England*. **London: DfES. Available at www.dcsf.gov.uk.**
This report similarly examines data on the relative achievements of male and female pupils, and considers the interrelationship between gender, ethnicity, class and achievement. There are also sections on gender and cognition, and international comparative data.

The General Teaching Council for England (GTCE) website area, Research for Teachers November 2002, summarises research by NfER: 'How are some schools tackling the differences in achievement between girls and boys?'

Teachers' TV features a programme *The Trouble with Boys*, also focusing on successful strategies for improving boys' achievement.

The 'Gender Agenda' area of **www.teachernet.gov.uk** is supported by a series of regional seminars. Reports on these, with links to other materials, can be found at **www.ttrb.ac.uk.**

If you are interested in issues relating to pupils' sexual orientation or homophobia:

Jennett, M. (2004) *Stand Up for Us: Tackling Homophobic Bullying in Schools*. **Wetherby: Health Development Agency. Available at: www.wiredforhealth.gov.uk.**
This resource, produced for the National Healthy Schools Standard, examines the range of ways in which homophobia can manifest itself in both primary and secondary schools and provides strategies to challenge and prevent its occurrence.

There is also a range of material relating to bullying, including homophobic bullying, at **www.dfes.gov.uk/bullying**, including the DfES publication *Don't Suffer in Silence*.

If you are interested in issues relating to the achievement of minority ethnic pupils:

Gillborn, D. and Mirza, H. (2000) *Educational Inequality: Mapping Race, Class and Gender. A Synthesis of Research Evidence*. **London: Ofsted.**
This report drew together the three main variables associated with underachievement for the first time, and argued that 'when comparing like with like, in terms of gender, class and ethnic origin, consistent and significant ethnic inequalities of attainment remain clear' (Gillborn and Mirza, 2000: 77)

DfES (2006) *Ethnicity and Education: The Evidence on Minority Ethnic Pupils aged 5–16*. **London: DfES. Available at www.dcsf.gov.uk.**
This report provides comprehensive data on the achievements of minority ethnic pupils and their attitudes to schooling and subjects.

Two Ofsted reports identify good practice in raising the achievement of Black Caribbean pupils. Both are available from **www.ofsted.gov.uk/publications**.

Ofsted (2002) *Achievement of Black Caribbean Pupils: Three Successful Primary Schools*. **London: Ofsted.**
Ofsted (2002) *Achievement of Black Caribbean Pupils: Good Practice in Secondary Schools*. **London: Ofsted.**
The GTCE website area, Research for Teachers September 2001, summarises work by researchers at the Open University: 'What do we know about the characteristics of successful multi-ethnic schools?'

Teachernet.gov.uk provides extensive case study materials and other information relating to issues relating to gender and achievement of minority ethnic groups.

The Standards Site (**www.standards.dfes.gov.uk**) has a micro-site dedicated to ethnic minority achievement, which includes a number of case studies and links to further documents and reports.

The Runnymede Trust (**www.runnymedetrust.org**) is a charitable organisation established to promote racial equality in Britain. The organisation publishes a number of books and pamphlets available via their website.

Woolfolk, A., Hughes, M. and Walkup, V. (2008) *Psychology in Education*, **Harlow: Pearson.**
This textbook contains a helpful chapter on motivation, and various sections referring to gender, ethnicity, self-concept and self-esteem in terms of psychological approaches.

Glossary

Kinaesthetic: applied to education, this term means being actively involved in learning through doing, rather than by listening or watching.

Self-concept: the set of beliefs about oneself, including attributes, roles, goals, interests, values and religious or political beliefs.

Self-esteem: how one feels about one's self-concept.

Socialisation: a term used by sociologists to define the process of learning to live within one's particular culture. This process of inducting individuals into values and assumptions about social roles enables social and cultural continuity to be maintained, but can also result in the continuation of stereotypical views about gender, ethnicity etc.

References

Berndt, T.J. and Keefe, K. (1995) Friends' influences on adolescents' academic achievement motivation: an experimental study, *Journal of Educational Psychology*, Vol. 82: pp. 664–70.

Bhavnani, R. (2006) *Ahead of the Game: The Changing Aspirations of Young Ethnic Minority Women*. Moving on up? Series. Manchester: Equal Opportunities Commission.

Blakemore, S. and Frith, U. (2005) *The Learning Brain: Lessons for Education*. London: Blackwell.

DfES (2006) *Ethnicity and Education: The Evidence on Minority Ethnic Pupils aged 5–16*. London: DfES.

Ecclestone, K. (2004) Learning or therapy: The demoralization of education, *British Journal of Education Studies*, Vol. 52, No. 2: pp. 112–137.

Gillborn, D. and Gipps. C. (1996) *Recent Research on the Achievements of Ethnic Minority Pupils*. London: HMSO.

Haynes, J., Tikly, L. and Caballero, C. (2006) The barriers to achievement for White/Black Caribbean pupils in English Schools, *British Journal of Sociology of Education*, Vol. 27, No. 5: pp. 569–583.

Jones, S. and Dindia, K. (2004) A meta-analytic perspective on sex equity in the classroom, *Review of Educational Research*, Vol. 74, No. 4: pp. 443–471.

Maslow, A.H. (1970) *Motivation and Personality*, 2nd edn. New York: Harper & Row.

Naama, A., Pike, A. and Barrett, M. (2004) Internalising and externalising problems in middle childhood: A study of Indian and English children living in Britain, *International Journal of Behavioral Development*, Vol. 28, No. 5: pp. 449–460.

Noyes, A. and Turner, T. (2005) Responding to diversity, in Capel, S. Leask, M. and Turner, T. (eds) *Learning to Teach in the Secondary School*, 4th edn. London: Routledge.

Pajares, F. and Valiente, G. (2001) Gender differences in writing motivation and achievement in middle school students: a function of gender orientation?, *Contemporary Educational Psychology*, Vol. 26: pp. 366–381.

Reay, D. (2001) The paradox of contemporary femininities in education: combining fluidity with fixity, in B. Francis and C. Skelton (eds) *Investigating Gender*. Buckingham: Open University Press.

Skelton, C. (2001) *Schooling the Boys*. Buckingham: Open University Press

Skelton, C. and Hall, I. (2001) *The Development of Gender roles in Young Children: A Review of Policy and Literature*. Manchester: Equal Opportunities Commission.

Skelton, C., Francis, B. and Valkanova, Y. (2007) *Breaking Down the Stereotypes: Gender and Achievement in Schools*. Manchester: Equal Opportunities Commission. Available at: **www.eoc.org.uk/research**.

Warrington, M. and Younger, M. (2003) 'We decided to give it a twirl . . .': single sex teaching in English comprehensive schools, *Gender and Education*, Vol. 15, No. 4: pp. 339–350.

Woolfolk, A., Hughes, M. and Walkup, V. (2008) *Psychology in Education*. Harlow: Pearson.

Wright, C. Weekes, D. and McGlaughlin, A. (2000) *'Race', Class and Gender in Exclusion from School*. London: Falmer.

Younger, M., Warrington, M. and Williams, J. (1999) The gender gap and classroom interactions: reality or rhetoric?, *British Journal of Sociology of Education*, Vol. 20, No. 3: pp. 325–341.

PART 2 Teaching for Learning

As a trainee teacher, or a teacher in the early stages of your career, you will be establishing your own professional practice within the context of the classroom. This part considers five key aspects of teaching that are likely to be important to most beginning teachers: creating a positive learning environment, knowledge of pupils' learning styles, classroom behaviour, assessment for learning, and inclusion. Your own practice in each of these areas will be informed by your values and beliefs, and will also be influenced by the range of factors discussed in Part 1. Additionally, *how* you teach will be affected by your personal views about the knowledge that teachers need in order to teach effectively. As your views about knowledge will affect your practice in all the areas considered in this part, we begin with a chapter examining teachers' knowledge and how different views about teachers' knowledge affect learning in the classroom.

CHAPTER 6

Teachers' Knowledge and Learning

In this chapter you will:

- Examine some of your personal beliefs about knowledge
- Consider the types of knowledge teachers need in order to teach effectively
- Reflect on the types of knowledge you will need to develop professionally
- Begin to consider the kinds of knowledge teachers may need in the future

Pearson Education Ltd/Rob Judges

What kind of teaching would you expect to see in the classrooms of the teachers quoted in Figure 6.1?

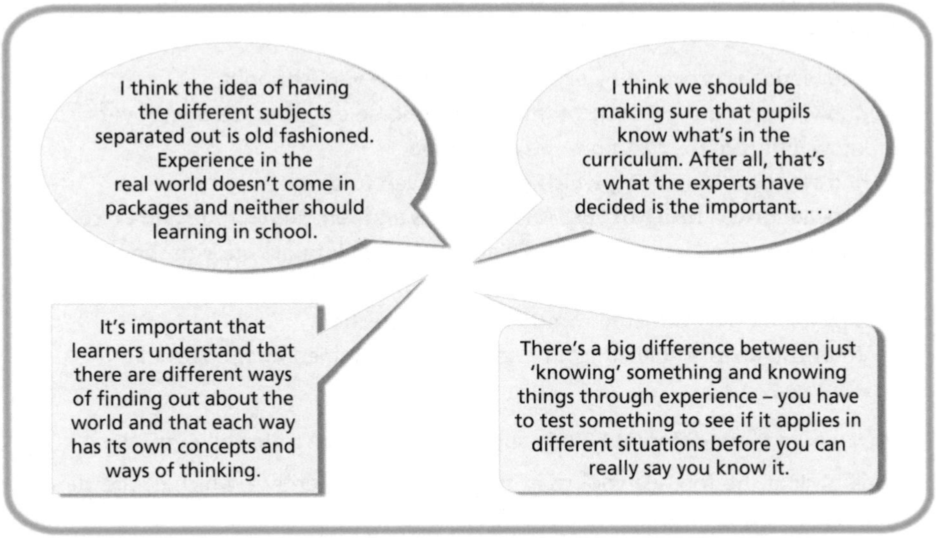

I think the idea of having the different subjects separated out is old fashioned. Experience in the real world doesn't come in packages and neither should learning in school.

I think we should be making sure that pupils know what's in the curriculum. After all, that's what the experts have decided is the important. . . .

It's important that learners understand that there are different ways of finding out about the world and that each way has its own concepts and ways of thinking.

There's a big difference between just 'knowing' something and knowing things through experience – you have to test something to see if it applies in different situations before you can really say you know it.

Figure 6.1
What kind of teaching . . . ?

Introduction

The importance of personal values and beliefs about education is an underpinning theme in this book, and was explored more fully in Chapter 2. However, it is worth reminding ourselves that all of us also hold beliefs and values associated with *knowledge* that will affect the ways in which we work in the classroom. We might not be as aware of our ideas about the nature of knowledge as we are about the views we hold of the purpose of education. However, the connections, and sometimes the contradictions, between the two are very important – at every one of the levels of influence on the classroom we considered in Part 1.

Although there are dictionary definitions of knowledge, these do not explore the difficult question about where knowledge originates. Although most of us do not tend to reflect on this question, our embedded assumptions about knowledge may in turn lead us to hold certain beliefs about teaching and learning and the purpose of education. Yet again, this is an area where our beliefs and values underpin all aspects of our classroom practice. If we do not bring these into the open in order to consider how they relate to new ideas and approaches, our effectiveness as teachers is likely to be far less.

Ideology: a set of values, ideas and beliefs about the way things should be organised within a particular society or culture.

Professional Standards for Teaching: the current government requirements that all teachers need to meet in order to be recognised as qualified teachers in England.

Qualified Teacher Status (QTS): a recognition that someone has met the first set of Professional Standards for Teaching in England and is able to start their Newly Qualified Teacher (NQT) year.

Core Standards (see Professional Standards below): the Core Standards apply to all teachers and must be met by Newly Qualified Teachers (NQTs) by the end of their first year in teaching.

THINKING IT THROUGH

What do you think are implications for teaching of these views about knowledge?

- Knowledge is provided by experts, for instance via textbooks.
- Knowledge is a fixed body of information, some of which we do not yet know, but is there waiting to be discovered.
- Knowledge is something which can be proved to be true.
- Knowledge is a result of cultural constructs and can vary in time and place.
- Knowledge is constructed by individuals through interaction with the environment.
- Knowledge is constructed through social interaction.
- What counts as 'knowledge' in a society is determined by the prevailing ideology.

How would these different beliefs about knowledge be reflected in teaching?

Look back at the four viewpoints at the start of this chapter – which of the views in this list do they most closely resemble?

Which views are closest to your own beliefs?

Knowledge for teaching

As the range of Professional Standards for teachers has developed (TDA, 2007) there is a danger that the identification of the areas of teachers' knowledge is increasingly being taken for granted. Many of the expectations in the **Professional Standards for Teachers: Qualified Teacher Status (QTS)** and the related **Core Standards** may seem intuitively obvious to new and intending teachers, but in fact these have gone through several versions over the past decade. Views of what teachers need to know in order to teach are not fixed, but are subject to revision and re-examination in the light of new learning and of changes in policy direction, although these two factors are not necessarily interdependent.

OVER TO YOU

Before continuing to read this chapter, make a list of the things *you* feel it is important for teachers to know, in order to teach effectively.

The question of what teachers need to know in order to teach effectively has been the focus of debate since the time of Plato in the fifth century BCE. In *The Republic* Plato discusses his ideal educational system, including the role of the teacher:

- The teacher should know his* subject, but also recognise the limits of his knowledge (*teachers in Ancient Greece were, of course, male).
- The teacher's role is to guide his students in the path of virtue, and to educate them through the use of dialogue.
- Through this process, the learner is supported to develop 'his' understanding through interaction with the more knowledgeable teacher, who also acknowledges that he has more to learn.

In this way, Plato suggests, knowledge is jointly constructed: 'knowledge will not come from teaching, but from questioning'. Put another way, Plato argues that teachers need subject knowledge, professional values and knowledge of how to support learners, nowadays often known as pedagogical knowledge. Today, these are still the key areas of the teaching Standards.

Each of these categories requires a considerable amount of further examination, however, and all the chapters in this book could be seen as an extended discussion of these topics. This chapter focuses particularly on the general area of teachers' knowledge, what this involves, and how it continues to develop during your teaching career.

'Subject' knowledge

Plato argues that the teacher needs to know his subject, and this view remains fundamental to philosophies of education in most parts of the world. Formal teacher education programmes generally involve, or require as a prerequisite for entry, the study of a subject or subjects to a much higher level than that expected of school-aged pupils themselves.

However, the relationship between teachers' personal knowledge and their ability to support the learning of others is not straightforward. If teachers 'know' aspects of a subject at their own level, will they automatically be able to enable children to develop knowledge and understanding in the subject field? For quite a large part of the twentieth century there was an assumption than this would be the case, and until the early 1970s there was no requirement for specific teacher training if secondary teachers already had a degree. Even after this date, much of the subject content element and the pedagogical element of teacher training were separate, even for primary teachers.

From the mid-1980s, educationalists began to look more closely at the interface between personal subject knowledge (or 'content knowledge') and pedagogy. Knowing how to transform personal content knowledge to make it accessible to learners became identified as a specific form of teacher's knowledge, and was referred to as 'subject application' in UK government documents (DES, 1989).

RESEARCH BRIEFING: THEORIES ABOUT TEACHERS' KNOWLEDGE: SHULMAN'S IDEAS

Lee S. Shulman gave a famous talk to the American Educational Research Association in which he argued that there was a 'missing paradigm' in previous discussions about subject knowledge, or 'content knowledge', and teaching. He pointed out that discussions about teaching had focused on general issues, rather than the more specific issues associated with teaching individual subjects.

Shulman (1995) proposed the existence of a category of teacher knowledge called 'pedagogical content knowledge' which involved a knowledge of ways of representing the subject, by analogy or example, to make it accessible to learners. It also included an understanding of the preconceptions and misconceptions learners might hold about aspects of the subject. Shulman also proposed a third knowledge category necessary for teachers – that of 'curricular knowledge', embodying relevant curriculum materials, resources and schemes or programmes appropriate for different subjects and different levels.

In Shulman's model teachers need three different forms of knowledge in order to teach:

content knowledge;
curriculum knowledge;
pedagogical content knowledge.

OVER TO YOU

Are Shulman's ideas represented in today's professional Standards and in current initial teacher education programmes?

Do they apply across the whole 7–14 age range?

Teachers' knowledge and educational policy

It has already been pointed out, in the introduction to this chapter, that views about what teachers need to know are not fixed, and are dependent on both new knowledge and new policies. In the UK in the 1980s the then Conservative government became concerned about the study of 'education' as part of teacher training courses. It was felt that teaching approaches which encouraged an **enquiry-based approach** to learning, or which adopted a **cross-curricular** or **topic-based** approach, were contributing to poor standards of learning and behaviour in pupils, and that a return to more strongly teacher-led and subject-focused approaches would raise standards. The introduction

Enquiry-based approach: an approach to teaching which involves pupils in working together to solve problems rather than working under the teacher's direction. The teacher's role becomes that of a facilitator, rather than an instructor.

Cross-curricular: approaches to teaching which seek to make links between different curriculum subjects.

Topic-based approach: a form of curriculum design where different subjects are linked by an overarching theme. Care is needed to avoid superficial connections being made between subjects.

of the National Curriculum in 1988, as part of the Education Reform Act (ERA), was intended to encourage a stronger emphasis on subject teaching in primary as well as secondary schools.

The ERA also established the school inspection body Ofsted, and the findings from early inspections of primary schools seemed to support the government's view. At that stage, many primary teachers appeared to lack the subject knowledge required to teach all subjects in the new National Curriculum (Ofsted, 1994), although it must be remembered that it had only recently been introduced. Further strength was given to the subject-led primary curriculum, and to the need for strengthening primary teachers' subject knowledge, by the publication of *Curriculum Organisation in Primary Schools* (Alexander, Rose and Woodhead, 1992). This report was commissioned by the government to examine how the curriculum was being managed, and how well different forms of organisation supported pupils' learning. The report argued in favour of subject-based teaching, rather than the cross-curricular approaches that had been popular in many primary schools.

As a result, government requirements for the content of teacher training were established in a series of circulars (DFE, 1992, 1993; DfEE, 1998), with a strong element of subject studies required for both primary and secondary student teachers. Although there have been substantial revisions to the National Curriculum, including the incorporation of the Primary and Key Stage 3 National Strategies, a strongly subject-based approach to teaching has dominated schools and initial teacher education for both primary and secondary phases, until very recently. However, both primary schools and secondary schools at Key Stage 3 are currently reviewing the ways in which they organise teaching of the curriculum, alongside new developments to the National Curriculum in Key Stages 1, 2 and 3. Local interpretations of these developments, either at local authority level or at school level, may vary considerably in different parts of the country.

WORKING IN THE CLASSROOM

How are schools with which you are familiar interpreting changes to the National Curriculum?

What are the implications of changes to the National Curriculum in terms of curriculum organisation? For example, are all subjects being taught discretely, or are there times when subjects are brought together?

OVER TO YOU

How far do you think that changes to the curriculum reflect a changing view of knowledge, for both pupils and teachers?

Some challenges to subject-based ideas of teachers' knowledge

There have been several challenges to the idea that content knowledge, or knowledge of the subject, is the core component of teachers' knowledge, on which other forms of knowledge depend. Some of these refer back to the work of Shulman who is accused of seeing subject knowledge as something objective, or external to the teacher. Critics argue that Shulman underestimated the importance of teachers' beliefs and values in relation to particular subjects, and that these have a strong influence on practice.

Photo 6.1
While it is important to know your subject, the values and beliefs you hold about it are just as significant for teaching

Source: Report Digital

For example, a teacher of art or music who believed that the purpose of their teaching was mainly to produce professional artists or musicians would have a very different approach to teaching compared to someone who wanted pupils to enjoy participating in artistic activity for its own sake.

CASE STUDY

Terry's ideas about teaching

Terry has two mathematics A levels and a good degree in maths. He is very enthusiastic about his subject and confident about his own knowledge because of his educational background. He has had previous experience working with young people and is looking forward to teaching in school.

Terry seems to see maths as a fixed 'body of knowledge': as a series of proofs and statements about how mathematics 'works'. He believes that mathematical knowledge is hierarchically constructed, so that each concept builds neatly on others. Several implications for his teaching arise from his beliefs about the nature of the subject, and about his own mathematical knowledge:

- Because he believes that his own mathematical knowledge is very good, the idea of modelling learning in an investigative way does not occur to him. He is unlikely to say to a class 'Let's find this out together', as this would position him in the role of a learner himself.
- Because he believes that maths knowledge is constructed in a particular way, he doesn't recognise that there are alternative ways to make connections between mathematical concepts. For Terry there may only be one 'right way' to do maths.
- Because he believes that maths knowledge is already 'out there', that people already know all there is to be known, he is less likely to value forms of learning that involve pupils discovering ideas and principles through investigation and problem solving. Terry will use problems in his teaching, but they are less likely to be open-ended and he is less likely to be involved in the problem-solving process as a partner with his pupils.

Source: This case study is based on a research article by Anne Meredith, focusing on an in-depth interview with a secondary PGCE student of mathematics: Meredith (1995)

Other critics feel that Shulman does not give sufficient weight to the ways in which knowledge is adjusted and constructed in different contexts, particularly in schools (Banks, Leach and Moon, 1996). For example, if we start with the idea of subject knowledge as being that which is studied in a university, this can be very different indeed from the form the subject takes within the school curriculum. In secondary schools, the choice of Examination Board for GCSE can make a significant difference to both what is taught in a subject and how it is taught. These differences may filter down in Key Stage 3 as the subject department may have developed a particular teaching approach to match the syllabus. In both primary and secondary schools, the choices teachers make about commercially produced textbooks and resources to support learning will also make a big difference to how the subject is presented, and thus to how knowledge in that area is conceived.

THINKING IT THROUGH

Based on your observations or experience in school, or on taught sessions during your training, how far do textbooks or commercially produced resources present a particular view of knowledge to pupils?

If possible, select a textbook or other commercially produced resource and try to identify the view of knowledge implied in the ways it produces information.

Are you comfortable with this view? Are there aspects of the subject you feel have been missed out?

What view of knowledge do you think is presented in *this* book?

The assumptions behind reforms of primary teacher training in the 1990s were that primary teachers would not teach effectively unless they had good subject content knowledge. However, some later research findings have suggested that this assumption may not be entirely well founded. Studies of effective teachers* of primary literacy and numeracy found that there was no direct relationship between teachers' own subject knowledge and the results their pupils gained in standardised tests (Askew *et al.*, 1997; Medwell *et al.*, 1998). Indeed, some apparently effective teachers either did not always appear to have strong subject knowledge at their own level, or were unable to make it explicit out of context (Poulson, 2001: 44–45). The researchers into effective numeracy teaching also found that 'there was little to distinguish highly effective teachers from the effective and moderately effective teachers in the sample in terms of formal knowledge of mathematical concepts' (Askew *et al.*, 1997).

'Effective teachers' in these studies knew strategies to make the subject accessible to their pupils, they had a good knowledge of pupils as individuals and they had an enthusiasm for their subject. They also understood how different aspects of literacy and numeracy fitted together and were able to make connections between these different areas, rather than teach them in isolation. In the research into effective mathematics teaching, the role of Continuing Professional Development (CPD) was also seen to be important. Teachers were more effective if they had attended extended CPD courses which focused specifically on teaching approaches in mathematics. We will return to the importance of CPD later in this chapter.

For primary teachers, at least, an alternative argument to the importance of subject content knowledge would place teachers' knowledge of *how* children learn before the *what*.

OVER TO YOU

Do you think there is a difference between the *kinds* of knowledge (not the amount!) needed to teach pupils in Key Stage 2 compared to Key Stage 3, or are they much the same?

Pedagogical content knowledge

It would appear that teachers' knowledge of teaching approaches, and their beliefs about how children learn in a subject, may be as important as their personal subject content knowledge, if not more so. However, it doesn't appear to be possible to develop effective pedagogical knowledge for a subject without some underpinning content knowledge, at the teacher's own level. Personal subject knowledge and pedagogical content knowledge are so intertwined that many educationalists have now given up trying to see them as separate.

---

* The definition of an 'effective teacher' in these research studies was that of a teacher whose pupils made measurably significant gains in achievement on the basis of test results. This would not be the only definition of teacher effectiveness in other contexts!

Unlike subject content knowledge, pedagogical content knowledge (sometimes known as PCK) needs an element of experience within the school and classroom context to develop fully, and cannot be taught in isolation from the teaching context. It has been suggested that teachers' pedagogical content knowledge develops over a period of several years and is composed of a range of different aspects.

RESEARCH BRIEFING: THEORIES ABOUT TEACHERS' KNOWLEDGE: MOVING BEYOND SHULMAN'S IDEAS

There have been a number of writers who have built on Shulman's initial ideas, one of whom is Rosie Turner-Bissett (2001). Turner-Bissett studied primary teachers who were seen as 'expert teachers' by their schools. She suggests that an amalgam of 11 types of knowledge can be identified as the constituents of the knowledge demonstrated by 'expert' teachers. These include:

- aspects of personal subject content knowledge, including the teacher's beliefs about a particular subject;
- knowledge of curriculum content and appropriate materials and strategies to support learning;
- general pedagogical knowledge, for example how to settle a class and maintain a learning atmosphere;
- the teacher's beliefs about teaching and learning, such as beliefs about how children learn;
- knowledge about learners, including knowledge of 'typical' 7 or 14 year olds and theories about how pupils learn and different stages of development;
- knowledge about the actual learners in the teacher's own classroom(s);
- knowledge about different educational contexts, in relation to catchment area, size of school etc;
- knowledge of their own educational aims or values: what the teacher believes the purpose of education to be;
- knowledge of oneself as a teacher, gained through deliberate reflection on practice.

OVER TO YOU

In training

Return to the list of things you felt it was important for teachers to know, which you wrote at the beginning of this chapter. How many of these can be related to the areas above?

Do you agree that all these areas are necessary for teachers to be able to teach effectively?

Starting your career

Although you will not have reached the 'expert' stage yet, and there will definitely be more you can learn, were there some of these kinds of knowledge that you feel you were able to bring to the beginning of your teaching career?

How do some of these kinds of knowledge match with the expectations in the Standards for QTS and Core Standards?

Investigating learning and teaching

The theme of teachers' beliefs about knowledge for teaching has been a recurring idea in this chapter.

The research of Askew *et al.* (1997) in primary mathematics and Medwell *et al.* (1998) in primary literacy provides further information about the ways in which teachers' beliefs about the nature of these subjects influenced the ways that they taught their pupils.

These research papers may also be of interest if you are mainly concerned with teaching at Key Stage 3, but if you have a particular subject area interest you will also find articles which look at the impact of teachers' beliefs on different subject areas by using search engines such as Google Scholar, or the Teacher training Resource Bank.

For example:

Article ID 13304 on ttrb.ac.uk is a review of research into views about knowledge for secondary PE teaching.
A chapter by Peter John in Glaxton *et al.* (1996) discusses the beliefs of 42 student teachers specialising in secondary history.

The changing nature of teachers' knowledge

So far this chapter has considered the kinds of knowledge that an individual teacher needs in order to teach effectively. It has been argued that knowledge for teaching is not static, but changes as a result of new policies and new knowledge about learning. There is, therefore, another kind of knowledge which impacts on our practice in schools and which forms a significant component of the knowledge base teachers are expected to have at the start of their professional lives: knowledge of current curriculum requirements, education policy initiatives and the role of educational research. The next four chapters in this book consider some areas of teachers' knowledge where there have been significant shifts in recent years, as a result of technological developments, educational research and new policy initiatives.

The ways in which changes to the body of teachers' knowledge develop are extremely complex, and there is much discussion about how far evidence from educational research impacts on government policy initiatives, or on practice in schools (Hargreaves, 1999; Cordingley, 1999), which we have already considered in Chapter 1. One significant area of current practice that has undoubtedly been influenced by research findings is that of assessment for learning (see Chapter 10), but there are many other examples in different areas. As we have seen, educational policy is also influenced by a number of other factors, international competitiveness being one. Major initiatives such as the Literacy and Numeracy Strategies (now part of the National Primary and Secondary Strategies) drew on evidence from outside the UK, and on international comparisons of pupil achievement. Although the accuracy of these comparisons has been contested, this does not mean that there are no useful lessons to be learned from other education systems, both now and in the future.

CONTROVERSY

Do teachers really change what they do as a result of new policies?

Although politicians would like teachers to adopt new policy initiatives on the basis of claims that pupil achievement will improve as a result, it appears to be the case that real change in teaching behaviour occurs only when a teacher's personal beliefs and values about teaching and learning are engaged.

Where this does not occur, teachers and schools may adopt the surface features of the new forms of practice, but not fundamentally change their ideas or underlying approaches (Alexander *et al.*, 1992). Alternatively, they may find ways of teaching in the ways they believe are best for their pupils by adapting aspects of the new policies through what has been called 'creative mediation' (Osborn *et al.*, 2000).

As a result of these different responses, even widespread, highly structured national initiatives such as the initial introduction of the Primary Literacy Strategy quickly emerged as having different interpretations in different schools.

THINKING IT THROUGH

On the basis of your observation and experience in schools, do some teachers pay only 'lip service' to new initiatives?

Should teachers resist or reshape national initiatives on the basis of their personal beliefs about teaching and learning?

THINKING IT THROUGH: *CONTINUED*

Think back to your responses to the questions about changes to the curriculum. Are you aware of any recent changes to curriculum, or policy initiatives, that have been welcomed by teachers? For example, many primary teachers have been enthusiastic about more 'creative' approaches to curriculum organisation.

Why have these teachers welcomed these changes?

Photo 6.2 Many primary teachers have welcomed increased opportunities to involve children in practical and creative approaches to learning.

Source: Pearson Education Ltd/Ann Cromack, Ikat Design

Teachers' learning

The changing nature of teachers' knowledge means that learning will continue to be part of your future professional life, and there is an expectation in all the Standards for teachers that you will regularly participate in CPD activities.

There is now a considerable amount of evidence about the kinds of CPD activity which work best for teachers and which have the greatest effect in terms of bringing about changes in classroom practice (see Table 6.1). As you identify areas for your own development it could be useful to bear these in mind.

Table 6.1 Effective components of CPD

- Wanting to make a difference to pupils' learning
- A focus on issues relevant to your own classroom practice
- A recognition of your existing knowledge and skills
- Opportunities for you to reflect on how new ideas relate to your existing beliefs about learning
- Opportunities for you to develop your own interpretation of the new ideas so that you become confident in their implementation
- Opportunities to work collaboratively with others, including through observation and discussion
- Using evidence from research into best practice to inform new approaches
- CPD activity sustained over a period of time in order for ideas to be implemented and evaluated
- Coaching or other kinds of feedback on your progress to help you sustain motivation
- Having support from senior staff within the school

Source: **www.teachernet.gov.uk**

OVER TO YOU

Compare the above components of effective CPD with the research findings about teachers' responses to educational change. What do you notice?

Look back to the different views about knowledge suggested at the start of this chapter. Are there any views expressed there which could make accepting change more difficult?

DCSF (Department for Children, Schools and Families): government department created in 2007, responsible for all matters affecting children and young people up to the age of 19, including child protection and education.

Many schools, particularly secondary schools, offer CPD programmes which include most or all of the above components, and which offer opportunities for peer mentoring and coaching to teachers beyond the induction year. Both the **DCSF** and the **General Teaching Council for England (GTCE)** provide access to digests of educational research they believe will be of interest to teachers, many of which include links to case studies of practice in schools, which could help to keep you up to date and inform your practice. Part 3 of this book examines the ways in which reflection, investigation and collaboration can enhance learning in more detail.

General Teaching Council for England (GTCE): the professional body for teaching in England.

Pupils' views of knowledge

In the first section of this book we emphasised the importance of recognising the factors that affect pupils and their abilities to engage with learning. Pupils' own views of what knowledge (and therefore learning) is, and their beliefs about its value, are also important factors in terms of their engagement with learning. By the time some pupils enter Key Stage 2, and certainly by the time they arrive in Key Stage 3, they will have preferences in terms of subject area, based on how easy or difficult they have found the work, and its intrinsic interest to them – perhaps based on out-of-school influences.

Pupils in the 7–14 age group are operating predominantly in the 'concrete' rather than the 'abstract' mode (see Chapter 4). Their concepts of knowledge and learning may be directly connected to subject content expressed as 'facts', rather than to conceptions of skills or knowing 'how to . . .'. Unless these forms of knowledge are clarified appropriately for pupils, misunderstandings about the nature and purpose of learning can arise, which may not initially be evident to the teacher concerned. Chapter 15 provides one such example: in one secondary school Year 8 pupils were asked to record their learning in a learning log. It quickly became evident that many pupils only recognised the 'facts' as learning, and ignored the other features of the lessons (e.g. learning to work co-operatively; learning to review and edit work).

Pupils may also hold implicit views about the nature of knowledge in terms of its provisionality. That is, how far knowledge is dependent on context, both in terms of the subject and also in terms of how knowledge in a particular area is being created. In simpler terms, this is the difference between believing that all answers are either right or wrong and recognising that in some contexts more than one response can be appropriate. While these are complex concepts for many pupils in the 7–14 age range to grasp, the foundations of this understanding need to be laid during this phase of development, in order to support pupils' learning in Key Stage 4 and beyond. Pupils whose view of knowledge remains at the level of right/wrong, true/not true are likely to find some subject areas difficult to understand as they progress further. Similarly, someone who believes that knowledge is a stable body of information that can be transmitted from teacher to learner may not appreciate the value of investigation, or the possibility that new knowledge can be created. 'Terry', whose case study we considered earlier in the chapter, may well be someone who still holds views of knowledge similar to these. Although he had been successful in his academic life, it appeared that he was less likely to be successful as a teacher.

WORKING IN THE CLASSROOM

How do we encourage pupils to develop an appreciation of these differences in the nature of knowledge?

What strategies have you observed, or used yourself, in schools that you recognise as helping (or perhaps accidentally hindering) this understanding?

Knowledge for the future

What kinds of knowledge will teachers need in the future? It seems certain that we will need to demonstrate qualities such as flexibility and adaptability and to be committed to continual learning and open to the possibility of change. The views that we hold about the nature of knowledge may help or hinder this process. The final part of this book considers some areas where significant change to teachers' working lives seems highly likely in terms of different working practices and the continued impact of new technologies.

Discoveries in brain-based science, or neuroscience, are informing our understanding about how information is processed by the brain, and influencing theories about classroom practice, as we have seen in Chapter 4. It seems likely that this area of scientific investigation will have more to offer education in the future. As we have already seen, and will explore in more detail later in this book, views of the curriculum and of the kinds of knowledge our pupils will need are also changing.

2020 Vision: The Report of the Teaching and Learning Review Group (DfES, 2006) identifies the following skills that adults will need in the year 2020, and recommends the necessary steps that will be needed to enable pupils currently in full-time education to develop these skills:

- being able to communicate orally at a high level;
- reliability, punctuality and perseverance;
- knowing how to work with others in a team;
- knowing how to evaluate information critically;
- taking responsibility for, and being able to manage, one's own learning and developing the habits of effective learning;
- knowing how to work independently without close supervision;
- being confident and able to investigate problems and find solutions;
- being resilient in the face of difficulties;
- being creative, inventive, enterprising and entrepreneurial.

The items in this list are skills and, rightly, there is no attempt to define the kinds of knowledge these skills will address. However, in many ways this vision of the purpose of education implies a shift in teacher–pupil relationships and a consequent shift in terms of the kinds of knowledge that will be important for teaching.

OVER TO YOU

How do you feel this vision of learning relates to the list of knowledge for teaching you developed earlier in the chapter?

How important do you believe subject content knowledge will be in the future?

SUMMARY

This chapter has considered ideas abut the knowledge that teachers need to be able to teach effectively, and has argued that our beliefs, and the beliefs of others, about the nature of knowledge have a direct effect on our work in the classroom.

SUMMARY *CONTINUED*

If we consider again the range of influences on the classroom discussed in Part 1:

Our beliefs about knowledge affect the ways we teach . . .
Our *pupils' beliefs* about school knowledge, and how it is presented to them, affects the way they learn . . .

Views about *knowledge in the curriculum*, developed by *schools, Local Authorities* and *national policies*, also impact directly on the classroom. They largely determine *what* we teach, although not always *how* . . .
National policy about curriculum and the beliefs about the knowledge pupils will need as future citizens is influenced by a range of factors:

public concerns about reading, for example, or about diversity in society;
international comparisons of pupil achievement;
globalisation and the need to develop a suitably productive workforce, able to respond to rapid changes . . .

it is clear that our professional practice needs to examine seriously the importance of knowledge for teaching, and the different forms of knowledge that teachers need now and in the future.

TAKING YOUR PRACTICE FURTHER

Select a lesson you have taught yourself, or one you have observed. Can you identify *specific* instances of where the different kinds of teacher knowledge were applied in the lesson? How far do these help you identify your beliefs, or the teacher's beliefs, about knowledge?

Are there areas of your own knowledge which you feel need to be extended or reconsidered?

TAKING YOUR THINKING FURTHER

This chapter has sought to set the stage for the remainder of this part, which examines some areas of learning and teaching in more detail. When you have finished this part of the book, review your ideas about teachers' knowledge again.

Have any of your beliefs about teaching and learning altered as a result of reflecting on your own classroom practice in the light of your reading?

Has this altered your views about aspects of teachers' knowledge, and what it is important for teachers to know?

Find out more

If you want to find out more about how the National Curriculum was developed, and the beliefs about knowledge that were held at the time it was introduced:

Ashcroft, K. and Palaccio, D. (1995) *The Primary Teacher's Guide to the New National Curriculum.* **London: Falmer.**
The National Curriculum referred to here as 'new' has long since been superseded, but this text provides a framework with which to examine later versions of the curriculum, and to interrogate the reasons why different subject areas rise (or fall) in importance.

If you want to think more about the place and value of your own subject area in the curriculum:

White, J. (ed.) (2004) *Re-thinking the School Curriculum: Values, Aims and Purposes.* **London: Routledge.**

This edited text was also identified at the end of Chapter 1. It considers how far different subjects are presently meeting the statement on Values and Purposes in the National Curriculum and what changes to the curriculum in each area needs to be made.

If you want to find out more about conceptions of teacher's professional knowledge:

Turner-Bisset, R. (2001) *Expert Teaching: Knowledge and Pedagogy to Lead the Profession.* **London: Fulton.**
This book develops the model of teacher knowledge, referred to earlier in this chapter, and provides examples of different kinds of knowledge through a number of case studies of classroom practice of both student teachers and more experienced teachers.

Glossary

Core Standards (see Professional Standards below): the Core Standards apply to all teachers and must be met by Newly Qualified Teachers (NQTs) by the end of their first year in teaching.

Cross-curricular: approaches to teaching which seek to make links between different curriculum subjects. The National Curriculum currently has a set of stated cross-curriculum dimensions for Key Stage 3 (qca.org.uk). This term is more commonly used in the first sense.

DCSF (Department for Children Schools and Families): government department created in 2007, responsible for all matters affecting children and young people up to the age of 19, including child protection and education. Changes to government policy over the years have meant that there have been several renamed departments concerned with education. DCSF replaced the Department for Education and Skills (DfES), which existed between 2001 and 2007. Prior to 2001 education was part of the remit of the Department of Education and Employment (DfEE), which was in turn created in 1995.

Enquiry-based approach: an approach to teaching which involves pupils in working together to solve problems rather than working under the teacher's direction. The teacher's role becomes that of a facilitator, rather than an instructor.

General Teaching Council for England (GTCE):
The General Teaching Council for England is the professional body for teaching in England. All trainee teachers are provisionally registered with the GTCE, and full registration is confirmed at the end of the induction year. The GTCE also provides a range of other services and resources for teachers, employers and parents. 'Our overall purpose is to work in the public interest to help improve standards of teaching and learning.'

Ideology: a set of values, ideas and beliefs about the way things should be organised within a particular society or culture.

Professional Standards for Teaching: the current government requirements that all teachers need to meet in order to be recognised as qualified teachers in England. They are organised in a progressive framework starting with those for **Qualified Teacher Status (QTS)** and moving on to the **Core Standards** by the end of the first year of teaching.

Qualified Teacher Status (QTS): a recognition that someone has met the first set of Professional Standards for Teaching in England and is able to start their Newly Qualified Teacher (NQT) year.

Topic-based approach: a form of curriculum design where different subjects are linked by an overarching theme. Care is needed to avoid superficial connections being made between subjects.

References

Alexander, R., Rose, J. and Woodhead, C. (1992) *Curriculum Organisation and Classroom Practice in Primary Schools*. London: HMSO.

Askew, M., Brown, M., Rhodes, V., Johnson D. and Wiliam D. (1997) *Effective Teachers of Numeracy*. London: Kings College London.

Banks, F., Leach, J. and Moon, B. (1996) *Knowledge, School Knowledge and Pedagogy: Reconceptualising Curricula and Defining a Research Agenda*. Paper presented at the European conference of Educational Research, Seville, Spain.

Cordingley, P. (1999) Constructing and critiquing reflective practice, *Educational Action Research*, Vol. 7, No. 2: pp. 183–191.

Department of Education and Science (1989) *Circular 28/89 Initial Training of Teachers*. London: DES.

Department for Education (1992) *Circular 9/92 Teacher Training (Secondary Phase)*. London: DfE.

Department for Education (1993) *Circular 14/93 Teacher Training (Primary Phase)*. London: DfE.

Department for Education and Employment (1998) *Circular 4/98 Teaching: High Status: High Standards*. London: Teacher Training Agency.

Department for Education and Skills (2006) *2020 Vision: The Report of the Teaching and Learning Review Group*. Available at: **www.teachernet.gov.uk/publications**.

Hargreaves, D. (1999) Revitalising educational research: lessons from the past and proposals for the future, *Cambridge Journal of Education*, Vol. 29, No. 2: pp. 239–249.

John, P.D. (1996) Understanding the apprenticeship of observation in initial teacher education. Exploring student teachers' implicit theories of teaching and learning, in Glaxton, G., Atkinson, T., Osborn, M. and Wallace, M. (eds) *Liberating the Learner. Lessons for Professional Development in Education*. London: Routledge: pp. 90–107.

Medwell, J., Wray, D., Poulson, L. and Fox, R. (1998). *Effective Teachers of Literacy: A Report of a Research Project Commissioned by the Teacher Training Agency*. University of Exeter.

Meredith, A. (1995) Terry's learning: some limitations of Shulman's pedagogical content knowledge, *Cambridge Journal of Education*, Vol. 25, No. 2: pp. 175–187.

Ofsted (1994) *Primary Matters*. London: HMSO.

Osborn, M., Croll, P., Broadfoot, P., with Pollard, A. and Triggs, P. (2000) *What Teachers Do: Changing Policy and Practice in Primary Schools*. London: Continuum.

Plato (2003) *The Republic*. London: Penguin Classics.

Poulson, L. (2001) Paradigm lost: subject knowledge, primary teachers and education policy, *British Journal of Education Studies*, Vol. 49, No. 1: pp. 40–55.

Shulman, L.S. (1995) Those who understand: knowledge growth in teaching, in Moon, B. and Shelton-Mayes, A. (eds) *Teaching and Learning in the Secondary School*. London: Routledge.

TDA (2007*) Standards for the Award of Qualified Teacher Status*. London: Training and Development Agency for Schools.

Turner-Bissett, R. (2001) *Expert Teaching: Knowledge and Pedagogy to Lead the Profession*. London: Fulton.

White, J. (ed) (2004) *Re-thinking the School Curriculum: Values, Aims and Purposes*. London: Routledge.

Websites

The Research Informed Practice Site:
http://www.standards.dfes.gov.uk/research/

GTCE Research for Teachers:
http://www.gtce.org.uk/research/rft/
Professional Development:
http://www.teachernet.gov.uk/professionaldevelopment

The Learning Environment

In the chapter you will:

- Consider the different aspects that make up the 'learning environment'
- Reflect on the effectiveness of the physical environment of the classroom and school as a support for learning
- Identify ways in which the physical environment could be improved to support learning
- Consider how learning outside the classroom extends and enhances pupils' understanding
- Consider how and when technologies can be used to improve learning
- Reflect on the effectiveness of the Interactive White Board, in particular, as a support for learning

What do we mean by a 'learning environment'?

Tick all the items in the following list which could apply:

- the ethos of the school;
- the physical arrangement of the classroom;
- the local environment;
- a virtual learning environment;
- the school buildings;
- the ways pupil learning is supported, e.g. through grouping, **differentiation** etc;
- physical factors such as lighting, heating and fresh air in the classroom;
- a physically and emotionally safe place;
- the nature and availability of resources;
- the home environment: access to space to work, to a computer, parental attitudes;
- the use of wall displays;
- the classroom 'climate' in terms of the teacher's beliefs about learning;
- education visit locations, such as museums, historic sites, field centres, outdoor activity centres etc.;
- anywhere.

Differentiation: the adjustment of the teaching process according to the learning needs of pupils.

Introduction

You have probably ticked every item in this list (possibly apart from the last one!). When we are talking about the nature of the learning environment, and the effect it may have on pupils' learning, we can be talking about any, or even all, of the above factors. The situation is further complicated as many of these factors can be inter-related, making it more difficult to identify exactly which aspect of the learning environment is significant in any particular situation.

The DCSF (Primary National Strategy, 2005) considers the learning environment to be composed of four factors, which we have expanded in the list below:

- physical: buildings, classroom layout and resources;
- relationships: between teachers and pupils, but also pupil to pupil;
- structures and expectations: school and classroom rules, but also the general school 'ethos' as discussed in Chapter 1;
- language and communication: both the use of language to motivate and create a positive learning climate (see Chapter 9) and also the ways in which communication is used around the school, which will be discussed later in this chapter.

The journal *Learning Environments Research* includes articles on teaching styles, teacher language, student co-operation and assessment, as well as those focusing on the physical or built environment. Some of these areas are considered elsewhere in this book in Chapters 8, 9, 10 and 11 and we will emphasise the interrelated composition of the effective learning environment in each section of this chapter. Underpinning the creation of an effective learning environment are the beliefs and values about teaching and learning held by the teacher and also promoted by the school. Although this chapter concentrates on the first of the four factors above, the teacher her/himself is the most powerful influence on the learning environment and shapes the experience of the learners in all four aspects.

This chapter concentrates firstly on the physical features of the learning environment: the way the clasroom learning space is arranged; the importance of the visual environment and on learning outside the classroom. We will then consider the use of Information and Communication Technologies (ICTs), and particularly the Interactive White Board (IWB) as a significant element of the classroom learning environment.

Interactive White Board (IWB): computer-linked classroom teaching aid that enables pupils and teacher to interact directly with material on the screen while providing a large-scale display visible to the whole class, thus increasing the potential for interactive learning. Can also be used to display pre-prepared materials.

THINKING IT THROUGH

Return to the list at the start of this chapter and annotate each item using the four factors comprising the learning environment suggested by the DCSF:

Physical;

Relationships;

Structures and expectations;

Language and communication.

You can attach as many factors to each item as you feel appropriate. What do you notice?

The physical environment

A survey of teachers' opinions about how well the learning environment in their school supported learning and pupil behaviour found that only 12% considered their school buildings effective (Teacher Support Network, 2007):

> According to the respondents, narrow corridors contribute to 'aggressive behaviour and arguments among students'; lack of 'a proper desk and chair' inhibit a teacher's ability to do their job; and lack of temperature control in classrooms up and down the country mean children are too cold or too tired from the heat to learn effectively.

(p. 1)

The 530 teachers in the survey identified classroom layout as the most important feature of the physical environment, followed by good ventilation and lighting. Over half the teachers reported that they were unable to rearrange the furniture in their classrooms to create more flexible arrangements to suit different approaches to teaching and learning. This seemed to be particularly the case in secondary schools, although some primary schools did not have sufficient space in the classrooms to allow for much flexibility either.

The teachers overwhelmingly considered that the physical environment had an effect on pupil behaviour. Poorly maintained classrooms gave the impression that pupils were not valued, too many pupils moving in confined spaces raised levels of aggression, and 'hot spot' areas such as unsupervised toilets also contributed to poor behaviour. Conversely, the factors that teachers felt improved learning included large, light and airy classrooms that were well maintained; adequate outdoor space for play and movement round the school; interesting wall displays using pupils' own work and adequate ICT resources.

OVER TO YOU

The survey asked teachers to describe their 'dream' learning environment. You can find out what they thought by accessing: **www.ttrb.ac.uk** article id 13531 and following the link to the survey report.

Why not write a description or draw a plan of your own 'ideal' classroom to compare with the results of the survey?

Later in this book, in Chapter 18, we will discuss new developments in school building and learning technologies, which seek to address some of these issues. However, in many schools the difficulties outlined above remain part of the day-to-day reality for teachers and pupils, and a range of approaches have been employed to minimise their effects. Careful timetabling, and one-way systems on staircases and corridors, can reduce crowding, and allocating specific toilet areas to different year groups in secondary schools can reduce problems in an area which is difficult to supervise.

The amount of input teachers are able to make to classroom layout and the physical environment varies between primary and secondary phases, and also between individual secondary schools and subject departments. Primary teachers usually 'own' their classrooms and will work in the same space, and with the same group of pupils, for at least a year, sometimes more. In Key Stage 3 some teachers may move to a different classroom for each lesson, while others are more regularly based in specialist teaching spaces. However, while it is the case that having your own teaching space is generally an advantage in developing an effective learning environment, there are still a number of issues to consider:

- The age of the pupils will make a difference to the organisation of space. For example, will you want a carpeted area where the whole class can sit, or will it be better if pupils remain in their seats? Will chairs be grouped around tables, or all facing the 'front'?

- Is the space for generalist or specialist teaching? Will there be room for group or individual work as well as space related to the needs of the subject?

- Your own beliefs about teaching and learning. How do you think pupils learn best in your subject, or at this age? How does this affect the use of space?

Jane McGregor, who researches the use of space in schools, argues that the taken-for-granted organisation of space in schools and classrooms reinforces and sustains certain types of power relations between teachers and pupils and between different groups of pupils (McGregor, 2004). The physical organisation of the school thus becomes part of its 'hidden curriculum'.

The amount of 'clutter' or 'busy-ness' in the environment is also claimed to have an adverse effect on learning. Watch the Teachers' TV programme **http://www.teachers.tv/ video/17831** for a debate between teachers with different views on this idea.

What is the effect of classroom layout on pupil learning?

The answer to this question is, of course, that it depends on both what, and how, you want pupils to learn. Furniture arranged in circles or around tables facilitates learning where discussion and collaboration are required, whereas tables or desks in rows are more suited to individual learning. Classroom layouts with 'multiple activity settings' enable pupils to work in whatever environment is best suited to the task in hand. An example of such a layout might be a primary classroom with a practical area, a carpet area and tables; or a secondary specialist teaching area with spaces for writing separated from areas for practical work or group discussion. While not all classrooms are large enough, or have suitable furniture to create these different activity areas, it can be well worth taking the time to rearrange furniture to suit the learning approach of the lesson – and worth taking the time to establish orderly furniture-moving routines with your pupils where age permits. This is especially important if the classroom is not your permanent base, and needs to be returned to its previous layout at the end of your lesson.

Pupil seating arrangements can also be regarded as part of the 'layout' of the classroom, even if this equates to the physical arrangement of people rather than furniture. In Chapter 9, we will see that 'relationships with others' are a significant factor in effective learning, and these can be fostered or hindered by classroom layout and seating plans. This emphasises yet again the importance of developing a good knowledge of your learners in a holistic sense: not just in terms of their academic achievement, but also their approaches to learning and their social skills. In one secondary school where seating plans are a common expectation for all classes, the pupils provided positive statements about the value of seating plans as part of a classroom display:

- To encourage proximal learning
- To encourage behaviour for learning
- To allow us to work with a range of people

(Andrew-Power and Gormley, 2007)

The language used by these pupils demonstrates their familiarity with a vocabulary about learning, supporting meta-cognition.

The creation of a 'teacher-zone' in the front of the room, reinforced by the interactive whiteboard, or laptop and projector, may continue to support the same teacher-centred approach which has been a feature of classrooms since the nineteenth century, unless we are consciously aware of this possibility. The furniture arrangements in rows or U-shapes, facing the 'front', found in many secondary classrooms also perpetuate

Hidden curriculum: a term used to denote the way in which schooling 'socialises' pupils into certain behaviours that are not made explicit.

Multiple activity setting: a learning space in which different activities can be carried out simultaneously, such as practical work, group discussion and independent work.

Proximal learning: learning involving others close by – paired or small-group-based learning.

Behaviour for learning: patterns of behaviour likely to bring about successful learning.

Meta-cognition: being aware of how we think and behave in learning situations.

this approach. In addition, this layout tends to focus the teacher's attention on the triangle of learners immediately in front of him or her, who receive 90% of the attention, while those at the sides and rear of the room tend to be ignored more often (Higgins *et al.*, 2005a: 6).

However, the apparently more 'democratic' furniture arrangement where pupils are grouped around tables, commonly used in primary classrooms, may also have disadvantages for learners at times. Research evidence suggests that table groups have an adverse effect on time on task for some primary-aged pupils where individualised learning tasks are concerned. When the classroom layout is changed to one where learners are not facing each other (but not necessarily facing the 'front'), time on task for individual work increases. The effect was especially noticeable for those pupils who spent less time on task when in group arrangements compared with other pupils (Hastings and Chantrey Wood, 2002: 41; Higgins *et al.*, 2005a: 26). While increased time on task does not necessarily mean that effective learning is taking place, it is clearly an important factor. Table groups are often used by primary teachers to facilitate ability groupings, regardless of whether the tasks pupils will be asked to undertake are collaborative or individualised. This evidence thus raises similar questions for primary teachers as the 'teacher-centred' layout does for secondary teachers: how far do we take these commonly used forms of classroom layout for granted?

The message from research into managing classroom space is that 'different forms of classroom arrangement facilitate or inhibit different forms of learning' (McGregor, 2007) and that, ideally, we need to recognise that planning for the classroom layout is an integral part of our planning for learning. Returning to the four factors that constitute the learning environment according to the DCSF, the *physical* arrangement of the classroom affects both the *relationships* between teacher and pupils and pupil to pupil, and the *structures and expectations* for learning.

The visual environment

Pupils, and their parents, often notice the strong contrast between visual environments as they transfer to secondary education. Traditionally, primary classroom walls and school corridors have provided space to celebrate pupils' work, to enrich the curriculum with images, maps and artefacts and to reinforce key concepts in subject areas. Once the same pupils move to the secondary school the visual environment often becomes less stimulating. The fact that primary pupils and their teacher spend most of their time over a year in one classroom, unlike their secondary counterparts, obviously goes some way towards accounting for this difference. So, too, does the teacher workload agreement which specifically identifies display as an activity which should be devolved to other staff. As there are relatively fewer teaching assistants in the secondary sector this clearly has an effect on the visual environments of many secondary classrooms. However, it is increasingly being recognised that the visual environment of public areas and classrooms conveys implicit messages about the learning ethos and the values of the school, and many secondary schools regard visual display as an important aspect of creating a learning environment and facilitate opportunities to develop it effectively.

OVER TO YOU

What messages are conveyed by the following?

- A well-produced and mounted sign on the front entrance of a junior school, 'Parents should not use this entrance'.

- A display in the school entrance with images of pupils from recent events or trips. The display is regularly updated to ensure images are current.

- Pupils 'self-portraits' mounted around the classroom, each with a statement beginning 'My name is . . . and I am good at . . .'.

- A flatscreen display in a pupils' social area that offers hints ands tips for revision in the period leading up to examinations, and gives positive messages of encouragement once the examinations begin.

- A permanent label on the staffroom door, 'No pupils allowed here'.

- 'Achievement boards' with photographs of pupils who have exceeded an agreed target, or overcome particular challenges. Pupils are carefully selected by teachers to represent the whole population of the school, not only academic high fliers.

- Positive statements on classroom doors with a focus on learning: for example, 'Welcome to science – prepare to be challenged'.

Source: some ideas based on an article by Kirstie Andrew-Power and Charlotte Gormley, 2007

Display can also help to compensate for some less than pupil-friendly architecture in older school buildings. Hanging items from the ceiling creates a less intimidating space for younger primary pupils, and displaying pupils' work and stimulus materials at pupil eye level implies pupil ownership, rather than teacher decoration! Display of materials that are intended as a longer-term resource, such as punctuation rule reminders, are better suited to display at higher levels where pupils can easily see them while seated, and from various parts of the classroom. Where possible, try to establish a temporary display area where you can support specific lessons or topics in the short term, with images or artefacts.

As with other aspects of the visual environment, thought needs to be given to the underlying messages of classroom or corridor display. What is its main purpose? To celebrate achievement or to support learning? If the former – what criteria will you use for including pupils' work? If the latter – what messages will be conveyed by what is displayed?

CASE STUDY

Wonky frames

An excellent example of a display which served both functions was observed by Guy Claxton in the foyer of a primary school, and used as an example in one of his public talks.

One class had been designing and making picture frames in their Design and Technology lessons. The display showed their 'wonky' frames – the ones that *didn't* work, alongside pupils' evaluations of their designs indicating what was unsuccessful and how this could be remedied in a further attempt.

The decision to display this work in the entrance of the school was a statement about the school's philosophy – that process was valued as much as the final product, and that key learning for pupils takes place through independent reflection and evaluation, rather than following instructions to make the 'perfect' frame first time.

Creating an effective and fairly robust display does take time, and therefore needs to be planned carefully – particularly where you may not be directly involved in the mounting of items or final creation on the board.

- Make sure you maintain any guidelines for mounting display items which have been agreed by the school: for example, the single or double mounting of items, the use of backing papers, borders etc. These guidelines will have been drawn up to create a consistent standard which reflects the values and ethos of the school.
- Identify the main purpose of the display in terms of any learning outcomes and/or intended outcomes for individuals and pupils' social and emotional learning.
- Give some thought to the visual variety of the display in terms of different sizes of items and the combination of maps, charts, photographs and written work.
- Items can be overlapped, provided essential information is not lost, or 'escape' from the frame for effect. These techniques also add visual variety.
- Other techniques include 3D effects with push-out letters, or artefacts pinned to the display. Make sure there are no desks or tables close enough to this display to result in damage to these types of item as pupils move round the classroom.
- Titles and any key words should be large enough to attract attention and encourage others to examine the display: font size 72 or larger. Use interesting fonts if you wish, but make sure they are still decipherable at a distance!
- Ensure that captions are informative for other pupils, teachers and visitors to the classroom.

Source: Ideas taken from Andrew-Power and Gormley (2007) and Beadle (2005)

The visual environment of the classroom and of the school as a whole has an impact on all four aspects of the learning environment. Well managed, it improves or changes the *physical* environment, sustains and helps to develop a positive ethos in terms of *structures* and *relationships* with pupils, and pupils' relationship with the curriculum. This is supported by the ways in which *language* is used to communicate with all members of the school community in the visual environment.

THINKING IT THROUGH

In training

As a trainee teacher it can be difficult to make major alterations to the physical environment to the classroom, but relatively small changes can make a difference to the learning environment.

Evaluate your primary classroom, or the main classroom(s) for your subject, as an environment for learning.

Is there one action you could take to influence the physical/visual environment of the classroom(s) during a teaching placement? How do you think this would impact on pupils' learning?

Starting your career

Carry out an audit of the physical/visual environment of your classroom, or rooms in which you frequently teach.

Are there aspects of the environment which might be barriers to learning for some pupils? If so, how might these barriers be reduced or overcome?

Investigating learning and teaching

Jane McGregor (2004), whose research was cited above, argues that power relationships between teachers and pupils are reinforced or reshaped through the use of physical space in the classroom. How far do you think that changing the physical layout of a learning environment can change relationships between teacher and pupils and pupil to pupil?

You might find the short article by McGregor (2007) useful to support your thinking. The website **http://www.teachernet.gov.uk/schoolsforthefuture/** also has links to projects across the UK, some of which involve new classroom designs. This topic will also be discussed further in Chapter 18.

Learning outside the classroom

Learning is not solely confined to the classroom, of course. Various kinds of informal and formal learning take place in the home and through clubs, societies and other activities with which individual pupils are involved. Many schools audit this range of involvement, to ensure they recognise and acknowledge the skills and talents possessed by pupils developed through such involvement. Schools themselves also provide lunchtime clubs and after-school activities, now part of the Extended Schools aspects of *Every Child Matters*.

All these opportunities are valuable and enriching for individual pupils, and can be seen as part of the personalisation agenda. However, there is also a place for planned learning opportunities that take all pupils beyond the classroom as part of a shared

Photo 7.1
Extending
the learning
experience
beyond the
classroom walls
develops pupils'
understanding
of real-life
contexts

Source: Pearson
Education Ltd/
Ian Wedgewood

educational experience. Following a period during which there had been some resistance to outdoor learning or 'school trips' by some parents and teacher unions, the *Learning Outside the Classroom Manifesto* was launched in 2006. This document had support from the Secretary of State for Education and was intended to stimulate involvement in seeking broader educational experience for all pupils.

> We believe that every young person should experience the world beyond
> the classroom as an essential part of learning and personal development,
> whatever their age, ability or circumstances.
>
> *(DfES, 2006)*

The range of possibilities for learning outside the classroom extends from using the school grounds as a resource, through examining aspects of the local community, visiting museums, galleries, heritage sites, zoos, wild life centres, theatres and music venues, to trips abroad, fieldwork and outdoor pursuits trips. Chapter 16 also suggests some ways in which partnerships can be developed to support learning outside the classroom more effectively. Since 2006 a website and a range of resources have been developed to support this area of work and a Council for Learning Outside the Classroom was established in January 2009 to promote this aspect of work further.

WORKING IN THE CLASSROOM

In training

The Professional Standards for QTS (Q30) expect those gaining Qualified Teacher Status to be able to 'identify opportunities for learners to learn in out of school contexts', although this does not necessarily require trainees to be directly involved in these opportunities.

On the basis of your observations in school, what opportunities are currently provided for pupils to engage in out-of-school learning?

Is this planned into the curriculum at least once per term, or are opportunities taken as the occasion arises?

Are all pupils able to participate? How are barriers to participation, such as those relating to pupils with physical disabilities, overcome?

Starting your career

How far do you see learning outside the classroom as a priority in your classroom or subject teaching? What do you see as the benefits of this learning? (You may want to access the *Education Outside the Classroom Manifesto* (DfES, 2006) or **www.lotc.org.uk** for further ideas.)

What are the policies or customs of your school regarding learning outside the classroom (see questions above)?

What would need to be considered in relation to each of the four factors outlined by DCSF (Primary National Strategy, 2005): physical; relationships; structures and expectations; language and communication?

Do you see any barriers to the successful use of learning outside the classroom? How can these be overcome?

Investigating learning and teaching

How would you make the case for the benefits of learning outside the classroom? The *Learning Outside the Classroom Manifesto* (DfES, 2006) argues for a range of educational benefits. How would you convince reluctant colleagues or parents that increasing the amount of learning outside the classroom would not adversely affect pupils' results in national tests or examinations?

   The review of the *Education Outside the Classroom Manifesto* on **www.ttrb.ac.uk** provides links to a few examples of successful projects, but you may need to draw on your own experience (see above) and on other reading to support your case. You may find this review and link to a document on informal learning helpful: **www.ttrb.ac.uk** article ID 13433. Although informal learning is not synonymous with learning outside the classroom, you may find some of the ideas helpful. You can also refer to the website designed to support the Manifesto: **www.lotc.org.uk**.

Technologies for learning

'Technology is not an option,' said Jim Knight, Minister of State for Schools and Learners, speaking at the launch of *Harnessing Technology: Next Generation Learning* (Becta, 2008a). This part of the chapter considers the role and use of technology as part of the learning environment. At the start of this chapter we argued that the teacher her/himself is the most powerful influence on the learning environment. This argument is just as true for the use of technology to support learning as it is for other aspects of the learning environment. It can sometimes seem as though the presence of technology alone can transform learning, but the evidence from research is indicating that this is certainly not the case.

At the start of the twenty-first century a number of briefings by government representatives provided an outline of their position about the use of technologies in education. The arguments were briefly as follows:

- In a new millennium, with a continually changing society, a rapid change in education was required.

- The UK had to compete in an increasingly competitive global marketplace. There would be fewer opportunities for unskilled, unproductive members of society; a society in which skills rapidly became obsolescent and the living wage increasingly difficult to attain.

- People were living longer and the change in demographics would have important effects on society. As the balance between young workers and older retired members of society changed, it would become increasingly difficult to maintain an adequate pension provision and health services.

- As a result of these demands a small nation such as ours had to make the most efficient use of its human capital. Our society had to move rapidly to a position in which the traditional boundaries between school, work and retirement would meld into a continuous process of lifelong and life-wide learning.

- The use of ICTs was seen to be pivotal to these economically driven changes.

DCSF: Department for Children, Schools and Families (formerly Department for Education & Skills, DfES). Main government department for education, with an extended remit to cover the requirements of Every Child Matters.

Government priorities for the use of technologies for learning are based around the key priorities of raising achievement and improving skills; narrowing gaps and supporting vulnerable learners; and improving capacity, quality and efficiency. Becta (formerly the British Educational Communications and Technology Agency) is a non-departmental body of the **DCSF**, charged with updating government strategy in ICT in education. In 2008 Becta published *Harnessing Technology: Next Generation Learning* (Becta, 2008a), which outlines a six-year plan aimed at schools, families and the Further Education and Skills sector.

Alongside the publication of this updated strategy, Becta also carried out a review of research and evidence on the current state of technology use (Becta, 2008b), which indicates some improvements over the past five years but also some areas that are still underdeveloped in terms of the strategy outcomes.

RESEARCH BRIEFING

The Becta strategy outlines five 'high level' outcomes for the next six years, which means they are intended to apply across the compulsory education sectors as a whole, The results of the review are summarised alongside each outcome.

Strategy 'high level' outcomes (Becta, 2008a)	Findings of review (Becta, 2008b)
Technology-confident, effective providers *Education and training providers able to make strategic and effective use of technology to achieve the best outcomes for learners*	Over the five years between 2002 and 2007 primary schools closed the gap with secondaries in this area. Twenty-eight per cent of primaries and 25% of secondaries are described as e-enabled and 39% and 43% respectively as 'enthusiastic'. However, 13% of primary schools and 8% of secondaries had low scores for this aspect.
Engaged and empowered learners *Learners able to access technology and the skills and support to use it to best effect inside and outside formal learning*	Ninety-two per cent of parents of school-aged pupils reported they had access to the internet and a computer at home. However, access varies in relation to socio-economic status and ethnic background. Pupils' access to computers at home is often shared with others, which may limit their individual use. Pupils' awareness of e-safety appears to be 'patchy' and dependent on the school they attend.
Confident system leadership and innovation *Education leaders enabled to lead technology to support their priorities and deploy innovative solutions to improve the quality of teaching*	Head teachers reported using technology for recording learner progress as their highest priority, followed by that of supporting independent learning (57% of primaries and 71% of secondaries). Personalised learning was regarded as a key priority for future development by 49% of primary and 66% of secondary head teachers. Communication with parents did not emerge as a high priority.

E-enabled: a measure of the ability of a school to make effective and strategic use of technology to improve learning. Judgements about a school's 'e-maturity' are made on the basis of the technical infrastructure and resources available, the confidence of staff to utilise technology effectively for both teaching and co-ordinating school activities and finally on how well technology engages the learners (see Becta, 2008b).

RESEARCH BRIEFING: *CONTINUED*

Learning platform: a software product which supports shared access to resources, communication and information internal to a school or other organisation (such as a local authority). **Virtual Learning Environments** (VLEs) or Course Management Systems are well-established examples of learning platforms.

Strategy 'high level' outcomes (Becta, 2008a)	Findings of review (Becta, 2008b)
Enabling infrastructure and processes *A technology infrastructure that offers learners and practitioners access to high-quality, integrated tools and resources at the best possible value for money*	More schools have access to learning platforms, but these are not yet widely used by teachers. The use and creation of digital resources has increased. Half of secondary teachers* and a third of primary teachers used self-created digital resources to support their teaching, although they use resources created by other teachers less frequently. Primary teachers are more likely to adapt materials created by other people. * Secondary teachers here cover the full secondary age range so results may be different for Key Stage 3.
Improved personalised learning experiences *Technology enabling improvements to learning and teaching, and tailoring of learning to suit the needs of learners*	In the 7–14 age groups there is little use of online learning or blended learning to allow learners to study at their own pace. The main use of technology in this area is to support assessment. Only 11% of primary teachers and 21% of secondary teachers* use technology to provide feedback to pupils. * Secondary teachers here cover the full secondary age range so results may be different for Key Stage 3.

Although there are still schools where the use of technology is still fairly under-developed, Becta takes a positive view of progress in using technologies to support learning, and this should mean that in most cases you will be in a good position to utilise ICTs in school. As you can see, however, there are several areas where schools and individual teachers may need to develop their practice further.

ICTs and learning – looking below the surface

The incorporation of technologies into the classroom as support for learning is now taken for granted, and sometimes it is also taken for granted that the use of Information and Communication Technologies (ICTs) will automatically improve learning. However, this is far from being the case:

Research in the area of ICT and classroom learning is now virtually unanimous in claiming that while new technologies can be used to enhance learning they are not sufficient in themselves to produce effective learning.

(Sutherland, Robinson and John, 2008: 29)

The utilisation of technology is not culturally or pedagogically neutral in schools or in other areas of our lives. The software we use, the way in which hardware is organised and accessed, the relationship of learners to each other and the learning tasks with which they engage grow from conceptions of learning, and perhaps unconsciously, of the society that we want to create and our perceptions of how this is to be accomplished. It is easy to forget that whichever software package is selected or hardware layout is used is underpinned by a series of assumptions about how learning takes place. For example, the use of **drill-and-skill** packages assumes that: knowledge is an object which can be broken into parts; learning is linear; children learn through the same small steps; and learners learn primarily through individual activity, in this case through interaction with technology.

Drill-and-skill: the learning of facts or simple skills through memorisation, reinforced by repetition.

An issue for critical consideration of such pre-packed learning systems is that of power, particularly where the power in the teaching–learning enterprise lies. The uncritical use of downloadable materials changes the power relationship between teacher and authority, providing the possibility for the teacher to become a mere supervisor of ready-made solutions. Similarly, the use of some software types can reduce the learner to a passive responder. Pre-packaged learning materials do not need to be commercially produced in order to increase the possibility of passive learning on the part of pupils. The increasing use of PowerPoint by teachers to structure lesson delivery also raises some difficult questions. PowerPoint was not originally designed for educational purposes, but as a presentation tool for business – particularly for sales and marketing. It supports a mode of delivery which is linear and predetermined, and which may not allow for pupil enquiry and constructed knowledge on social constructivist principles. Here, all the power remains with the teacher as creator of the presentation.

As teachers we need to investigate the potential of different forms of ICTs by familiarising ourselves with the features that are available, and by matching these features to the learning needs of our pupils and the intended outcomes of our lessons. There are other elements which also need consideration in terms of the successful use of ICTs to support and enhance learning – most importantly the pupils' own expectations of ICT, based on both their in-school and out-of school experiences, as the following case studies illustrate.

CASE STUDY

Always expect the unexpected!

Case studies based on examples from
Sutherland, Robinson and John (2008)

Case Study 1

A Year 7 class were engaged in a geography
activity based of the local area. Over several
lessons they were asked to use mind-mapping
software to generate ideas about whether it is a
good place to live; to support their initial ideas
through web-based research and fieldwork;
and to present their findings in groups, using
PowerPoint or MS Publisher.

By the end of the lesson sequence, only half
the groups had completed the task because of
the time taken in discussing presentational
features. The teacher commented: '. . . they
spent absolutely ages deciding what font and
colour looked best. So whereas I'd envisaged
the computerised graph construction making
things far quicker than if they'd done it by
hand, I don't think it was any quicker at all.
In fact it might even have taken longer.'

Case study 2

A primary teacher decided to use a software
package (VirtualFishtank) to support science
teaching about the features of living things.
She asked pupils to design a virtual fish with
as many features as possible that would try
to ensure it survived for a long time. She
introduced the activity as a simulation, and
explained that this was 'like a game'. In the
ensuing lesson pupils focused on the competitive
element of seeing how long 'their fish' could
survive, rather than on identifying the features
of their fish that aided its survival, or otherwise.

Mind mapping: a term initially coined by Tony Buzan to describe visual representation of interlinked ideas.

THINKING IT THROUGH

What were the pupils' expectations for the use of ICTs in these lessons?

How had these expectations developed? Why did the pupils in Case Study 1 tend
to focus on presentation? Why did the pupils in Case Study 2 become so competitive?

What could these teachers have done differently (or in a subsequent lesson) to
avoid these unintended outcomes?

For many pupils, there will be a gap between the quality of the hardware and software they experience at home and what they use in school – and the comparisons will not usually be in the school's favour. The novelty factor of most learning technologies has now worn off, and we need to adopt a more critical stance towards the ways in which they support learning in the classroom. While individual primary teachers use technology more often in their lessons than secondary teachers, perhaps because of the relatively greater availability of appropriate software for primary-aged pupils (Becta, 2008b: 34), teachers in both primary and secondary schools use technology mainly to support whole-class teaching as a display and presentational tool. Only about 30% of teachers in both primary and secondary schools report using technology in other ways. This raises one of the key questions about the use of ICTs to support learning: are teachers 'doing different things with ICTs' or are they just 'doing the same things differently' (Sutherland, Robinson and John, 2008)?

In order to 'do things differently' we need to identify exactly what it is that ICTs offer us that is not available through other media. Technologies offer their users a range of opportunities, often called affordances, although they can also engender constraints. These opportunities do not lie within the technologies themselves, although it is sometimes hard to recognise that this is not the case, but in the *interactions* between users and the affordances of a particular technology. As a simple example, word processing software offers the opportunity for easy revision of text, or provisionality. However, in the early days of computer use in classrooms, pupils were often encouraged to use it to type out their work in 'best', precisely as if the word processor was the same as a typewriter. In order for the affordance of provisionality to be recognised by pupils, it also needed to be acknowledged by teachers, who had to rethink their views of learning and teaching with ICT. The benefit existed in the interaction *between* the learner and the software, between the *understanding* that written text can be changed and improved and the *facility* to do this quickly and easily.

WORKING IN THE CLASSROOM

In what ways might ICTs be 'doing the same things differently' or 'doing different things'?

Drawing on your experiences in schools so far, and on your experience as a pupil, if this is relatively recent, list the ways in which you have noticed the following ICTs being used to support learning across the curriculum, or in subject areas other than specific ICT lessons:

> Computer software, other than word processing
> Digital still or video cameras
> Internet access
> Interactive White Boards
> Tape recorders or digital voice recorders
> Video-conferencing
> Virtual Learning Environments
> Word processing software.

What other ICTs have you observed in use?

In what ways was the use of ICT enabling *teachers* to work more efficiently or effectively?

In what way(s) was the use of ICT changing the learning experience for *pupils*?

Would it have been possible for learners to achieve the same learning outcomes *without* the use of ICT?

How far do you think the use of ICT directly contributed to achieving the intended outcomes for the learners?

(Please turn to the end of this chapter for some possible answers to these questions.)

Affordances: opportunities that enable different forms of interaction, made available by particular technologies.

Provisionality: the concept that electronic text can be seen as a provisional, rather than permanent text form, unlike handwritten text which needs to be rewritten if changes are made; an **affordance** of word processing, and some other forms of software.

Virtual Learning Environment (VLE): see learning platform. A software product providing shared resources and information, with communication through e-mail and discussion boards, which is internal to a school organisation, but accessible remotely via password.

Transforming learning with ICTs

Initially, ICTs were presented as an enabling tool, that is, as a more efficient means of meeting traditional educational ends. More recently, policy documents have moved beyond this to suggest that technology may have a more 'transformational' role in providing appropriate educational settings for the twenty-first century (DfES, 2003).

Avril Loveless (2007), an expert in learning technologies at the University of Brighton, has reviewed ways in which digital technologies have contributed to creative activities in terms of:

physical and virtual learning environments;
developing ideas;
making connections;
creating and making;
collaboration;
communication and evaluation.

Responses to *physical environments* can be created through images, sound and text, using information gathered from digital cameras (still or video), mobile phones, Personal Digital Assistants (PDAs) and Global Positioning Systems (GPS). Using these simple technologies a variety of learning experiences are possible: pupils can simulate a 'moonwalk' in the school grounds, using actual images from the moon's surface; maths trails, story trails and history trails can be created to support learning outside the classroom. See **http://www.createascape.org.uk/** for examples of existing work by teachers and pupils, and advice on developing your own 'mediascapes'.

A wide range of digital tools exists to support pupils in *developing ideas* and testing outcomes through simulations. These tools also provide a means of engagement for pupils in terms of offering opportunities for experimental and open 'play', but the use of them does not, in itself, guarantee creative outcomes. Some tools also 'shape' the end product and could perhaps be seen as limiting some aspects of creative thinking. There is also a need for informed teacher support to ensure that pupils gain the maximum benefit from these types of activities. (For a further, more detailed exploration of this area, see Loveless, 2007: 9–10.)

In terms of *making connections*, the range of possibilities is too large to be detailed here. They extend from online access to museums and galleries through to YouTube and social networking sites. Similarly, the potential of digital technologies to support pupils in *creating and making* activities is enormous, in terms of both visual and sound-based technologies and the associated editing software which is now easily available. In one primary school, the pupils in Key Stage 1 had developed their own puppet play. They wanted to share this with others in the school, but were too nervous to feel able to present it in a traditional assembly. One of the Year 6 pupils had experience in using the Moviemaker application, from home, so with the help of digital video the puppet play was recorded in the familiar classroom environment and presented to the whole school as a DVD which could also be taken home and shared with parents.

Digital technology also offers the potential for *communication and collaboration* over distances. Pupils halfway across the world from each other can create a shared story book together, or indeed share a geography lesson, as easily as pupils from the next

Photo 7.2
The range of digital technologies now available in schools makes it possible for pupils to create materials and communicate with others using a range of media. This enables learners with a range of needs and abilities to participate fully in activities and to demonstrate their understanding

Source: Pearson Education Ltd/ Ann Cromack. Ikat Design

class. Artists can link with pupils in schools on collaborative projects, and virtual artists' studios can be created. Currently in development, Virtual Puppeteers allows pupils in different locations to create virtual 3D puppets and stage settings and collaborate to create and perform plays in real time that can be watched by a networked audience.

(See **www.futurelab.orguk/projects/virtual_puppeteers**)

OVER TO YOU

These examples offer exciting possibilities, but the technology can also be seductive.

Is this all creativity?

How far can the facility to capture, compose and reproduce images be seen as truly creative?

In what ways is developing a virtual puppet play different from developing one with puppets in the classroom as teachers have done for many years?

What do you see as the particular advantages for creative learning provided through the use of digital technology? How do these apply to subject teaching in Key Stage 3?

Various forms of technology are well-established aspects of the learning environment. How well they are deployed, both in terms of *physical* arrangement and in terms of underlying assumptions about *structures and expectations* for learning, significantly impacts on classroom *relationships*, both between teacher and pupils, and pupil to pupil. The next section will also consider the potential of one particular form of learning technology to affect *language and communication* within the classroom.

The Interactive White Board

This next section of the chapter discusses the use of the Interactive White Board (IWB) in some detail as it is the technological development that reportedly has had the greatest effect on teaching and learning in recent years. Many of the underlying questions raised in this section could also be applied to other forms of ICT, however.

The introduction of IWBs into classrooms over the past 10 years or so has made a substantial contribution to changing teachers' attitudes to the use of ICTs to support learning, indicated in the Becta review outlined above (Becta, 2008b). IWBs can offer vastly improved display facilities, engage pupils directly through interactive functions and enable the collection and analysis of pupils' work in ways that were previously far more cumbersome. The IWB can help with modelling activities, for example modelling different kinds of writing, or approaches to mathematical problem solving. It provides visual support for learners who may find some concepts too abstract: for example by enabling rotation of shapes, or building on map contours. The IWB may support a range of pupil learning styles, and they are widely reported to improve pupils' attention spans and motivation (Smith *et al.*, 2005; Moss *et al.*, 2007; Kennewell and Beauchamp, 2007). So, you might ask, what's not to like?

Part of the answer is that these benefits depend heavily on teachers' pedagogical values and beliefs and do not automatically follow from merely having the IWB available in the classroom. The IWB can also reinforce **didactic** teaching from the front and teacher control of the lesson, as suggested earlier in this chapter (Somekh *et al.*, 2006). In order for the IWB to enhance learning, we need to understand how it can be used to develop more interactive, collaborative learning opportunities, rather than act as a cosmetic improvement for essentially traditional pedagogy.

Didactic:
teaching through direct instruction or demonstration with little pupil involvement.

Within the policy literature on the potential for the use of ICT in schools, and for IWBs in particular, the terms 'multimodality', 'pace' and 'interactivity' are frequently used (Kennewell, 2006). It is argued that successful IWB use should take advantage of these capacities.

Each of these terms deserves closer examination:

- **Multimodality**: this is the capacity for the integration of text, image and sound which is generally regarded as engaging learners, and helping some less able pupils understand more difficult concepts as they can be represented visually.

- **Pace**: the ability to maintain pupils' engagement through varied activities. In practice, 'pace' is reflected in the opportunities the IWB provides to move rapidly between screens or programs and the ability to revisit material (both teacher developed and pupil developed) for review. The ability to preload materials to the

IWB is also seen as contributing to 'pace' (Kennewell, 2006: 5). However, it is worth considering whether the opportunities that the IWB presents for 'pacy' work might sometimes work against 'thinking time' and the opportunity for deeper learning that this offers. This idea will be raised again, as we consider the concept of 'interactivity'.

- **Interactivity**: this is the most important, and the most contested, claim for the way in which the IWB enhances learning. The use of the IWB to enable pupils to manipulate objects and interact directly with the screen in view of the whole class is claimed as a powerful tool for directly engaging pupils in learning, but while this certainly *can* be true, recent research indicates it is not always necessarily so, as the next examples indicate.

The educational thinktank Futurelab produced a report on the use of IWBs in the classroom in 2007 which explores the issues around interactivity, and raises some challenging questions:

> There is sometimes the misguided assumption that because theoretically a technology has the functionality embedded within it to promote greater interactivity and collaboration, that this will automatically translate into more interactive classroom practice. The reality is, of course, that the design, the positioning, the school ethos, teacher experience and understanding, and so forth, can all mediate the extent to which it is used as a truly interactive pedagogical tool.
>
> *(Rudd, 2007: 7)*

Knowledge for teaching, as we have seen in Chapter 6, involves both subject or content knowledge and pedagogical knowledge, and for the IWB to be used effectively, both are essential.

Dr Gemma Moss and colleagues from the Institute of Education in London carried out research in London secondary schools to provide a report for the DfES on the impact of IWBs on pupil performance. The researchers found little evidence for improvements in attainment as a result of IWB use, unlike primary schools where the use of IWBs has been claimed to raise standards (Moss *et al.*, 2007).

In some cases they felt the IWB was 'window dressing' for poor teaching technique. One science lesson observed by Dr Moss's team was intended to explore the gravitational force of a jump jet. As part of the lesson pupils were asked to move arrows on the board to show where they thought the force was coming from.

> This had nothing to do with explaining gravitational force. The images may have engaged pupils in the exercise but did not help them to understand about gravity.
>
> *(Guardian, 4 December 2007)*

Interactivity which encourages deeper learning may require the teacher to relinquish some of their control over the shape and direction of the lesson, in order to allow pupils to explore ideas and to engage with the construction of knowledge rather than merely receiving it. The IWB has the potential to support exploratory learning, supplemented by two-way dialogue (Alexander, 2008) in which there is a more equal relationship between the teacher and the pupils. However, this potential is not always realised.

RESEARCH SUMMARY

Between 2002 and 2004 researchers observed 187 lessons with Year 5 and 6 pupils where IWBs had been introduced into the schools about two years previously. They found that the use of IWBs did not bring about a fundamental change in teachers' pedagogy and the majority of teachers continued to use a traditional question and answer approach in the lessons observed.

Closed questions were initially used three times more frequently than open questions. During the second year, although initial questions were often more open, pupils' responses were briefer than in lessons observed previously without IWB use, and there were fewer 'uptake' questions (feedback which makes connections with other aspects of the lesson).

The researchers concluded that IWBs engaged pupils and generated a faster pace in lessons, but often at the expense of longer, more detailed pupil answers. They also noted that pedagogical changes took time to become embedded, and that an increased use of probing questions only became evident at the end of the two-year period. This suggested that teachers needed time and possibly further training in order to realise the potential of IWBs for dialogic teaching.

A detailed summary of this large-scale research investigation, supported by case studies of effective interactive use of IWBs from both primary and secondary settings, is available at **http://www.gtce.org.uk/teachers/rft/curriculum0908/** under 'Interactive teaching and interactive whiteboards' (September, 2008). The summary is based on research by Smith, Hardman and Higgins (2006).

Dialogic teaching: a term coined by Robin Alexander to denote a particular approach to teaching through talk which operates to stimulate and extend pupils' thinking through the disciplined use of key strategies.

The strategies that can encourage deeper learning dialogue, such as allowing longer response time to questions, encouraging peer-to-peer feedback and engaging genuinely with pupils' ideas and feedback, are not dependent on the use of the IWB. However, IWB technology does offer genuine benefits for teachers if lessons are planned with higher-order thinking skills in mind, and there are opportunities for pupils to share in the directing and development of the lesson.

Higher order: thinking or questions that involve deductive or inferential thinking, or that seek explanation or justification rather than repetition of known facts.

CONTROVERSY

Can we really develop interactive learning in the current educational climate?

This quotation is taken from part of the Futurelab report on IWBs which identifies the constraints operating in classrooms that act against utilising the full potential of IWBs to support learning.

Higgins et al. [2005b] and Hall and Higgins (2005) further note that the degree to which pupils are able to participate in interactive learning and teaching practices is limited by the emphasis on rigid curricula and 'teaching to test' under a standards agenda that engenders a perceived 'need' amongst many teachers to stringently control the classroom. This can result in pupils' views often being overlooked as the need to deliver curriculum content prevails and the likelihood of many teachers to encourage greater active pupil participation diminishes . . . In short, it may be argued that the culture and focus on current national educational priorities, and the accountability that accompanies them, could reduce the likelihood of greater interactivity in schools and in the classroom.

(Rudd, 2007: 7)

OVER TO YOU

How far do you agree with the last sentence in this extract?

Is the principle of active pupil participation being sacrificed to the need to meet nationally determined performance outcomes?

Can these two agendas be reconciled?

SUMMARY

This chapter has considered the importance of four aspects of the learning environment, as identified by DCSF, in terms of the physical and visual environment of schools and classrooms and the impact of technologies for learning. We have emphasised that the aspects of the learning environment are interconnected, and that, for example, the physical environment also has an effect on relationships within the school and on structures and expectations for learning.

We have argued that your values and beliefs about learning and teaching can strongly determine the kind of physical and visual environment you create as a teacher, and will most certainly impact on the ways in which you use technologies to support learning. If new technologies are indeed going to transform learning (DfES, 2003) it will not be the technology itself that achieves this, but your knowledge and understanding of how it can be used to best effect.

THINKING IT THROUGH

In training

Having read the section on Technologies for Learning in this chapter, what actions could you take now, while still in training, to ensure you are 'doing things differently with ICTs' to support learning, rather than 'doing the same things differently'?

Where the opportunity arises, discuss this issue with your mentor and, if possible, arrange to observe other teachers using ICTs in different ways.

Starting your career

Review the range of ways in which you currently use ICTs to support learning and evaluate how far you feel these encourage interactive teaching or promote pupils' thinking and problem-solving/creative skills. Are there areas where you feel you could improve your practice?

Ask your mentor or another colleague to observe one of your lessons to compare their observations with your self-evaluation.

Investigating learning and teaching

What do we really mean by 'interactive teaching' in connection with ICTs, especially the IWB? The GTCE *Research for Teachers* summary mentioned above (**http://www.gtce.org.uk/teachers/rft/curriculum0908**) provides some suggestions in relation to the use of teachers' questions and development of 'dialogic teaching', but interactivity implies more than this, as the work of Kennewell (2006), also mentioned above, makes clear.

You could investigate teachers' and student teachers' conceptions of 'interactive teaching' through the use of interviews or questionnaires (see Chapter 13) and compare your results with some of the research mentioned in this chapter or in the additional materials given below.

GTCE: The General Teaching Council for England is the professional body for teaching in England. All trainee teachers are provisionally registered with the GTCE, and full registration is confirmed at the end of the induction year. The GTCE also provides a range of other services and resources for teachers, employers and parents. 'Our overall purpose is to work in the public interest to help improve standards of teaching and learning.'

SOME POSSIBLE ANSWERS TO THE QUESTIONS ON PAGE 153

For teachers ICTs can:

- save time by enabling the sharing of ideas and resources;
- improve lesson design;
- engage pupils with a wide range of resources and techniques to support critical thinking;
- support both individual and collaborative work;
- support whole-class discussion regarding first-hand observation;
- enable more effective communication with parents and pupils regarding out of school learning;
- be used to examine assessment data to increase personalised learning (depending on the quality of the data!).

For pupils ICTs can:

- allow them to investigate or be creative in ways not possible otherwise;
- give them access to information not otherwise readily available;
- engage them in the selection and interpretation of information;
- help them review, refine, re-draft and modify work in progress;
- enable them to see patterns or behaviours more clearly;
- add reliability or accuracy to measurements;
- save time, for example spent on measuring, recording or writing.

TAKING YOUR PRACTICE FURTHER

There are a large number of textbooks and handbooks on the use of ICT to support learning in different curriculum areas. For example, David Fulton Publishers have a series for primary teachers, 'Teaching ICT in the Primary Curriculum', with separate books on Science, Art, Mathematics and English and also books on 'creative approaches' to ICT in Mathematics and English. However, there are many other similar texts.

For secondary teachers, Woollard, J. (2007) *Learning and Teaching Using ICT in Secondary Schools*, Exeter: Learning Matters, or Leask, M. and Pachler, N. (2nd edn) (2006) *Learning to Teach using ICT in the Secondary School*, London: Routledge, could be places to start, although subject-specific textbooks are also likely to contain chapters on the use of ICTs.

Teachers TV has a specific area devoted to the use of ICT under four categories: subjects, learning, resources, and management.

QCA also provide guidance on the use of ICT in subject teaching.

TAKING YOUR THINKING FURTHER

If you want to find out more about ways to develop the physical and visual environment, including the use of seating plans, **http://www.teachingexpertise.com/topic/learning-environment** offers free downloads of articles from the publication *Curriculum Briefing* on these topics, some of which are referred to in this chapter.

If you want to explore issues relating to the use of technologies to support learning, **www.ictliteracy.info** is an international portal providing a range of research-based and other materials on digital literacies, with a specific teacher-focused area.

Use **http://www.ictliteracy.info/whiteboardtechnology.htm** to locate abstracts and links to a number of research articles on 'interactions between students, teachers and technology' using IWBs.

The journal *Learning, Media and Technology*, Vol. 32, No. 3, 2007, is a special issue on 'The Interactive Whiteboard Phenomenon'.

Find out more

Two Teachers' TV programmes which might be of interest:

They Didn't Teach Me That: Classroom Environment (primary focus)
http://www.teachers.tv/video/3239

Professional Skills – Positive Learning Environment (primary)
http://www.teachers.tv/video/17831

This programme challenges some of the 'accepted wisdom' about the primary classroom environment.

The booklet *Primary Ideas: Projects to Enhance Primary School Environments* by Leo Care and Prue Chiles (2006), published by The Stationery Office, contains ideas about ways in which schools have enhanced entrances, playgrounds, signs and displays.

If you want to make connections between a positive school and classroom environment and aspects of social and emotional learning, including behaviour for learning strategies, these connections are explored in the Primary and Key Stage 3 National Strategies: Behaviour, Attendance and SEAL strands:
http://nationalstrategies.standards.dcsf.gov.uk/node/86931.

The Teachers' TV programme, *Every Child Matters: Emotional Literacy at Marlowe Academy*, can be viewed at **http://www.teachers.tv/video/30099**. This includes brief information about the way in which this school in a deprived area supports transition from Key Stage 2 for both pupils and parents.

Emotional health and well-being initiatives, which overlap, but are not synonymous with Social and Emotional Aspects of Learning (SEAL), are considered on the Healthy Schools website:
http://www.healthyschools.gov.uk/.

The booklet *Promoting Emotional Health and Wellbeing* (2005) can be downloaded using the reference DfES 0180-2005 PDF3.

The Resources area of the Healthy Schools website provides a link to four case studies of schools that appeared in recent *Teachers TV* programmes.

If you want to find out more about how ICT is impacting on teaching and learning: Becta publish regular updates at **www.becta.org.uk**, including an annual award for ICT excellence. There is a dedicated area for schools, with areas on curriculum and learning and teaching.

Glossary

Affordances: opportunities that enable different forms of interaction, made available by particular technologies.

Behaviour for learning: patterns of behaviour likely to bring about successful learning.

DCSF: Department for Children Schools and Families (formerly Department for Education and Skills, DfES). Main government department for education, with an extended remit to cover the requirements of Every Child Matters.

Dialogic teaching: a term coined by Robin Alexander to denote a particular approach to teaching through talk which operates to stimulate and extend pupils' thinking through the disciplined use of key strategies (see **www.robinalexander.org.uk/dialogicteaching**).

Didactic: teaching through direct instruction or demonstration with little pupil involvement.

Differentiation: the adjustment of the teaching process according to the learning needs of pupils.

Drill-and-skill: the learning of facts or simple skills through memorisation, reinforced by repetition.

E-enabled: a measure of the ability of a school to make effective and strategic use of technology to improve learning. Judgements about a school's 'e-maturity' are made on the basis of the technical infrastructure and resources available, the confidence of staff to utilise technology effectively for both teaching and co-ordinating school activities and finally on how well technology engages the learners (see Becta, 2008b).

GTCE: The General Teaching Council for England is the professional body for teaching in England. All trainee teachers are provisionally registered with the GTCE, and full registration is confirmed at the end of the induction year. The GTCE also provides a range of other services and resources for teachers, employers and parents. 'Our overall purpose is to work in the public interest to help improve standards of teaching and learning.'

Hidden curriculum: a term used to denote the way in which schooling 'socialises' pupils into certain behaviours that are not made explicit. Can be used in a critical sense to denote forms of social control.

Higher order: thinking or questions that involve deductive or inferential thinking, or that seek explanation or justification rather than repetition of known facts.

Interactive White Board (IWB): computer-linked classroom teaching aid that enables pupils and teacher to interact directly with material on the screen while providing a large-scale display visible to the whole class, thus increasing the potential for interactive learning. Can also be used to display pre-prepared materials.

Learning platform: a software product which supports shared access to resources, communication and information internal to a school or other organisation (such as a local authority). **Virtual Learning Environments** (VLEs) or Course Management Systems are well-established examples of learning platforms.

Meta-cognition: being aware of how we think and behave in learning situations. Ultimately this implies active control over the process of thinking, for example: planning the way to approach a learning task, monitoring comprehension, and evaluating progress towards the completion of a task.

Mind mapping: a term initially coined by Tony Buzan to describe visual representation of interlinked ideas. There are a number of software packages which enable 'mind maps' to be created, amended and linked to other electronic resources.

Multiple activity setting: a learning space in which different activities can be carried out simultaneously, such as practical work, group discussion and independent work.

Provisionality: the concept that electronic text can be seen as a provisional, rather than permanent text form, unlike handwritten text which needs to be rewritten if changes are made; an **affordance** of word processing, and some other forms of software.

Proximal learning: learning involving others close by – paired or small-group-based learning.

Virtual Learning Environment (VLE): see learning platform. A software product providing shared resources and information, with communication through e-mail and discussion boards, which is internal to a school organisation, but accessible remotely via password. Different VLEs have varying facilities such as options for learners to create personal online portfolios, upload assignments etc.

References

Alexander, R. (2008) *Dialogic Teaching*, 4th edn. York: Dialogos.

Andrew-Power, K. and Gormley, C. (2007) On display: wall to wall learning, *Curriculum Briefing 5*. Available at: **http://www.teachingexpertise.com/topic/learning-environment**.

Beadle, P. (2005) Look what I can do Mum. Available at: **http://www.guardian.co.uk/education/2005/apr/12/teaching.schools**.

BECTA (2008a) *Harnessing Technology: Next Generation Learning*. Coventry: Becta.

BECTA (2008b) *Harnessing Technology Review 2008: The Role of Technology and Its Impact on Education*. Coventry: Becta.

DfES (2003) *Fulfilling the Potential: Transforming Teaching and Learning through ICT in Schools*. Annesley: DfES. Available at: **http://publications.teachernet.gov.uk**.

DfES (2006) *Learning Outside the Classroom Manifesto*. Nottingham: DfES.

Hall, I. and Higgins, S. (2005) Primary school students' perceptions of interactive whiteboards, *Journal of Computer Assisted Learning*, Vol. 21, No. 2: 102–117.

Hastings, N. and Chantrey Wood, K. (2002) *Re-organising Primary Classroom Learning*. Buckingham: Open University Press.

Higgins, S., Hall, E., Wall, K., Woolner, P. and McCaughey, C. (2005a) The impact of school environments: a literature review, *The Centre for Learning and Teaching*, School of Education, Communication and Language Science, University of Newcastle. Available via: **http://www.cfbt.com/PDF/91085.pdf**.

Higgins, S., Falzon, C., Hall, I., Moseley, D., Smith, F., Smith, H. and Wall, K. (2005b) *Embedding ICT In the Literacy And Numeracy Strategies: Final Report*. Newcastle: Newcastle University.

Kennewell, S. (2006) *Reflections on the Interactive Whiteboard Phenomenon: A Synthesis of Research*. Swansea School of Education. Available at: **http://www.aare.edu.au/06pap/ken06138.pdf**.

Kennewell, S. and Beauchamp, G. (2007) Features of interactive whiteboards, *Learning Media and Technology*, Vol. 32, No. 3: pp. 227–241.

Loveless, A. (2007) *Creativity, Technology and Learning – A Review of Recent Literature*. Futurelab. Available at: **http://www.futurelab.org.uk/resources/publications-reports-articles/literature-reviews/Literature-Review382**.

McGregor, J. (2004) Space, power and the classroom. *Forum (for promoting 3–19 comprehensive education)*, Vol. 46, No. 1: pp. 13–18.

McGregor, J. (2007) Understanding and managing classroom space, *Curriculum Briefing 5*. Available via: **http://www.teachingexpertise.com/topic/learning-environment**.

Moss, G., Jewitt, C., Levaãiç, R., Armstrong, V., Cardini, A. and Castle, F. (2007) *The Interactive Whiteboards, Pedagogy and Pupil Performance Evaluation: An Evaluation of the Schools Whiteboard Expansion (SWE) Project: London Challenge*. Institute of Education, University of London/DfES, London.

Primary National Strategy (2005) *Behaviour and Attendance Materials: Positive Behaviour and the Learning Environment*. London: DfES.

Rudd, T. (2007). *Interactive Whiteboards in the Classroom*. Future Lab Report. Available at: **http://www.futurelab.org.uk/resources/documents/other/whiteboards_report.pdf**.

Smith, F., Hardman, F. and Higgins, S. (2006) The impact of interactive whiteboards on teacher–pupil interaction in the National Literacy and Numeracy Strategies. *British Educational Research Journal*, Vol. 32, No. 3: pp. 443–457.

Smith, H.J., Higgins, S., Wall, K. and Miller, J. (2005) Interactive Whiteboards, boon or bandwagon? A critical review of the literature, *Journal of Computer Assisted Learning*, Vol. 21, No. 2: pp. 91–101.

Somekh, B., Underwood, J. *et al.* (2006) *Evaluation of the ICT Test Bed Project Annual Report*. March. Coventry: Becta. Available at: **www.evaluation.icttestbed.org.uk/files/ict_test_bed_evaluation_2005.pdf**.

Sutherland, R., Robinson, S. and John, P. (2008) *Improving Classroom Learning with ICT*. London: Routledge.

Teacher Support Network and British Council for School Environments (2007) *Report on the School Environment Survey Results 2007*. Available at: **http://www.teachersupport.info/files/upload/docs/0607_School_Environments_Report.pdf**.

CHAPTER 8

Learning Styles and Teaching Repertoires

In this chapter you will:

- Consider the evidence to support theories about learning styles, preferences and approaches, including popular theories such as 'VAK'
- Relate learning style theory to emerging evidence from neuroscience
- Consider the implications of these theories for your own classroom teaching
- Link these theories to the range of additional factors which could influence pupils' learning
- Reflect on these issues in the context of current educational policy on 'personalisation'

How do you learn?

a) Do you like to approach a writing task such as an essay piece by piece, gradually finding out how the sections fit together as you write, or do you like to have a broad idea of the whole essay before you begin?

b) When you are thinking about something, or working your ideas out, do you find yourself thinking through images, or do you think mainly in words?

c) Do you feel you need to have direct experience of something before you can really understand the ideas behind it?

d) Are you comfortable drawing on abstract ideas in order to experiment to solve problems?

As you read on through this chapter, you will be able to associate these questions, and your answers, with some different theories about learning styles and learning strategies.

Introduction

Our own educational experiences tell us that individuals learn in different ways, long before we encounter the range of theories about learning and learning styles that have proliferated over the past 30 years. If we believe as teachers that we have a responsibility to develop each pupil's potential, then recognising these different approaches to learning will be an extremely important element in our classroom practice. Additionally, current educational policy is emphasising the importance of 'personalised learning' as outlined by the former Minister for School Standards, David Miliband:

> Decisive progress in educational standards occurs where every child matters; careful attention is paid to their individual learning styles, motivations and needs; there is rigorous use of pupil target setting linked to high quality assessment; lessons are well paced and enjoyable; and pupils are supported by partnership with others well beyond the classroom. This is what I mean by 'Personalised Learning'.
>
> *(North of England Speech, January 2004)*

It is important to distinguish between theories about how learning takes place, that is, theories about how information is processed by the brain, and theories about how individuals prefer to learn. These two ideas are closely related, but not the same. An individual's learning preference can help or hinder information processing, depending on the learning context, which is why it is important for teachers to be aware of pupils' learning styles and preferences. However, this chapter suggests that the process of identifying such preferences is not as straightforward as is sometimes claimed, and a number of other factors also need to be considered.

Learning styles, preferences and approaches

Psychologists have developed a range of theories related to learning styles, some of which are very familiar in school contexts, others perhaps less so. **Cognitive learning theories** focus on ideas about the different ways in which people approach learning, in terms of the strategies they predominantly use to process information. These are sometimes referred to as 'learning styles'. Some theories suggest that cognitive learning styles may be relatively fixed (Riding and Raynor, 1998), while others suggest that while individuals will have preferences for one or two learning strategies, most learners are able to adopt different strategies in different contexts (Kolb, 1985; Honey and Mumford, 1992).

The term 'learning style' is often used as a generic term, rather than one with a precise psychological definition, and may be used when referring to either of the following:

- the inherent ways learners process information (the psychological definition of cognitive style);
- how learners cope with different tasks and learning situations (a more general definition).

You will most probably be more familiar with the concept of learning styles in terms of the second meaning, rather than the first, although these two ideas are not mutually exclusive. Over the past few years, schools and Further Education Colleges have used various learning styles 'tests' or 'inventories' with students (you may well have completed one of these yourself). The intention has been to develop pupils' **metacognitive** understanding of how they learn, in order to increase their independence. However, such tests or inventories can lead to underestimation of pupils' learning potential if they are taken too literally, by either pupils or teachers.

> **Cognitive learning theory:** a theory that seeks to explain how learners process information.

> **Meta-cognition:** being aware of how we think and behave in learning situations. Ultimately this implies active control over the process of thinking: for example, planning the way to approach a learning task, monitoring comprehension, and evaluating progress towards the completion of a task.

RESEARCH BRIEFING: KEY THEORIES ABOUT LEARNING STYLES: 'FIXED' COGNITIVE STYLES

The term 'cognitive style' refers to the preferred way an individual processes information.

Riding and Raynor (1998) suggest that cognitive styles may be relatively fixed for each individual. According to Riding and Raynor, individuals tend to process information either in parts (analytics) or in wholes (wholists). They also represent information during thinking either through mental pictures (imagers) or in words (verbalists) (see Figure 8.1).

RESEARCH BRIEFING: *CONTINUED*

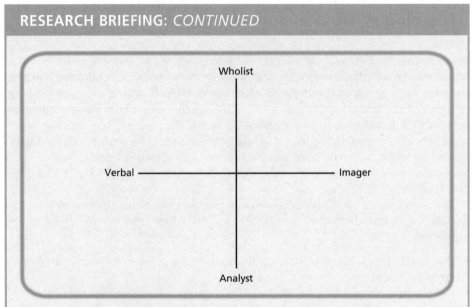

Figure 8.1 **Riding and Raynor's continuum**

Individuals will demonstrate combinations of both dimensions of this model (wholist-verbaliser; analytic-imager etc.) and may be located anywhere along the spectrum.

OVER TO YOU

How would you describe your own cognitive style using this framework? Look back to your answers to questions a) and b) at the start of this chapter.

WORKING IN THE CLASSROOM

Would it help pupils to be able to recognise their own cognitive style?

In what ways does classroom practice already support these ideas?

For example, by providing clear learning outcomes, pupils with a 'wholist' approach are helped to see the 'big picture' of the lesson or topic, while 'analysts' would be helped by being able to summarise learning at key points. What other examples relating to Riding and Raynor's framework can you identify?

The second way in which the term 'learning styles' is used refers to the strategies used by individuals to cope with different learning situations – both in formal (in school) learning and less formal learning contexts. Since these contexts vary considerably, the different strategies learners use also vary. Key theorists in this area argue that effective learners are able to use a range of styles or strategies to solve problems and incorporate new learning into their existing knowledge bases. Where learners demonstrate a preference for one approach over others, it is argued that they should be encouraged to extend their repertoire through supportive teaching.

RESEARCH BRIEFING: KEY THEORIES ABOUT LEARNING STYLES: LEARNING STRATEGIES

Kolb (1985) suggests that learners potentially move through a four-stage cyclical process in experiential learning which combines *perception* and *processing*.

The learner is immersed in the new experience at the *concrete experience* stage, then *reflects* on their observations before developing more *abstract conceptualisation* which is used to support *active experimentation* to solve problems or make decisions (see Figure 8.2). However, many learners have a preference for one of these four stages and may need to be supported in extending their learning strategies to encompass the full cycle.

Experiential learning: involves making meaning, or developing understanding, from direct experience, sometimes called 'learning by doing'.

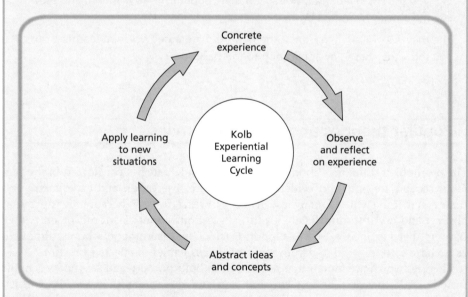

Figure 8.2 Kolb's experiential learning cycle
Adapted from Smith (2001)

Honey and Mumford (1986) identified four approaches to learning in adults which have a relationship with Kolbs' experiential learning cycle:

RESEARCH BRIEFING: *CONTINUED*

- *activists*, those who 'learn by doing' and can be impatient when asked to plan or repeat activities;
- *reflectors*, who tend to want to collect as much information as possible, and prefer to see the 'big picture';
- *theorists*, who like to see how new information fits with other knowledge, and prefer to work logically, one step at a time;
- *pragmatists*, who look for the practical application and value of new ideas, and will not tend to waste time analysing why things went wrong.

They suggest that effective learners should be able to adopt the approach suited to complete a given learning task. Learners who are unable, or reluctant, to utilise one or more approaches will be not be as successful as those who can operate in all four.

THINKING IT THROUGH

Can you see any relationships between these approaches to learning, and the cognitive styles identified by Riding and Raynor?

The theories of Kolb and Honey and Mumford are based on adult learners. Do you think they have any application to the classroom?

Popular theories about learning styles

The psychological theories about learning styles and strategies considered in the previous section are based on evidence gained from observation and experiment, and draw together the work of many researchers. However, perhaps because they are rather abstract and do not immediately lead to suggestions about classroom practice, they have not been explicitly used to support teaching and learning in schools, although, as we have seen, they do underpin many of the principles of effective practice.

Theories which are more often referred to in both primary and secondary schools include 'VAK' theories, 'Brain Gym' and 'accelerated learning' theories, all of which have been popularised through books and commercial training programmes. These theories claim to be based on evidence from either psychological or neurological research – sometimes both.

VAK: the acronym used to refer to the theory that learners have preferred ways of receiving information through the senses.

The idea that learners have a preferred learning style based on the senses underpins the popular Visual–Auditory–Kinaesthetic (**VAK**) theory. This idea was originally developed by proponents of Neuro-Linguistic Programming (NLP) which claims to be able to 're-programme' certain types of behaviour (phobias, for example). It was believed that individuals have preferred ways of interpreting the information they receive from the outside world, through one of the senses. This belief was influential in establishing the VAK theory, where learners are assumed to learn predominantly through Visual means, Auditory means (by listening) or Kinaesthetic means (through physical activity).

VAK theory is widely believed to be an important influence on pupil learning in many schools. It is not unusual to find lesson plan formats in use which require specific identification of aspects of the lesson aimed at each of these styles. However, some recent psychological research tested recall of information which was presented to pupils in the three VAK styles. The results indicted no benefits from having materials presented in the learners' preferred learning style, and concluded that attempts to focus teaching on learning styles was wasted effort (Kratzig and Arbuthnott, 2006, cited in Howard-Jones, 2006). It is important to note, however, that these findings do not challenge the idea of VAK preferences in themselves.

The use of multi-sensory approaches to learning also underpins 'accelerated learning' strategies. The work of psychologist Alistair Smith (1996, 1998) is well known in this area and claims to bring together evidence from studies of the brain and psychological theories.

THINKING IT THROUGH

As you consider the '7 stage cycle' advocated by Alistair Smith, what connections can you identify with others already considered in this book, such as constructivism, or the work of Riding and Raynor, or Kolb, outlined in this chapter?

OVER TO YOU

Smith's '7 stage cycle'

A prerequisite for the effective use of accelerated learning is the establishment of a supportive learning environment.

Stage 1: Connect the learning: provide opportunities for pupils to make explicit connections with previous work, before any new ideas are introduced. Examples of this strategy include jotting down main facts or ideas or engaging in quick activities to remind pupils of key terms from the previous lesson.

Stage 2: The big picture: share an overview of the whole topic so that learners can see where the lesson content fits. (This element draws on the ideas of Ausubel, 2000.)

Stage 3: Describe the outcomes: identify specific lesson outcomes and success criteria and enable pupils to set personal targets.

Stage 4: Input: new information is provided using VAK approaches. This section should be relatively short.

Stage 5: Activity: provide pupils with opportunities to process information in a variety of ways, drawing on multiple intelligence theory (Gardner, 1999). Keep activity sessions short, or 'chunked', although pupils could undertake more than one activity in a lesson. A brief learning review should follow each activity period.

Stage 6: Demonstrate: Pupils demonstrate their understanding using a variety of presentation techniques, including peer teaching, hot seating, role play, display or mini-whiteboards.

Stage 7: Review for recall retention: the final review of learning includes the use of memory and recall techniques and previews the next stage of learning.

How many of these stages do you recognise from observation in schools, or your own teaching?

Do you think this approach applies to all subjects?

Where might it be particularly useful?

Proponents of accelerated learning, including Alistair Smith, claim to be drawing on scientific evidence to support particular elements of their recommended approach. These include:

- allowing pupils free access to water during lessons on the basis that dehydration affects brain processing capability;
- providing 'brain breaks' or opportunities for physical action on the basis that increasing oxygen flow to the brain improves concentration;
- the use of music to influence pupils' emotions while learning, or to improve learning by connecting the left and right sides of the brain and by creating new pathways between the two halves;
- 'Brain Gym' activities also claim to improve learning by making connections between the two halves of the brain, and by activating 'brain buttons' to improve reading and writing capability.

However, neuroscientific evidence does not fully support these claims.

RESEARCH BRIEFING: WHAT DO NEUROSCIENTISTS SAY ABOUT THESE POPULAR THEORIES?

Allowing free access to water throughout the day

Dehydration does lead to loss of cognitive ability. However, studies on adults show that *too much* water can have the same effect. 'Encouraging children to drink water when they are thirsty may be a more sensible approach than constantly monitoring the amount of water they consume. Exercise and unusually hot weather are the exception to this rule, when there is evidence that children's

RESEARCH BRIEFING: *CONTINUED*

own monitoring systems are less reliable and they should be encouraged to drink in order to avoid dehydration.'

Improving connections between the two sides of the brain

'Except in the rare case of brains which have been lesioned, pathways exist permanently between the left and right hemispheres, most notably via the corpus callosum. At present, there is no scientific evidence to suggest we can voluntarily create new ones.'

Increasing oxygen flow to the brain to aid concentration

'No part of the brain is ever normally inactive in the sense that no blood flow is occurring. Furthermore, performance in most everyday tasks, including learning tasks, requires both hemispheres to work together in a sophisticated parallel fashion.'

Brain Gym

Neuroscience has not established the existence of 'brain buttons' and many of the claims made for Brain Gym exercises are described as 'pseudoscience'.

Source: All quotations from Howard-Jones (2006)

Lesioned: deliberately cut. In this context the term refers to very rare brain operations on patients with severe epilepsy, where cutting through the **corpus callosum** alleviates the major symptoms.

Corpus callosum: a mass of fibres located in the middle of the brain which connects the two hemispheres and allows communication between them.

It would seem that some of the 'scientific' claims made on behalf of these popular theories may not be well founded. Nevertheless, many teachers continue to be convinced of their merits, because their own experience indicates that learning improves when some aspects of these theories are employed. It is unlikely that so many teachers are mistaken – so what explanations might there be for the differences in learning that teachers have observed, if neuroscience does not support the claims made by supporters of these theories?

OVER TO YOU

Some possible explanations could include:

- Physical exercise does improve alertness – and research indicates that short sessions of Brain Gym improve response times.
- Riding and Raynor's verbalist-imager dimension of cognitive style might have a relationship to visual/aural preferences.
- Using a range of teaching approaches is more likely to engage and interest learners.
- Pupils in the 7–14 age range are developmentally more likely to benefit from concrete, hands-on approaches to learning. Kolb suggests that this is part of the cycle of experiential learning.

A final word about accelerated learning

'Cognitive acceleration' programmes in primary science and mathematics have been shown to bring about improvements in pupils' understanding and achievement (Adey and Shayer, 1994). These programmes are based on well-established principles of constructivist and social constructivist learning, and do not make the same claims to be based on brain research as 'accelerated learning' programmes. Since the terms are similar, it is important to recognise that they refer to very different approaches to teaching and learning.

What can neuroscience tell us about learning?

So far we have only considered the lack of evidence from neuroscience to support claims about learning and learning styles. However, neuroscience is providing some valuable new information about how the brain develops and the implications for education. In Chapter 4 we reviewed the evidence for 'activity spurts' in brain development, and the impact this has in early adolescence. The information may partly explain the typical adolescent behaviours and the difficulties some young adolescents have in concentrating and retaining information.

RESEARCH BRIEFING: MESSAGES FROM NEUROSCIENCE

Numeracy and Literacy learning

The human brain appears to be 'hard-wired' for language acquisition, insofar as the brain structures to support language are present at birth. However, there are no structures to support numeracy or literacy learning. Neural pathways are therefore shaped to fit literacy and numeracy functions through experience.

- Research suggests that the brain processes written words along one of two complementary pathways, either by converting letters/words into sounds, as in phonic approaches, or by directly transferring whole words or phrases into meaning. This 'dual-route' theory suggests that a balanced approach to the teaching of reading would be beneficial to most learners.

- Research also indicates that the neural circuits for number and space are intertwined so that teaching methods which link the two (number lines, rods, games etc.) are more likely to be effective.

Source: Based on a GTCE research review in *Neuroscience*, April 2009

Learning and the emotions

The combination of synaptic pruning (see Chapter 4) and the release of sex hormones in adolescence can lead to difficulty in regulating emotions, which in turn affects learning.

RESEARCH BRIEFING: *CONTINUED*

Positive emotions, such as fascination, absorption and amusement, trigger the motivation to learn, and the messages for teachers here are, obviously, that the more we can engage these positive emotions in learners the more focused their attention is likely to be (Fredrickson, 2001). This has led to claims about the importance of 'happiness' in fostering learning.

It is certainly the case that being stressed can prevent learning, but certain levels of stress hormone in the brain can actually improve memory. Research in Australia has found that we are more creative when we are happy, but are less careful in how we perceive things. If we are slightly irritable or apprehensive, we are more critical, and pay more attention to details (Ciarocchi, Forgas and Mayer, 2001).

Working memory and the limits of memorisation

Researchers into neuroscience and mathematics have found that different teaching methods create neural pathways that are more or less efficient, depending on whether drill learning or 'strategy learning' is involved. An over-emphasis on memorisation encodes knowledge as facts, but does not necessarily foster understanding. Simple right/wrong assessment systems are unlikely to discover whether pupils have knowledge encoded as facts or through the use of strategy, and teachers need to develop methods which uncover pupils' strategies and assumptions, in order to assess understanding effectively (GTCE research review, *Neuroscience*, April 2009).

Other discoveries by neuroscientists throw light on the operation of working memory, indicating that when new processes are being learned this places considerable demands on the areas of the brain involved. Once the process has been mastered, brain activity in this region decreases as the process becomes more automatic, and working memory capacity is released to enable other tasks to be completed (Howard-Jones, 2006).

There are two implications for the classroom based on this evidence:

firstly, an explanation for why some learners find it difficult to retain several new ideas or instructions at once, especially in the primary years when the relevant area of the brain is still developing;

secondly, it suggests that pupils should be encouraged to show their working of problems, since external recording can alleviate pressure on working memory until the process has been assimilated and become more automatic.

In this respect, some ideas from accelerated learning have a basis in scientific evidence.

Drill learning: the learning of facts through memorisation, reinforced by repetition. Sometimes also called rote learning.

Strategy learning: learning based in the developing and understanding of problem-solving strategies, rather than memorisation (see drill learning above).

Other factors influencing learning

As we have already discussed in the previous part of this book, individual learners are influenced by many factors, apart from their approaches to learning in terms of learning style(s). As important, if not more important, is their belief about learning and its value, and the perception they have of themselves as a learner. These issues were discussed in Chapter 5, but it is important to remind ourselves of the significance of these beliefs in relation to learning styles. The cumulative experiences that any learner brings to a new learning encounter affects they way they approach it. They may be reluctant to engage with new concepts, or to take risks on the basis of previous 'failures', or conversely they may be confident enough to experiment and open to support.

There is considerable evidence to suggest that pupils are more successful if they are aware of the strategies they employ in order to learn: that is, if they develop meta-cognitive awareness. This is an important dimension of assessment for learning, which is discussed in Chapter 10. Discussion about preferred approaches to learning is an essential part of this process, whether couched in terms of VAK or using other frameworks such the learning style inventory developed by Honey and Mumford. However, such discussions have the potential to be counter-productive, as well as valuable, if they reinforce pupils' negative conceptions of themselves as learners.

Learning style theory is valuable insofar as it reminds us that pupils are individuals, each of whom has a different sense of their identity as a learner. Consequently, employing a variety of methods of conveying information and engaging learners is more likely to bring about successful learning. If learning style theory leads to labelling, then options may close down for individual learners rather than open up. Worse still, pupils (and teachers!) may come to regard such labels as deterministic and believe they are incapable of learning in other ways.

Behaviourist: a theory of learning based on the idea that our behaviour is shaped by the feedback (or 'reinforcement') we receive. In school contexts this often takes the form of pupils being rewarded for successful learning (merit points, prizes etc.) and the application of sanctions if behaviour is not satisfactory.

Implications for the classroom

Taking a positive view of learning style theories, they can remind us to utilise a broad and varied repertoire of teaching strategies. The recent indications from neuroscience, as well as from established educational theory, are that effective learning takes place when new information is linked with existing knowledge. This appears to happen most effectively when the learner is actively engaged with learning, rather than acting as a passive recipient. Considering pupils' possible learning styles, without being limited by assumptions about them, can offer us a range of opportunities for active engagement.

A recent government publication (DfES, 2007) identifies three main teaching and learning models, based on prominent learning theories.

- Direct teaching models, based in the behaviourist tradition, are recommended where pupils need to learn new skills and procedures, including aspects of reading and writing and some academic content.

- Cognitive teaching and learning models 'help pupils learn to process information, build concepts, generate and test hypotheses and to think creatively'.
- Social models help pupils construct new knowledge and understand concepts through collaborative learning. (DfES, 2007: 4)

Each of these models has an associated repertoire of teaching strategies to support learning, although key skills such as questioning and explaining are common to all three.

Photo 8.1
Thinking aloud as you model the process under study is a vital aspect of effective modelling

Source: Pearson Education Ltd/ Rob Judges

Direct teaching strategies can be utilised positively through modelling and demonstrating skills and procedures. A significant aspect of effective modelling is the use of 'thinking aloud' by the teacher, to provide a commentary on the decisions taken or the necessary steps or stages in a procedure. Without this commentary, pupils may learn to copy, but not to understand, the reasons for the processes involved. It is also useful to identify possible problems or pitfalls in a procedure when modelling or demonstrating, as the direct teaching model does not lend itself to 'learning by mistakes' in the same way as constructivist approaches to learning.

Other direct teaching strategies include:

the use of simulations, where the characteristics of a situation are predetermined in order to allow pupils to practise certain skills;

some forms of direct interactive teaching recommended in the Primary and Key Stage 3 Strategies.

WORKING IN THE CLASSROOM

Think of a recent lesson you have observed, or one you have taught, which you feel contained characteristics of direct teaching, such as modelling or demonstration.

Reflect on your use of 'thinking aloud' as part of the process.

Did you offer pupil opportunities to evaluate how well they had demonstrated the new learning, and what they would need to do to improve?

Can direct teaching cater for a range of learning *styles*?

CONTROVERSY

Is direct interactive teaching effective?

Despite the high profile given to direct interactive teaching in the National Strategies, some research findings indicated that the quality of pupils' learning did not improve and may actually have suffered as a result. Detailed observations of 10 teachers during the Literacy Hour found that traditional patterns associated with whole-class teaching were maintained, despite the surface appearance of new organisational arrangements:

> the teachers were using the same discourse style regardless of the year group they were teaching and whether they were working with the whole class or with a group of pupils on a guided reading or writing task. Teacher presentation and teacher-directed question and answer therefore dominated most of the classroom discourse. There was also a notable absence of the higher order questioning and teacher-led discussion which is said to characterise interactive whole class teaching so as to allow pupils to develop more complete or elaborated ideas.
>
> (Mroz, Smith and Hardman, 2000: 384–5)

A slightly later research investigation into the effectiveness of whole-class interactive teaching (Smith and Higgins, 2006) also found that while the number and pace of pupils' contributions increased during Literacy lessons, there were fewer opportunities for extended interactions or higher-order thinking. Compared with the study above, interaction had increased, but higher-order thinking had still not been developed.

OVER TO YOU

In training

Try to arrange to observe an experienced teacher using a whole-class, interactive approach for part of a lesson. With their permission, note down the incidence of closed and open questions they ask the class. What kinds of questions promote deeper thinking and more extended responses in pupils? How does the teacher support and encourage deeper thinking?

As your training progresses, you could also undertake the activity below, perhaps through collaborating with another trainee teacher.

Starting your career

Either set up a tape recorder to record part of one of your lessons where you intend to use a whole-class interactive approach, or arrange for your mentor or another colleague to observe the lesson and to note down the range and type of questions used.

What do you notice about your own use of questions?

Which strategies were more or less effective in promoting deeper thinking and more extended responses?

Investigating teaching and learning

Access the following research summary from the *Research Informed Practice Site*, and also, if possible locate and read the original research (Smith and Higgins, 2006), 'Effective classroom interaction: use of questions and feedback to generate discussion', **http://www.standards.dfes.gov.uk/research/themes/ speakandlisten/interaction/**.

Compare the findings of this research with that reported in a GTCE *Research for Teachers* summary: 'Effective talk in the primary school', **http://www.gtce.org.uk/teachers/rft/talk_prim0506/**.

What are the implications for practice outlined in these research studies?

Both studies are based in primary schools. How far do you think these implications apply to teaching at Key Stage 3?

Closed questions: questions for which there is either a single right answer, or questions that are answerable by yes/no responses.

Open questions: questions with more than one possible answer, or questions designed to encourage reflection and further thought.

Induction: in education, the process by which the learner develops their own conceptual understanding by being supported to generalise or recognise causal connections, or draw analogies with previous experience.

The teaching strategies associated with *cognitive teaching and learning models* (DfES, 2007) rely largely on the teacher's capacity to use effective listening and questioning techniques in order to support pupils' reasoning and concept acquisition through enquiry and induction. Inductive techniques involve supporting pupils to draw their own conclusions on the basis of experience or evidence; these might involve generalisation, making causal connections or prediction.

Dialogic teaching: a term coined by Robin Alexander to denote a particular approach to teaching through talk which operates to stimulate and extend pupils' thinking through the disciplined use of key strategies.

Listening is as important as questioning, in determining how to support pupils' reasoning. Dialogic teaching (Alexander, 2006) requires the teacher to pay careful attention to pupils' answers in order to help build on them, rather than to accept an answer and move on to another question.

How does 'dialogic teaching' work?

In dialogic teaching, the teacher supports pupils' contributions through the strategy of cumulation, where pupils respond to each other's ideas to build collective understanding.

Strategies for supporting cumulation include:

- re-phrasing and summarising pupil contributions in order to encourage other pupils to contribute further ideas;
- explicitly linking pupils' ideas together, with further questions – this strategy, known also as 'chaining', can lead to the creation of coherent lines of enquiry, where one response builds on another to deepen understanding;
- probing questions and redirecting questions to other pupils are also helpful strategies in developing cumulation.

Cumulation: evaluating and building on pupils' responses through careful listening so that pupils' answers are built into subsequent questions to create a 'chain' of coherent enquiry.

Research has indicated that teachers tend to address questions mainly to the V-shaped wedge in the centre of the room (Brown and Wragg, 1993), so that care needs to be taken to ensure the involvement of as many pupils as possible, through the use of directed questions, rather than the 'hands-up' approach.

It is not necessarily easy for teachers to engage in dialogic teaching. In one case study, outlined in the GTCE *Research for Teachers* summary: 'Effective talk in the primary school', mentioned above (**http://www.gtce.org.uk/teachers/rft/talk_prim0506/**):

Probing questions: questions that encourage respondents to think more deeply or provide additional information or justification.

> Teachers found it hard at first to relinquish control of the classroom talk and to adopt instead, a type of dialogue in which responsibility for the dialogue was shared with the pupils. Teachers needed to walk a fine line between feeding in ideas and developing discussions that had got stuck in a loop and taking over.

WORKING IN THE CLASSROOM

Based on your observations, or reflection on your own teaching, can you think of an example where pupils' responses were extended through techniques such as probing or chaining?

Which aspects of the primary curriculum, or your subject area, do you feel would benefit most from the use of cognitive methods?

Social models of learning (DfES, 2007) involve different forms of collaborative group work. Group work offers opportunities for:

- focused input by the teacher to scaffold learning;
- peer scaffolding as learners collaboratively discuss or investigate issues;
- the development of a range of social skills, including the use of turn taking, active listening, supportive questioning and respectful response to the ideas of others.

Both the Primary and Key Stage 3 Strategies promote the use of group work as an essential feature of learning, and additionally the Primary Strategy emphasises the importance of supporting pupils to develop the necessary skills for effective discussion. These ground rules will continue to need reinforcement in Key Stage 3.

Photo 8.2
The focus of collaborative group work needs to challenge and motivate learners. This requires careful planning and an effective introduction to the task

Source: Pearson Education Ltd/ Ann Cromack. Ikat Design

Even when pupils have been adequately prepared, genuinely collaborative group work remains a very challenging strategy to implement, given the range of learning needs, pupil abilities and personalities often found in the average classroom. Some factors which are more likely to lead to successful learning include:

- Making the goals of the activity clear, and ensuring that pupils have a shared understanding of the outcomes within the group, and are aware of success criteria.
- Depending on the activity involved, pupils should be encouraged to develop an action plan before commencing the task.
- During the activity itself, pupils should be encouraged to review progress against the action plan, and intended outcomes and success criteria.
- On completion, pupils should consolidate their learning by reviewing the process and evaluating the quality of the outcome, or summarising what they have learned.

OVER TO YOU

How can a range of learning *styles* be accommodated within social models of learning?

Is it better to form groups on the basis of our understanding of pupils' preferred styles in order to allow them to capitalise on strengths?

Alternatively, should we deliberately look for opportunities to encourage pupils to move outside their 'comfort zone'?

What other factors will we need to consider, in addition to preferred learning style, if we adopt this approach?

Personalisation and learning to learn

Personalised learning/ personalisation: Current policy developments towards enabling education to match the needs and interests of learners.

The **personalisation** agenda includes attention to more than just individual learning styles and we will be considering some of the other aspects, identified by David Miliband (2004) in the earlier extract, in Chapter 10 and also in the final part of this book. An awareness of each individual's preferred approaches to learning, and perhaps the need to support them in extending their repertoire of styles, is undoubtedly an important element in ensuring that each of our pupils can reach their potential. The significant theme underpinning personalisation is that of *informed choice*. The implication of this is that pupils need to develop their own understanding of how they learn, and of the advantages and possible disadvantages of particular learning styles in different contexts. As we have already discussed, labelling, or attributing apparently fixed learning styles to pupils, can only be counter-productive in terms of this development.

There are several important aspects connected with helping pupils develop their meta-cognitive awareness – understanding how they learn. A very significant aspect is the effective use of formative assessment, explored in Chapter 10 of this book, but other aspects include developing personal qualities or dispositions such as 'resilience' and 'resourcefulness' as well as being able to learn along with others and to reflect on learning (Claxton, 2002). Engaging pupils in reflective discussion about their own learning in a range of contexts, as advocated in the Primary and Key Stage 3 Strategies, is an important part of this process. This includes pupils reflecting on their participation, and that of others, in group activities, as well as providing feedback on their individual learning experiences. The use of mechanisms such as 'traffic lights,' 'smiley faces' or 'thumbs up' is now common in many schools, particularly in primary classrooms, but such responses carry little value unless they are interrogated by the teachers. Engaging with personalisation and utilising learning style theory to move learning forward requires a listening and analytical stance in order to build on what our pupils tell us about their learning.

SUMMARY

This chapter has considered a range of theories about learning styles. These have included cognitive theories which are focused on how information is processed and theories about preferred learning strategies, which focus on how individuals approach learning tasks. We have taken a more critical stance towards some popular approaches to 'learning styles' which claim to be based in scientific evidence. In many cases, there is little or no evidence from research to support some of the claims made by these approaches, which should therefore be treated with caution.

We have also considered some recent evidence from neuroscience, which may help us review some assumptions about teaching and learning, particularly with young adolescents. We have also discussed the implications for learning and learning styles of three main approaches to teaching: direct teaching models, cognitive models and social models. Each of these has strengths and can support different kinds of learning, and will also impact differently on pupils' preferred learning styles. Thus we have emphasised the importance of helping to develop pupils' meta-cognitive understanding of their own learning approaches, and of the potential benefits of other approaches, in order to extend their choice of learning strategies.

TAKING YOUR PRACTICE FURTHER

Although you will decide for yourself how much emphasis you wish to place on different ideas about learning styles, this might be a good opportunity for you to review your own beliefs or assumptions about your pupils and about your own teaching, or to consider the implications of the views of teachers whom you have observed.

- Do you tend to categorise individuals in terms of the ways they learn, or have you observed other teachers doing this, even inadvertently?

- Do you sometimes deliberately encourage pupils to approach learning in a different way, or have you observed this in the classroom? If so, how are pupils supported to ensure they do not become discouraged or de-motivated?

- Do you involve pupils in discussion about how they learn, as well as what they learn, or have you observed this in school?

- Do you feel you have (or might have) a predominant teaching approach? Remember that the research of Mroz *et al.* indicated that teachers were actually teaching in the same ways as before, even though they appeared to be implementing new approaches. You might find it useful to work with your mentor, or another teacher as a peer observer, to examine this question.

TAKING YOUR THINKING FURTHER

The concept of 'personalisation' has been developed in a number of ways since David Miliband's North of England speech in 2004, quoted at the start of this chapter.

How has it been translated into action through different policy developments over the past 5 years?

You might want to consider areas such as:

- developments in the National Strategies (see DfES, 2007 for example);
- changes to the curriculum;
- changes to assessment (see Chapter 10);
- increasing pupil participation in education (see Chapter 15).

How do these developments relate to the ideas expressed by educational writers such as Charles Leadbeater (2004) and those explored by the National College of School Leadership (NCSL, 2005)?

Find out more

If you want to find out more about learning styles:

A number of general textbooks have chapters or sections on learning styles:

Woolfolk, A. (2008) *Psychology in Education*. Harlow: Pearson.

Pritchard, A. (2005) *Ways of Learning; Learning Theories and Learning Styles in the Classroom*. London: Fulton.

Hoult, S. (2005) *Secondary Reflective Reader: Professional Studies*. Exeter: Learning Matters.

Capel, S., Leask, M. and Turner, T. (2005) *Learning to Teach in the Secondary School*, 4th edn. London: Routledge.

If you want to find out more about how neuroscientific research can help educational understanding:

Blakemore, S.-J., and Frith, U. (2005) *The Learning Brain*. Oxford: Blackwell.

This very accessible book explains how neuroscientists examine the brain, and is honest about the limitations of neuroscience as far as education is concerned. It has chapters on focusing on the brain and literacy, the brain and mathematics, and reading difficulties as well as on the operation of memory and adolescent brain development.

The Teaching and Learning Research Programme (TLRP) has published a helpful booklet on neuroscience and education, which examines what is currently known about the brain that has relelvance for education, and also examines some of the popular theories also discussed in this chapter.

Howard-Jones, P. (2006) *Neuroscience and Education: Issues and Opportunities. A Commentary by the Teaching and Learning Research Programme*. Available at: **www.tlrp.org/pub/commentaries.html**.

The General Teaching Council for England has published a summary of a lengthy international review on neuroscience, drawing on a number of research projects. The summary contains several case studies of linked research showing educational relevance and also addresses a number of 'neuromyths' – such as the idea that we only use 10% of our brains, or that learners can be regarded as 'left brained' or 'right brained'. Available at: **www.gtce.org.uk/teachers/rft/neuroscience/**.

If you want to find out more about effective questioning strategies, including dialogic teaching approaches:

Alexander, R.J. (2008) *Towards Dialogic Teaching: Rethinking Classroom Talk*. York: Dialogos.

This booklet was first published in 2004 and there have been three further editions. The fourth edition of March 2008 has additional material and recommendations for further reading. The booklet provides detailed guidance on developing dialogic talk in classrooms and spells out the differences between this approach and the more common forms of classroom dialogue.

Brown, G. and Wragg, E. (1993) *Questioning*. London: Routledge.

Despite the date of publication, this book is still a classic text on the area of questioning. It identifies different types of question and their value for learning, and emphasises the importance of 'take-up time' – that is, allowing pupils time to reflect on their answers before being expected to respond to higher-order questions.

There is also a Teachers' TV programme with Ted Wragg on questioning: programme ID 11807, which suggests that teachers, rather than pupils, still take up most of the classroom talk time and that little has changed since the research on which the book above was based.

There is also an EPPI systematic review on 'What characterises effective teacher initiated teacher–pupil dialogue to promote conceptual understanding in mathematics lessons in England in Key Stages 2 and 3', published in 2008. This can be accessed via **www.ttrb.ac.uk** article ID 14241. The findings suggest that teacher–pupil interaction in mathematics is largely confined to traditional short response and feedback patterns rather than more extended use of talk.

Glossary

Behaviourist: a theory of learning based on the idea that our behaviour is shaped by the feedback (or 'reinforcement') we receive. In school contexts this often takes the form of pupils being rewarded for successful learning (merit points, prizes etc.) and the application of sanctions if behaviour is not satisfactory.

Closed questions: questions for which there is either a single right answer, or questions that are answerable by yes/no responses.

Cognitive learning theory: a theory that seeks to explain how learners process information.

Corpus callosum: a mass of fibres located in the middle of the brain which connects the two hemispheres and allows communication between them.

Cumulation: evaluating and building on pupils' responses through careful listening so that pupils' answers are built into subsequent questions to create a 'chain' of coherent enquiry.

Drill learning: the learning of facts through memorisation, reinforced by repetition. Sometimes also called rote learning.

Dialogic teaching: a term coined by Robin Alexander to denote a particular approach to teaching through talk which operates to stimulate and extend pupils' thinking through the disciplined use of key strategies (see **www.robinalexander.org.uk/dialogicteaching**).

Experiential learning: involves making meaning, or developing understanding, from direct experience, sometimes called 'learning by doing'.

Induction: in education, the process by which the learner develops their own conceptual understanding by being supported to generalise, or recognise causal connections, or draw analogies with previous experience.

Lesioned: deliberately cut. In this context the term refers to very rare brain operations on patients with severe epilepsy, where cutting through the **corpus callosum** alleviates the major symptoms.

Meta-cognition: being aware of how we think and behave in learning situations. Ultimately this implies active control over the process of thinking, for example: planning the way to approach a learning task, monitoring comprehension, and evaluating progress towards the completion of a task.

Open questions: questions with more than one possible answer, or questions designed to encourage reflection and further thought.

Personalised learning/personalisation: this is now a widely used term in a range of contexts. Broadly, it reflects current policy developments towards enabling education to match the needs and interests of learners more closely than in the past, through a number of initiatives, many of which are discussed in this book. See **www.ttrb.ac.uk** article id 12406 for a commentary on the concept of 'personalised learning' with further links to other resources.

Probing questions: questions that encourage respondents to think more deeply or provide additional information or justification.

Strategy learning: learning based in the developing and understanding of problem-solving strategies, rather than memorisation (see drill learning above).

VAK: the acronym used to refer to the theory that learners have preferred ways of receiving information through the senses: visual, auditory or kinaesthetic.

References

Adey, P. and Shayer, M. (1994) *Really Raising Standards*. London: Routledge.

Alexander, R. (2006) *Towards Dialogic Teaching: Rethinking Classroom Talk*, 3rd edn. York: Dialogos.

Ausubel, D.P. (2000) *The Acquisition and Retention of Knowledge: A Cognitive View*. Boston, MA: Kluwer Academic Press.

Brown, G. and Wragg, E. (1993) *Questioning*. London: Routledge.

Ciarocchi, J., Forgas, J. and Mayer, J. (eds) (2001) *Emotional Intelligence in Everyday Life: A Scientific Enquiry*. Philadelphia: Psychology Press.

Claxton, G. (2002) *Building Learning Power*. Bristol: TLO Ltd.

DfES (2007) *Pedagogy and Personalisation*. London: DfES.

Fredrickson, B. (2001) The role of positive emotions in positive psychology; the broaden and build theory of positive emotions, *American Psychologist*, Vol. 56, No. 3: pp. 218–26.

Gardner, H. (1999) *Intelligence Reframed: Multiple Intelligences for the 21st Century*. New York: Basic Books.

GTCE (April 2009) Neuroscience. Available at: **http://www.gtce.org.uk/teachers/rft/neuroscience/**.

Honey, P. and Mumford, A. (1986) *Using Your Learning Styles*. Maidenhead: Peter Honey.

Honey, P. and Mumford, A. (1992) *The Manual of Learning Styles*. Maidenhead: Peter Mumford.

Howard-Jones, P. (2006) *Neuroscience and Education: Issues and Opportunities*. Teaching and Learning Research Programme, Institute of Education.

Kratzig, G.P. and Arbuthnott, K.D. (2006) Perceptual learning style and learning proficiency: a test of the hypothesis, *Journal of Educational Psychology*, Vol. 98, No. 1: pp. 238–246.

Leadbeater, C. (2004) *Learning about Personalisation. How can we put the learner at the heart of the system*. DfES. Available via: **www.teachernet.gov.uk** online publications or **www.innovation-unit.co.uk**.

Miliband, D, (2004) North of England speech. Available at: **http://www.innovation-unit.co.uk/about-us/background/north-of-england-speech.html**.

Mroz, M., Smith, F. and Hardman, F. (2000) The discourse of the Literacy Hour, *Cambridge Journal of Education*, Vol. 30, No. 3: pp. 379–390.

NCSL (2005) *Leading Personalised Learning in Schools*. Nottingham: NCSL. Available at: **www.teachernet.gov.uk**.

Riding, R. and Raynor, S. (1998) *Learning Styles and Strategies*. London: Fulton.

Smith, A. (1996) *Accelerated Learning in the Classroom*. Stafford: Network Educational Press.

Smith, A. (1998) *Accelerated Learning in Practice*. Stafford: Network Educational Press.

Smith, H. and Higgins, S. (2006) Opening classroom interaction: the importance of feedback, *Cambridge Journal of Education*, Vol. 36, No. 4: pp. 485–502.

Smith, M.K. (2001) 'David A. Kolb on experiential learning', *The Encyclopaedia of Informal Education*. Available at www.infed.org/biblio/b-explrn.htm

In this chapter you will:

- Consider the differences between 'behaviour management' and 'behaviour for learning' approaches
- Consider how approaches to behaviour management are embedded in a broader set of values and beliefs about learning
- Develop your understanding of strategies to support learning behaviours
- Reflect on the importance of 'emotional intelligence' in relation to behaviour and learning

What would you do?

You have just settled the class down to work quietly and independently when Kieran arrives late. He flings the door open and pushes past several pupils to get to his usual seat without acknowledging your presence.

Do you:

- Say loudly 'Kieran, how dare you come in like that? Get up, go back out and come in properly. What should you say to me?'

- Ignore him until he has settled in his seat and then go to him quietly explain the task.

- Follow him to his seat and say quietly but clearly, 'Kieran, what are the rules when people come in late? Right now I want you to get on with this task, but I need you to stay behind at the end of the lesson so that we can talk about this'.

What might you need to know about Kieran in order to select an appropriate course of action?
What will Kieran learn from each of these responses?
What will other pupils in the class learn?
What does each response say about your priorities as a teacher?

Introduction

The purpose of this chapter is to focus on approaches which encourage behaviour that promotes learning, rather than on strategies for controlling or managing behaviour that is unacceptable to the teacher. This is not to say that teachers, and schools, do not need systems and strategies for classroom discipline, but that the underpinning values of these systems and strategies can result in very different outcomes in terms of pupil learning.

This book, and others in the series, has taken the view that one of the aims of education is to enable learners to become autonomous, socially responsible individuals. The foundations for these qualities are laid in the early years of schooling and reinforced during the primary and early secondary school phases: encouraging the development of behaviours for learning is an important part of the process. The following extract is taken from a review of research literature about learning and behaviour that we will consider in more detail later in this chapter:

> The stance taken by the review team, informed from background literature, was that there is an interdependent relationship between behaviour and learning. . . . The team also held the view that the fostering of learning behaviour or 'behaviour for learning' is the foundation for effective behaviour management. This contrasts with a view that 'learning to behave' is the central focus of behaviour management in schools.
>
> *(Powell and Tod, 2004: 82)*

The use of the term 'learning behaviour' is important, in that it seeks to reduce the perception that promoting learning and managing behaviour are two separate issues.

It serves to shift the focus from unwanted behaviours to those behaviours that are necessary for learning in group settings.

The management of pupil behaviour is an aspect of professional practice which is high on most teachers' agendas. For new teachers and teacher trainees this is particularly the case, as surveys of Newly Qualified Teachers (NQTs) indicate. Rightly, the Professional Standards for Teachers: Qualified Teacher Status (QTS) require new teachers to know a range of strategies for managing behaviour, and to be able to employ these to maintain an orderly learning environment. However, the Professional Standards go further than this: new teachers are expected to 'manage learners' behaviour constructively and promote their self-control and independence' (Q31: TDA, 2007). This emphasises how important it is to consider what else we may be teaching through the strategies we employ in order to bring about an orderly environment. As the initial activity suggests, we need to consider the messages we might inadvertently convey about teaching and learning.

OVER TO YOU

What values and beliefs about teaching and learning might be embedded in terms such as 'behaviour management' and 'classroom control'? How might these terms position both the teacher and the learner?

The implication might be that it is the teacher, rather than the learner, who is doing the managing and controlling. The learner is implicitly seen as someone who is unable to take responsibility for their own learning behaviour, or who actively wishes to avoid learning. Inevitably, this conception of the learner will also relate to perspectives on learning and to the teaching and learning strategies employed within the classroom.

'Discipline' and control

Bill Rogers, a well-known writer in the field of behaviour management, points out the distinction between discipline and control (Rogers, 1997). According to Rogers, discipline involves pupils' agreement to, or acceptance of, the behaviours which are appropriate in the learning context, whereas control implies that all the power remains in the hands of the teacher. Establishing discipline in this sense may take time, but will ultimately be more fruitful in terms of creating a learning environment than the continued operation of control strategies.

Of course, as a trainee teacher or a teacher encountering a new class you have to establish yourself as someone capable of bringing about a disciplined learning environment. This establishment phase is significant in fostering the development of a learning community within the class or group, which will, in turn, support learning behaviours. For the trainee teacher, who does not always meet the class at the start of a school year, this phase normally involves identifying and employing the already established routines of the class, and of the school's discipline policy. For the new teacher this phase will coincide with the start of the new school year and will be an important part of the development of a long-term relationship: not just between teacher and pupils, but between the pupils and learning.

Schools will vary in the amount of autonomy granted to individual teachers; there will already be a whole-school behaviour policy in place, which may be more or less detailed according to context. Whether you are a trainee or a new teacher, you need to demonstrate consistency with existing practice within the school. However, in both cases the employment of these existing routines needs to be accompanied by critical reflection. You should consider (and preferably discuss with colleagues) *why* these approaches have been adopted, and evaluate how far they can be employed to support the development of learning behaviours. Understandably, as a new or a trainee teacher, or someone facing a challenging situation, you may look for quick solutions, but unless strategies are located within an overall framework, which is consistently upheld, the evidence is that they will cease to be effective within a very short time.

Rogers (1997) identifies three types of discipline: preventative, corrective and supportive:

- Preventative discipline strategies aim to minimise the opportunities for disruption to occur.
- Corrective strategies are those which are employed to correct behaviour which is deemed to be disruptive.
- Supportive discipline strategies are those which seek to correct behaviour in such a way that a positive classroom atmosphere is maintained.

Corrective discipline strategies are the least successful in the long term. They frequently focus on negative rather than positive factors and may contribute to poor self-esteem and motivation in some pupils. Corrective strategies are characterised by the use of sanctions or the threat of sanctions as a major strategy for classroom control, and by negative language use ('Stop talking' 'Don't get out of your seat'). In some circumstances, the use of corrective strategies can exacerbate tensions within the classroom and increase disruption, rather than reduce it. Even where they appear to be effective in maintaining an apparently orderly classroom, it is less likely that a predominantly corrective approach will create an environment in which learning behaviours can be developed.

WORKING IN THE CLASSROOM

Reflect on the strategies you have observed in schools, or used in your own teaching, and try to locate each of them under one of these three headings. What does this activity tell you about the underlying approach to behaviour management?

The messages from key literature in the field of behaviour management are consistent: in order to establish and maintain a positive environment that will support learning you need to plan for it. Although there may be teachers who intuitively or charismatically maintain order, a consciously developed plan which identifies the development of learning behaviour as its focus is more likely to be effective.

Establishing a positive learning environment: preventative and supportive strategies

Chapter 6 emphasised the importance of the varieties of knowledge for teaching which support effective professional practice. Your own subject knowledge and your knowledge of the range of effective teaching strategies within the subject will underpin effective lesson planning. Additionally, your understanding of what you can expect from pupils within the age and ability range you are teaching is also important. Fundamentally, if your lesson is not matched to the needs of the pupils, and does not have the potential to engage their interest and motivate them to learn, difficulties with pupil behaviour are more likely to result. This should go without saying.

Organisational planning will also be important, in terms of ensuring resources are ready and that you have considered the most effective (i.e. least disruptive) way to distribute them when they are needed. Any additional adults who may be in the classroom may require briefing in respect of their roles and responsibilities during the lesson. You may also wish to consider the physical arrangement of the classroom in relation to the demands of the planned lesson. Will there be room for pupils to move easily, if this is going to be necessary? If pair or group work is part of the lesson, does the arrangement of furniture help or hinder this process, and how will pupils be helped to maintain their engagement with the lesson if some alteration to arrangements is necessary? These issues were considered in Chapter 7.

Planning the lesson content and the organisation are both forms of preventative discipline. There are other forms of preventative planning which could also have an impact on the success of your teaching, and these might be less obvious.

Consider the possible effects on the classroom environment and learning of:

- planning to meet and greet particular pupils in a positive way as they enter the classroom;
- planning how you will deal with pupils who arrive late to your lesson, to minimse disruption;
- planning how you will deal with pupils who do not have the required equipment to carry out a task;
- planning how you will deal with pupils who are returning after absence, or who may return;
- identifying likely opportunities to praise pupils for maintaining expected behaviour (e.g. settling to work quickly; moving from the carpet to tables in the primary classroom);
- consciously looking for opportunities to use descriptive praise with individual pupils who appear to be making progress in their learning behaviour (e.g. 'Well done S, you have remembered to put your hand up every time today');
- congratulating the class for specific learning behaviour at the end of the lesson (e.g. 'You worked well with your talking partners today, thank you').

Source: Based on Ellis and Tod (2009)

In almost all lessons there will be points at which pupils may lose focus if you have not considered how you will manage the situation. This will depend on how well established certain 'learning behaviours' are within the class. To some extent, this will also depend on how well you know the pupils, but there are some fairly predictable occasions where good planning is likely to minimise low-level misbehaviour.

THINKING IT THROUGH

This is a list of possible 'learning behaviours' that pupils will need to have developed to ensure the smooth operation of a lesson:

Waiting their turn   Accessing equipment   Sharing a space
Listening to others   Problem solving if stuck   Sharing equipment
Listening to others and the teacher   Working with others in a group
Ignoring distractions   Responding to teacher questions

Which will they need to apply at the different points of the following lesson?

Teacher input to whole class or
Teacher input to whole class on carpet

Moving to tables

Independent task

Group task

Plenary

How would you work to strengthen any learning behaviours that were not well established?

Supportive discipline strategies are those which seek to maintain pupils' sense of self-worth, while also requiring them to recognise agreed rules and routines. There are a number of well-known texts on behaviour management that explore such strategies in depth, indicated in the section on Further Reading at the end of this chapter. Some valuable advice using real-life case studies is also provided on *Teachers' TV*, also listed at the end of this chapter.

Supportive discipline strategies are rooted in the development of an effective relationship between teacher and pupils. In most classrooms this is established through the implementation of some key principles:

- Establishing shared principles for behaviour, based on learning.
- Establishing and maintaining clear expectations, generally expressed as rules and routines.
- Using positive language to give directions about behaviour.
- Maintaining a positive body stance.

Behaviourist: a theory of learning based on the idea that our behaviour is shaped by the feedback (or 'reinforcement') we receive.

Assertive discipline: a term given to particular form of 'behaviour management' system first developed in the USA by Lee and Marlene Canter. Lee Canter was a psychiatric social worker.

Extrinsic: in this case, external to the learner, as opposed to the internal satisfaction of doing good work or maintaining effective learning behaviour.

- Offering pupils the choice to behave responsibly, and *providing take-up time* (this means giving pupils sufficient time to make their choice without losing face; Rogers, 2002; Hook and Vass, 2002).
- Providing *motivational feedback*: such as 'I like the start of your story. I wonder what the children felt when . . .'.
- Avoiding confrontation through the use of techniques such as *partial agreement* (for example, if a pupil objects to a reminder about behaviour, saying that other people have done the same thing: 'Maybe they did but I need you to . . .').
- Using rewards and sanctions in a consistent manner.
- Being prepared to admit to mistakes if they are genuine – and saying sorry!

It has been argued (e.g. Porter, 2007; Kohn, 2001) that strategies for classroom management which adopt a strongly **behaviourist** approach, such as some versions of '**assertive discipline**,' do not have a lasting effect on either behaviour or motivation, despite the fact that they apparently encourage positive behaviours. These methods involve the use of **extrinsic** motivational strategies, whereby individuals earn points towards tangible rewards for the whole class. The awarding of points is made in a public manner, using individual names in order to make clear the desirable behaviour to the rest of the class, since behaviorist approaches operate on the basis of positive reinforcement. However, research indicates that pupils generally prefer to receive both praise and rebuke in private rather than through public means such as names on the board (Kendall-Seatter, 2005). It is also the case the some 'rewards' could be seen as undermining other values promoted by the school. For example, having time off lessons by earning 'golden time' as a reward might well convey the message that lessons are not seen as valuable by the school.

Photo 9.1 Positive relationships can be fostered through the use of quiet praise or reminders of acceptable behaviour, rather than more public interventions

Source: Pearson Education Ltd/ Ian Wedgewood

OVER TO YOU

Most schools do find it necessary to use extrinsic reward systems to support their behaviour policies. What learning implications might there be for these types of reward, all of which have been used within primary or secondary schools?

- The award of points to individuals leading to the award of a certificate in an assembly.
- Chocolate.
- Points awarded to individuals being collected on behalf of the class to earn a class treat: such as a cake and soft drink 'party' at the end of term, or similar event selected by the pupils.
- Money.
- Points awarded to individuals being allocated to teams or 'houses'.
- The award of points to individuals leading to a congratulatory postcard being sent home, or similar system.

Which of the above would you wish to use yourself (depending on the age of the pupils with whom you are concerned) and why?

CASE STUDY

Private rewards – public results

The 'Steer Report' was commissioned by the government to identify good practice and make further recommendations on improving behaviour in schools. The author was Sir Alan Steer, a former head teacher with a successful record in this area. This extract is taken from the report (DfES, 2005: 18) as an example of effective practice.

> We introduced reward postcards. Each day every teacher was expected to send one reward postcard home to a set of parents/carers. The focus for the reward would change on a weekly basis to ensure that the widest possible number of students became eligible.
>
> One week the focus might be on best homework produced, on another biggest improvement in effort, or highest quality of work achieved today. This had the effect of improving relationships with parents who were tired of receiving letters and phone calls when things went wrong.

This is a good example of the type of positive relationship building with parents that was discussed in Chapter 3.

Acceptable and unacceptable behaviour

It would be highly surprising if you have not already experienced differing expectations of acceptable behaviour in different schools and even classes within the same school, either in your own experience as a pupil or during your training. The same 'lively' class can be regarded positively by one colleague and as challenging or even disruptive by another. While the school's behaviour policy establishes a baseline for expectations, there can still be a wide spectrum of interpretation within this framework. Where does this leave individual pupils, in terms of developing their own understanding of appropriate behaviours in learning contexts?

In some classrooms, pupils' understanding of what is, or is not, acceptable is based on their experience of the teacher's expectations, rather than being rooted in broader principles related to their own learning and the learning of others. Pupils across the 7–14 age range will vary in their ability to appreciate and articulate the factors which support learning, but they should all have the opportunity to contribute to the discussion. Supportive discipline strategies, mentioned above, usually include opportunities for teacher and pupils to agree on a set of positive behaviours which will support learning. These discussions need to be set within the context of the whole-school policy, but also contextualised for the particular classroom or subject area. The differing demands placed on pupils by the organisation of space or the specific activities required in some subject areas mean that the conventions for effective participation need to be established and rehearsed before strategies such as 'rule reminding' can be effective.

WORKING IN THE CLASSROOM

Consider classroom(s) or subject area(s) with which you are familiar.

How do the environment or the subject-specific pedagogies impact on learning behaviours?

What strategies have you observed, or used yourself, to engage pupils in differentiating their learning behaviours according to context?

Qualifications and Curriculum Development Agency (QCDA): the official body responsible for all aspects of curriculum development and statutory assessment in England. It is sponsored by the Department for Children Schools and Families (DCSF).

QCDA (2001) set out benchmarks for identifying acceptable and unacceptable behaviour in order to move away from more arbitrary personal judgements by teachers. Criteria are established for assessing learning, conduct and emotional behaviours, so that these can be accurately and consistently described. This enables clearer targets to be set and also helps to maintain the focus on the behaviour, not the pupil, which avoids negative labelling (**http://www.qca.org.uk/downloads/pupils_emot_behav_diff.pdf**).

Although clear description of unacceptable behaviours is very important, this does not in itself indicate which strategies will be most appropriate to support the development of more positive behaviour in the pupil. Hayes (2004: 266) identifies three broad categories of unacceptable behaviour in primary age pupils:

- those who are regularly mischievous, but are generally harmless;
- those who misbehave willfully;
- those who are non-conformists.

Hayes argues that teachers need to be careful to distinguish between non-conformism and wilful misbehaviour. In the first instance the pupil may not recognise the need to conform, or have sufficient maturity to be able to do so. In the second case the pupil is aware of the rules and possible consequences, but makes a deliberate choice to mis-behave. The same behaviour observed in two different pupils (such as unacceptable movement around the classroom) might thus have a different explanation and require a different response.

OVER TO YOU

How helpful do you think these categories are?

What attitude towards a pupil might be implied by the phrase 'wilful misbehaviour'?

Hayes identifies these categories in the primary school context. Do they also apply to younger secondary pupils?

How would your use of strategies differ in each case?

Maintaining a learning atmosphere

If a key principle in your classroom is that of encouraging learning rather than merely controlling unacceptable behaviour, then strategies which maintain a learning atmos-phere will be important. If you frequently interrupt the class in order to focus on individuals, even if this is to praise rather than correct behaviour, you will disrupt the general learning atmosphere. For some pupils such interruptions break concentration, lower motivation and may even lead to off-task behaviours. You should always aim to deploy the least intrusive strategy available for positive correction and to maintain learning behaviour. An intrusive strategy is one which is likely to interrupt the learn-ing of pupils other than the individuals whose behaviour is not conducive to learning.

THINKING IT THROUGH

Re-order the following strategies from least to most intrusive – some of these strategies could be used in combination:

- Moving to the area of the classroom near the pupil(s) concerned
- Identifying the pupil(s) by name with a rule reminder* or behavioural direction+, across the classroom

THINKING IT THROUGH: *CONTINUED*

- 'Tactical ignoring' followed by positive reinforcement if the pupil returns to task
- Making eye contact with the pupil ('the look')
- Approaching the pupil(s) and identifying them by name with a rule reminder or behavioural direction
- Publicly praising a nearby pupil for desired behaviour
- Approaching the pupil(s) and reminding them of the consequences of further misbehaviour – allow 'take-up' time
- The 'look' plus recognised non-verbal signal such as rotating hand for 'face the front'
- Quietly approaching the pupil(s) and asking them how they are getting on with the work
- Offering the pupil(s) a controlled choice of behaviour, plus 'take-up' time

*A 'rule reminder' example: 'Peter, what is our rule for asking for help?'
+ A behavioural direction example: 'Sally facing the front, thanks'

Source: Based on the work of Rogers (2002) and Hook and Vass (2002)

There will inevitably be those pupils whose first response is to deny the action, or to point out that other pupils initiated the problem. This type of response is particularly common with older primary and secondary pupils entering adolescence, with its attendant resistance to authority. It is important to remain focused on the key outcome – engaging the pupil with the learning task – and not to be distracted by these 'secondary behaviours'. Common advice in these situations is to offer partial agreement – 'Maybe you didn't, but I need you to face the front now. Thanks.' Hook and Vass (2002) suggest that the frame 'maybe . . . and' is more effective than 'maybe . . . but'. Each has its uses in different situations.

Unfortunately, there will sometimes be occasions when the unacceptable behaviour continues, despite rule reminders and reminders of the consequences of continued misbehaviour. This may be due to a lack of self-control on the part of the pupil or to what Hayes (2004) refers to as 'wilful' misbehaviour. If you have already established clear rules for learning behaviour with the class as a whole, and have used the 'rule reminder' strategy with the pupil(s) concerned, it is unlikely that the unacceptable behaviour is due to a lack of understanding about appropriate behaviour convention. You may then have no option but to invoke the sanctions which are part of the behaviour policy of the school.

Sanctions have not proved to have a long-lasting effect on pupils' behaviour, however. As Mujis and Reynolds (2001) note, there is no guarantee that the unacceptable behaviour will not be repeated for other teachers, or that the pupil will engage more fully with learning as a result. Where pupils are disaffected, lack self-control or find it difficult to interact effectively with others, the use of sanctions will offer only a temporary respite, not a solution. A longer-term approach may be required, involving a consideration of the range of factors which may be affecting the pupil's learning behaviour.

RESEARCH BRIEFING: WHAT ARE THE CAUSES OF INAPPROPRIATE LEARNING BEHAVIOURS?

Educational researchers Sacha Powell and Janet Tod (2004) undertook a **systematic review** of research into how theories explain learning behaviours in school contexts. The purpose of the review was to support trainee teachers in developing their understanding of the behaviour of pupils, as opposed to merely seeking strategies to control unwanted behaviour. The review involved an examination of 46 research studies, and in-depth analysis of five studies which were identified as having a high evidence weighting (i.e. studies which were well designed and likely to produce trustworthy evidence).

The review process was informed by the view that learning and behaviour are interdependent and form a dynamic relationship. Evidence from the in-depth analysis of five studies supports this position, and suggests that 'learning behaviour develops from the interaction of the individual with contextual and social factors' (Powell and Tod, 2004: 83.) The reviewers identified three main types of learning behaviour observed in the research studies, and suggest that these can be placed in three *interdependent* categories.

Systematic review: an approach to examining a number of research articles or reports in order to evaluate the reliability of the evidence presented against a set of given criteria. Only research which meets the criteria is then discussed in the final review article. It has been argued that this approach sometimes excludes research that could offer valuable insights into difficult areas.

Product (on-task) centred learning behaviours	Participation (social) centred learning behaviours	Person centred learning behaviours
motivation	responsiveness	self-regard
self-discipline	participation	self-esteem
engagement with task	communication	independent activity
	collaboration	responsibility

Influences on the development of learning behaviours are not confined to the classroom. Powell and Tod (2004) identify a 'triangle of influence' of social, emotional and cognitive factors which have a reciprocal influence on learning behaviours. In Figure 9.1 these are identified as the social context in which the learner is placed, the feelings and interpretations of the learner (emotional factor) and the influences of the curriculum or task (cognitive factor). ▶

RESEARCH BRIEFING: *CONTINUED*

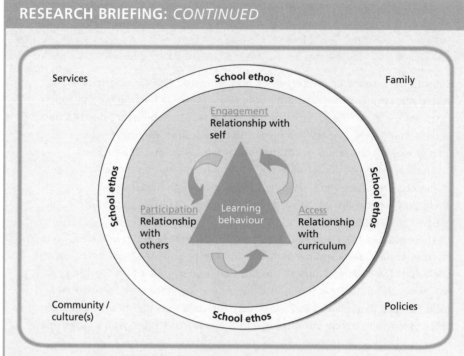

Figure 9.1 **Learning behaviour conceptual framework**
Source: Ellis and Tod (2009), adapted from Powell and Tod (2004)

The interdependence of the categories of learning behaviour and the need to consider all three corners of the triangle of influence mean that there is no 'one size fits all' approach which can be applied to supporting the development of learning behaviours.

The three relationships of the behaviour for learning triangle

Powell and Tod's research review (2004) suggests that there are three areas where learners may experience difficulty in developing effective learning behaviour, all of which need to be considered.

- Is the pupil willing and able to access, process and respond to the learning opportunities available though the curriculum?
- Is the pupil willing and able to interact socially and academically with others, including the teacher and other adults?
- Is the pupil willing and able to include themselves in the learning opportunities and relationship on offer in the classroom and wider school context? This relationship area includes how the learner feels about themselves, their self esteem, self-efficacy,

Self-esteem: how one *feels* about one's **self-concept**.

self-concept, resilience and their own perceptions of the relevance of school learning.

The terminology of 'willing and able' acts as a reminder that each of these three areas (or 'relationships' as they are termed by Powell and Tod, 2004) involves both dispositions (see Claxton, 2002) and skills.

Since the publication of the research review, Powell and Tod's initial ideas have been developed further in terms of the application of the behaviour for learning framework by Ellis and Tod (2009). At the level of day-to-day classroom practice this framework does not seek to replace or supersede existing positive approaches to behaviour management described by Rogers (e.g. 2002), Hook and Vass (2002) and others. Rather it encourages teachers to consider the extent to which their day-to-day behaviour management strategies impact positively on pupil learning. At this level of use, the emphasis for the class teacher is on ensuring that all aspects of their classroom practice protect, enhance but, at the very least, do not impact negatively on the three relationships within the framework.

By explicitly acknowledging the interdependence of social, emotional and cognitive aspects of learning, the behaviour for learning framework also enables teachers to make informed choices about which strategies are likely to be most effective for groups and individual pupils whose behaviour presents particular difficulties in the classroom. It is possible to identify the learning behaviour to promote and consider whether this would be best achieved by strategies and approaches that seek to develop or work via the learner's relationship with the curriculum, relationship with others or relationship with self. The following case study provides an introduction to this level of use. More detail on the core and extended use of the behaviour for learning conceptual framework is provided by Ellis and Tod (2009).

Self-efficacy: an individual's judgement of his/her ability to carry out a task or sustain behaviours that will lead to a certain outcome.

Self-concept: the set of beliefs about oneself, including attributes, roles, goals, interests, values and religious or political beliefs.

Resilience: the ability to accept being unsuccessful in a task, and to persist in attempting to master a skill or understanding.

CASE STUDY

Samantha – applying the framework of relationships

Samantha often disrupts lessons by talking to others around her, even when they are clearly engaged with their work. She gets out of her seat at inappropriate moments, and sometimes calls out while the teacher is talking.

Although Samantha appears to understand the subject matter of lessons, she is slow to produce written work. If required to stay behind after lessons, however, she can complete tasks to a reasonable standard.

She often forgets or loses items needed for school work, fails to complete homework and needs frequent reminders about the school conventions for presentation, such as use of underlined headings, date etc.

Samantha has not established long-lasting relationships with other pupils in her year group. In the past she has become 'best friends' with several different girls, but these friendships have often ended argumentatively when she has not had her own way. At this stage she has no apparently close friends, and some pupils in the class are noticeably reluctant to work with her as they find her behaviour distracting.

Source: Adapted from original scenario in Ellis and Tod (2009)

THINKING IT THROUGH

In your opinion, what learning behaviours should Samantha be helped to develop?

How do these relate to the table of learning behaviours suggested by Powell and Tod?

(For example, if you feel she needs to be supported to develop the product-centred behaviour of 'engagement with task', how might this relate to person-centred behaviours, such as 'responsibility' or 'self-esteem', and social-centred behaviours such as 'participation'?)

What strategies or interventions might you use to promote one of these learning behaviours?

For example, if you decided to work on social-centred behaviours you might plan a lesson that required small-group or paired activity. You would identify working pairs or groups, to avoid Samantha being rejected by others, and select pupil(s) whom you felt would sustain engagement with the task as Samantha's partner(s). You would identify clear roles for individual pair or group members, supporting these with checklists or similar resources.

This is just one example. What other approaches could be developed?

Emotional intelligence: generally taken to embrace both being self-aware about one's own emotions and likely reactions to different situations, and being able to respond appropriately towards others.

Emotional literacy: similar to emotional intelligence, but preferred by some writers (such as Weare, 2004) because the use of the term 'literacy' is felt to place greater emphasis on personal empowerment.

How important is 'emotional intelligence'?

You may recognise some elements of Powell and Tods' framework as being similar to the social, emotional and behavioural skills identified in the Behaviour and Attendance strand of the National Strategies as *Social and Emotional Aspects of Learning* (SEAL). These are based in the work of American psychology journalist Daniel Goleman (1996) in his influential book *Emotional Intelligence*. It is suggested that pupils with good social and emotional skills are more able to manage strong feelings and persist in the face of difficulties (DfES, 2003). These emotional skills enable them to be more effective learners both independently and collaboratively, as they are able to resolve conflicts, sustain friendships and work or play co-operatively.

In order to be able to manage feelings and to be resilient in the face of challenges, pupils need to be sufficiently self-aware to recognize their emotional condition and to employ strategies to manage their feelings, if necessary. This capacity is sometimes referred to as **emotional intelligence** (Goleman, 1996) or **emotional literacy** (Weare, 2004). It has become regarded as a significant aspect of positive behaviour management in schools (Weare, 2004). The relationship between emotional intelligence, self-regard and self-esteem is significant. An individual who does not value themselves as an individual or have a belief in their own ability is less likely to be motivated to succeed or to overcome difficulties. However, it should be noted that high self-esteem in itself is not necessarily positive in all circumstances. Pupils who bully others, or who abuse alcohol or drugs, have been identified as sometimes having high self-esteem, but not necessarily a realistic self-concept (Weare, 2004).

Teachers can support individual pupils to manage their anxiety or frustration by encouraging them to remain calm and approach tasks step by step and by reminding them of what they already know, which will help them with the task in hand. Careful use of motivational feedback will also help to counter negative responses in pupils with low self-esteem. This type of feedback is not the same as indiscriminate praise, which is eventually de-motivating (see Chapter 10 on Assessment for Learning), but nor does it imply that the work is lacking in some essential aspects.

Hook and Vass (2002) give the example 'What else could you add to the picture?' as an example of implicitly negative feedback. Contrast this approach with providing a factual description of what has been achieved, followed by encouragement to extend further: 'Good. You've included some detail on the type of furniture which would have been in the house. I wonder what other items might have been there to show the kind of person who lives there . . .'.

The *Social and Emotional Aspects of Learning* (SEAL) programme has been generally very well received in schools, and is now seen as contributing towards the 'well-being' of both staff and pupils. This voluntary programmme has a very comprehensive website area within the National Strategies site, as part of the *Behaviour and Attendance* strand: **http://nationalstrategies.standards.dcsf.gov.uk/inclusion/behaviourattendanceandseal**. The SEAL programme is based around five areas described as skills:

- Self-awareness
- Managing feelings
- Empathy

Photo 9.2
'Circle time' can give pupils an opportunity to explore and express their feelings about issues such as friendship or bullying

Source: Dan Sullivan/Alamy

Multiple intelligence: a concept developed by Howard Gardner (1983). The idea that humans possess a number of discrete 'intelligences' such as linguistics intelligence, musical intelligence, spatial intelligence. Gardner first proposed seven intelligences, but later increased this number.

- Motivation
- Social skills

These are based on the work of Goleman (1996) and the ideas of American psychologist Howard Gardner (1983) who developed the concept of 'multiple intelligence'. Gardner suggested that individuals possess a broader number of 'intelligences' than the dominant linguistic, mathematical and logical intelligences valued by society. Gardner's first book proposed musical, spatial and kinaesthetic intelligences, and also inter- and intra-personal intelligences. That is, the ability to understand other people and how to relate to them and the ability to understand oneself in order to function effectively in society. He did not intend his ideas to be applied directly to education, however, although his later writings have explored this connection (for example, Gardner and Hatch, 1989). Goleman integrated these last two 'intelligences' with some evidence from neuroscience and psychology research to produce his popular book.

OVER TO YOU

In training

What connections can you see between the three areas of relationship from the 'behaviour for learning' triangle of influence and the five areas of skill from the SEAL programme?

How far do you feel these skills can be developed as a separate aspect of the curriculum?

Starting your career

Select two or three pupils who appear to be having difficulties with aspects of learning, but who are not identified as having Special Educational Needs (SEN). Apply the framework of the 'behaviour for learning' triangle to each pupil. What adjustments could you make to your teaching to support the development of learning behaviours?

If the SEAL programme is used in your school, how can you draw on it to support these pupils?

Investigating teaching and learning

How helpful are notions of 'multiple intelligence' for education?

Gardner's ideas have been criticised for several reasons, and each of these areas are worthy of exploration in order to clarify how far we can adopt his theory.

Do they lead to labelling (s/he has a particular kind of intelligence) which could narrow the curriculum for a learner rather than broaden it?

Do they take developmental issues into account? A 5 year old might demonstrate more 'kinaesthetic intelligence' than a 50 year old!

Can they be measured? Gardner himself rejects the notion of testing for multiple intelligences, but there are many 'self-report' inventories available. How reliable are these?

What does neuroscience say about the idea of multiple intelligences? There is no current evidence for different pathways in the brain, corresponding to the different intelligences, as originally supposed.

Use one or more of the texts in the *Find Out More* section of this chapter to investigate these issues.

CONTROVERSY

Does emotional intelligence exist?

You may remember the article by Professor Frank Furedi, from Chapter 5, in which he expresses his concerns about the development of the 'therapeutic culture' in education.

Professor Guy Claxton from the University of Bristol, famous for his work on 'learning to learn' (Claxton, 2002), also has some reservations.

Claxton was asked to produce a booklet about Emotional Intelligence by the Association of Teachers and Lecturers (Claxton, 2005) in which he points out some of the difficulties and dangers of accepting the idea of emotional intelligence uncritically:

- He points out that by using terms such as 'intelligence' or 'literacy' alongside the word 'emotional' the impression is given that this is a respectable concept, but which also appeals to those who feel that the curriculum has gone too far in one direction. Nevertheless, these terms encompass such a broad range of attributes as to have very little meaning as concepts in their own right.

- There are no reliable measures of emotional intelligence. Students are often asked to complete self-report questionnaires, involving questions such as 'I am good at recognising other people's feelings'. However, when the results of self-report methods were compared with experiments where pupils were shown a number of photographs and asked to name the emotions, the correlation between their self-report scores and scores on this activity were low.

- The evidence that possessing emotional intelligence helps learning is variable. Being 'happy' can make people more creative, but also more careless and less logical. The emotions do indeed affect what and how people learn, but not necessarily in the slightly simplistic ways suggested by some emotional intelligence proponents. Claxton argues that we can carry the ideas too far: being resilient in the sense of being willing to try something more than once is a helpful trait, but refusing to give up might not be!

These are only some of the issues raised by Claxton, and you may wish to download this publication to read more. Full details are given at the end of this chapter.

Social and Emotional Aspects of Learning

The SEAL programme materials are careful to stress that the approach is not intended as therapy for pupils, nor are phrases such as 'happiness' used in relation to any of the materials. The ideas of both Claxton and Furedi should cause us to be cautious about claims for 'miraculous' changes in pupils' behaviour, but nevertheless there is some evidence to suggest that the systematic development of pupils' emotional and social competence within a whole-school context does have an effect. There is research evidence which links rates of exclusion with key policies on learning and behaviour (Hoult, 2005). Weare (2004) quotes Southampton City Local Authority exclusion statistics which declined from 113 in 1997 to 22 in 2000 as a result of a policy of placing emotional literacy 'at the heart of the process'.

The SEAL programmme in primary schools is designed to extend over the whole school year, and is supported by teaching materials based on seven themes such as 'Say no to bullying' and 'Good to be me'. The materials are developed so that these themes can be revisited with pupils at different ages, throughout the primary years. The SEAL materials extend into Key Stage 3, with a unit specifically designed for Year 7 called 'A Place to Learn' intended to support pupils during the transition period. Materials and teaching suggestions are provided for three more themes for Years 7, 8 and 9, which focus on motivation, social skills and empathy and managing feelings. The themes are also supported by assembly ideas. Depending on the school organisation, these materials can be used during pastoral periods, in 'form time' or in Personal, Social and Health Education (PSHE) periods.

However, SEAL is intended as a whole-school approach and not one that should be ignored by other subject teachers. All teachers should be aware of the ways in which the teaching and learning ethos in their classrooms supports motivation and fosters self-esteem and positive relationships: for example through the use of assessment for learning strategies (see Chapter 10) or methods for improving pupil participation (see Chapter 15). The ideas presented earlier in this chapter are intended to support this development. Nevertheless, just as with the ideas in the 'behaviour for learning' triangle, some pupils will be identified as needing additional support on either group or individual levels. These levels are referred to in the National Strategies as 'Wave 2' and 'Wave 3', where 'Wave 1' refers to high-quality provision for *all* pupils. Where pupils have been identified as Wave 2 or Wave 3 in terms of their needs within the SEAL framework, subject teachers need to be aware of ways in which they can build on the work that is being developed in focus group or individual sessions.

RESEARCH BRIEFING: WHAT WORKS IN DEVELOPING CHILDREN'S EMOTIONAL AND SOCIAL COMPETENCE AND WELL-BEING?

Katherine Weare and Gay Gray from the University of Southampton were commissioned to investigate this question. Their report involved a literature review, case studies, based on the work of five local authorities and interviews with teachers and other professionals (Weare and Gray, 2003).

The recommendations include advice to the DfES about prioritising work in this area (which has since been implemented through SEAL) and on actions for schools. These are:

- Taking a whole-school approach – aimed at all pupils, with additional support for those with behavioural and emotional problems (see Wave 2 and Wave 3 above).

- Ensuring coherence, teamwork and the involvement of parents: making sure that all agencies work together, as required by ECM.

- Starting early and taking a developmental approach: implementing programmes to support emotional and social competence *before* problems arise, and recognising that this is a long-term commitment.

- Creating appropriate environments: this means one with an emphasis on positive relationships and expectations, but with clear rules and boundaries that are consistently maintained.

- Introduce explicit teaching and learning programmes: such as SEAL. Promote teachers' competence and well-being: look for ways of reducing teacher stress, and ensuring that teachers' needs are part of a whole-school programme.

In some cases whole-school approaches may stop at the level of what Weare (2004) calls a 'traditional special needs approach', that is, focusing on those pupils whose needs are immediate and paramount. She argues that for longer-term, sustainable impact all aspects of school life should be included in order to develop an 'emotionally literate school'. These include parental involvement in decisions which affect the whole school community, and systems to ensure teachers' well-being as well as that of pupils. These views are supported by Watkins (2008) who makes the following points:

- Proactive schools that aim to pre-empt difficulties have better behaviour.
- Schools with a strong sense of community have better behaviour.
- Schools with teacher collaboration have better behaviour.
- Schools that promote pupil autonomy have better behaviour.

Ofsted (2005) also identified behaviour as 'significantly better in settings which have a strong sense of community and work closely with parents . . . a strong lead by senior managers who set high standards and provide close support to staff contributes significantly to the effective management of behaviour'.

Some of these issues have already been discussed in earlier chapters in this book, and others will be considered in the following part, particularly Chapters 14 and 15.

SUMMARY

This chapter has argued that the teacher's responsibility is to support learning first and foremost and that any systems for managing behaviour within schools and classrooms should make this the main priority. In order to promote 'behaviour for learning' teachers need to adopt both 'preventative' and 'supportive' strategies: to minimise difficulties through effective planning of lessons and organisational strategies to support pupils as individuals or groups in developing and maintaining learning behaviour.

We have examined the framework developed by Powell and Tod (2004) and developed further by Ellis and Tod (2009), which considers three areas of relationship that can affect learning behaviour, and related this to the idea of 'emotional intelligence' and the SEAL programmme currently used in many schools.

Finally, we have emphasised that developing positive behaviour is a whole-school matter which involves all staff and parents – not only in terms of abiding by a 'discipline policy' but in terms of actively fostering improved relationships with learning.

TAKING YOUR PRACTICE FURTHER

This chapter has argued that the employment of behaviour management strategies should lead to the development of effective learning behaviours. This may also involve reviewing our beliefs about learners and learning.

- Apply the 'triangle of influence' model to learners in class(es) with which you are familiar.
  - In terms of the 'triangle of influence', why are some learners more successful?
  - Considering less successful learners, do any patterns emerge which might inform teaching? For example, is the pupil provided with a range of opportunities to foster participative behaviours, such as group working skills, that are explicitly identified and valued?
- In a teaching context, review the language you use during a typical lesson, or during interactions with particular pupils. You could do this by leaving a tape recorder running unobtrusively, or by asking your mentor or another teacher with whom you have a peer coaching relationship to observe and record key language verbatim.
  - Could you utilise more positive forms of language in your interactions with the class, and especially with individuals?
  - Do you sometimes become side-tracked by 'secondary behaviours'?
  - Do you sometimes interrupt the work of the whole class to respond to individual behavioural issues?
  - Do your teaching interactions with individuals promote self-esteem?

TAKING YOUR THINKING FURTHER

Many books are published on the topic of behaviour management, not all of which have been referred to in this chapter.

A recent 'post' on the Times Educational Supplement website suggested the following as a 'top 5'. What does each title suggest about attitudes to teaching and learning and to pupils?

1. Blum, P. (1998) *Surviving and Succeeding in Difficult Classrooms*. London: Routledge.
2. Rogers, B. (1997) *You Know the Fair Rule*. London: Pitman.
3. Cowley, S. (2003) *Getting the Buggers to Behave*. London: Continuum International.
4. Rogers, B. (2002) *Classroom Behaviour*. London: Paul Chapman.
5. Leaman, L. (2006) *Managing Very Challenging Behaviour*. London: Continuum International.

If possible, select at least one of these texts and consider how far the author is concerned with 'managing' behaviour and how far they are concerned with developing 'learning behaviours'.

Find out more

If you want to find out more about behaviour for learning:

Your first stop should be the website **www.behaviour4learning.ac.uk**. There is a link directly from the front page of **www.ttrb.ac.uk** – 'associated sites'.

The behaviour4learning site provides articles and research on the topic of behaviour and well-being, resources for initial teacher education and a series of videos on effective strategies aimed at secondary teachers.

Behaviour4learning now also has its own YouTube channel.

Teachers' TV also has a programme series focusing on aspects of behaviour management. You will need to decide how far you agree with the underlying philosophies of some of these programmes, a number of which are also reviewed on the behaviour4learning website.

Key series: *Teaching with Bayley* for secondary teachers and *Teaching with Cowley* for primary teachers.

Teaching with Kellington has a focus on Key Stage 3 pupils who are underachieving.

You might also be interested to read Watkins, C. (2008) *Managing Classroom Behaviour,* London Association of Teachers and Lecturers. This is freely available to download from **www.atl.org.uk/publications**.

This booklet covers a range of issues and provides sound advice in line with the behaviour for learning approach. However, it was first written in 1997 and the references do not appear to have been updated.

Key texts on behaviour management

Ellis, S. and Tod, J. (2009) *Behaviour for Learning: Proactive Approaches to Behaviour Management*. Abingdon: Routledge.
Hook, P. and Vass, A. (2002) *Teaching with Influence*. London: Fulton.

Rogers B. (1990) *You Know the Fair Rule*. London: Pitman.

Rogers, B. (2002) *Classroom Behaviour*. London: Paul Chapman.

Rogers, B. (2004) *How to Manage Children's Challenging Behaviour*. London: Paul Chapman.

If you want to read about critiques of multiple intelligence theory:

Schaler, J.A. (ed) (2006) *Howard Gardner Under Fire: The Rebel Psychologist Faces His Critics*. Open Court.

White, J. (1998) *Do Howard Gardner's Multiple Intelligences Add Up*? London: Institute of Education, University of London.

Waterhouse, L. (2006a) Multiple Intelligences, the Mozart Effect, and Emotional Intelligence: A critical review, *Educational Psychologist,* Vol. 41, No. 4: pp. 207–225.

Waterhouse, L. (2006b) 'Inadequate evidence for multiple intelligences, Mozart Effect, and Emotional Intelligence theories, *Educational Psychologist*, Vol. 41, No. 4: pp. 247–255.

If you want to find out more about 'emotional intelligence':

Claxton, G. (2005) *An Intelligent Look at Emotional Intelligence*. London: Association of Teachers and Lecturers.

This is freely available to download from **www.atl.org.uk/publications**. This publication takes a well-informed and appropriately critical look at the concept of emotional intelligence to separate the 'hype' from the evidence. It is based in research evidence and provides a good introduction to a complex area where neuroscience and psychology meet. It also contains a very good list of additional reading.

Glossary

Assertive discipline: a term given to particular form of 'behaviour management' system first developed in the USA by Lee and Marlene Canter. Lee Canter was a psychiatric social worker. In this system the teacher takes control of the classroom using a discipline plan with clearly laid down rules, rewards and sanctions which must be followed by the pupils. It is based on **behaviourist** assumptions about learning and was highly authoritarian when first developed in the mid-1970s, although it has since been modified to a more co-operative approach.

Behaviourist: a theory of learning based on the idea that our behaviour is shaped by the feedback (or 'reinforcement') we receive. In school contexts this often takes the form of pupils being rewarded for successful learning (with ticks, stars, prizes etc.) or behaviour (merit points, prizes etc.) and the application of sanctions if behaviour is not satisfactory.

Emotional intelligence: a term made famous by Goleman (1996). Although definitions of the concept vary, it is generally taken to embrace both being self-aware about one's own emotions and likely reactions to different situations, and being able to respond appropriately towards others, by being empathetic and displaying social skills.

Emotional literacy: similar to emotional intelligence, but preferred by some writers (such as Weare, 2004) because the use of the term 'literacy' is felt to place greater emphasis on personal empowerment.

Extrinsic: in this case, external to the learner, as opposed to the internal satisfaction of doing good work or maintaining effective learning behaviour.

Multiple intelligence: a concept developed by Howard Gardner (1983). The idea that humans possess a number of discrete 'intelligences' such as linguistics intelligence, musical intelligence, spatial intelligence. Gardner first proposed seven intelligences, but later increased this number.

Qualifications and Curriculum Development Agency (QCDA): the official body responsible for all aspects of curriculum development and statutory assessment in England. It is sponsored by the Department for Children Schools and Families (DCSF).

Resilience: the ability to accept being unsuccessful in a task, and to persist in attempting to master a skill or understanding. Can also include the idea of having strategies to support persistence, such as a willingness to try different approaches.

Self-concept: the set of beliefs about oneself, including attributes, roles, goals, interests, values and religious or political beliefs.

Self-efficacy: an individual's judgement of his/her ability to carry out a task or sustain behaviours that will lead to a certain outcome. Can relate to emotional issues such as anger as well as an individual's belief in their intellectual or physical capacities to undertake a task.

Self-esteem: how one *feels* about one's **self-concept**.

Systematic review: an approach to examining a number of research articles or reports in order to evaluate the reliability of the evidence presented against a set of given criteria. Only research which meets the criteria is then discussed in the final review article. It has been argued that this approach sometimes excludes research that could offer valuable insights into difficult areas.

References

Claxton, G. (2002) *Building Learning Power*. Bristol: TLO.

Claxton, G. (2005) *An Intelligent Look at Emotional Intelligence*. London: Association of Teachers and Lecturers. This is freely available to download from **www.atl.org.uk/publications**.

DfES (2003) *Primary National Strategy (Social, Emotional and Behavioural Skills)*. London: DfES.

DfES (2005) *Learning Behaviour* (the 'Steer Report'). London: DfES. Available via: **teachernet.gov.uk**.

Ellis, S. and Tod, J. (2009) *Behaviour for Learning: Proactive Approaches to Behaviour Management*. Abingdon: Routledge.

Gardner, H. (1983) *Frames of Mind*. London: Heinemann.

Gardner, H. and Hatch, T. (1989) Multiple intelligences go to school: Educational implications of the theory of multiple intelligences, *Educational Researcher*, Vol. 18, No. 8: pp. 4–9.

Goleman, D. (1996) *Emotional Intelligence: Why It Can Matter More Than IQ*. London: Bloomsbury.

Hayes, D. (2004) *Foundations of Primary Teaching*, 3rd edn. London: Fulton.

Hook, P. and Vass, A. (2002) *Teaching with Influence*. London: Fulton.

Hoult, S. (2005) *Secondary Professional Studies: Reflective Reader*. Exeter: Learning Matters.

Kendall-Seatter, S. (2005) *Primary Professional Studies: Reflective Reader*. Exeter: Learning Matters.

Kohn, A. (2001) *Beyond Discipline*. Upper Saddle River, NJ: Prentice Hall.

Mujis, D. and Reynolds, D. (2001) *Effective Teaching: Evidence and Practice*. London: Paul Chapman.

Ofsted (2005) *Managing Challenging Behaviour*. London: Ofsted.

Porter, L. (2007) *Behaviour in Schools*. Maidenhead: Open University Press.

Powell, S. and Tod, J. (2004) *A Systematic Review of how Theories Explain Learning Behaviour in School Contexts*. London: EPPI Centre Social Science Research Unit, Institute of Education.

QCA (2001) *Supporting School Improvement: Emotional and Behavioural Difficulties*. Sudbury: QCA. Available at: **http://www.qcda.gov.uk/libraryAssets/media/pupils_ emot_behav_diff.pdf**.

Rogers, B. (1997) *You Know the Fair Rule*. London: Pitman.

Rogers, B. (2002) *Classroom Behaviour*. London: Paul Chapman.

Rogers, B. (2004) *How to Manage Children's Challenging Behaviour*. London: Paul Chapman.

TDA (2007) *Standards for the Award of Qualified Teacher Status*. London: Author.

Watkins, C. (2008) *Managing Classroom Behaviour*. London: Association of Teachers and Lecturers.

Weare, K. (2004) *Developing the Emotionally Literate School*. London: Paul Chapman.

Weare, K. and Gray, G. (2003) *What Works in Developing Pupils Social and Emotional Competence and Well-Being?* Research Report 456. Nottingham: DfES.

In this chapter you will:

- Consider the differences between assessment *of* learning and assessment *for* learning
- Examine the impact of different approaches to assessment on pupils' motivation and achievement
- Consider how approaches to assessment are embedded in a broader set of values and beliefs about learning, which are informed by learning theory
- Evaluate your own beliefs about the purposes of assessment
- Consider current developments in national policy and practice on assessment for learning

Pearson Education Ltd/Rob Judges

Why do we assess pupil learning in schools?

Please tick the following statements on the basis of your *immediate* response
These purposes of assessment are:

	Very important	Quite important	Not very important
a) to help group or set pupils appropriately			
b) to help set targets for pupil learning			
c) to diagnose errors in pupils' learning			
d) to monitor pupils' progress			
e) to provide information for parents			
f) to provide feedback for pupils on how they can improve			
g) to provide information for other teachers			
h) to measure pupils' achievement against local and national expectations			
i) to help adjust our teaching			
j) to inform school improvement planning			
k) to compare pupils within the class or set			
l) to help pupils take responsibility for their own learning			
m) to inform our planning			
n) to help evaluate our own teaching effectiveness			
o) to provide information for local authority target setting			
p) to motivate pupils			
q) to help develop skills of lifelong learning			
r) to acknowledge pupils' efforts			
s) to find out what pupils know, understand or can do at the start of a new unit of learning			
t) to identify underachievement			

It is unlikely that you will have decided that all these statements are 'very important', although you might not have wanted to tick the 'not very important' column. Where you have placed your emphasis will depend to some extent on your role within your school context and your stage of professional development and also on your own values and beliefs about learning.

You might like to consider whether the pattern of ticks would be different for a senior manager, subject leader or head of department.

Formative assessment: where the purpose is to help in decisions about how to advance learning and the judgement is about the next steps in learning and how to take them.

Introduction

This chapter focuses on the relationship between assessment and pupil learning, and on current views of the most appropriate ways to improve learning and achievement through effective assessment strategies. Currently, most teachers working with the 7–14 age range are likely to be familiar with a range of both **formative** and **summative** assessment approaches in their classroom. Summative approaches are normally used at the end of blocks of work, often as tests or examinations, to provide a final or summary indication of the pupil's achievement. All schools are involved in summative assessment through the form of **standardised** national tests where pupils' results are set alongside those of pupils from other schools.

Summative assessment: where the purpose is to summarise the learning that has taken place in order to grade, certificate or record progress.

Formative approaches involve giving feedback on work either orally or through written comments on an ongoing basis. The phrase 'assessment for learning' (AfL) is now commonly used to denote ongoing assessment practices, which are generally regarded as formative for pupil learning. Formative assessment and AfL are not always the same thing, however, although sometimes the terms are used interchangeably. Some formative assessment practices do not necessarily promote effective learning unless they are also embedded in a set of beliefs about the ways assessment and learning are interrelated. AfL is thus more than a set of guidelines about how to assess pupils' learning: it also involves examining our values and beliefs about teaching.

The principles of AfL have now been integrated into both the Primary National Strategy and the Key Stage 3 Strategy and schools are being asked to audit their assessment practice and involve teachers in staff development activities to promote the use of AfL across the curriculum (DCSF, 2008). In order to understand why, we will examine the evidence that explains why views about effective assessment have changed over recent years.

Standardised: criteria for success are established through an initial process of testing materials with large numbers of pupils in different schools and areas to arrive at agreement on levels of achievement (i.e. agreed standards).

Assessment *of* learning

The majority of teachers have experienced assessment during their own schooling in the form of tests and examinations. Indeed, you will have been successful in these types of assessment activity in order to obtain the necessary grades to enter Higher Education and qualify as a teacher. It is probable that the feedback you received on your work in primary and the early years of secondary school took the form of marks or grades, crosses and ticks or smiley faces, and comments such as 'good work' or 'try harder'.

These assessment practices fall into the category of assessment *of* learning. Assessment of learning makes a judgement on the basis of completed achievement, whether this is a public examination such as GCSE or A Level, or a piece of written work produced as part of the normal timetable. This is what most people, parents and governors as well as teachers, have regarded as assessment, because of their past experiences. This view of assessment has also been promoted through government policy over the past 20 years, and remains a powerful influence in the daily lives of teachers and pupils.

The National Tests (often known as 'SATs') have impacted on the lives of pupils and many teachers, whether or not they have been teaching pupils in Years 2, 6 or 9. In many schools pupils sat the optional QCA tests in Year 4, or sat the Key Stage 3 national tests a year early to allow more time to cover the GCSE syllabus. Pupils' achievements in national tests at Key Stages 2 and 3 and QCA tests have been used as benchmarks to measure their progress in learning and, increasingly, to measure teacher effectiveness. Schools' reputations may stand or fall on the basis of their published national test results. Assessment of learning appears to be the dominant indicator of educational achievement and standards (for good or ill) in the eyes of the media. It is hardly surprising that it has had a significant impact on teaching and learning, as we discussed in Chapter 1. However, the amount of national testing is currently being reduced. Revisions to tests have taken place at ages 7 and 11 in Scotland and Northern Ireland, and at 7, 11 and 14 in Wales. Either national tests in these countries are being abolished or the role of teachers' involvement is increasing. In England, teacher involvement in assessment has been increased for tests at the end of Key Stage 1 and the national tests at the end of Key Stage 3 became non-statutory in 2008.

All schools are required to have systems for recording assessment data in order to track individual progress against national standards. In this way, teachers and school leaders can identify trends in pupil performance and initiate action as required. For example, the information can be used to examine the relative performance of boys and girls, or of pupils from ethnic minority backgrounds, and to identify if, and where, any action is necessary to ensure these pupils can reach their potential. This use of assessment information is an important part of ensuring effective inclusive practice within the school. However, research has suggested that an over-emphasis on summative assessment may not be helpful in improving achievement.

THINKING IT THROUGH

If you gave high importance to answers e, g, h, j, k and o in the opening activity, these responses apply particularly to the idea of assessment *of* learning.

This is not to say that these responses are in any way inappropriate: teachers do indeed need to use assessment for these purposes. However, if you gave these responses a higher priority than others in the list it may be helpful for you to reflect on some of the ideas explored further in the rest of this chapter.

Giving higher importance to any of the other answers indicates that you place a value on formative assessment.

Responses f, l, p and q might indicate that you place a value on developing pupils' meta-cognition, or on helping them 'learn how to learn'.

Meta-cognition: being aware of how we think and behave in learning situations. Ultimately this implies active control over the process of thinking, for example: planning the way to approach a learning task, monitoring comprehension, and evaluating progress towards the completion of a task.

Assessment of learning and classroom practice

The argument underpinning the policy developments surrounding national testing at ages 7, 11 and 14 was that standards of achievement in schools would improve. Comparison with other countries suggested that pupils in England and Wales were lagging behind in terms of achievement, and it was felt this would have an adverse effect on economic development.

Testing was seen as an incentive for pupils and teachers, in terms of rewards or penalties. It was also assumed that schools would realise they had to show continual improvement through the publication of results so they would try harder and thus pupils would benefit (ARG, 2002a). While this has been true for some pupils and some schools, questions are raised about what is being learned through this process, both by those who succeed and those who do not.

Concerns about the effects of these types of assessment on learning led to the formation of a research group in 1989, which was renamed the Assessment Reform Group (ARG) in 1996. This group of educationalists was sponsored by the independent Nuffield Foundation to investigate the relationship between effective learning and assessment methods and to bring the research evidence to the attention of policy makers (**http://www.assessment-reform-group.org/**). The ARG have produced several influential publications, drawing on careful examination of research evidence. Educational writers had previously identified the adverse effects of national testing on pupils' motivation and self-esteem (Gipps,1994) and this is emphasised in research reviews and related ARG publications (Harlen and Deakin Crick, 2002; ARG, 2002a). The 'high stakes' for schools and individual pupils associated with national testing encourages the narrowing of the curriculum as a result of 'teaching to the test'; practice testing further undermines the confidence and motivation of less successful pupils and also encourages the development of test-taking strategies which reduce higher-level thinking, even in more able learners.

The review of research evidence into the effects of tests on motivation and learning found that teachers' teaching styles were also affected by pressures associated with high-stakes testing. They were more likely to transmit knowledge than to provide more open, active or creative learning experiences, and also to focus more on summative assessment with their pupils, for example by providing marks to indicate pupils' likely performance in test conditions. These tendencies are likely to reduce pupils' learning opportunities.

'High stakes' assessment: where summative assessment is used for making decisions that affect the status or future of students, teachers or schools.

THINKING IT THROUGH

The following quotation is taken from an editorial, written in 2002, from the journal *Assessment in Education*. As you read, consider how far you think the sentiments expressed here still apply in schools with which you are familiar. These may be schools you have attended as a pupil as well as schools where you have had teaching placements or other experience.

CONTROVERSY

Should education work to an 'industrial' model?

The requirement to give an account, to meet standards, to measure up well against performance targets and to be compared against others is now so pervasive that its presence in society is hardly remarked. Part of the motivation behind all this activity is a laudable quest for more transparency, higher quality and greater accountability. However, another element is the belief that the competition it inevitably provokes, both in relation to the standard itself and in relation to the performance of others, is a valuable way of 'driving up' standards of 'delivery' and of 'performance' – the vocabulary itself is rooted in models of industrial production.

In no aspect of public life have these pervasive assumptions had more impact than in the world of education. Assessment activity now shapes the goal, the organisation, the delivery and the evaluation of education. For children starting school, every aspect of their lives is likely to be framed and shaped by the demands of assessment, whether this is the assessment activities they themselves are subject to – such as weekly class tests, national testing sweeps at regular intervals, mandatory diagnostic testing, public examinations or entrance examinations – or the results of the assessments that their teachers and schools are subject to, the effects of which are likely to be felt in terms of curriculum priorities, teaching methods, homework policies, classroom organisation and so on.

Source: Editorial (2002) *Assessment in Education*, Vol 9, No 3

OVER TO YOU

The writer implies that competition and the vocabulary of 'industrial production' are inappropriate for the educational context. Do you think it is possible to have the positive benefits of greater transparency and accountability without comparisons and competition between institutions?

The suggestion in the second paragraph is that assessment activity dominates all aspects of school life, including what and how children are taught. Is this statement true in your experience?

Is it possible to strike a balance between having a curriculum which is 'assessment led' and one where assessment is a 'bolt-on'?

Formative assessment strategies and improvements in achievement

A number of research projects developed from the work of the Assessment Reform Group, and in 1998 a review of research into the use of formative assessment methods was published. *Inside the Black Box* (Black and Wiliam, 1998) has been a highly influential publication in terms of its impact on classroom practice and national policy in the UK as a whole. Black and Wiliam considered over 250 research studies into the use of formative assessment strategies with learners from five years old to university students and concluded that these studies showed that learner achievement improved as a result. They then went on to consider evidence about assessment practices being used in schools at the time of writing and argued that many teachers were over-using tests which encouraged superficial, rote learning; they were giving marks or grades to pupils without giving advice about how work could be improved and this was leading to the demoralisation of pupils with consistently low marks. Many teachers were not using the results of their assessments to identify pupils' learning needs and adjusting their teaching as a result.

Finally, the pamphlet examined evidence about how formative assessment could be improved on the basis of a synthesis of evidence from the research studies. This was developed into a set of recommendations for practice:

- providing effective feedback to pupils;
- actively involving pupils in their own learning;
- adjusting teaching to take account of the results of assessment;
- recognising the influence assessment has on motivation and self-esteem, both of which are crucial for learning;
- considering the need for pupils to be able to assess themselves and to understand how to improve.

These recommendations were then tested in further research with schools in projects with two local authorities, and *Working Inside the Black Box* (Black *et al.*, 2002) reported on the outcomes of the school-based projects. As a result, further recommendations for practice were proposed, involving:

- an improved use of questioning strategies (as discussed in Chapter 8), with more 'take-up time' and more opportunities to extend pupils' understanding;
- careful feedback through marking and oral comments, to indicate what has been done well, what needs further improvement and how improvements can be made, along with opportunities for pupils to follow up these suggestions (discussed below);
- the use of peer- and self-assessment, supported by clear aims for pupils' work and clear criteria for success (discussed below);
- the formative use of summative tests (discussed below).

In all cases, the effective use of these approaches rested on careful planning of tasks, the identification of suitable questions and time taken to share the learning objectives and intended outcomes, or success criteria, with the pupils.

Photo 10.1
Ongoing feedback and discussion about pupils' work can help learners identify their own areas for improvement or development

Source: Pearson Education Ltd

The term 'assessment *for* learning' was coined by the ARG as a deliberate counter-point to the notion of assessment *of* learning, discussed above. Their definition of 'assessment for learning' continues to be used in all policy and curriculum documents by DCSF, QCA, Ofsted and the National Strategies. Assessment for learning (AfL) is defined as:

> the process of seeking and interpreting evidence for use by learners and their teachers, to identify where the learners are in their learning, where they need to go and how best to get there.

(Assessment Reform Group, 2002b)

Using the outcomes from the school-based projects the ARG produced a poster outlining 10 principles of Assessment for Learning which the evidence demon-strates can improve the quality of pupil learning and achievement (ARG, 2002b) (**http://www.assessment-reform-group.org/publications.html**).

The ARG has argued that summative assessment strategies can also be utilised formatively, and that teachers and schools should make greater use of these (ARG, 2002a). Classroom tests can provide positive learning opportunities as well as nega-tive ones, where pupils are encouraged to use the results diagnostically, and not as a means of comparing themselves with others. Teachers working in schools involved in developing the ideas outlined in *Inside the Black Box* (Black and Wiliam, 1998) found that pupils benefited from activities such as peer marking tests, either using a marking scheme provided or developing their own, and from setting some of their own test questions in order to develop their understanding (Wiliam *et al.*, 2004). Ofsted (2003) also found that effective assessment strategies in secondary schools included dis-cussing and analysing National Curriculum-level descriptors with pupils so that these were incorporated into relevant personal targets, using the principles of AfL.

What model of learning is implicit in AfL?

Constructivism: a view of learning that emphasises the active role of the learner in building understanding, and making sense of information from experience.

Social constructivism: the theory that learning is constructed through active participation with others within the contexts of the socio-cultural group.

Behaviourist: a theory of learning based on the idea of positive (or negative) reinforcement. Pupils are rewarded for successful learning (with ticks, stars, prizes etc.) or behaviour (merit points, prizes etc.). Sanctions are applied if behaviour is not satisfactory.

We have suggested earlier that there is a relationship between our beliefs about learning and assessment methods. Our beliefs about learning are based on theories about how learning occurs and about the nature of learners themselves, which are often implicitly held. A detailed discussion of the relationship between assessment and theories of learning is provided by Mary James (James, 2006), but essentially AfL practice is located within the constructivist and social constructivist perspectives on learning. These perspectives are based particularly upon the work of Piaget and Vygotsky, which was discussed in Chapter 4.

In summary, the learner is not seen as a blank page or 'empty vessel' but as someone who constructs meaning from his or her experiences from early infancy (or even from before birth). Learning is therefore an active process. Learning is successful when the learner can make connections between new experience and previous learning, leading to *understanding*. If prior knowledge is insufficient, the learner's capacity to learn new material will be reduced and the possibility of misunderstanding is increased. Social interaction is also seen as an important element in successful learning – learners learn from the people around them as well as through their own direct experience and both teachers and other learners have a significant role to play in this process.

If effective learning needs to be related to previous knowledge then it is essential that teachers undertake formative, ongoing assessment in order to find out what learners do and do not understand about a topic. Only then can the teacher give learners appropriate opportunities to test and apply their new knowledge in different situations or contexts in order to embed their understanding. This principle is already well established in schools.

So too is the principle of providing feedback to promote motivation in learners. However, the way feedback is used can be very different depending on the theory of learning which underpins the teacher's teaching, or possibly an entire education system. A behaviourist view of learning uses both praise and criticism to promote learning. Learners learn what kinds of actions promote a positive response from the teacher and which are likely to produce negative responses. However, this type of learning tends to develop learner dependency, because learners are not encouraged to consider what counts as effective learning for themselves, but reproduce behaviour to please the teacher. In fact, even where teachers maintain that they are attempting to develop reflective and independent learners, they can undermine this process if they provide inappropriate feedback.

Feedback needs to be specifically focused on the goals of the learning activity and the success criteria provided. Merely telling a student that they have produced good work does not help them as they do not know why it is good. Similarly, giving marks or grades for work without a means of enabling the learner to identify why the mark or grade has been awarded will not help them to make progress.

A numerical mark does not tell pupils how to improve their work, so an opportunity to enhance their learning has been lost.

(Black et al., 2002)

Just as different approaches to assessment are based in different theories of learning, the use of different assessment methods can develop different beliefs about learning in the learners who experience them. In the UK, researchers in schools noticed that many pupils did not look at the teacher's comments on work when it was returned, but only at the grade awarded. This attitude implies quite a passive view of learning as the pupils were regarding the outcome of their work as fixed (by the grade) and did not appear to consider that they could continue to learn by reviewing the teacher's comments to identify where they had done well or where improvement was needed. Effective AfL should involve pupils in reflection on their work and give them time to make suitable improvements, or to internalise what they have learned through feedback. Even the most helpful comments will have little effect if the learner cannot see how they can be applied in future.

THINKING IT THROUGH

Reflect back on your own experience as a learner so far.

Can you think of examples of feedback, whether from a teacher, instructor or other experienced person, that helped you understand how something could be improved? (This might be academic work, or sporting technique, or a personal interest such as gardening or carpentry!) What made this feedback effective?

What opportunities were *you* given to identify where improvement could be made in academic or other work? How did you know what would count as 'improvement'?

If you are unable to identify any examples from your own experience, can you identify an example of where specific feedback *could* have helped you, even if you did not receive it at the time?

Giving feedback

Feedback can be either oral or written, and both have an important place in supporting learning. The advantage of oral feedback is its immediacy, but this can also be a disadvantage if the pupil does not remember what was said and so fails to take the advice on board. Positive feedback can also be immediately motivating, but may also lose its effectiveness if praise is used indiscriminatingly (Dweck, 2000).

Oral feedback	
Advantages	**Possible disadvantages**
Immediate	Pupil(s) may not have time to reflect on implications for their work in the future
	Pupils may not understand what is meant
Adaptable	Unplanned oral feedback may not be well considered to support learning
Stimulating	Pupils may not have time to consider their responses
Personalised	Pupil may not remember it. Other pupils may not appreciate that it can also apply to them
Motivating	Pupils may feel embarrassed by public feedback

Written feedback has a number of advantages over oral feedback in terms of time for both teacher and pupil to reflect on their responses, but it does of course lose the immediacy of oral feedback which can be important for keeping pupils motivated and on task during the lesson. Both types of feedback are necessary to support AfL effectively, but to be effective *they must be based on the lesson objectives and learning outcomes (success criteria) that have been shared with the class.*

The National Strategy materials identify the following factors are being important in written feedback:

- focusing on the learning objectives selectively;
- confirming that pupils are on the right track;
- stimulating the correction of errors or improvement of a piece of work;
- scaffolding or supporting pupils' next steps;
- providing opportunities for pupils to think things through for themselves;
- commenting on progress over a number of attempts;
- avoiding comparisons with other pupils;
- providing pupils with the opportunities to respond.

Source: some suggestions above based on training material on assessment for learning in the Secondary National Strategy: Unit 4. Available at:
www.nationalstrategies.standards.dcsf.gov.uk

WORKING IN THE CLASSROOM

Feedback can be seen as positive or negative and specific or non-specific. To be effective, it needs to be both positive and specific, in terms of providing suggestions for further improvement. For example: 'This work is unsatisfactory' is both negative and non-specific.

How would you characterise the following examples of feedback?

WORKING IN THE CLASSROOM: *CONTINUED*

1. This is a really good opening section. You have used the proper vocabulary and you have made the order of events clear by using words such as 'firstly', 'secondly' and 'then'. You could improve the next section further if you take another look at your use of special vocabulary.
2. This work could be much better. You have not included the proper vocabulary we talked about in the lesson in the second section.
3. This is good work, but you need to include more of the proper vocabulary we talked about in the lesson.
4. Well done, you have tried really hard with this work.

What is your response to no. 3? How helpful is the 'target'? What is the effect of the use of 'but' here?

OVER TO YOU

In training

Draw up a checklist for providing effective written feedback on pupils' work. This will vary depending on the age of the pupils concerned and whether you are teaching in Key Stage 2 or 3.

As the opportunity arises, compare your list with the assessment and marking policy of schools with which you are familiar. How does your checklist compare with assessment practice in the school?

Starting your career

How far does your own marking reflect the principles above?

Are there areas where you feel your feedback could improve?

What might be the effect on your pupils, and how might you need to prepare them for changes to your marking practice?

Investigating teaching and learning

The above suggestions for effective written feedback are based on research evidence from a variety of sources. Assessment for Learning is an area of research that has had a direct impact on national policy.

Using some of the research literature suggested at the end of this chapter, compare the findings with the key recommendations for the use of AfL as outlined in the National Primary and Secondary Strategies.

How closely do you feel these are related? Would you want to add to, or change any of the policy recommendations?

Meta-cognition: being aware of how we think and behave in learning situations. Ultimately this implies active control over the process of thinking, for example: planning the way to approach a learning task, monitoring comprehension, and evaluating progress towards the completion of a task.

One of the important principles of AfL is that of placing an emphasis on **meta-cognition**. This means that the learner needs to have some understanding of their own learning processes. Supported by effective feedback from the teacher, they are then increasingly able to take responsibility for improving their work through reviewing the objectives of the activity and the success criteria which have been identified.

The evidence from the school-based projects, reported in *Working Inside the Black Box* (Black *et al.*, 2002), is that peer assessment supports and develops self-assessment, and that this in turn increases learners' motivation to learn and their interest in what they are learning. Peer assessment, where learners review the work of others against given criteria, thus *precedes* self-assessment and helps to establish the skills of self-monitoring and self-assessment. However, this developmental sequence is sometimes lost, and pupils are asked to assess their own work without having had the opportunity to learn to distance themselves through peer assessment activities.

In many ways the key principles for developing peer- and self-assessment are similar to those for the effective use of oral and written feedback:

- Opportunities for peer- and self-assessment need to be planned into lessons.
- Pupils need to understand the purposes (objectives) and intended outcomes (criteria) against which work is to be evaluated.
- Pupils need to be given time to carry out both peer- and self-assessment activities.

To be effective, pupils need to learn how to assess the work of others, and their own, in small, incremental steps. This means they need to be supported to focus on the next stage of development for the work, and on specific rather than general features.

Photo 10.2 Peer assessment needs to be supported by guidance about the purpose and intended outcomes of the work. Learning to undertake peer assessment can help pupils assess their own work more effectively

Source: Pearson Education Ltd/Rob Judges

How can this be supported in the classroom?

Depending on the age of the pupils you are teaching, you could:

- Work with the whole class to review an anonymised piece of a pupil's work against *one or two specific* criteria. This should be a good piece of work, but still with some room for improvement. Pupils need to know what the expected standard is, not to be shown poor work as an example!

- Provide a *short* list of success criteria for a task as a handout or on the board, depending on context. Pupils review each other's work in pairs. This can also be very useful for group-based or problem-solving tasks, as well as independent work – pupils then discuss how well the criteria were achieved as a group.

- Work with groups and individuals during the working process to encourage reflection on the work and to seek suggestions from pupils as to how it could be developed further against shared criteria. This is not quite the same as giving oral feedback in the ways outlined above, since the key focus is to elicit pupils' views rather than to provide targets yourself. You will need to be clear about your own role in order not to confuse asking the pupils for feedback with giving it yourself!

- Involve pupils in leading plenaries. At the start of a lesson, ask a group to be prepared to lead the plenary. Support them in reviewing the lesson objectives and commenting on what has been achieved and what still needs to be done.

    You will have needed to model the use of plenary sessions previously, and to have encouraged the active participation of pupils in reviewing progress in order for this strategy to be effective.

- Older pupils could be involved in the shared development of assessment criteria for a given task, based in their familiarity with tasks of a similar type.

- Pupils could be asked to write their own questions on a given topic to match the learning outcomes, and to indicate what they would expect in an answer. This activity will help to indicate their level of understanding of the topic, as well as distinguishing between learning objectives and learning outcomes.

Source: some suggestions above based on training material on assessment
for learning in the Secondary National Strategy: Unit 5. Available at:
www.nationalstrategies.standards.dcsf.gov.uk

CONTROVERSY

Have assessment for learning strategies become a gimmick?

In an article in the *Times Educational Supplement* (17 October 2008) it is suggested that AfL strategies are being used in many schools in a superficial way, with little real change in teachers' practice.

> *Bill Boyle, professor of educational assessment at Manchester University, said many schools were introducing gimmicks but not changing their practice.*
>
> *About 80 per cent of the 480 heads he surveyed said AfL was a very high priority. But follow-up visits to 24 schools found little evidence that teachers were using the technique's principles in their day-to-day practice . . . .*
>
> *Professor Boyle said: 'During the course of roll-out, the principles (of AfL) got reduced to a shopping list of things to do, which could be memorised:*   ▶

sharing learning objectives with the pupil; using written comments to feed back to pupils rather than supplying marks or grades; using open questioning rather than closed; involving pupils more in their own learning process, and introducing peer and self-assessment strategies.'

When he visited schools, he observed classrooms with learning objectives on the board and some peer assessment, but found that teachers still controlled the learning rather than giving pupils more active involvement. This was partly because of misunderstandings about AfL, he felt, but also because national tests straitjacketed schools.

Shirley Clarke, the author of several books on using AfL (see Find Out More section in this chapter) has also expressed concerns about the way in which some of these strategies have been adopted in schools. In her initial work with schools she suggested using acronyms such as WALT (we are learning to) and WILF (what I'm looking for) to help teachers and children focus on learning objectives and success criteria. She now feels the use of these acronyms is counter-productive:

Ms Clarke said that when she started the work in 1998, the idea of learning objectives (what pupils were learning) and success criteria (whether they had learnt it) were new. 'So Walt, Wilf and Oli, at that time, were wonderful,' she said. 'Teachers were making them into characters – into dogs or cats.'

'Walt you can't really go wrong with, but Wilf was a bit of a disaster – it meant teachers were giving children the success criteria instead of asking children to generate them. It made children think, "This is about doing what the teacher wants us to do." Even worse, using animals meant some young children were saying, "We're learning this for the dog."

'So now on all courses and books, I say get rid of them. It has blighted me. There may be teachers still using them, but they ought to be throwing them away. I now talk about learning objectives and success criteria.'

There are some popular strategies which are claimed to support pupils' self-assessment and which are widely used in classrooms, particularly in primary schools. However, in some cases these may also have become a gimmick, like WALT and WILF, and we need to consider their use carefully.

Show me your thumbs

At the end of the lesson, pupils are asked to show their thumbs held up, down or across to indicate how well they believe they have achieved the learning outcomes.

Advantages:

quick to operate;
provides teacher with a snapshot of the whole class.

Disadvantages:

could give superficial and inaccurate picture of learning, if not followed up with other forms of assessment;

teacher may not recall or record those pupils who have made inappropriate assessments of their own learning;

some pupils may not wish to show their lack of understanding in public.

This last point can be partly overcome through the use of small whiteboards where pupils hold up their response so that only the teacher can see.

Traffic lights

Pupils place coloured dots against parts or all of their work to indicate how well they feel they have achieved the learning outcomes.

Advantages:

private response on part of pupil;

teacher can respond directly to pupil's own assessment with written feedback;

teacher can assess how well the pupil has understood the learning outcomes.

Disadvantages:

some teachers feel this is more time consuming;

less effective if not introduced through use of peer assessment and/or modelling what would count as good work in some form.

WORKING IN THE CLASSROOM

What strategies have you observed for encouraging pupils to self-assess their work?

How effective do you feel they have been?

What are their advantages and possible disadvantages?

If you have seen examples of the two specific strategies above, do you agree with the advantages and possible disadvantages identified? Would you want to add anything to these lists?

The implications of AfL for teaching and learning

Properly implemented, assessment for learning challenges beliefs about learning for teachers *and* learners. Accepting the evidence that implementing the key ideas of AfL in schools will improve the quality of pupils' learning is just the first step. The teachers involved in the school-based projects found that implementing the AfL approach involved more than just applying some new rules. Both they and their pupils had to reconsider their approaches and beliefs about effective learning:

> implementing assessment for learning/formative assessment may require a teacher to re-think what effective learning is, and his or her role in bringing it about.
>
> *(James, 2006: 49)*

The teachers had to let go of the idea that they needed to control all aspects of the pupils' learning, and to accept that their pupils were capable of making judgements about their own learning which would lead to improvement (see Figure 10.1). Conversely, pupils had to learn to take responsibility for their own learning rather than passively accept the teacher's judgement in the form of marks or grades. Pupils also had to learn to move away from relying on marks or grades as indicators of achievement, and to review their work against comments based on agreed criteria. For many teachers and learners these are radical shifts of perspective.

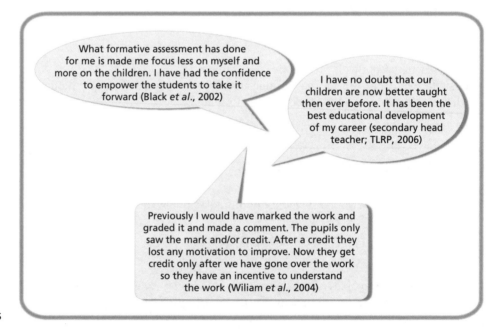

Figure 10.1 Teacher's voices: some responses from school-based projects

OVER TO YOU

Educational writers and policy makers use the term 'effective learning' as though we all agree on what this means. This book has encouraged you to reflect on your own views of the purpose of education and your beliefs about teaching and learning.

The *teachers* in the school-based projects seem to have moved their own ideas about effective learning from a focus on the teacher towards a focus on the learner.

Policy makers might regard effective learning as learning that achieves good results, as measured through standardised tests or comparisons with other countries.

What is *your* view of effective learning? Can we bring these two perspectives together?

Bringing formative and summative assessment closer together?

In the 'controversy' discussion box you were asked to consider whether it is possible to strike a balance between having a curriculum which is 'assessment led' and one where assessment is 'bolted on' and is not integrated into teaching and learning. In 2007 the *Making Good Progress* pilot scheme brought formative and summative approaches to assessment closer together. This involved over 450 schools working with pupils at Key Stages 2 and 3. Teachers were asked to monitor pupils' progress in reading, writing and mathematics through the year, using specific, standardised criteria. These are laid out in materials developed by QCDA entitled *Assessing Pupils' Progress* (APP). 'Single level tests' for National Curriculum levels 3–8 were available twice during the year so that teachers could confirm their assessment of the level at which individual pupils were working. These were based on the same standardised criteria as the teacher assessment being used throughout the year. Funding was made available for pupils to have 'progression tutoring' where they entered a Key Stage behind expectations, or were making slow progress.

In 2008 the Assessment for Learning Strategy was published (see Figure 10.2), with the intention of embedding the principles of assessment for learning and the use of APP criteria in all schools, but with a particular focus on Key Stage 2 and 3 (DCSF, 2008).

Formative and summative assessment is brought together at three levels:

1 Day-to-day assessment in which learning objectives are made explicit to pupils; they are given immediate feedback and are supported to use self- and peer-assessment.

2 Periodic assessment reviews a pupil's achievement across a subject to inform planning and further targets.

3 Transitional assessment, which may involve national tests, provides more formalised assessment information that can be shared with parents or carers and teachers in the next year group or school.

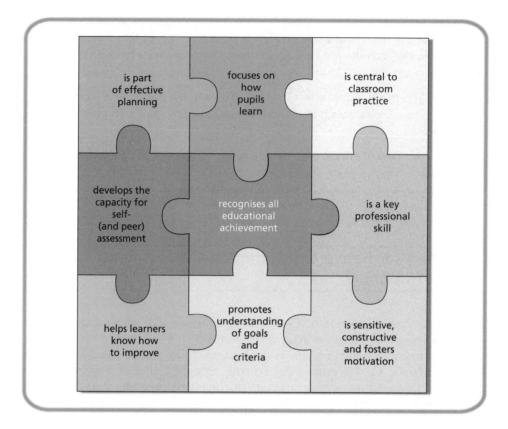

Figure 10.2
Assessment for learning strategy
Source: DCSF (2008), p. 5

OVER TO YOU

Assessment for Learning has been adopted as national policy in England, and is supported by the National Primary and Secondary strategies.

The APP criteria are developed for each level and sub-level at Key Stages 2 and 3, and will be developed to include foundation subjects as well as the core subjects in the National Curriculum.

Can schools successfully maintain the pupil-focused principles of AfL alongside the criteria for APP? Is there any danger that using APP may once again encourage 'teaching to the test'?

SUMMARY

This chapter has compared ideas about assessment *of* learning and assessment *for* learning, and posed the questions as to how far these two ideas can be brought together. We have examined the conclusions of the work of the Assessment Reform Group, which suggest that formative assessment has a strong impact on successful learning, and looked at strategies for supporting the use of formative assessment with pupils. However, the use of AfL strategies without deeper consideration of effective learning could result in the adoption of surface features but no real change in teaching and learning.

As with other approaches to teaching and learning discussed in this part of the book, we argue that teachers need to be self-aware, and to examine their own beliefs and values in order to support learners towards taking responsibility for their own learning. Assessment for learning strategies can be a significant part of this process, when they are used within a positive classroom environment.

TAKING YOUR PRACTICE FURTHER

Using the ideas outlined in this chapter, audit your current assessment practice and decide on your next steps in terms of developing the use of AfL in your teaching.

Areas you may wish to consider in detail could include:

- sharing and developing success criteria with pupils, which are clearly linked to lesson objectives;
- reviewing approaches to marking and feedback;
- involving pupils in peer assessment activities;
- involving pupils in identifying relevant targets for development and monitoring their own progress;
- making formative use of summative assessment strategies such as class tests or preparation for external testing.

TAKING YOUR THINKING FURTHER

The following books and articles provide a starting point for looking at the research evidence for assessment for learning approaches:

Gardner, J. (ed) *Assessment and Learning*. **London: Sage.**
This edited book contains articles by educational researchers on a range of topics.

The journal *Assessment in Education* contains many relevant articles: for example

Wiliam, D., Lee, C. Harrison, C. and Black, P. (2004) Teachers developing assessment for learning; impact on student achievement, *Assessment in Education*, **Vol. 11, No. 1.**
The journal *Research Papers in Education* has a special issue devoted to the Learning How to Learn Project, which grew out of the work of Black and Wiliam and the ARG. *Research Papers in Education* (2006), Vol. 21, No. 2.

There are a number of research digests on assessment for learning on The Research Informed Practice Site (TRIPS):
http://www.standards.dcsf.gov.uk/research/themes/assessment_for_learning/
There are also research digests on the GTCE Research for Teachers site:
http://www.gtce.org.uk/teachers/rft/.
'Assessment for learning: putting it into practice' created in 2004
Learning How to Learn through AfL strategies' created in 2007
These reviews include detailed case studies and suggestions for further reading.

A research report from one of the two local authorities involved in the school-based projects discussed in this chapter is available at: **http://www.aaia.org.uk/pdf/Gillingham1.pdf**.

Find out more

Some key texts on using assessment for learning in schools include:

Black, P. Harrison, C., Lee, C., Marshall, D. and Wiliam, D. (2003) *Assessment for Learning: Putting It into Practice*. **Maidenhead: Open University.**

Clarke, S. (2005) *Formative Assessment in the Secondary Classroom*. **London: Hodder and Stoughton.**

Clarke, S. (2005) *Formative Assessment in Action: Weaving the Elements Together*. **London: Hodder and Stoughton.**

Clarke, S. (2001) *Unlocking Formative Assessment: Practical Strategies for Enhancing Pupils' Learning in the Primary Classroom*. **London: Hodder and Stoughton.**

Questioning is a key strategy in the effective use of assessment for learning. Look back at Chapter 8 for some suggestions about reading and resources.

Teachers' *TV* has a number of programmes focusing on assessment for learning in both primary and secondary schools. Some of these have also been reviewed on **www.ttrb.ac.uk**.

TTRB review ID no 13086 takes a critical look at one such *Teachers' TV* programme, focusing on a secondary setting, and compares it with another programme with a primary focus. Links to both programmes and further reading are embedded in the review.

Glossary

Behaviourist: a theory of learning based on the idea of positive (or negative) reinforcement. Pupils are rewarded for successful learning (with ticks, stars, prizes etc.) or behaviour (merit points, prizes etc.). Sanctions are applied if behaviour is not satisfactory.

Constructivism: a view of learning that emphasises the active role of the learner in building understanding, and making sense of information from experience.

Formative assessment: where the purpose is to help in decisions about how to advance learning and the judgement is about the next steps in learning and how to take them.

'High stakes' assessment: where summative assessment is used for making decisions that affect the status or future of students, teachers or schools.

Meta-cognition: being aware of how we think and behave in learning situations. Ultimately this implies active control over the process of thinking, for example: planning the way to approach a learning task, monitoring comprehension, and evaluating progress towards the completion of a task.

Social constructivism: the theory that learning is constructed through active participation with others within the contexts of the socio-cultural group.

Standardised: criteria for success are established through an initial process of testing materials with large numbers of pupils in different schools and areas to arrive at agreement on levels of achievement (i.e. agreed standards).

Summative assessment: where the purpose is to summarise the learning that has taken place in order to grade, certificate or record progress.

References

'Editorial' (2002) *Assessment in Education*, Vol. 9, No. 3.

Assessment Reform Group (2002a) *Testing Motivation and Learning*. ARG.

Assessment Reform Group (2002b) *Assessment for Learning: 10 Principles*. ARG.

Black, P. and Wiliam, D. (1998) *Inside the Black Box*. London: nferNelson.

Black, P., Harrison, C., Lee, C., Marshall, B. and Wiliam, D. (2002) *Working Inside the Black Box*. London: nferNelson.

DCSF (2008) *The Assessment for Learning Strategy*. Nottingham: DCSF. Available at: **http://publications.teachernet.gov.uk/eOrdering Download/DCSF-00341-2008.pdf.**

Dweck, C. (2000) *Self Theories: Their Role in Motivation, Personality, and Development*. Philadelphia: Routledge.

Gipps, C. (2004) *Beyond Testing: Towards a Theory of Educational Assessment*. London, Falmer.

Harlen, W. and Deakin Crick, R. (2002) A systematic review of the impact of summative assessment and tests on students' motivation for learning' in *Research Evidence in Education Library*. London: EPPI-Centre, Social Science Research Unit, Institute of Education, University of London.

James, M. (2006) Assessment, teaching and theories of learning, in Gardner, J. (ed.) *Assessment and Learning*. London: Sage.

Ofsted (2003) *Good Assessment in Secondary Schools*. London: Office for Standards in Education.

TLRP (2006) *Enriching the Experience of Schooling: A Commentary by the Teaching and Learning Research Programme*. Available at: **www.tlrp.org.uk/publications**.

Wiliam, D., Lee, C., Harrison, C. and Black, P. (2004) Teachers developing assessment for learning; impact on student achievement, *Assessment in Education*, Vol. 11, No. 1: pp. 49–65.

11 Including All Learners: Developing Independence

In this chapter you will:

- Reflect on your understanding of the term 'inclusion'
- Consider the implications of some different models of inclusion
- Identify ways in which inclusive classroom practice can be developed, to increase the independence of all learners
- Consider ways in which schools can develop an inclusive ethos

Introduction

This chapter discusses some of the issues that teachers need to address when considering questions of inclusive practice, and how all learners within our classrooms can develop independence and participate fully in educational experiences.

What do we mean by 'inclusion'?

What do *you* think of when someone uses the term 'inclusion' in an educational context?

- Supporting pupils with Special Educational Needs (SEN) in mainstream schools?
- Providing equal opportunities for all learners?
- Ensuring the learning and participation of all those subject to exclusionary pressures?
- Including pupils with social and emotional difficulties in mainstream classrooms?
- Ensuring that minority groups within the school are valued and respected?

All of these? Some of these? None of these?

Although inclusion is often taken to refer only to the integration of pupils with SEN into mainstream schools, as in the Ofsted report *Special Educational Needs and Disability: Towards Inclusive Schools* (2004), other definitions have a wider scope.

As just a few examples from official documents, definitions of inclusion are provided by the Qualifications and Curriculum Development Agency (QCDA, available at: **http://www.qcda.org.uk/qcda_13580.aspx**), the Department for Education and Skills (2004: 28) and Ofsted (2001). All these definitions emphasise the view that the concept of inclusion applies to all pupils to ensure their entitlement to high-quality teaching and learning experiences. It is not to do with a particular type of school, but about how all pupils are supported to achieve and participate fully in school life. Explicitly or implicitly, these definitions refer to the range of factors affecting different groups of pupils. For example, Ofsted (2000) identifies the following groups of pupils as requiring particular consideration:

- girls and boys;
- minority and ethnic faith groups, Travellers, asylum seekers and refugees;
- pupils who need support to learn English as an additional language (EAL);
- pupils with special educational needs and/or disabilities;
- gifted and talented pupils;
- children 'looked after' by the local authority;
- other children, such as sick children; young carers; those children from families under stress; pregnant schoolgirls and teenage mothers; and
- any pupils who are at risk of disaffection and exclusion.

(Ofsted, 2000)

We will return to the value, or otherwise, of categorising pupils into groups later in this chapter.

Sebba and Ainscow (1996: 9) have described inclusion as the 'process by which a school attempts to respond to all pupils as individuals by reconsidering its curricular organisation and provision', and the *Index for Inclusion* (Booth *et al.*, 2000) provides a wide-ranging set of conditions for the identification of an inclusive school (**www.csie.org.uk**).

What these definitions have in common is the view that inclusion is about the learning of *all* pupils, based on the principle of human rights (Mittler, 2000). However, Sebba and Ainscow (1996) and the *Index for Inclusion* make it clearer that it is the *school* that has to change its cultures, policies and practices and not the pupil who has to 'fit in' with the culture of the school. This involves teachers in re-examining their own beliefs and understanding about inclusive education, which will be the main thrust of this chapter.

While there are many more definitions of 'inclusion' than those given above, what they all have in common is the idea that one or more groups of individuals are being excluded from access to education in some way or other. Without 'exclusion', the concept of 'inclusion' would make no sense. The term exclusion is often used in the context of pupils who have been excluded from full-time education, as a result of behaviour which the head teacher and governing body deem to constitute an unacceptable risk to staff, other pupils or the individual pupils themselves. As used within debates on inclusive practice, however, the term has a broader meaning.

Hidden curriculum: this term is used to identify the ways in which schools can transmit implicit norms, values and assumptions through their organisational features and the attitudes and values displayed by the school staff.

Exclusion in this broader sense occurs in a variety of ways, some of which have already been explored in earlier chapters of this book. For example: pupils may experience exclusion on the basis of gender, sexual orientation, ethnicity, religion, socio-economic status, ability or disability and on any combination of these. Exclusive actions may be deliberate, for example where individuals are excluded from playground activities by other pupils, or ignored or rejected during classroom activities, but they can also be inadvertent or the result of particular beliefs held by pupils and teachers. For example, in Chapter 5 we saw that teachers' beliefs about Asian girls could affect their expectations of the girls' participation in lessons. The curriculum and visual environment within a school may exclude or ignore the cultures of some pupils, thus devaluing their own experience, or school systems may not take some cultural or religious practices into account. The 'hidden curriculum' of school ethos and expectations of pupils' behaviour, or relationships between staff and pupils, may also be exclusive, as we discussed in Chapters 2 and 3.

OVER TO YOU

In what ways can adjustments to be made to accommodate a wide range of individual needs? What about the physical aspects of the school, school organisation, the curriculum, approaches to learning and teaching?

Some adjustments by schools are required by law, such as access for disabled pupils or the appointment of a Special Educational Needs Co-ordinator (SENCo) to co-ordinate provision for pupils with special educational needs. Other adjustments will be specific to individual schools.

In training/starting your career

Based on your experience in schools so far, what adjustments have you noticed which are designed to include different groups of pupils with individual needs? If you are already working in a school, what do you know about the range of individual needs within the school and the adjustments made to accommodate them?

Are there any groups of learners for whom you feel further adjustment could be made?

Investigating learning and teaching

What are the barriers to developing inclusive practice faced by primary and secondary schools? Which of the following do you feel are particularly significant?

Teacher attitudes
Pressure from high stakes testing
Parental pressure
Funding and resource issues (including staffing)

You may want to support your thinking by reading the National Union of Teachers study: *The Costs of Inclusion*: MacBeath *et al.* (2006).

High stakes testing or assessment: where summative assessment is used for making decisions that affect the status or future of students, teachers or schools.

CASE STUDY

Haslina and Ferenc are both 12 years old and recent arrivals in the UK, from different parts of the world. Although both attended school in their home countries and made good progress in their learning, neither of them learned English. Their secondary school does not have a teacher with specific responsibility for English as an Additional Language (EAL). In order to provide them with individual support, they have been placed with a small group of other pupils, all of whom are on the school's SEN register. Some members of this group have behavioural difficulties, while others have a range of learning difficulties.

- How well are the needs of Haslina and Ferenc being met?

- What assumptions about these pupils may be being made?

- In what ways may they be being excluded from full participation in learning?

- What other information would you need in order to ensure their participation in learning?

- What barriers to participation might exist for these pupils, within the school?

International agreements on inclusive education

Access to education is regarded as a fundamental human right, outlined in the United Nations Convention on the Rights of the Child (UNCRC) (1990) in article 28. Additionally the UNCRC states that 'Education should develop each child's personality, talents and abilities to their fullest potential as well as develop respect for parents, other members of human society and the environment' (Article 29). The United Kingdom signed the convention in 1990, and its requirements came into force in 1992. This involves periodic reporting to the United Nations about how these rights are being implemented.

So the right of every child to an education that enables them to reach their full potential is enshrined in both national and international agreements and legislation. Additionally, the idea that, as far as possible, all pupils should be educated in inclusive schools, rather than segregated according to definitions of 'special need', is outlined in further international agreement.

The Salamanca Statement

In 1994 representatives from 92 governments and 25 organisations met in Salamanca in Spain to draw up a policy statement to 'promote the approach of inclusive education, namely enabling schools to serve all children'. The Salamanca Statement focused particularly on pupils with special educational needs, but the meeting was underpinned by the idea of '"schools for all" – institutions which include everybody, celebrate differences, support learning and respond to individual needs' (UNESCO, 1994: iii).

The key principles

We believe and proclaim that:

- every child has a fundamental right to education, and must be given the opportunity to achieve and maintain an acceptable level of learning,
- every child has unique characteristics, interests, abilities and learning needs,
- education systems should be designed and educational programmes implemented to take into account the wide diversity of these characteristics and needs,

Child-centred pedagogy: an approach to teaching which focuses on the learning needs of the children in the class, rather than on following a pre-set curriculum with objectives determined by the teacher or administrators.

- those with special educational needs must have access to regular schools which should accommodate them within a **child-centred pedagogy** capable of meeting these needs,
- regular schools with this inclusive orientation are the most effective means of combating discriminatory attitudes, creating welcoming communities, building an inclusive society and achieving education for all; moreover, they provide an effective education to the majority of children and improve the efficiency and ultimately the cost-effectiveness of the entire education system.

(UNESCO, 1994: viii–ix)

The Salamanca statement goes beyond considering the rights of all children to receive a suitable and inclusive education, and argues that inclusive schooling is a prerequisite for an inclusive society. This, in itself, is a challenging and controversial idea.

Social inclusion

Increasingly, government policy has also become concerned with what might be termed 'social inclusion' – the need to ensure that certain groups within the population, such as disaffected young people, or those living in areas with high unemployment (sometimes described as 'marginalised groups'), become more productively involved with society, both to increase the economic prosperity of the country and to improve their personal conditions. There have been a number of policy initiatives aimed at promoting social inclusion, such as *Excellence in Cities* (DfEE, 1999) and the establishment of *Education Action Zones*. Although funding for both of these initiatives has now come to an end, they represent a further conception of inclusion, in addition to that concerned primarily with SEN and to that of entitlement to participation for all pupils. In both cases these initiatives were aimed at 'socially and economically deprived' communities with the view of increasing the educational engagement of children and young people, and their parents. These initiatives included funding for **learning mentors** in schools, to support pupils deemed to be 'at risk' for a variety of reasons; funding for schemes such as 'Aim Higher' which encourages young people with no family experience of Higher Education to consider it as a serious option for their future, and various types of family support programme ranging from 'parenting classes' to **family literacy** support.

This then is a 'different view of what it means to be "included" – a view which is about acquiring essential skills, surviving in a competitive labour market and active engagement with a stakeholder democracy rather than about participating as an equally valued member of a common social institution' (Dyson, 2001: 28).

Learning mentor: a person working within a primary or secondary school to support pupils identified as being 'at risk' of academic failure. They form a bridge between pastoral and academic concerns.

Family literacy: the use of structured literacy programmes shared by several members of the family.

CASE STUDY

Where do you stand?

Sarah, Angela and Derek, all members of the school governing body, are discussing how to promote an inclusive ethos within the school:

Sarah: We need more in-service training to help teachers raise their expectations of SEN pupils and to give them strategies for overcoming barriers to learning for our pupils with physical disabilities. We can't call ourselves an inclusive school just because we have wheelchair ramps and wider classroom doors!

Derek: Of course I agree with what you're saying, but I don't think this goes far enough. Inclusion isn't just about SEN nowadays. What about our under-achieving pupils, like some of the boys? And the Traveller families? I don't think we're getting it right for them – they don't seem to think school has anything to offer them and I worry about what's going to happen to them later on. What's the future going to be like for people with no qualifications? We need to be putting more effort into raising standards for these sorts of pupils.

Angela: This isn't just about underachievement. We won't tackle underachievement when some of our pupils feel excluded from education because it doesn't seem to relate to their points of view and where they have to make all the compromises. I think we have to go back to the basics of how we think about teaching and learning – that would make a difference to all our pupils, with or without SEN.

THINKING IT THROUGH

Whose views do you sympathise with most?

Do you think it is possible to respond to all the points made by Sarah, Derek and Angela within the current school context?

The importance of independence

This chapter is subtitled 'developing independence' for several reasons. As we have seen, some conceptions of inclusive educational practice are primarily concerned with ensuring that learners will feel part of our broader society as active citizens, and contribute to the prosperity of the country. Others are more concerned with changing attitudes and behaviours within society as a whole to recognise and value diversity, and yet others are concerned with ensuring that pupils identified as having SEN are enabled to reach their fullest potential. Regardless of which of these perspectives you see as a priority, pupils will need to be supported to develop as independent learners and thinkers in order to participate fully in education and society.

Independent learners are more able to take responsibility for their own learning, to solve problems and to maintain resilience in the face of initial difficulties. These attitudes are increasingly valued by employers, and underpin current changes to the curriculum both in primary schools and at Key Stage 3. However, being an independent learner does not necessarily mean always learning on one's own. The skills of working collaboratively with others, but without immediate adult direction, are also important, and enabling all learners to participate in collaborative learning of this nature, as well as individual activities, is an important aspect of effective teaching and of developing independence of a different kind.

Some of the ways in which pupils can be supported towards independence have been explored in earlier chapters of this book. Chapter 10 on *Assessment for Learning* considered ways in which pupils can be supported in taking responsibility for improving their own learning. Assessment for Learning approaches also develop pupils' understanding of how they learn, and this understanding can help to develop more independence. The *Behaviour for Learning* triangle (Powell *et al.*, 2004), discussed in Chapter 9, reminds us of the three dimensions that need to be considered in identifying appropriate strategies to help pupils engage with learning:

* their relationship with the curriculum: its relevance and accessibility;
* their relationships with others: how well individuals are able to work collaboratively;
* their relationship with themselves: their self-belief in terms of learning and their resilience.

These dimensions could also be applied to the concept of developing independence through inclusive practice:

* What strategies have been adopted to ensure that all pupils are able to access a relevant curriculum with the minimum of adult support?
* How does the ethos of the classroom, and the school, encourage collaborative working, tolerance and respect for the opinions of others?
* In what ways do teachers develop motivation and perseverance in learning by reducing barriers, while avoiding dependence?

The role of the Teaching Assistant

Within most primary classrooms, and in increasing numbers of Key Stage 3 classrooms, Teaching Assistants (TAs) are deployed to support the learning of pupils with SEN. However, while TAs are a highly valuable resource, if they are deployed as a

Photo 11.1
The effective deployment of teaching assistants can support inclusive practice

Source: Pearson Education Ltd/ Ian Wedgewood

Differentiation /differentiated planning: the adjustment of the teaching process according to the learning needs of pupils. Differentiated planning is generally taken to mean the matching of work to the differing capabilities within the class, matched to an overall intended learning outcome. Differentiation may operate by varying the type of tasks set for different groups of pupils, by varying the resources provided, varying expectations of the outcome or providing higher levels of adult support.

substitute for **differentiated** planning based on effective assessment of pupils' needs, their presence may limit the development of independence in learning. In an Ofsted report on progress towards inclusive schools the deployment of TAs was not always seen as being effective:

> In some cases it (the use of TAs) was having two negative effects: it reduced the extent to which the teacher planned tasks so that pupils with SEN could undertake them successfully; and it often meant that pupils had too few opportunities to work independently. In over half of lessons seen, the explanations and activities were well matched to most pupils' needs, but pupils with SEN depended on teaching assistants to break the tasks down further so that they could participate. In these lessons the focus of the teachers' planning was on how the pupils with SEN could be kept engaged, rather than on what the pupils needed to learn next. There was not enough stress on how to improve their understanding and skills. This was a common reason why a significant number of pupils with SEN made too little progress, despite good teaching for the majority of the class.

> *(Ofsted, 2004: 16)*

In some cases pupils spend the majority of their learning time working with the TA rather than the class teacher, which could be seen as a form of 'within-class segregation' (Wedell, 2005: 5) or 'casual exclusion' (DCSF, 2008). This may inadvertently encourage other pupils to regard some pupils with forms of SEN as 'different' and prevent the development of friendships. In some cases this could also lead to bullying and victimisation of pupils with disabilities or SEN who may not have developed the social skills to assert themselves and exercise control over their situation as a result of having spent too great a proportion of time with adults rather than their peers.

WORKING IN THE CLASSROOM

Based on your observations or experience in schools, are the comments made by Ofsted in 2004 still appropriate, or has the way in which TAs work in classrooms changed since then?

How far do you agree with the suggestion that some pupils experience 'casual segregation' as outlined above? What strategies could you use, or have you observed, that are intended to prevent this?

Pupil voice: a term used to identify a range of strategies utilised to gather pupils' views about all aspects of school life. See Chapter 15.

Crucially, we also help to develop independence by creating opportunities for pupils' views to be heard so that we can learn from what they tell us. The concept of pupil participation involves the right of pupils to express an opinion, as well as the right to be helped to learn across the school curriculum. Chapter 15, in the next part of the book, also discusses the topic of '**pupil voice**', but as it is particularly important to ensure that the voices of pupils in danger of exclusion or marginalisation are heard, this is also part of the inclusion debate.

The *Special Educational Needs Code of Practice* (DfES, 2001a) is the legal document that identifies the rights and entitlements of pupils identified as having specific learning needs. This requires the views of parents and pupils to be taken into account when decisions are made about whether the pupil should be educated within a mainstream or special school setting. The booklet entitled *Enabling Pupil Participation* (DfES, 2001b) emphasises the importance of ensuring that you are aware of pupils' views and feelings as part of your ongoing practice. In order for all pupils' voices to be heard, they may need to be supported in learning how to express their opinions. For younger pupils this could involve ensuring that they have opportunities to make simple choices about issues immediately affecting them, to increase their participation and to develop their confidence that their views will be listened to. It will also be important to look for ways to increase the participation of pupils with SEN in structures such as school councils. For some pupils with communication difficulties, schools may need to involve a facilitator, such as a signing interpreter, but the choice of when to involve another adult should be the pupil's, as much as possible – and not the school's. Other strategies for increasing participation and consultation are discussed in Chapter 15.

> **School councils:** bodies established to provide a forum for pupil representatives to raise issues of concern, and to enable the school management to consult with pupils on issues directly affecting their learning, well-being and experience in school. See Chapter 15.

As we have already discussed within this book, pupils with SEN are not the only pupils who may be marginalised within the school or classroom, and even where established mechanisms for consultation with pupils exist, these are not a guarantee that all the perspectives within the school will be represented, or valued. Teachers need to be constantly looking for curriculum opportunities and teaching strategies that enable all pupils to feel valued and able to express their opinions without anxiety.

Models of inclusion and SEN: deficit versus social models

Different approaches to inclusion and SEN in schools can often be traced back to one of two underlying models of individual need. Within the *medical* or *deficit* model, the difficulty is seen to reside within the pupil, who is regarded as having some kind of problem requiring treatment, or who deviates in some way from a 'normal' standard (Skidmore, 2004). This view regards the pupil as essentially passive, and as a person requiring expert or professional support in order to access educational opportunity. In the model there is no need for schools or individuals to change their attitudes as they have no responsibility for the problem, which remains with the pupil.

In contrast, *the social model* focuses on the ways in which society creates barriers for the individual pupil, through negative or discriminatory attitudes and exclusive actions. This view calls on society to change its practices and regards the pupil as someone who is being denied opportunities for choice and independence. In schools, the social model focuses on changing expectations, identifying alternative teaching strategies and approaches, and identifying and challenging school policies and practices that might act as barriers to inclusion.

SUMMARY

Dimension	Normative or deficit model	Social model
Location of difficulty	The problem is seen as 'within-child'	Society creates the 'problem'
Theory of 'educability' (how much a child is able to learn)	Hierarchical – some pupils are intrinsically more able than others	All pupils have an open-ended potential for learning
Explanation of educational difficulty	The focus is on the impairment or deficit	The focus is on an insufficiently responsive curriculum or pedagogy
Theories of teaching	The professional is seen as the expert There may be a cycle of dependency	The young person has rights Independence is seen as a priority
School response	Support for learning should remediate weaknesses of individual students	Support for learning should seek to reform curriculum and pedagogy across the school
Curriculum model	An alternative curriculum should be provided for the less able	A common curriculum should be provided for all students
Views of society as a whole	Stereotypical views may be held	Negative views are reinforced by language, the media and those who hold power.

Source: **Based on Skidmore (2004) and CWDC (2005)**

While these models have mainly been applied to SEN pupils, it could be argued that they are also applicable to other groups, such as looked after children or refugee or asylum seeker pupils who in some ways deviate from the 'norm'.

OVER TO YOU

Do you think pupils such as refugees or looked after children could be regarded in similar ways to the deficit or normative model suggested in the table above?

What might the table look like if applied to yet other groups of pupils? For example, boys or ethnic minority pupils? How would their 'educational difficulty' be defined?

What might this tell us about the ways in which society thinks about learners and learning?

How helpful are categories of individual need?

Earlier in this chapter we noted a list of different groups of pupils, identified by Ofsted (2001) as requiring particular consideration for ensuring inclusive practice. The practice of categorising different groups of individuals can be seen either as bureaucratic 'labelling' which reduces individuals to stereotypical designations or as part of a process to ensure that appropriate resources and support are available for all those at risk of social and/or educational exclusion. Maintaining a balance between these positions requires both individual teachers and whole school communities to evaluate not only their observed practice, but also their underlying values and attitudes towards learners as individuals. This process can sometimes be personally challenging for those involved.

THINKING IT THROUGH

Has anyone identified a pupil, or pupils, to you in the following way: 'He is a Traveller' or 'She is epileptic'?

How would this make you feel about the pupil or pupils?

Tick any of the following responses that apply. Try to be as honest as you can about your first reaction.

A. Concerned – you may not have enough knowledge to be able to deal with this type of pupil

B. Worried – you know this will create additional work for you

C. Unsure – about how this type of pupil can really fit in with work in your classroom because of their difficulties

D. Unclear – you need more specific information to support this pupil's learning

E. Positive – you have been wanting more experience with this type of pupil

F. None of the above – insert your own response

THINKING IT THROUGH: *CONTINUED*

Some comments on the above responses

A. While it is true that some pupils' learning needs, such as EAL, require specific knowledge, it is not always the case that different kinds of knowledge or pedagogy are required to support a range of learning needs. This will be explored later in this chapter.

B. This will be true if you believe that differentiated teaching always means giving different work as opposed to providing appropriate support. You may wish to discuss this with your mentor or tutor, or another colleague.

C. Try not to make assumptions about what pupils can or cannot do. In most cases there will be teaching approaches which can be used to involve all learners to the best of their ability. Take advice about curriculum areas where health and safety issues are involved, but do not automatically exclude a pupil from participation.

D. You are right. You need information on the pupil's previous achievement in as much detail as possible. Look for what this pupil *can* do, in order to identify the next stage of learning. It will be little help to you to know what s/he cannot do!

E. This is a helpful response in terms of extending your professional experience, but be careful you aren't inadvertently 'collecting' different categories of learner, without recognising them as individuals.

F. If your initial response was different from any of the suggestions, why was this? Was it because you feel confident in addressing the needs of all pupils, regardless of their nature, because you rejected the way language was used to describe the pupil, or for some other reason?

When we allocate learners to categories, we thereby ensure that they have features in common and it may become more difficult to regard them as individuals. It is also the case that labelling does not automatically help us to support the learner: there is rarely if ever only one teaching approach that will be appropriate for any given learning need.

We need to consider the possibility that some individual learners who have been grouped together may actually be more dissimilar to each other than similar, despite their common label. For this reason, labelling or categorising learners can sometimes be counter-productive. Another effect of creating categories of learners is that we inadvertently separate them from each other, by emphasising differences rather than similarities. It could be argued that this becomes a form of segregation or exclusive practice, even if it is intended to be the opposite. Attaching labels to individuals or groups may also present them as a 'problem' to be dealt with, or as a deviation from some notion of 'normality', rather than valuing diversity within the learning community and regarding it as a resource.

Are there advantages for learners of identifying various categories of learning need? Some individual learners clearly benefit from the allocation of additional resources to enable them to participate fully in education. Systems are needed to enable these resources to be provided, which leads to the identification of different categories of individual need. An additional argument could certainly be that identifying categories of individual need helps us recognise the ways in which some learners are marginalised within education and society and brings them to our attention in a positive way. Another argument is that we cannot discover how well our education system is providing for different groups of learners unless we monitor their achievement as distinct groups. We can then target research and resources where they are most needed. However, even where we recognise that there may be some benefits from identifying particular types of individual need, we should be extremely careful to avoid using language that suggests that the label is the most important thing about them, as in the activity above.

Woolfolk, Hughes and Walkup (2008: 130–131) draw on the work of Meece (2002) to argue for 'person first' language, whereby the focus is on the learner, rather than the nature of the individual need or challenge. Thus 'He is a pupil *with* special educational needs' rather than 'He *is* SEN' and 'She is a pupil *with* epilepsy' rather than 'She *is* epileptic'.

OVER TO YOU

Has reading the above section encouraged you to re-evaluate any of your previous thoughts or actions?

If so, in what ways will this make a difference to your attitudes and/or behaviour in future?

Bearing in mind the drawbacks associated with labelling or categorising learners, the next sections of this chapter will examine some issues that apply particularly to certain groups of pupils.

Including pupils with Special Educational Needs: issues and questions

The *Salamanca Statement* calls for the accommodation of pupils with special educational needs in 'regular' or mainstream schools, and this is reiterated in the revised SEN Code of Practice (DfES, 2001a). This emphasises the right of every child to a place in a mainstream school, and strengthens the involvement of children and their parents in decision-making processes affecting their educational provision. Pupils with SEN should be offered full access to a 'broad, balanced and relevant curriculum' in the line with the statutory Inclusion statement of the National Curriculum. This sets out three basic principles that all teachers and schools should follow:

- setting suitable learning challenges;
- responding to pupils' diverse learning needs;
- overcoming potential barriers to learning and assessment for individuals and groups of pupils.

(www.qcda.org.uk)

Note that the statement requires schools and teachers to overcome *potential* barriers to learning and inclusion; that is, to be proactive in assessing the learning context, rather than waiting for any difficulties to emerge and then seeking to remediate them.

These developments arise from a series of policy developments that can be traced back to 1978, when the prominent educational thinker, Mary Warnock, was commissioned to draw up a report on the education of pupils with disabilities of various kinds. The so-called 'Warnock Report' (DES, 1978) replaced the previous 10 statutory categories of 'handicap' with the term 'special educational needs'. The Report suggested that 'one in five' pupils might fall into this category, but that the majority of pupils could have their needs met in mainstream schools. Since then, there have been a series of policy documents focusing on SEN, with an increasing emphasis on inclusive practice, defined as the practice of integrating SEN pupils into mainstream classes wherever possible.

There are questions, however, as to how effective these policies have been. Some of the reasons for current concerns about provision for SEN pupils relate to uneven provision nationally – what is referred to as a 'post code lottery' where the amount of funding available to schools varies from local authority to local authority (Audit Commission, 2002; Ofsted, 2004). Perhaps even more importantly, there are also variations in the local definitions of SEN which may have an adverse effect on pupils' learning.

A pupil is defined as having special educational needs if he or she has a learning difficulty which requires special educational provision to be made for him or her. *The Education Act* of 1996, section 312, identifies a pupil as having learning difficulty if:

> He has a significantly greater difficulty in learning than the majority of children of his age,
> He has a disability which either prevents or hinders him from making use of educational facilities of a kind generally provided for children of his age in schools within the area of the local authority.
> (www.everychildmattters.gov.uk/glossary) *(gendered language in original)*

Ainscow and Muncey (1989) found that some schools were designating the 'bottom' 20% of their pupils as having SEN, on the basis of Warnock's estimate of one in five pupils having special educational needs, rather than on the basis of identified learning difficulty. More recently, an Ofsted survey produced similar findings (Ofsted, 2004). If schools inappropriately identify pupils as having SEN rather than as 'low achievers', this can result in lowered expectations and less attention being paid to improvements in learning for low-achieving pupils (Ofsted, 2004). There is obviously a continuum between low achievement and 'significantly greater difficulty in learning' along which individual pupils might be located, but once again, the critical issue will be that of considering the learner as an individual, rather than a member of a category.

The Ofsted survey of 2004 also found that while most mainstream schools were committed to including pupils with SEN and physical or sensory disability, only a minority were doing so successfully. The majority of schools were not yet adapting the curriculum or deploying adult support effectively enough to ensure the academic progress or increased independence of SEN pupils. In many cases provision for physical or sensory impairment had concentrated on issues to do with accommodating pupils physically, for instance by widening doors or equipping teachers with devices to support pupils with hearing impairment. Less emphasis had been placed on ensuring pupils' access to, and participation in, the curriculum.

(Ofsted, 2004: 5)

CASE STUDY

In each case, consider the following questions:

- How well are the needs of these pupils being met? In what ways have the schools sought to remove barriers to learning for these pupils?

- Do you consider that some barriers to full inclusion still remain for either of these pupils?

- In what ways are these pupils being enabled to develop independence?

- Are there further actions these schools might consider which could further develop independent learning for either of these pupils?

Gordon was born with spina bifida and uses a wheelchair for much of the day. He also requires special toilet routines as his condition affects his bladder and bowels. A Teaching Assistant (TA) is available to assist Gordon with access to the disabled toilet if he needs it, but during lessons the TA works with other pupils, as agreed with the class teacher. Gordon's wheelchair is located at the side of the classroom near the clasroom door, to ease his entry and exit, and for safety reasons.

Samantha in Year 4 has difficulties with speech and language, although this is improving. In the classroom she works with two other pupils who have learning difficulties with literacy and numeracy. All three pupils are regularly supported by a trained TA, who is familiar with their Individual Education Plans (IEPs). During whole-class sessions, the teacher aims to include Samantha and her fellow pupils in discussions, but Samantha rarely responds to direct questions or invitations to contribute, although she will answer via the TA who then tells the rest of the class what she has said.

How can we address these issues in our own classrooms?

While some aspects of improving inclusion for pupils with SEN will need to be addressed on a whole-school basis, there is a great deal that individual teachers can do to encourage the engagement and independence of all pupils. Many of the strategies are also likely to benefit other learners, including those who are low achievers but who do not necessarily have a learning difficulty.

In an examination of *Inclusion and Pupil Achievement*, conducted for the DfES (Dyson *et al.*, 2004) the researchers found no significant differences between effective classrooms containing pupils with SEN and those that did not. '. . . Apart from the fact that a relatively high proportion of classrooms (with SEN pupils) had access to TAs . . . there was nothing unusual in terms of resources or teaching techniques or organisation in these classrooms' (Dyson *et al.*, 2004: 74). However, what *was* observed was 'how familiar techniques were used to enhance the sorts of *flexibility and individual responsiveness* which also tended to characterise the structure of provision in these schools' (*op cit.*, italics ours).

RESEARCH BRIEFING: EFFECTIVE AND INCLUSIVE CLASSROOMS

The researchers noted that the teachers in the effective* and inclusive classrooms demonstrated some or all of the following characteristics:

- clear learning objectives;
- a sound knowledge of what the pupils already knew;
- sensitive support which did not single out individuals on the basis of their ability;
- flexible deployment of teaching assistants;
- the same curriculum for all pupils, but with some differentiated tasks;
- differential expectations, with praise given for individual achievement (but not indiscriminately);
- effective use of explanations and modelling of tasks;
- tasks could be completed in different ways, according to ability;
- flexible use of grouping and whole-class teaching;
- the use of a wide range of learning and teaching strategies: sorting cards, drawing, writing, graphical representation; verbal explanations by pupils.

Very similar findings were reported in the Ofsted survey report on inclusive schools (Ofsted, 2004: 15), with the use of multi-sensory resources for each part of the lesson, personal targets incorporated into the learning objectives and opportunities for independent learning embedded in the planning.

* 'Effective' classrooms were deemed to be those in schools with a comparatively high proportion of pupils with SEN, compared to other local schools, but which were identified as 'high performing' on the basis of the average measured attainment of their pupils.

Source: Dyson *et al.* (2004), p. 52

Multi-sensory resources: aids to learning that incorporate visual and auditory materials, and, where appropriate, opportunities for physical manipulation of items, such as mathematical equipment, or the use of aids for sequencing events to support writing.

What these two reports show is that inclusive teaching is based in good practice, and in an inclusive ethos where the teacher plans on the basis of knowledge of individual learners. These effective teachers used different forms of grouping to avoid segregation of pupils with SEN, and reduced over-dependency on adult support through planning for independent learning.

'Gifted and Talented' pupils

As with low-achieving pupils and those with SEN, it could be argued that flexible organisation and effective differentiation should be sufficient to cater for more able pupils, including those designated as academically **gifted**. The inclusive classrooms identified by Ofsted (2004) and Dyson *et al.* (2004), referred to above, engaged higher-ability learners as effectively as the less able, and provided opportunities for pupils to support each other's learning.

However, it is not always easy to recognise that an individual pupil falls into the 'gifted' category, as many pupils in this group actually underachieve *in terms of their potential*. This may mean that their academic performance appears 'average' or even lacking in effort. This underachievement can result from a range of factors, some of which have been referred to in earlier chapters. These can include peer pressure leading to an unwillingness to stand out from the group; low self-esteem, perhaps resulting from low expectations on the part of teachers or parents; or frustration resulting from a lack of challenge in the work provided. Pupils with particular talents that are unrecognised, especially if they are in less well-known sports or areas of music or dance, can also become frustrated since their school experiences do not reflect the

Gifted (and talented): there are no precise definitions of what it means to be academically gifted, but the term is broadly used to identify those pupils who demonstrate a significantly higher level of ability than most pupils of the same age.

Photo 11.2 The talents of pupils whose activities lie outside the 'mainstream' of school life can sometimes go unrecognised. It is important for schools to find ways to discover, and celebrate, these achievements

Source: Pearson Education Ltd/Photodisc. Lawrence M. Sawyer

aspects of their lives that are of most interest to them. (See, for example, the case study of 'John' available at **www.qcda.org.uk/qca_2049.aspx**. Other case studies are also available at **www.qcda.org.uk**; search on gifted and talented and follow links to Guidance on teaching the Gifted and Talented; case studies).

There are forms of checklist for helping to identify gifted and talented learners, but many gifted and talented pupils fall outside these parameters, especially if they also have one or more learning disabilities, such as dyslexia, or visual or hearing impairments, or if they exhibit challenging behaviour. Pupils whose first language is not English are particularly prone to have their academic abilities underestimated. Thus, while such checklists can be helpful, it will be important for teachers to keep an open mind about individuals, rather than to attempt to fit them into preconceived structures. Individuals may not fit these descriptions precisely *because* they are gifted or talented in particular ways!

 **CASE STUDY**

David was the youngest of three children, and his older siblings were academically successful at school. However, during his primary school years David struggled with all aspects of the curriculum. At the age of 7 his level of reading was well below average and he displayed no particular interest in any curriculum area. His school acknowledged his lack of engagement, but at that time no further support was forthcoming. At home he exhibited a fascination with the mechanical aspects of household items, which he was able to dismantle and re-assemble, but his primary education offered him few opportunities to apply these abilities in school. He was finally motivated to improve his reading through his own desire to read the book of *1001 Dalmations*, after seeing the cartoon film – until that point he had appeared to be unaffected by his apparently low level of literacy. David's mother reported that he had persisted with reading the book night after night, and read it three times before he was satisfied.

David lived in an area with selection at the age of 11, and unlike his older bother and sister, he failed to reach the standard required for grammar school entry. His parents made the decision to place him in a small independent school, believing that the smaller class size might be supportive. However, for the first few years David did not appear to make substantial academic improvements. He was antagonistic to some teachers, made few friends and exhibited little interest in learning most subjects.

Around the age of 13, David was introduced to science in a practical way that engaged his interest for the first time. This became the main focus of his educational life, and motivated him to improve his achievement in other curriculum areas in order to achieve the necessary examination results which would admit him to a local sixth form. There he obtained good A level results and gained a university place for a science degree. He then went on to study for a PhD, and is now a highly successful professional scientist.

OVER TO YOU

This true story took place a number of years ago. Could these events happen now?

How would you describe David's individual needs as a learner?

Could he be described as gifted, as having SEN, or are neither of these categories appropriate?

On the basis of your experience so far, or using other reading, can you suggest teaching strategies which might be appropriate for a pupil such as David, and which would help him to engage more fully with the curriculum at an earlier stage?

Pupils who are identified as gifted may experience forms of pressure associated with this identification, in much the same way that some pupils labelled as 'SEN' respond to categorisation. Since 'giftedness' may be associated with some curriculum areas more than others, it is important not to expect high levels of performance in all subjects, or to transmit such expectations to the pupil concerned. It is also important not to assume that all very able or gifted pupils can work independently, or that they are self-motivated to learn.

The evidence suggests that the majority of very able, or gifted, pupils have learning needs that are broadly similar to those of other learners where differentiation is used effectively:

- they flourish in a supportive learning environment, where they feel secure to ask questions, and are encouraged to do so;
- where they are provided with appropriately challenging tasks, and learn to accept failure as well as success;
- where they receive focused praise related to their personal achievements and are involved in setting targets for their learning development.

Very able or gifted pupils may also need to be supported in developing social and team-working skills, and respecting the views and contributions of others, through sensitive planning of collaborative learning.

However, as has been indicated above, some gifted pupils do experience difficulties in school:

> For some pupils, educational progress is less straightforward than it is for others, and their learning needs call for careful consideration. The most common categories identified in the literature are those gifted and talented pupils who:
>
> - have unbalanced profiles, eg good oral but poor written skills
> - experience motivational problems, and may underachieve or truant
> - find organisation and/or time management a problem
> - lack support and encouragement for their learning
> - find their ability difficult to handle.
>
> *Source*: **www.brookes.ac.uk/schools/education/rescon/ cpdgifted/docs/unit1/1-2-individualneeds.pdf**

In such cases there are a range of strategies that may need to be employed, including the involvement of learning mentors or other support, or provision of focused study support. Identifying the appropriate strategy will normally be the responsibility of the school's Gifted and Talented co-ordinator, whose role it is to ensure that pupils identified as being very able or having particular talents are appropriately supported. As with any other pupil, you will need to be sure that you are familiar with the nature of the support that is being provided and how you can ensure that the pupil(s) concerned can access it to best advantage in relation to your own teaching.

OVER TO YOU

In training

Have you encountered any pupil(s) identified as very able or gifted in a particular area? What provision have you made, or observed, to support such pupils within normal lessons? In the light of the previous section of this chapter, do you feel this support could have been developed further?

Starting your career

Are you aware of any pupils in your class(es) who might be underachieving in terms of their potential, as discussed above? How would you consider altering your own planning in order to support such pupils in the future? What systems exist in your school to offer further support for these pupils?

Investigating learning and teaching

Why is the underachievement of gifted and talented pupils such an area of concern? What is the role of teacher expectations in the (mis-)identification of gifted and talented pupils? What factor might prevent teachers from recognising the learning potential of some pupils?

The 'Launchpads' area of **http://www.brookes.ac.uk/schools/education/ rescon/cpdgifted/** provides useful information about the underachievement of gifted and talented pupils in both primary and secondary schools.

Withdrawal: the practice of withdrawing pupils from classroom activities to provide additional support in relation to an identified need.

Acceleration: the practice of 'speeding up' an individual pupil's academic development.

Curriculum enrichment: providing work within the normal classroom to extend the thinking of very able pupils, rather than 'moving the learner on' as with acceleration.

Withdrawal, acceleration and 'curriculum enrichment': a challenge to inclusion, or a means towards achieving it?

The practice of withdrawing pupils from classroom activities to provide additional support in relation to an identified need operates in a variety of forms, and in many schools. Such support lessons include focused literacy teaching sessions for low-achieving pupils, which are currently recommended as good practice to improve pupil achievement, and specialised provision of English lessons for pupils with English as an additional language. Lessons such as these should be regarded as 'intervention' programmes: that is, a short-term strategy for overcoming a temporary barrier to progress. They should have clear objectives which are regularly assessed against agreed criteria and a planned exit strategy, which identifies how and when the pupil will be expected to be reintegrated into full lessons. According to the Primary National Strategy website, 'Focused, time limited support of this kind is the best way of securing long-term curriculum entitlement' (**http://www.standards.dfes.gov.uk/primary/faqs/ inclusion**).

The situation may be different where pupils with more significant learning difficulties are concerned. Some periods of withdrawal for specialised teaching (for instance in Speech and Language Units, or units for hearing-impaired pupils attached to schools) complement their experience in mainstream classrooms. However, such long-term withdrawal activities need to be carefully managed or they can have detrimental effects, as pupils can become isolated from their peers and lose opportunities to benefit from learning from others as well as possibly lacking a broader curriculum experience.

CASE STUDY

A lonely experience. . . .

In some schools the arrangements (for pupils with significant learning difficulties) meant that the pupils remained out of the class group for much of the day, isolated from their peers and deprived of access to a broad curriculum. Additionally, those pupils who needed contact with the best teaching, whatever the personal qualities and skills of the teaching assistants, were denied it. In one primary school, a pupil with profound and multiple learning difficulties was taught for most of each day by a teaching assistant on her own as there were no other pupils with similar needs and the mainstream lessons were unsuitable. The school did find some opportunities in music and art to include her with her peers but, overall, she had a lonely experience each day.

(Ofsted, 2004: 17)

OVER TO YOU

This situation was clearly unsatisfactory for the pupil concerned.

However, the SEN Code of Practice (DfES, 2001a) gives parents and pupils the right to opt for an education in a mainstream school.

What are the tensions for schools that arise from situations such as the one described in this case study?

Acceleration and curriculum enrichment: another kind of withdrawal?

Some schools have also taken the decision to support academically very able or gifted pupils through the use of withdrawal groups, or through curriculum acceleration. 'Acceleration' usually means moving a pupil into a year group higher than that for their chronological age for all or part of the curriculum, but can also mean providing individual work within their own classroom designed to meet learning objectives for older years. This process overlaps with curriculum 'enrichment' approaches. Critics of some forms of acceleration express concerns about social isolation where younger pupils may not have developed the social maturity to interact effectively with their older peers.

Curriculum enrichment involves providing work within the normal classroom which extends the thinking of very able pupils by considering the area under study in more depth, rather than 'moving the learner on' as with acceleration. Enrichment activities can also occur outside the regular curriculum, taking place after school, at weekends or during the holiday period. This provides more opportunities to involve pupils in experiences which are not confined to particular curriculum areas, as well as enabling them to follow up deep personal interests. However, the benefits of such programmes are unclear and critics of such enrichment activities provided for very able pupils argue that the principles of inclusive practice are being ignored. A review by the National Foundation for Educational Research found 'little evidence of the long-term benefits of enrichment. There are also few criteria for evaluating the coherence of enrichment activities in relation to the whole curriculum' (White, Fletcher-Campbell and Ridley, 2003).

CONTROVERSY

Not everyone agrees with current policies concerning Gifted and Talented pupils. Read the following extracts from a newspaper article by Bethan Marshall.

Bethan Marshall: Why should the gifted and talented be favoured?

The Independent newspaper: Thursday, 10 August 2006

. . . The Government's 'gifted and talented' policy . . . uses the idea that these two words appear synonymous, so lending them the veneer of parity, but exploits the fact that they have a slightly different resonance . . . The difficulty is that the words themselves are not synonymous. They have a kind of pecking order. Gifted feels better than talented and the policy, which was allegedly designed to encourage a broader view of what it means to excel, has become focused on a very small elite of clever children.

What makes this all the more problematic is the narrowness of the way these children are identified. . . . Secondary schools tend to use national curriculum tests and cognitive aptitude tests to select the small coterie of pupils picked in any given year-group. . . . Moreover, there are few mechanisms to reappraise a child's rating as gifted and talented. Once pupils are picked up as special at 11, there is little attempt later in their school career to change that description. Yet they have more money spent on them than children who are not singled out in this way. . . .

Some of the arguments against the scheme are the most obviously egalitarian. It is unclear why very able children should get special privileges, such as additional trips and workshops denied to the vast majority of pupils. . . . the dangers of labelling pupils extend well beyond a threat to equality. What is so damaging about our national obsession with ability is not the idea of differential ability per se, but the implication that ability is fixed and immutable.

. . . In the end, all such views are anti-educational. The purpose of school must be that learning and the acquisition of knowledge makes you smarter. But the metaphor of an intelligence quotient is it implies there are only so many 'smart' cells to go around. Half a century's worth of evidence suggests this is a mistake, cognitively and socially.

The perversity of the 'gifted and talented' register is it negates aspiration and builds into the structures of education lower expectations of 95 per cent of children. This must change.

The message of school should be that education matters because we can all improve; not that life is sweet if a test tells you that you are bright.

THINKING IT THROUGH

(This article was written in 2006, and there have been some changes to policy regarding Gifted and Talented pupils in the meantime. However, the key points are still worth considering.)

How far do you agree or disagree with the writer's arguments?

For example: do you agree that the term 'gifted' sounds superior to that of 'talented'?

If so, why might that be the case?

Look back at the table comparing the *medical/deficit* model of inclusion with the *social* model. Where is the author suggesting that the advocates for Gifted and Talented policies stand?

How can schools develop an inclusive ethos?

This is a difficult question to answer directly, as there appear to be a wide range of routes towards whole-school inclusive ethos. However, it is unlikely that inclusive attitudes will be adopted towards pupils if there is not also a collaborative and participatory culture amongst the staff, supported by the school leadership.

Booth and Ainscow, the authors of the *Index for Inclusion*, suggest that inclusion is a process, not a system: 'It is an ideal to which schools can aspire but which is never fully reached. But inclusion happens as soon as the process of increasing participation is started' (Booth *et al.*, 2000: 3). In other words, there is not a fixed 'checklist' that will indicate when a school has achieved inclusive status, because the views and values of those within the school will change as they reflect on their own practice. This relies on a critical examination of the values of the school as a whole, and of individual teachers within it, and will be reflected not just in its policies but in everyday practices in teaching, learning and assessment and in the school's management practices.

Constructivist/ constructivism: a view of learning that emphasises the active role of the learner in building understanding, and making sense of information from experience.

RESEARCH BRIEFING

A research review into school actions that promoted participation by all students (Dyson, Howes and Roberts, 2002) found that high levels of collaboration amongst staff, commitment to equality of opportunity and a respect for difference were important aspects of inclusive cultures. Although these did not automatically lead to enhanced student participation, they were clearly prerequisites. Teachers in these schools were more likely to respect diverse students, and were more likely to utilise constructivist, 'problem solving' approaches to teaching and learning which facilitate participation. More inclusive schools were also more likely to adopt forms of school organisation that enabled pupils to learn together rather than being separated into specialised groups. The importance of good links with parents and the local community was also evident, but it was suggested that here, too, diversity needed to be recognised and valued, rather than seeking to arrive at complete agreement in all areas. This enabled different groups to be more willing to consider a range of possible solutions to complex problems.

However, the review also noted some barriers to the development of inclusive schools in terms of local and national policy initiatives, such as the encouragement of setting by ability and the importance placed on high stakes testing.

OVER TO YOU

In training

Drawing on the various activities in this chapter, what features would you look for in an inclusive school?

Starting your career

How far do you feel your school reflects an inclusive culture?

In what ways does your classroom practice support the culture within the school?

Are there areas of your own practice you would like to change after reading this chapter?

Investigating learning and teaching

Research suggests that whole-school agreement on the nature of inclusive practice is important, but there are likely to be differing opinions within a school community as to what inclusion means. What might be the implications for pupils if differing views exist within a given school?

You may find it useful to support your thinking by reading Sikes, Lawson and Parker (2007).

SUMMARY

This chapter has focused on just a few of the groups in danger of marginalisation.

Others, such as looked after children, teenage mothers and refugee and asylum seeker pupils, are also identified as having specific needs. However, as we have argued earlier, the more we separate our pupils into groups with apparently related needs, the less we might see them as individuals, and thus fail to find out their real needs as individual learners. We have tried to emphasise the importance of approaches to teaching and learning that are flexible and responsive to the needs of all pupils, whatever their current abilities.

TAKING YOUR PRACTICE FURTHER

Research into barriers to participation suggests that teachers' misplaced assumptions about what their pupils can do are a significant element (Ainscow, Booth and Dyson, 2006). How well do you know what pupils in your class(es) *can* do, as opposed to what you think they can't?

The same research found that accessing pupils' perspectives challenged teachers' accepted beliefs, and helped them reconsider they ways that they taught. Chapter 15 considers the ways in which 'pupil voice' contributes to a better understanding of effective learning. How could you find out more about how your pupils experience learning? See Research Briefing Number 6 at **www.tlrp.org/pub/research.html** for one such example.

TAKING YOUR THINKING FURTHER

This chapter has asked you to evaluate your own attitudes and classroom practice in relation to inclusion, and to consider that of others. This is a challenging area, with constant ongoing debate.

The texts given below in 'Find out more' will introduce you to the range of discussions.

For example: Norwich, B. (2008) *Dilemmas of Difference, Inclusion and Disability. International Perspectives and Future Directions*. London: Routledge.

While this book focuses particularly on special educational issues, broader questions about the nature of inclusion in more general education are raised.

Find out more

There are a large number of helpful books focusing on inclusive practice, of which the list below is a small sample:

Ainscow, M., Booth, T. and Dyson, A. (2006) *Improving Schools, Developing Inclusion*. **London: Routledge.**
This text uses the experiences of 25 schools participating in a research project to explore ways in which schools might develop more inclusive practice.

Farrell, P. and Ainscow, M. (2002) *Making Special Education Inclusive*. **London: David Fulton.**
This is an edited collection of chapters examining a wide range of issues associated with inclusive practice.

Norwich, B. (2008) *Dilemmas of Difference, Inclusion and Disability. International Perspectives and Future Directions*. **London: Routledge.**
This thought-provoking text explores the concept of 'difference' as applied to Special Educational Needs through examination of practice in three different countries, and from a number of different theoretical perspectives.

Skidmore, D. (2004*) Inclusion – the Dynamic of School Development*. **Maidenhead: Open University.**
This text develops case studies of practice in secondary schools and examines the tensions between theoretical positions on inclusion and teachers' experiences and attitudes.

Soan, S. (2004) (ed) *Additional Educational Needs – Inclusive Approaches to Teaching*. **London: David Fulton.**

This is a very good introductory textbook, with a wide focus, including bilingual learners and gifted and talented pupils. It includes case studies and supporting activities.

The Teacher Training Resource Bank (**www.ttrb.ac.uk**) also provides a wide range of resources related to inclusion. TTRB also has a sub-portal spcifically focused on SEN issues accessed via the TTRB main site (**http://sen.ttrb.ac.uk**).

www.Multiverse.ac.uk focuses on the educational achievement of pupils from diverse backgrounds in relation to ethnicity, social class, EAL, religious diversity, refugee and asylum seeker pupils, and Traveller and Roma pupils.

Glossary

Acceleration: the practice of 'speeding up' an individual pupil's academic development. Usually means moving a pupil into a year group higher than that for their chronological age for all or part of the curriculum, but can also mean providing individual work within their own classroom designed to meet learning objectives for older years.

Child-centred pedagogy: an approach to teaching which focuses on the learning needs of the children in the class, rather than on following a pre-set curriculum with objectives determined by the teacher or adminstrators. It is closely linked, but not identical, to differentiation, which can also be employed in the context of a predetermined curriculum.

Constructivist/constructivism: a view of learning that emphasises the active role of the learner in building understanding, and making sense of information from experience.

Curriculum enrichment: providing work within the normal classroom to extend the thinking of very able pupils, rather than 'moving the learner on' as with acceleration. Enrichment activities may also take place outside the regular curriculum: after school, at weekends or during the holiday period.

Differentiation/differentiated planning: the adjustment of the teaching process according to the learning needs of pupils. Differentiated planning is generally taken to mean the matching of work to the differing capabilities within the class, matched to an overall intended learning outcome. Differentiation may operate by varying the type of tasks set for different groups of pupils, by varying the resources provided, varying expectations of the outcome or providing higher levels of adult support.

Family literacy: the use of structured literacy programmes shared by several members of the family. The intention is to raise the literacy levels of all family members through a focus on supporting the literacy development of one or more children.

Gifted (and talented): there are no precise definitions of what it means to be academically gifted, but the term is broadly used to identify those pupils who demonstrate a significantly higher level of ability than most pupils of the same age. This ability could be displayed in one or more curriculum areas, or as physical or artistic talent.

See **http://www.brookes.ac.uk/schools/education/ rescon/cpdgifted/docs/unit1/1-1- definitionsofabilityunit1.pdf** for a detailed discussion of this contested area.

Hidden curriculum: this term is used to identify the ways in which schools can transmit implicit norms, values and assumptions through their organisational features and the attitudes and values displayed by the school staff. The term is usually used in a critical sense, to suggest disagreement with the values and assumptions being transmitted. The term usually implies the operation of exclusionary practices or forms of social control: often both.

High stakes testing or assessment: where summative assessment is used for making decisions that affect the status or future of students, teachers or schools.

Learning mentor: a person working within a primary or secondary school to support pupils identified as being 'at risk' of academic failure. They form a bridge between pastoral and academic concerns. The learning mentor may be a qualified teacher or a member of the support staff who has received specific training.

Multi-sensory resources: aids to learning that incorporate visual and auditory materials, and, where appropriate, opportunities for physical manipulation of items, such as mathematical equipment, or the use of aids for sequencing events to support writing.

Pupil voice: a term used to identify a range of strategies utilised to gather pupils' views about all aspects of school life. See Chapter 15.

School councils: bodies established to provide a forum for pupil representatives to raise issues of concern, and to enable the school management to consult with pupils on issues directly affecting their learning, well-being and experience in school. See Chapter 15.

Withdrawal: the practice of withdrawing pupils from classroom activities to provide additional support in relation to an identified need.

References

Ainscow, M., Booth, T. and Dyson, A. (2006) *Improving Schools, Developing Inclusion*. London: Routledge.

Ainscow, M. and Muncey, J. (1989) *Meeting Individual Needs in the Primary School*. London: David Fulton.

Audit Commission (2002) *Statutory Assessment and Statements of SEN: In Need of Review?* London: Audit Commission.

Booth, T., Ainscow, M., Black-Hawkins, K., Vaughn, M. and Shaw, L. (2000) *Index for Inclusion: Developing Learning and Participation in Schools*. Bristol: Centre for Studies in Inclusive Education (CSIE).

Children's Workforce Development Council (2005) *Learning Mentor Training Module 2*. London: CWDC.

DCSF (2008) *Bullying Involving Children with Special Educational Needs and Disabilities*. Annesley: DCSF.

DES (1978) *Special Educational Needs (The Warnock Report)*. London: HMSO.

DfEE (1999) *Excellence in Cities*. Available at: **www.standards.dfes.gov.uk/sie/eic**

DfES (2001a) *Special Educational Needs Code of Practice*. Nottingham: DfES.

DfES (2001b) *SEN toolkit; section 7 'Enabling Pupil Participation'*. Annesley: DfES.

Dyson, A. (2001) Special needs in the twenty first century: where we've been and where we're going, *British Journal of Special Education*, Vol. 28, No. 1: pp. 24–29.

Dyson, A., Farell, P., Polat F., Hutcheson G. and Gallannaugh, F. (2004) *Inclusion and Pupil Achievement*. DfES Research Report RR578. Nottingham: DfES.

Dyson, A., Howes, A. and Roberts, B. (2002) *A Systematic Review of the Effectiveness of School Level Actions for Promoting Participation by All Students*, EPPI Centre. London: Institute of Education.

MacBeath, J., Galton, M., Steward, S., MacBeath, A. and Page, C. (2006) *The Costs of Inclusion: Commissioned and Funded by the National Union of Teachers*. Cambridge: University of Cambridge, Faculty of Education.

Meece J.L. (2002) *Child and Adolescent Development for Educators*. New York: McGraw-Hill.

Mittler, P. (2000) *Working towards Inclusive Education*. London: David Fulton.

Norwich, B. (2008) *Dilemmas of Difference, Inclusion and Disability. International Perspectives and Future Directions*. London: Routledge.

Ofsted (2000) *Evaluating Educational Inclusion: Guidance for Inspectors and Schools*. London: Ofsted.

Ofsted (2004) *Special Educational Needs and Disability: Towards Inclusive Schools*. London: Ofsted. Available at: **www.ofsted.gov.uk**.

Powell, S., Tod, J., Cornwall, J. and Soan, S. (2004), *A Systematic Review of how Theories Explain Learning Behaviour in School Contexts*. EPPI Centre. London: Institute of Education.

Sebba, J. and Ainscow, M. (1996) international developments in inclusive schooling, *Cambridge Journal of Education*, Vol. 26, No. 1: pp. 5–18.

Sikes, P., Lawson, H. and Parker, M. (2007) Voices on: teachers and teaching assistants talk about inclusion,

International Journal of Inclusive Education, Vol. 11, No. 3: pp. 355–370.

Skidmore, D. (2004) *Inclusion: The Dynamic of School Development*. Maidenhead: Open University Press.

UNCRC (1990) *United Nations Convention on the Rights of the Child*. Available at: **http://www.unicef.org.uk/ publications/pub_detail.asp?pub_id=210**.

UNESCO (1994) *The Salamanca Statement and Framework for Action on Special Needs Education*. Available at: **http://www.unesco.org/education/ pdf/SALAMA_E.pdf**.

Wedell, K. (2005) Dilemmas in the quest for inclusion, *British Journal of Special Education*, Vol. 32, No. 1: pp. 3–11.

White, K., Fletcher-Campbell, F. and Ridley, K. (2003) *What Works for Gifted and Talented Pupils? A Review of Recent Research*. London: NFER.

Woolfolk, A., Hughes, M. and Walkup, V. (2008) *Psychology in Education*. Harlow: Pearson.

Pearson Education Ltd/Studio 8. Clark Wiseman

PART 3 Enhancing Teaching for Learning

The previous part of this book considered some fundamental aspects of classroom practice. We now consider further areas that can have a positive impact on your teaching and on pupils' learning experiences. Reflection on your own teaching will help to identify areas for development or improvement, and you can enhance pupils' learning still further by building on these ideas developed as part of a small-scale, systematic classroom investigation. This part also considers how collaborating with others within and beyond the school, and consulting with pupils about aspects of their learning and experience in school, can have a positive impact on your own professional development and pupils' engagement with learning.

12 Reflecting on Learning

In this chapter you will:

- Reflect on your understanding of the terms 'reflection on practice' or 'reflection on learning'
- Recognise that reflection on practice can take different forms
- Consider whether reflection on practice *necessarily* enhances teaching and learning
- Evaluate your own use of reflection on practice in enhancing learning
- Consider ways to assess how the outcomes of reflection on practice may bring about improvements in pupils learning and achievement

What does reflection on practice mean?

If you were asked to explain what reflection on practice means to you, which of these ideas would you select (more than one is possible!)

1. Writing down what you did in the lesson	2. Discussing what you have done with others	3. Understanding yourself better as a teacher
4. Learning from your mistakes	5. A waste of time	6. Identifying where to go next in your teaching
7. Something you had to do for your ITT course	8. Improving your practice	9. Examining your actions compared to your values
10. Considering the role of education in society	11. Thinking about pupils' learning	12. Learning from observation of other people's teaching

Introduction

This chapter considers the importance of improving learning through critical reflection on aspects of our own and others' practice, and on pupils' learning. It examines some definitions of reflective practice and offers suggestions for ways of supporting reflection on practice, and of evaluating whether the outcomes of reflection contribute to improvements in pupils' learning. You will find a number of slightly different phrases or terms about reflective practice used in different books, including in this chapter. We have tended to use the phrase 'reflection on practice' to encompass reflection on our own practice, reflection on our pupils' learning and reflection on what we learn by observing others. However, it is important to remember that the improvement of learning is always the main focus of the process.

It is very unlikely that anyone who is currently being trained as a teacher in the UK, or who has been trained within the past 30 years or so, has not heard or read the terms 'reflective practice' and 'reflection on practice'. Current and previous Standards for Qualified Teacher Status in England have expected prospective teachers to 'reflect on and improve their practice'. Teacher training courses expect student teachers to demonstrate this capacity by providing reflective comments on their classroom teaching on placement, and sometimes through reflective commentary during their taught courses through the use of journals or learning logs. Many Continuing Professional Development programmes also advocate the use of learning journals as an aid to professional reflection. The belief that reflection leads to improvement in practice is very strongly established in the educational cultures of the UK, Australia, New Zealand, North America and many other countries.

However, believing that reflection on teaching and learning, and on educational issues in general, is important is not the same as saying what it *is*. Twenty years ago the educational writer James Calderhead warned that 'the phrase has become a slogan, disguising numerous practices' (Calderhead, 1989: 46). Thus different kinds of activity can be described as reflective practice, but lead to different outcomes and are based in different beliefs about teaching and learning. Some of these different views are suggested in the activity at the start of this chapter.

OVER TO YOU

Go back to your responses to the opening activity in this chapter. Can you develop your personal definition of reflection on practice based on your choices from the list of options?

Are there ideas missing from the list that you feel are important to complete your definition?

Some background

The concept of the importance of reflection dates back to the influential work of John Dewey (1933), one of the pioneers of modern educational thinking. Dewey contrasted ideas of 'routine action' with those of 'reflective action'. Routine actions are carried out 'because we've always done it this way' or 'because that's what we've been told to do'. They rely on tradition, instructions from a higher authority or institutional expectation and can lead to a relatively static situation where response to changing priorities or events can be difficult. In contrast, 'reflective action' is based on self-appraisal and critical examination of context and purpose, which enables flexibility, responsiveness to change and social awareness. Dewey's concepts have been applied to teaching by a large number of authors and have formed the basis of significant theories of teacher knowledge and professional development, including those associated with teacher research which is considered in Chapter 13.

What does Dewey mean by 'routine action'? No-one would deny that certain routines are vital in contexts where large numbers of young people are moving around buildings and engaging in a range of activities where individual safety and access to learning need to be ensured. However, Dewey's idea of 'routine action' is not only concerned with what we normally refer to as classroom or school routines, but refers to any actions or behaviours we might adopt in an unthinking manner. These could include the adoption of teaching behaviours based on our own memories of being at school, or in imitation of other teachers, but could also include behaviour based on assumptions around issues such as gender, socio-economic status, ethnicity etc.

One example of a routine classroom action might be the common practice of insisting that pupils raise their hand to answer a question.

The intended outcomes are to maintain an orderly atmosphere by avoiding 'calling out', and also to encourage individual pupils to recognise that everyone should have a chance to participate, which is denied if they call out answers before others have had a chance to respond.

However, an unintended outcome of the 'hands up' routine might be that some pupils 'learn' that if they don't raise their hands, they need not engage with the lesson as they will not need to know the answer. Most teachers become aware of this possibility and vary their questioning style appropriately. However, they have often had to have the potential drawback pointed out to them during their initial training, since this routine is strongly ingrained as a 'teacherly' behaviour, often on the basis of their own memories of being a pupil.

WORKING IN THE CLASSROOM

Can you identify any 'routine actions' that you have noticed in school so far? Why do you think such routines are observed? What do you think are the intended outcomes of these routines for pupils? Are there any possible *unintended* outcomes?

More recently, the influential work of Schön (1983) has examined reflective action as applied to teaching. Schön is well known among educationalists for his distinction between 'reflection-in-action' and 'reflection-on-action': the first being the capacity for making rapid judgements about how to respond in a given situation, and the second being deliberate consideration after an event. In his book *The Reflective Practitioner* (1983), Schön also discusses different ideas about teachers' knowledge and how teachers develop their own theories for application in the classroom. He rejects the idea that teachers act as technicians who apply the theories of others ('technical rationalism') and argues that teachers' professional knowledge is constructed through reflection on what they actually do in specific contexts and then applied in practice, becoming 'knowledge-in-action'. This is not to say that teachers should not be aware of, and examine, the ideas of other people, but that teachers have a particular kind of personal knowledge, developed in and through practice, that should be recognised and valued.

The influential writers we have so far referred to were concerned with examining broad principles of knowledge and teachers' knowledge in particular. They were not concerned with exploring what teachers actually reflect on, or suggesting what they *should* reflect on. This is a more difficult and contested area that is intimately bound up with questions of values and beliefs about the purpose of education. Thus two people who hold quite opposing views about educational issues could both be equally convinced of the importance of reflective practice.

RESEARCH BRIEFING: TYPES OF REFLECTION

Zeichner and Tabachnik (2001) discuss four main traditions that have emerged in discussions of reflective teaching. These traditions are not mutually exclusive, but represent the different focus or priority that has been identified in each case.

RESEARCH BRIEFING: *CONTINUED*

The *academic tradition* is concerned with the importance of subject knowledge, and of the importance of reflecting on the most appropriate ways of enabling learners to understand the subject.

The *social efficiency* tradition focuses on the application of teaching approaches that have been seen to be effective through research and evidence. In this tradition, the role of reflection is to make judgements about the application of the suggested practice to the specific school context.

The *developmentalist tradition* is based on the belief that deciding what should be taught, and how it should be taught, relates first and foremost to the developmental stage of the learner. In this tradition, reflection concerns itself with the learning of individual children or groups of children.

The *social reconstructionist tradition* is concerned both with the teacher's own action and with questions of social justice and the improvement of society. Here the reflective teacher examines issues within the school and their own classroom concerned with equality, democracy and social relationships: race, gender and social class, and how the process of schooling does, or does not, bring about a more equitable society. This tradition also often involves collaboration with others, and values the development of 'learning communities'. This tradition in particular also requires the reflective teacher to examine their own implicit assumptions, and to consider the difference between what one says one believes and what one does in practice. Thus reflection on self, or 'reflexivity', is an important aspect of this form of reflective practice.

THINKING IT THROUGH

Examples of how these traditions may operate in practice might be as follows: imagine a situation where an examination of pupils' work indicates that many of them have not understood an important concept within a particular subject area.

- Operating within the *academic tradition*, the teacher would focus their reflection on trying to find ways of improving their pupils' understanding of the subject by trying different teaching strategies, and might perhaps read books or articles to get ideas. The focus would be on the *subject*.

- Operating within the *social efficiency tradition*, the teacher would look for ways to increase their pupils' subject understanding through looking for teaching methods that seemed to have been proven to be effective, and then deciding which they felt would work best with these pupils in this school context. The focus would be on the *proven effectiveness* of the teaching approach.

THINKING IT THROUGH: *CONTINUED*

- Operating within the *developmentalist tradition*, the teacher would consider the learning needs of individual pupils or groups of pupils to decide whether they were ready for this next stage in learning, or whether they needed further reinforcement of previous learning to consolidate their understanding. The focus would be on the *pupils*.

- Depending on the subject area, operating within the *social reconstructionist tradition* might involve the teacher reflecting on whether the subject matter had been presented in such as way as to include all pupils within the class, in terms of gender, ethnicity and/or social class. The focus would be on the *role of education in society*.

OVER TO YOU

Where would you place yourself in terms of these four traditions?

What role do the other traditions play in your thinking?

Each of these traditions can also clearly be recognised within educational policy and practice for the 7–14 age group, although it has to be said that not everyone will agree with the ways they are manifested. The *academic tradition* is reflected in the content of national curricula and the National Strategies in England, and on discussions about the most effective ways to support learning in different subject areas, while the *social efficiency tradition* can be linked to the current belief in 'evidence-based practice' which underpins government thinking about education in the UK, and in England in particular. It is also the tradition that most closely matches the conception of reflection on the Standards for Qualified Teacher Status in England. The *developmentalist tradition* underpins much practice within primary education throughout the UK, and also within Key Stage 3 in England with the increasing introduction of Project Based Learning. Work being undertaken in many English schools in response to *Excellence and Enjoyment* (DfES, 2003) in terms of a more integrated and 'creative' curriculum could also be termed *developmentalist*. Changing curricula in Scotland, Northern Ireland and Wales also reflect this trend. Finally, the *social reconstructionist tradition* is represented in a number of ways within government policy on education, and is reflected in the National Curriculum statement of values in England and in similar statements in the rest of the UK.

In their book on reflective teaching, teacher educators Ghaye and Ghaye also identify four main focuses or areas for reflection on practice, in response to the different starting points that might initiate a teacher's reflective thinking (Ghaye and Ghaye, 1998). As with the traditions identified by Zeichner and Tabachnik, these are not exclusive of one another. For example:

Qualified Teacher Status (QTS): a recognition that someone has met the first set of Professional Standards for Teaching in England and is able to start their Newly Qualified Teacher (NQT) year.

- You may have strong beliefs about the purpose of homework, or the teaching of your subject, or policies about pupils with special needs, and be reflecting on your *values* in relation to those held by others.
- You may be trying to analyse why a specific teaching approach, such as group problem solving, does not appear to be effective at the present time, and how you might need to change your own *practice*.
- You may be concerned by the results of assessment of pupils' learning in an area of the curriculum and be looking for ways to bring about *improvement*.
- You may be looking for ways to communicate better with parents within the school *context*.

OVER TO YOU

In training

Can you identify examples of these four areas for reflection on practice from your own experience, observation in school or discussion with fellow trainees or student teachers?

Starting your career

Where are you focusing your attention at this stage of your career? Take a moment to stand back to consider the areas you have been reflecting on most often. Ghaye and Ghaye do not suggest that teachers should necessarily be reflecting on all four areas, but it might be helpful for you to consider other aspects of learning and teaching if you have been concentrating mainly on one of these areas.

Investigating learning and teaching

Based on your own experience, observations in school or discussion with colleagues or fellow student teachers, can you identify examples of the four areas for reflection identified by Ghaye and Ghaye? How might you relate these to the 'traditions' identified by Zeichner and Tabachnik? Any such relationship would be specific to the particular example – each of these areas might be interpreted in terms of all four traditions.

For example, reflecting on the possible tensions in the relationship between AfL and APP (see the end of Chapter 10) might be initiated by your *values*, by reflection on your *practice*, or reflection on the *improvement* of pupils' learning.

Taking the area of *values*, your reflection might relate to the *developmentalist* tradition in terms of considering the value of different forms of assessment for pupils at particular ages, or to the *social reconstruction* tradition if your values lead you to question the use of some forms of standardised assessment.

What about the area of values in relation to the *academic* or *social efficiency* traditions? How could reflection focusing on your *practice* or the *improvement* of pupils' learning relate to Zeichner and Tabachnik's traditions in the context of this example?

Dewey (1933) argued that reflective thinking requires open-mindedness, responsibility and whole-heartedness. We suggest that the common ground shared by these 'traditions' or areas for reflection is that of an enquiring stance, a refusal to take things for granted and, above all, a commitment to continued learning – both that of your pupils and your own.

How can reflection on practice be developed?

Reflective practice should be understood as a disposition to enquiry. It is not just a collection of methods for eliciting evidence about practice. It is not a toolbox that consists of things such as critical incident analysis pro-formas, guidelines on how to keep learning journals and conduct school experience debriefs. These are important, but should be seen as part of the bigger reflective process.

(Ghaye and Ghaye, 1998: 17)

As Ghaye and Ghaye point out, there are no quick-fix methods through which one can become a 'reflective teacher': someone who regularly considers various aspects of their own practice and the learners' experience. Increasing experience is of course an important part of the process, but not sufficient in itself – this can just as easily lead to 'routine action' as to 'reflective action'. Being able to shift your focus away from yourself and your 'teaching behaviour' towards the learning behaviour of your pupils is extremely important, but in fact very hard to do. Being able to identify or clarify areas for development or improvement is essential if appropriate action is to be taken, although at first you may not know which actions are likely to be effective. Thus, drawing on the practice of others through observation or reading is also a contributory element. However, this needs to be applied to your specific teaching context, based on your knowledge of the pupils, and evaluated in terms of its effectiveness.

The most common ways in which trainee teachers and new teachers are expected to demonstrate their capacity to reflect on and improve their practice are through written lesson evaluations and/or lesson observation and evaluative discussions with their mentor, line manager or course tutor. Training programmes provide general guidance on the sorts of comments that are expected in written evaluations: a focus on evidence of learning rather than description of the lesson, and identification of areas for future improvement or continued development. While this written evidence is required as evidence for assessment purposes, that is not its major function, although it can sometimes be regarded in this mechanical light by trainee teachers! The conscious analysis and evaluation of elements of your practice is a discipline that the training process seeks to establish through the process of written reflection. Writing also enables others involved in supporting your training to have access to your thinking, and thus to engage in focused discussion on your development.

However, written evaluations often tend to focus on the immediacies of the lesson, and the pressures of moving on to the next session sometimes mean that these reflections operate in isolation. The focus of mentoring or performance management discussions can sometimes also be on a single observed lesson, as noted by educational researchers Edwards and Protheroe (2003) in their investigation into mentoring conversations. Although these discussions are valuable, they do not always support the full range of reflective thinking suggested by Ghaye and Ghaye (1998) above. Some mentoring and performance management discussions are also constrained by the context of assessment against given standards, whether for awarding Qualified Teacher Status or other national standards, completing the NQT year or linked to expectations from school inspection. These are important and necessary aspects of the context within which your professional practice will develop, but they sometimes act as constraints on some types of more open, questioning discussion. For example, researchers Jones and Straker (2006) found this occurring in the content of many mentoring discussions.

Photo 12.1 Observing other teachers can be a powerful way of enhancing reflection on your own practice, as well as providing an opportunity for professional discussion as part of a mentoring or coaching relationship

Source: Pearson Education Ltd/ Ian Wedgewood

Should this be the case, there are still likely to be a number of opportunities for you to engage in both formal and informal discussions in school which will both stimulate further reflection and enable you to discuss your ideas with other colleagues. Some forms of Continuing Professional Development activity, either within or beyond your school, will also provide opportunities for discussion and reflection on your practice that enable you to consider broader issues of values and educational purpose. What is important is that you should maintain your own 'disposition to enquiry'. Chapter 14 provides some suggestions about getting the most from these opportunities, and also discusses the benefits of peer observation and co-coaching to support reflection and develop your practice.

Reflection on practice takes the form of a conversation – whether one you hold with yourself, or one undertaken with another person or with several others. How much you develop your ideas through reflection will depend on how seriously you undertake your 'conversations' and how much you 'listen' – that is, how far you apply your own self-awareness or reflexivity. Some training and professional development programmes ask you to 'reflect on your reflections' at key stages in the course, in order to develop the capacity for meta-analysis – standing back from the immediacies of the individual lesson to identify broader trends in your practice and responses, and to recognise challenges and paradoxes in your role. For example, you may notice a gap (or gaps) in the areas you have been writing about, suggesting that there is an aspect of your practice which you have not been considering as fully as some others.

David Tripp worked as a university tutor with teachers on Continuing Professional Development programmes, and noticed that sometimes quite small events triggered major reviews of teachers' thinking. He encouraged teachers to try to identify moments when they had experienced a shift in their perspectives on learning and teaching. Tripp (1993) refers to these as 'critical incidents'. These may be classroom (or staffroom) events that are not 'dramatic or obvious' but which in some way indicate or represent a teacher's underlying ideas or beliefs which they had not been fully aware of previously. It may be difficult to distance yourself from your own practice sufficiently to recognise such events, which is why the role of an observer, or your later reflection on your notes, can be valuable.

CASE STUDY

The class teacher was concerned that her class were unable to sustain co-operative discussion. She therefore divided the class into two groups and set up a debate, with groups taking opposing positions. Her intention was to encourage the pupils to work together in order to develop their co-operative skills, but as the lesson developed she realised that she was fostering competition, not co-operation, through her choice of activity.

In later reflection she identified this teaching episode as a 'critical incident' as it made her re-evaluate some of her own assumptions about the effects of different teaching strategies on learners.

Source: based on Tripp, 1993: 15

OVER TO YOU

What assumptions about learning are implicit in her decision to set up a debate? What questions might you want to ask about her decision?

For example: will establishing an implicitly competitive environment foster co-operation?

Will asking pupils to adopt a one-sided position which they don't necessarily agree with, and which places them in opposition to others, foster co-operation?

For the teacher in this case study, the realisation that her teaching approach could have the opposite effect to the one for which she was aiming meant that she had to re-examine her own values and her implicit assumptions abut co-operation. 'Critical incidents' do not have to be negative, as in this example. One colleague of ours talks about a moment early in her career when she suddenly realised in the middle of a lesson that she didn't have to get everything 'right' in her teaching – that there would always be something more to learn. She describes this as a most positive and liberating experience!

WORKING IN THE CLASSROOM

Can you identify an occasion, or more than one occasion, when you realised something new about yourself as a teacher, and which you feel changed something about your professional practice afterwards? It does not need to be a dramatic moment or a major change of direction in your teaching. Professional learning is often made up of many small steps.

In her book entitled *Expert Teaching*, Rosie Turner-Bissett (2001: 16) talks about 'knowledge of self' as one of the necessary aspects of knowledge for teaching (see also Chapter 6), and in Daniel Goleman's well-known work on 'emotional intelligence' (Goleman, 1995), knowing one's emotions and having self-awareness are seen as the key characteristics on which other aspects of emotional intelligence are based. Undertaking this process of reflection honestly can sometimes be difficult, and it may require both the open-mindedness and the whole-heartedness referred to by Dewey to acknowledge your own responsibility for any difficulties you have experienced, as opposed to locating the 'fault' within the pupils or the school systems.

What strategies do you use to develop your own reflective practice?

Are you making the most of both formal and informal learning opportunities (see Table 12.1)?

Which of these opportunities have you already experienced?

Are there further opportunities that are available to you at your current stage of professional development but which you have not yet experienced?

Table 12.1 Formal and informal learning opportunities

Formal opportunities	Informal opportunities
Seminar and tutorial discussions with tutors and peers	Sharing ideas with peers outside formal taught sessions
Written reflections on your own teaching or observation of others	A personal learning journal, not used as part of course assessment
Observations of your teaching and subsequent discussion with your mentor or tutor	Informal discussions with your mentor or class teacher
Structured opportunities to observe other teachers	Listening to teachers talking about their teaching, in staffrooms or school meetings
Being involved in peer mentoring or co-coaching activity	
Attending school-based training events	
Attending courses outside the school	Meeting teachers from other schools and sharing ideas
Learning walks (see next Case study) Planning and undertaking a classroom-based research investigation (see Chapter 13)	Informal observation of classrooms and the learning environment around your school
Undertaking a course of accredited study	

CASE STUDY

What is a learning walk?

The National College for School Leadership says:

. . . organised and highly structured collaborative enquiry 'walks' through the classrooms of a school by colleagues from that (and other) school(s) in order to identify evidence of progress and areas for development. They include short visits to classrooms by a team of people who work together to collect evidence, learn about what is happening and ask questions. They are intended to be constructive rather than judgemental and aim to help the school understand how teachers teach, how learners learn and what gets taught to whom and when.

Many schools are now engaging in 'learning walks', both within their own schools and visiting others. A learning walk might also be conducted by parents and school governors, or by pupils of the school (see Chapter 15 on 'pupil voice').

The ground rules for an effective learning walk are:

- A clear purpose and previously agreed focus (e.g. learning of pupils with English as an Additional Language, deployment of Teaching Assistants, sharing good practice).

- Short periods of classroom observation (maximum 15 minutes).

- Agreed rules for questioning of teachers and pupils so that lessons are not disrupted.

- The 'walkers' prepare a short report based on the agreed focus. This might identify relative strengths and areas for development and enable good practice to be extended and/or an action plan for development to be drawn up.

Individual teachers might also carry out a learning walk, by agreement with colleagues. For example, one primary school ICT co-ordinator took a learning walk through her school with a camera and photographed all the evidence of ICT use she could identify during the course of a morning.

Photo 12.2
Professional discussion enhances reflection on your own practice. This does not always need to be as part of a mentoring relationship, but could also involve peer observation or co-coaching activities, where each of you share an area of expertise with the other

Source: Pearson Education Ltd/ Ian Wedgewood

How can we recognise a reflective teacher?

As we can't 'see' the process of reflection, we rely on the evidence of outcomes expressed in words or actions. It is unlikely that we would characterise someone as a reflective teacher if we never observed any changes in their practice, even if they insisted that they constantly reflected upon it. So it seems as though change of some kind is a necessary part of being recognised as a reflective teacher. There also needs to be a relationship between words and actions, as it is a lot easier to say what one believes than it sometimes is to put it into practice! Russell (1993) has written extensively in the area of reflective practice, and warns:

> . . . we may be able to articulate principles with little or no understanding of what it means to express them in practice. One result is that it is far too easy to believe that one is expressing one's beliefs in one's teaching, even to believe that this is the meaning of 'putting theory into practice'. Those who have observed teachers at length and worked to compare beliefs with actual practices, tend to be very aware of *the significant gaps between beliefs and actions*.
>
> *(Russell, 1993: 147, italics ours)*

It is important to stress here that the comment above is not intended to imply that teachers are in any way dishonest or hypocritical, but that it is extremely difficult to be sufficiently self-aware, as we have discussed earlier. However, despite these often observed gaps, the teacher who is able to articulate *why* they operate in a particular way, based on their values and their knowledge of various kinds, as discussed in Chapter 6, is more likely to be someone who reflects and analyses their practice.

If some kind of change or development in our practice is a necessary element of being a reflective teacher, then we need to be able to focus closely on exactly what it is that needs to change. In the early stages of professional development, this focusing process is usually supported by a more experienced colleague acting as a mentor, but increasingly schools are developing collaborative learning relationships between teachers at all stages of their careers. More and more teachers are also listening to their pupils' views about teaching and learning, through various feedback mechanisms, often callled 'pupil voice' strategies. These are discussed further in Chapter 15. Feedback from our colleagues and our pupils may help to identify areas for consideration, although sometimes you may need to enquire more deeply into an issue in order to gain a specific focus for development. Discussions with colleagues are a central part of this process, and can involve challenges for both participants. Being told, for example, that you 'need to improve your use of questions' may not be sufficiently helpful for you to understand both what actions are required and why they are important (see the Case study of 'Claire' later in this chapter). In order to develop your practice, you will need to probe more deeply into what is meant by such a comment, by asking questions of your mentor or other colleague, or asking for examples of points in the lesson which exemplified the issue. Such questions are likely to help your observer articulate their own understanding further, so that the conversation becomes more meaningful for both of you as you construct understanding together. This process is discussed in more detail in Chapter 14.

Transmission
a view of
teaching and
learning where
information
is given
(transmitted).

**Enquiry-based
model:**
an approach to
teaching which
involves pupils
in working
together to
solve problems
rather than
working under
the teacher's
direction.

In his writing about reflective teaching, Russell also argues that the changes in practice implemented by a reflective teacher do not always have to be successful. What is significant is the process of evaluation (Russell, 1993: 146). This is an important point, as much of the writing about reflective practice (and the implications from the teaching Standards) is that reflective practice *automatically* leads to improvement. Russell is helpful in reminding us that this is not always the case, and that we have not been unsuccessful as reflective teachers if we find that our actions do not bring about the outcomes we had hoped or expected. The question as to what might constitute an improvement in practice is discussed later in this chapter.

We judge how far an individual is or is not reflective about their practice mainly on the basis of what they say, and on what they then do. Reflective teaching is often characterised as being cyclical, or spiral, in which teachers constantly monitor, evaluate and adjust their practice. This is the view taken by the requirements of the Standards for the Award of QTS and the Core Standards for Teachers in England, and the assumption is that if it is carried out conscientiously this process will almost certainly lead to development in your practice and probably to improvements in pupils' learning. However, this may not always be the case.

CASE STUDY

Tabachnik and Zeichner (1986) describe two teachers in their first year of teaching, both of whom state at the beginning of the year that they intend to encourage active learning by pupils and to respond to pupils' interests in order to increase motivation. At the start of the year, both are teaching in relatively routine ways:

'Beth'	'Hannah'
Beth's teaching becomes more teacher dominated and she alters her earlier beliefs about encouraging active pupil participation in learning. She begins to include more use of worksheets, practice exercises and tests through which pupils become increasingly passive as learners. By the end of the year Beth is operating within a transmission model of teaching and learning, where pupils have little opportunity for active participation.	As the year progresses Hannah consciously tries to develop her teaching to increase pupil participation and active learning opportunities. By the end of the year there are clear differences in the ways in which learning is planned and implemented in her classroom and Hannah is operating within an enquiry-based model of learning. Pupils are able to learn through investigation, and are actively involved in formulating the questions which direct their work.

Both Beth and Hannah were thinking about their teaching. Are they both reflective teachers?
Source: Based on Zeichner and Tabachnik (2001: 82)

How we answer the question at the end of this case study depends both on our own beliefs about learning and also on whatever views of effective practice exist in our own particular culture. In today's climate, with an emphasis on independent learning and personalisation, Hannah would be more likely to be described as a reflective teacher. However, in the not so distant past within the UK, Hannah's more 'open' approach based on pupil participation might well have been criticised as inefficient and lacking clear focus or specific learning outcomes, and Beth's focus on knowledge acquisition might have been seen as better teaching.

Thus reflective teachers cannot separate themselves from broader issues of educational context and purpose. We need to ask *why* one approach is deemed to be better than another at the same time as (or before) we decide to change certain aspects of our practice. This question may lead us to consider other factors, such as evidence from research and practice and/or government policy and its ideological basis, as well as considering our own knowledge of our pupils and their context.

How do we recognise improvements in our practice?

The answer to this question depends, of course, on our definition of 'improvement' and what kinds of evidence we believe would indicate positive development of our practice. It also depends on what we already understand about the area identified for improvement, and whether the impetus has come from self-evaluation or from feedback from another person, such as a mentor or a senior colleague. Trainee teachers or newly qualified teachers are often asked to identify possible improvements to their teaching, either in writing, or verbally during post-lesson discussion. This can sometimes be experienced in a negative manner, as if one's teaching is automatically not good enough, although this may be far from the intention of the training institution or the observer of the lesson.

In order to be able to bring about improvements to our practice, we need first to be able to identify our relative strengths and weaknesses in terms of supporting learning, and also the strengths and weaker areas in our pupils' achievement in order to decide where to focus our attention. As a trainee teacher, you will gain some indications of things you are doing well, as well as areas for further development, during your training process, and you will also identify some targets for professional development during your induction year as an NQT. These targets will be your starting point, but in order to be sure you are able to identify your own improvement you will need to clarify and break down these targets further, perhaps through reading or discussion with your mentor or other teachers.

Claire has established a very good relationship with her pupils. She works hard to involve them in learning and makes sure that she encourages responses from most, if not all pupils at some point in the lesson through the use of directed questions. Her mentor is very positive about her development, but suggests that she needs to develop a greater range of questioning strategies to encourage higher-order thinking in her pupils. Claire is confused as she thought she had been doing this already. She knows about 'closed' and 'open' questions and she has been deliberately asking questions that she believes to be 'open' in type. She has asked pupils to explain the difference between groups of objects; she has encouraged them to express their opinions on the topics studied. Surely this is what she is meant to be doing?

Claire feels she has a good relationship with her mentor, and is able to express her confusion and ask for advice. Her mentor suggests that Claire observes another teacher and writes down *all* the questions asked during the lesson, whenever they are asked and whatever form they take. Claire's mentor will do the same thing on one of Claire's lessons after Claire has undertaken the observation and had time to think about what she has seen.

Claire returns from her observation with a very long list of questions, which she can quickly see fall into different categories: some are about classroom rules or procedures ('Have you all got your books ready?'), a few are about recalling information ('What did we find out about . . . last time?'), and some are about analysing previous learning ('So what important things did we learn from this?'). The teacher asks the pupils' opinions about aspects of learning ('So what do we think might happen next?') just as Claire feels she does with her own pupils, but Claire realises that this teacher does not always accept the pupils' initial answers and ideas, but asks additional questions ('Why do you think this might be the case?' 'Is there any evidence for this?').

In her subsequent lessons Claire tries to put these strategies into practice and her mentor agrees that the pattern of her questions has changed from the previous observation. Claire still needs to develop her own understanding of how types and sequences of questions can support her pupils' thinking skills, rather than just copying the practice of others, and her mentor suggests that she should now read more about higher-order thinking skills and questioning techniques to consolidate her learning.

Claire becomes very interested in this topic, and is determined to keep developing her teaching to improve pupils' thinking skills – but how will she know if she is succeeding?

How can Claire evaluate further improvements in her practice?

Table 12.2 offers some possible sources of evidence, not all of which will be helpful for Claire, although they could be useful to evaluate other developments in practice. Which would you choose in order to evaluate how successful changes to her questioning strategies have been, over time? You will need to consider what sort of evidence might indicate that development in thinking skills has taken place, in relation to the age group(s) of pupils with which you are familiar in the 7–14 age range, as the evidence will obviously vary.

THINKING IT THROUGH: *CONTINUED*

Table 12.2 Some sources of evidence to identify improvements in practice

Evidence	Strengths	Possible weaknesses
Assessment of pupils' work on an ongoing basis	Fairly quick feedback, depending on nature of intended improvements. Can help refine further changes to pedagogical approaches.	Might encourage attention on short-term gains without addressing longer-term issues, leading to possible fragmentation of learning.
Observation of pupils' responses to changes in practice	If conducted systematically and maintained over time, can provide rich information.	It can be easy to see what we want to see.
Formal assessment of pupils' work through summative assessment such as end of Key Stage testing.	Regarded by others as reliable evidence of improvement in pupil achievement.	Long term. May not focus on areas which you believe are most important.
Observation of your teaching with an agreed focus for the observer	Provides a more objective view of your pedagogical practice and the pupils' response, which can be compared with your own impressions.	Not establishing shared understanding about key concepts beforehand. Confusion about purpose of observation if feedback is also concerned with judgement on performance.
Feedback from pupils	Can provide valuable insight into learners' feelings about certain experiences, barriers to learning and learning preferences.	May not be part of school culture. Pupils may feel they need to provide a 'right' answer.
Reviewing evaluative writing, e.g. in a learning journal	Can offer opportunities to clarify thoughts and ideas and to interpret actions through subsequent reflection.	Has to be maintained and has to be meaningful to the individual, not seen as an externally imposed task.

SUMMARY

At the beginning of this chapter you were offered some ideas about reflection on practice. By now you may have realised that to some extent all of the statements could be true, depending on the purpose and outcomes of the process. In the following paragraph, numbers in brackets refer back to the table at the start of the chapter.

Activities such as writing an account of the lesson, discussing your teaching with others, learning from your mistakes and observing the teaching of others (1, 2, 4 and 12) can lead towards a better understanding of yourself, clearer understanding of pupils' learning and thus identifying where to go next in your teaching (3, 11 and 6). However, these actions may not improve your practice (8) without a clear understanding of what would constitute an improvement and *why* this would be an improvement. This could in turn lead you to consider your actions in relation to your values (9) and the role of education in society (10). Without these broader considerations, we suggest that much reflection on practice could become a 'routine' action rather than a truly reflective one which would remain at the level of 'something you had to do for your ITT course' (7) and thus – a waste of time (5).

OVER TO YOU

Now look back at your definition of reflection on practice. Is there anything you would want to change?

TAKING YOUR PRACTICE FURTHER

Ghaye, A. and Ghaye, K. (1998) *Teaching and Learning through Critical Reflective Practice*, London: Fulton.

If you want to support your reflection on practice through journal writing, Chapter 5 in explores a range of forms journals can take. This text has a primary focus but can usefully be read by teachers working in Key Stage 3 since although the examples are rooted in primary practice, the discussion apples to reflection on practice in general.

Moon, J.A. (2006) *Learning Journals: A Handbook for Reflective Practice and Professional Development*. London: Routledge.

Jenny Moon is a well-known author in the field of using journals and personal writing for professional development and this book contains many suggestions for different approaches to keeping learning journals.

TAKING YOUR PRACTICE FURTHER *CONTINUED*

The topic of developing your learning through reflective discussion with others is further explored in Chapter 14.

There are many helpful texts which can inform aspects of your reflection on practice:

Pollard, A. (2008) *Reflective Teaching: Evidence Informed Professional Practice*, 3rd edn. London, Continuum. This is probably one of the best-known general texts.

This is also supported by a website, RTWeb, with a further range of reflective activities.

Dillon, J. and McGuire, M. (eds) (2007, 2nd edn.) *Becoming a Teacher: Issues in Secondary Teaching*, Buckingham: Open University Press. This contains articles which place the role of the teacher in a broader social context. Although this is aimed at secondary teachers, many of the articles raise issues that apply equally to primary practitioners.

The following two texts provide extended readings from a range of educational writers to develop understanding of a range of topics, including pupils' learning styles, planning, assessment, and behaviour for learning:

Hoult, S. (2005) *Reflective Reader: Secondary Professional Studies*. Exeter: Learning Matters.

Kendall-Seatter, S. (2005) *Reflective Reader: Primary Professional Studies*. Exeter: Learning Matters.

TAKING YOUR THINKING FURTHER

Educational writers and researchers have suggested that student teachers, and teachers in the early stages of their careers, develop their reflective practice along a continuum (Furlong and Maynard, 1995).

The suggested pattern is for novice teachers to begin by focusing mainly on themselves and how well they are teaching, then to begin to recognise some of the challenges involved in teaching, but often to ascribe difficulties to the pupils rather than to aspects of their own teaching, and then to re-focus their attention on the needs of the learners, rather than their own needs as teachers. Furlong and Maynard suggest that at this stage many novice teachers 'plateau', as they have found a fairly successful way to operate in the classroom. Some choose to remain in their 'comfort zone' and do not continue to develop their practice. ▶

TAKING YOUR THINKING FURTHER *CONTINUED*

Thus, not all of them progress to Furlong and Maynard's next stage of reflection on the wider purposes of education and its role in society.

Donald McIntyre, who has spent many years researching teacher development, suggests that beginning teachers may not yet be ready to consider the wider questions of the role of education in society and how their teaching relates to this (McIntyre, 1993).

How far do you think Furlong and Maynard's pattern of progression is accurate in your experience?

How might you identify whether you had reached a 'plateau' in your own practice? What evidence might you use?

Do you agree with McIntyre that student teachers and beginning teachers are not really ready to reflect on the wider issues?

Find out more

There is a substantial literature on the nature of reflective teaching, some of which has been referred to in this chapter.

Most writers consider that growth in teacher knowledge through reflection on practice requires sustained commitment and increasing experience. For a discussion of this view:

McIntyre, D. (1993) Theory, theorisation and reflection in initial teacher education, in Calderhead, J. and Gates, P. (eds) *Conceptualising Reflection in Teacher Education*. London: Falmer. This book also contains a number of other interesting articles.

For a discussion of the difference between 'novice' and 'expert' teachers' behaviours, which can be related to Schön's 'reflection-in-action', see:

Berliner, D. (1995) Teacher expertise, in Moon, B. and Shelton-Mayes, A., *Teaching and Learning in the Secondary School*. London: Routledge.

A further examination of the differences between more and less experienced teachers' classroom practice can be found in:

Tochon, H. and Munby, F. (1993) Novice and expert teachers' time epistemology: a wave function from didactics to pedagogy. *Teaching and Teacher Education*, Vol. 9, No. 2: pp. 205–218.

Glossary

Enquiry-based model: an approach to teaching which involves pupils in working together to solve problems rather than working under the teacher's direction. The teacher's role becomes that of a facilitator, rather than an instructor.

Transmission: a view of teaching and learning where information is given (transmitted) by the teacher to the pupils, as opposed to involving pupils more directly in their learning; often associated with behaviourist learning theory.

References

Calderhead, J. (1989) Reflective teaching and teacher education, *Teaching and Teacher Education*, Vol. 5, No. 1: pp. 43–51.

Calderhead, J. and Gates, P. (1983) (eds) *Conceptualising Reflection in Teacher Education*. London: Falmer.

Dewey, J. (1933) *How We Think*. Chicago: Henry Regnery.

DfES (2003) *Excellence and Enjoyment: A Strategy for Primary Schools*. London: DfES.

Edwards, A. and Protheroe, L. (2003) Learning to see in classrooms: what are student teachers learning to teach in schools? *British Educational Research Journal*, Vol. 29, No. 2: pp. 227–242.

Furlong, J. and Maynard, T. (1995) *Mentoring Student Teachers: The Growth of Professional Knowledge*. London: Routledge.

Ghaye, A. and Ghaye, K. (1998) *Teaching and Learning through Critical Reflective Practice*. London: Fulton.

Goleman, D. (1995) *Emotional Intelligence*. New York: Bantam Books.

Jones, M. and Straker, K. (2006) What informs mentors' practice when working with trainees and newly qualified teachers? An investigation into mentors' professional knowledge base, *Journal of Education for Teaching*, Vol. 32, No. 2: pp. 165–184.

McIntyre, D. (1993) Theory, theorisation and reflection in initial teacher education, in Calderhead, J. and Gates, P. (eds) *Conceptualising Reflection in Teacher Education*. London: Falmer.

Russell, T. (1993) Critical attributes of a reflective teacher: is agreement possible?, in Calderhead, J. and Gates, P. (eds) *Conceptualising Reflection in Teacher Education*. London: Falmer.

Schön, D. (1983) *The Reflective Practitioner: How Professionals Think in Action*. New York: Basic Books.

Tabachnik, B.R. and Zeichner, K. (1986) Teacher beliefs and classroom behaviours; some teacher responses to inconsistencies, in Ben-Peretz, M., Bromme, R. and Halkes, R. (eds) *Advances of Research on Teacher Thinking*. Berwyn, PA and Lisse, W. Germany: Swets and Zeitlinger.

Tripp, D. (1993) *Critical Incidents in Teaching*. London: Routledge.

Turner-Bissett, R. (2001) *Expert Teaching: Knowledge and Pedagogy to Lead the Profession*. London: Fulton.

Zeichner, K. and Tabachnik, B.R. (2001) Reflections on reflective thinking, in Soler, J., Craft, A. and Burgess, H. (eds) *Teacher Development: Exploring Our Own Practice*. London: Paul Chapman.

In this chapter you will:

- Consider why systematic investigation of teaching and learning can develop professional practice
- Begin to identify areas in your own practice that might benefit from further investigation
- Identify suitable approaches to support investigation within the classroom
- Understand how your chosen approach relates to your focus for investigation
- Consider what kind of evidence would be needed in order to draw conclusions from your investigation
- Become aware of some of the ethical issues associated with classroom-based investigation
- Consider ways in which it could be possible to share the outcomes of your investigation with others

Pearson Education Ltd/Studio 8. Clark Wiseman

Investigating learning

One way of creating education entails repeating what has been done before: basing today's action on the way it was done last week or last year; or following curriculum guidelines devised by someone else. Most of us work this way much of the time, arguing that there is no opportunity to do otherwise.

Playing hunches is a second way of creating education: using intuition without challenge and without monitoring the consequences. Most of us work this way sometimes.

There is another way. It is creating education by asking questions and searching for evidence. It is creating education by challenging and developing one's own personal theories of education – by asking 'how do I improve my practice?' and 'how do I help you improve your learning?' It is creating education by asking about intentions, by determining their worth, by appraising resources, by identifying alternative strategies and by monitoring and evaluating outcomes.

It is creating education through critical and systematic enquiry: creating education through research.

If we all did this just occasionally, and reported the outcome to other teachers via the internet, we would be not only striving to improve our own practice, but, by sharing our discoveries, working for a better educational world.

Source: This is a synopsis of Michael Bassey's 1991 presidential address to the British Educational Research Association. Available at: http://www.teachernet.gov.uk/research/Learning_about_research/

OVER TO YOU

The ways in which you can answer the following questions will depend on your current level of teaching experience, but we would like to argue that the third way of working depends more on your values as a teacher rather than on your experience.

- How often do you work in the first way outlined by Bassey, above? Do you agree that there is little opportunity to do otherwise?

- How often do you work in the second way? Do you consider this to be an effective way to work?

- How often do you ask questions about your own practice and your pupils' learning, to which there are no answers that can be easily obtained by seeking other people's opinions or advice?

Introduction

Systematic enquiry: a planned approach to investigating a question of interest to your professional practice, involving the selection of an appropriate research method, the collection of evidence or information relating to your focus question and an evaluation of your evidence leading to some form of conclusion and possibly a recommendation for future practice.

This chapter considers the value of undertaking critical and systematic enquiry into learning within, and perhaps beyond, the classroom, or as Michael Bassey (above) argues: creating education through research. Previous chapters have offered a number of suggestions for considering specific aspects of learning in more depth, and whether these involved considering the learning behaviour of individuals and groups of pupils or developing pupils' understanding of their own learning through the use of assessment for learning strategies, the necessity for critical reflection on your own practice has always been present. The previous chapter discussed the process of professional reflection and its importance for improving the quality of learning and teaching as part of your professional development. We suggested that effective reflection on learning is likely to raise some questions that cannot be immediately or easily answered. One of the options for developing your professional understanding in these circumstances is to undertake a structured investigation into an aspect of learning and teaching that you would like to understand more about, in order to improve your professional practice. This chapter will introduce you to some ways in which such an investigation could be planned and implemented.

Within this chapter we have used the term 'investigating learning' in preference to the word 'research'. Some practitioners find the latter term off-putting, and assume it means having to undertake time-consuming study involving statistics, or large-scale surveys, and that it has little relevance to classroom practice (McNamara, 2002). However, we want to argue, like Michael Bassey at the head of this chapter, that systematic investigation into aspects of teaching and learning, either within your own classroom or within your school, *is* a form of educational research, just as much as the larger or more complex studies conducted by professional researchers. Such investigations need not be separate from your normal practice, nor create large amounts of additional work, if they are well planned.

As a trainee teacher or an NQT you should have the support of your mentor, who will be able to advise you, and many schools continue to offer opportunities for mentoring and coaching beyond the formal induction year. We discuss the importance of mentoring and coaching for professional development in Chapter 14 in this part of the book. However, while you or your mentor may be able to suggest possible answers to your questions or concerns about improving learning, it will be up to you to implement any suggestions and to evaluate their effectiveness.

Action Research: The essential feature is that the researcher is actively involved in the process of problem solving, rather than standing outside events in a 'traditional' researcher role.

The TDA Core Standards (**www.tda.gov.uk/teachers/professionalstandards/**) require all teachers to 'Have a creative and constructively critical approach towards innovation; being prepared to adapt their practice where benefits and improvements are identified' (Standard C8). The rest of this chapter offers some ideas as to how you might approach the process of critical evaluation, and argues that investigating learning should be seen as an integral element of your continuing professional practice, rather than a 'one-off' or isolated activity undertaken as part of your initial training or as part of a CPD course.

Teachers' classroom-based research is often referred to as Action Research, although this term has come to be used rather more loosely than its originators intended (Hopkins, 2002: 50). This chapter will follow Hopkins in using the term 'classroom research' rather than 'action research', although many of the processes discussed will be based on the ideas of various action research practitioner, such as Kemmis and McTaggart (1988), Elliot (1991) and McNiff (2002).

Why investigate?

Throughout this book we have emphasised the importance of articulating your own professional values and beliefs, and reflecting on the kind of teacher you wish to be. Although the educationalist Eric Hoyle developed his well-known descriptions of the 'restricted' and the 'extended' professional before the introduction of the National Curriculum in England and Wales (Hoyle, 1980), they are still worth examination. Although 'restricted professionals' have many good qualities, they rarely look beyond the immediacies of the classroom context in order to evaluate the effectiveness of their teaching or to consider the relationships between their own practice and the context of the school and of society.

- **The restricted professional – characteristics:**
  - a high level of classroom competence
  - child-centredness (or sometimes subject-centredness)
  - a high degree of skill in understanding and handling children
  - derives high satisfaction from personal relationships with pupils
  - evaluates performance in terms of his/her own perceptions of changes in pupil behaviour and achievement
  - attends short courses of a practical nature
- **The extended professional – characteristics**
  - views work in the wider context of school, community and society
  - participates in a wide range of professional activities, e.g. subject associations, teachers' meetings, conferences
  - has a concern to link theory and practice
  - has a commitment to some form of curriculum theory and mode of evaluation.

While it is understandable that your main concerns during your training and early years of teaching will focus on these immediacies, there are some dangers in being wholly focused on the classroom: it is easy to develop the habit of narrowed vision that is concerned only with practical issues, or to become complacent as you arrive at a comfortable position where everything seems to be running smoothly. In order to continue to develop professionally, we argue that you need to look beyond the classroom, and perhaps also beyond the priorities identified in the school's own training programme, in order to question and evaluate practice for yourself.

This can be challenging in the face of well-established centralised directives and perhaps a culture operating within the school that makes questioning accepted practice difficult. However, being able to come to a reasoned professional judgement (not a knee-jerk rejection) about educational priorities is the mark of a thinking teacher in Hoyle's 'extended professional' sense.

In his book on classroom research, David Hopkins, a well-known educational writer, justifies the importance of teachers continuing to investigate their own teaching in a climate of more centralised control over the curriculum:

> Successful implementation of any centralised innovation requires adaptation by teachers at the school level. It is not an either/or situation or a straight choice between 'top-down' or 'bottom-up' – it is a combination of both . . .
>
> . . . the claim of teaching to be a profession lies in the ability and opportunity for teachers to exercise their judgement over the critical tasks involved in their role, namely curriculum and teaching. Most centralised school systems prescribe what is to be taught to pupils, but require the teacher to put the curriculum into practice. At a very basic level this involves the teacher in some form of 'translation' of the curriculum policy into schemes of work or lesson plans. More emphasis on research-based teaching would, I believe, result in better 'translations' of centralised curriculum into practice and in teachers who are more confident, flexible and autonomous.
>
> *(Hopkins, 2002)*

You might also wish to read sections on Teachernet entitled 'Why research', which give further reasons why classroom teachers should become involved in researching their own practice and/or collaborating with others in order to do so. Available at: **http://www.teachernet.gov.uk/research**.

THINKING IT THROUGH

In training/starting your career

How far do you think that the schools you have experienced so far offer opportunities for teachers to become 'extended professionals'?

Although this can be a difficult question to judge at an early stage of your training, or even perhaps as an NQT, you might want to consider the culture or ethos of the school as it relates to encouraging all staff to develop their professional knowledge and providing opportunities for open discussion about educational issues.

Starting your career

What actions would you need to take to develop your own learning at this stage in your career, e.g. joining a subject organisation (if you have not already done so), finding out about any local educational networks?

What areas or issues that affect the learning of your pupils do you feel you need to understand better?

Investigating learning and teaching

You might find it useful to find out more about the wide range of school- or classroom-based research that is being carried out by teachers across the UK, funded by the National Teacher Research Panel, by accessing the short reports available at: **http://www.standards.dfes.gov.uk/ntrp/**.

What is the difference between reflection on learning and investigation into learning?

In the previous chapter we discussed the qualities of the 'reflective practitioner' as a person who is committed to continually developing and improving their own practice.

If this is the case, at first sight there may not seem to be much difference between reflection on learning of the kind we discussed, and investigating learning in the classroom. However, there are some differences between the two kinds of professional activity, although it might be difficult at times to identify the point at which one shades into the other.

Although we emphasised that reflection on learning involves reflection on the learning of your pupils as well as on your own practice as a teacher, the outcomes of your reflection may well be aimed at relatively short-term and often very specific ends. For example, you may be identifying particular pupils on whom you feel you need to focus more closely in a subsequent lesson, or reviewing a part of your lesson to decide how you could present the topic differently in future. An investigation into an aspect of classroom practice would normally focus on a slightly broader issue and be conducted over a longer period of time (subject to your circumstances in the school). Most crucially, your investigation will be *planned* and *systematic*: you will decide on a particular approach that you believe may meet the focus question or resolve an issue you have identified, you will monitor your progress and evaluate the outcome in an appropriate way. Thus classroom investigation is more formalised than reflection on learning, although it will usually be from your reflections that your investigation will develop.

You might also draw on other people's experience of classroom investigation to help you shape your own at the planning stage. This might involve reading case studies from educational websites, or looking at research digests, also available via websites, or reading research articles in professional journals or educational journals. Some suggestions for research digest websites are given at the end of this chapter.

Making classroom investigation part of your everyday life

Many teachers say that they don't have the time to 'do research on top of teaching', perhaps because they feel that 'research' is something separate from their everyday work. Conversely, we have argued that investigating learning is both a form of research and also an essential part of teaching. As teaching is your main job, any research investigation needs to be seen as an integral part of your daily life in school, rather than something additional to, or outside, it. The focus that you choose for your investigation will thus need to take into account the time you have available in school and your personal context. This will depend upon whether you are undergoing your initial teacher training, if you are in your NQT year, or whether you are now in your second or subsequent year of teaching.

Routes into teaching such as a BA or PGCE course usually require trainee teachers to undertake a small-scale investigation into an aspect of learning, based in school experience, but the amount of time you have to focus on such an investigation will usually be short – anything from one week to seven or eight weeks. On some Initial Teacher Training programmes, the outline of your school-based investigation will have been given to you in the course materials, while on others you may have a fairly free rein. If you are training on the Graduate Teacher Programme, there may not be any requirement for you to conduct such an investigation, but you will have more time based in school to enable you to identify your own area of interest, or to base your investigation on feedback from your mentor, particularly towards the end of your training year, although the time you have available may still be relatively short. In these contexts, your choice of focus and your methods of gathering information need to be carefully planned in order to be manageable within the timescale. You will need to appreciate that any conclusions you draw from investigations with relatively short timescales should be tentative, but this should not deter you from undertaking a small-scale investigation. You may have further opportunities to repeat or refine your work in your first teaching post, and even if this opportunity does not arise you will be able to build on your experience with a different focus.

WORKING IN THE CLASSROOM

The following are examples of ideas that might be the focus of small-scale investigations which could be carried out over a relatively short timescale. Ideas about how these investigations could be carried out and what evidence would be needed in order to draw conclusions are discussed later in this chapter.

- Improving pupils' skills in listening and responding to each other's ideas in discussion, or developing their skills of peer review.
- Investigating pupils' views about how well they feel some aspect of classroom practice helps them learn: for example, the seating arrangements you normally use (see Chapter 7) or an assessment for learning strategy that has been established within the school, such as peer assessment (see Chapter 10).

As your NQT year progresses and you become established within your school, you may begin to identify issues or aspects of teaching and learning which you wish to investigate further, either with guidance from your mentor or other colleagues, or based on your own reflections on learning and on evidence from pupil assessment. As you become more experienced as a teacher, you may also find that questions about pupil learning arise from discussions with other colleagues which could lead to more extended, or collaborative, investigation. More extended investigations will enable you to draw on more evidence, and to come to conclusions which may be more reliable than those based on the shorter-term research undertaken during your training. Examples of these types of investigation could include evaluating the success of new initiatives within the school, or seeking to bring about changes in learning behaviours over a longer period of time than a few weeks. Such investigations can also be incorporated into more formalised CPD programmes, leading to further qualifications, such as Post-graduate Diplomas or Master's degrees.

Investigating learning: identifying a focus

Making sure we have a clear focus for investigation is one of the most challenging aspects of improving classroom practice. In the previous chapter we discussed the importance of identifying highly specific personal targets for improvement, as opposed to making blanket statements such as 'improve the use of questions', and of establishing some criteria for evaluating the success of changes to classroom practice. This process applies equally to that of developing a systematic investigation into any aspect of teaching and learning, and the process of reflection on pupils' learning will necessarily precede any decision as to your focus area.

John Elliot, one of the key writers on 'action research', emphasises the importance of 'reconnaissance' before developing your plan of action and putting it into practice. This period of fact-finding and analysis is crucial to the success of the investigation (Elliot, 1991). Your initial idea may be based on reflection on your teaching, on evidence from assessment of pupils' work and/or on observation of pupils' engagement with learning in certain situations or (most probably) on several types of evidence. Jean McNiff, another very influential writer on classroom research, suggests that your focus question might typically begin 'How do I . . . ?' as you seek to develop aspects of your own practice in order to improve learning. However, you need to be prepared for the possibility that your focus may change as your investigation continues:

> Be aware that the research question might change as you develop the research. The question 'How do I help my students concentrate?' might transform into the question 'How do I make my lessons more interesting so that my students want to learn?' As you reveal issues through studying your practice you will come to new understandings about yourself and the problematics of your situation and begin asking new questions.
>
> *(McNiff, 2002: 86)*

However, your focus does not need to be that of a 'problem'. Hopkins (2002) notes that some action research literature tends to use terms such as 'problem' and 'improve' as if the only purpose of classroom investigation is to correct a deficit. An equally valid reason for engaging in an investigation would be to introduce a new idea or approach to your teaching, even where no 'problem' is evident. The Guidance notes on the Core Standards (**www.tda.gov.uk/teachers/professionalstandards/**) encourage teachers to 'apply constructive criticism to new ideas, research and approaches and contribute to change and innovation by taking informed risks to promote and adopt them'.

Having identified your initial idea, you need to analyse the ways in which it would be possible to bring about the change or development in learning that you want. There will rarely be only one suitable approach, but you will need to be realistic about what can be achieved within your own classroom. This is likely to involve recognising limitations as well as possibilities, for example in terms of resourcing or the availability of physical space. Your fact finding should involve asking the opinions of your mentor and/or other colleagues as well as referring to books and websites, so that you can draw on their experience of the learners in your school as part of your evidence base for deciding on the most appropriate action. The fact-finding process will also help you to refine your ideas and clarify the focus of your investigation.

CASE STUDY

The following extract is taken from a teacher's evaluation of a writing project, linking journalistic writing and RE with a Year 5/6 class (full case study available at **http://www. standards.dfes.gov.uk/primary/casestudies/ literacy/403685/622147/918439**).

> Redrafting was another area that some children found difficult. They were able to come up with ideas for improving someone else's writing during the whole class session but, on the whole, were not able to identify ways in which their own writing could be improved. Part of the problem may be the difficulty of 'decentering' from a piece on which they have spent a lot of time. Given more time, I would have spent longer working on this. I think I will explore the idea of developing regular, writing partners with whom children can share the editing task.

Here the problem is clearly identified, along with a suggested explanation for the pupils' difficulties in identifying ways in which their own writing could be improved, accompanied by a proposed line of action which takes the explanation into account.

You may wish to consider whether there were other lines of action this teacher could have considered, in addition to that of writing partners.

A *sustained investigation* into developing children's abilities to re-draft their work would need to identify specifically how the use of writing partners would be introduced, and how the outcomes of the investigation would be evaluated. One you have read the later sections in this chapter, you may wish to return to this case study to consider which strategy or strategies would be most suitable in this example.

CASE STUDY

A teacher is concerned by what she perceives as socially inappropriate behaviours exhibited by different sub-culture groupings within the same mixed ability Year 8 class. These mutually exclusive sub-cultures impact on some forms of collaborative learning, since members of one sub-group are vociferously reluctant to work with those of another.

While recognising that this is not an issue that can be adequately addressed by a single teacher, she decided to investigate different approaches to support group-based learning as she felt this would contribute to effective learning in her subject area.

She considered the following strategies:

- Working in pairs or trios as this would break down the larger sub-groups.

- Allowing pupils to work in 'friendship' groups initially but using strategies such as 'envoying' where individual group members needed to visit and talk to other groups to obtain necessary information, and 'rainbowing' where group members each have a designated responsibility. New groups are then formed around the different areas and the original groups re-form to apply the knowledge obtained.

- As some members of the Year 8 class were also in her form tutor group, she considered addressing the issue through PSHE, and sought advice from the Year Leader on a suitable approach.

Which of these strategies would you adopt? Can you think of other approaches that could be tried?

Collecting and evaluating your information

What kind of information you collect as part of your investigation will depend, of course, on the nature of your focus question, and on the outcomes you hope to achieve. Just as with your focus question, however, you may find that the kinds of evidence you find useful may change as your investigation progresses. For this reason it is important to evaluate the progress of your investigation regularly, to reflect on your progress in bringing about the changes in pupils' learning you wish to implement, and to make any necessary alterations to your action plan. The 'action research' tradition conceptualises this as a spiral (Kemmis and McTaggart, 1988) (see Figure 13.1) or cyclical (Elliot, 1991; McKernan, 1996) process. This is a useful model to apply, since it acknowledges that the process of your investigation is likely to directly affect events and responses in the classroom, so that the situation at the beginning of the process is not the same as the situation part way through.

Hopkins (2002) outlines six principles for successful classroom research, of which the first three are particularly relevant to the process of **data collection**:

- The first is that the teacher's primary job is to teach, and any **research method** should not interfere with or disrupt the teaching commitment.

- The second criterion is that 'the method of data collection must not be too demanding on the teacher's time. As a corollary, the teacher needs to be certain about the data collection technique before using it.'

- The third principle is perhaps the most contentious. The **methodology** employed must be reliable enough to allow teachers to formulate hypotheses confidently and develop strategies applicable to their classroom situation.

(Hopkins, 2002: 52–53)

The first source of data is the *naturally occurring information* gained as part of your normal teaching: the pupils' work and your assessment and recording of their achievement and your lesson plans and evaluations.

Data collection: the systematic gathering of information/ evidence to support your investigation.

Research method: the way in which data is collected. Some examples of research methods are given later in this chapter.

Methodology: the overall approach taken to gathering and analysing data.

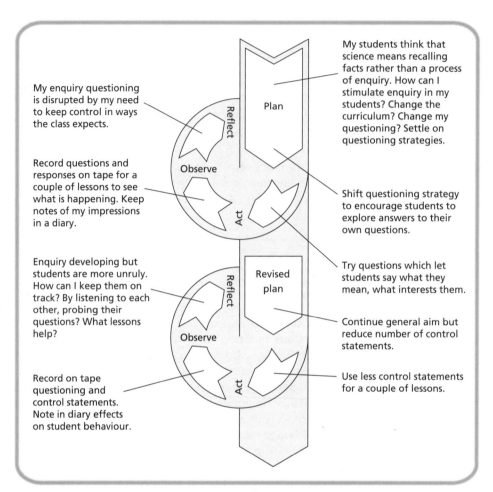

Figure 13.1
The 'action research spiral' (based on Kemmis and McTaggart, 1988, p. 14).

Source: Hopkins, D. (2002) *A Teacher's Guide to Classroom Research*, 3rd edn. Buckingham: Open University Press

My enquiry questioning is disrupted by my need to keep control in ways the class expects.

Record questions and responses on tape for a couple of lessons to see what is happening. Keep notes of my impressions in a diary.

Enquiry developing but students are more unruly. How can I keep them on track? By listening to each other, probing their questions? What lessons help?

Record on tape questioning and control statements. Note in diary effects on student behaviour.

My students think that science means recalling facts rather than a process of enquiry. How can I stimulate enquiry in my students? Change the curriculum? Change my questioning? Settle on questioning strategies.

Shift questioning strategy to encourage students to explore answers to their own questions.

Try questions which let students say what they mean, what interests them.

Continue general aim but reduce number of control statements.

Use less control statements for a couple of lessons.

Reflect
Observe
Act
Plan

Reflect
Observe
Act
Revised plan

Photo 13.1
Normal classroom practice provides a wealth of information on which you can draw to inform your investigation

Source: Pearson Education Ltd/ Ian Wedgewood

Assessment information

Your assessment of pupils' work can provide a rich evidence base for reviewing the effectiveness of your teaching in individual lessons and over time. In addition to using your assessment information to inform your planning for future learning, you will also be comparing the achievement of your pupils with that of others within the school, or in similar schools, as part of your normal practice in relation to the QTS or Core Standards Q13 or C13 and C14. This information may help you to identify a focus for investigation, or provide evidence about the effectiveness of your teaching strategies. However, It may take some time for you to be able to make secure judgements about your pupils' achievement in terms of statistical comparison. Your ongoing analysis of pupils' learning and progression within your own classroom can also provide you with valuable insights:

- Recording pupils' achievements in terms of specified learning outcomes will quickly provide patterns for both individual pupils and aspects of your own teaching which may have been either more or less successful than others.

- Close analysis of pupils' work, or of sections of longer examples, may also reveal patterns relating to misunderstandings, or limitations on understanding, which can then form the focus of further investigation.

- Analysis of patterns from the targets you identify for individual pupils, resulting from the use of assessment for learning approaches, can also be informative.

Lesson plans and their related evaluations can also offer opportunities to notice patterns: Do some teaching strategies apear to be more effective than others in helping you achieve your intended objectives? What explanations might there be for these differences? How will you investigate these possible explanations?

Observation of teaching and learning, undertaken either by yourself or by another colleague, also provides very valuable information, if it is gathered and recorded in a systematic way:

- Where you are working with a mentor, or in a school where peer observation is established practice, discuss your research focus with your observer so that written feedback and the subsequent discussion can become part of your evidence base.

- If you are working with a Teaching Assistant, it may be possible for your assistant to record specific information about selected pupils' responses to given parts of a lesson. In many schools this would be part of normal practice.

- In some schools, the establishment of 'teaching laboratories' makes it possible for video recordings to be made of lessons, so that you are able to analyse your teaching approaches and pupils' responses. These are speciallly designed classrooms fitted with closed circuit video cameras that enable the lesson to be recorded from several angles. The lesson can be observed 'live' elsewhere in the school by video link and also recorded for later viewing and discussion with a coach or mentor. As many people find their first viewing of their teaching rather embarrassing, and need to be able to distance themselves in order to analyse the lesson effectively, you will need to set time aside to watch the video recording at least twice, and probably several times.

- Pupil observation of lessons. In some secondary schools, pupils have been trained to observe teaching sessions and to provide feedback. This is discussed in more detail in Chapter 15. It is also possible to engage primary-aged pupils in observation and reporting back on learning where the activity and the purpose of the observation are carefully planned and understood by all pupils.

- Your own observational notes, jotted down during or immediately after lessons in a notebook carried only for this purpose. It is useful to write your notes on the left-hand side of the double page, keeping the right-hand side for additional reflective comments at a later stage. It is important to remember that these notes are likely to be only a partial record of events, and will not record very specific information, such as the detail of conversations, unless you have been able to focus on a small group of learners, and that your account may be over-subjective. Bell (2005) reminds us that 'familiarity may cause you to overlook aspects of behaviour that would be immediately apparent to a non-participant observer seeing the situation for the first time' (Bell, 2005: 187).

Photo 13.2
It may be difficult to observe small-group learning for a sustained period. How else might you gather information about their learning processes?

Source: Pearson Education Ltd/ Ian Wedgewood

Audio recording

Tape-recording elements of your own lessons, in order to focus on a particular aspects of your teaching and/or the pupils' responses, can provide you with some of the detail that observational notes cannot capture. As with video recording, the experience of hearing yourself may be uncomfortable at first, so you need to set time aside to listen to the recording several times in order to analyse it effectively. If you decide to make a written transcript of conversations this is also time consuming, although transcription does help you to identify issues that you may not pick up so easily through listening alone.

Although there are now very effective small voice recorders which can be used unobtrusively, if you wish to record children's conversations without an adult present you will have to allow time for them to become accustomed to the idea so that their responses are not affected by the presence of the recording device. It is also absolutely vital that you gain the permission of *everyone involved* (adult or pupil) before using any kind of recording of a lesson, video or audio. This issue is discussed later in the chapter under the 'Ethics' heading.

All this comes down to the point that you need to focus your use of audio recording carefully in order to make the best use of it as a data-gathering strategy. Despite the caveats above, the tape recorder can provide valuable evidence to support assessment of learning and to inform your future teaching.

CASE STUDY

In a geography class with able 11 year olds, the teacher asked the pupils to work in groups to examine four different sketch maps and to decide which was 'best'. She tape-recorded one group's discussion and was able to identify the kinds of criteria the pupils were using to make their decisions, and to identify gaps in their understanding.

In a subsequent lesson, she asked groups to feed back to the whole class and tape-recorded this element of the lesson so that she had results from more than one group.

Although she lost some of the spontaneity of the individual group discussion, she was still able to identify patterns in the pupils' thinking and to review her materials and teaching approaches on the basis of this information.

Source: Hull *et al.* (1985), cited in Hopkins (2002: 106–107)

Pupil learning diaries or evaluations

Current emphases on 'learning to learn' have encouraged some schools to establish pupil diaries or logs in which they record their own views about their learning strategies, either electronically or on paper. As these are the pupils' personal views, their comments may not always be relevant to your own focus of investigation, but they may provide a valuable alternative insight into some aspects of your teaching and could act as a form of **triangulation** of aspects of your research. As with video and audio recording, there are ethical implications associated with the use of pupils' learning diaries, but if they are already established as part of normal school practice these issues should have been resolved. Similarly, where schools engage in lesson evaluation by pupils as part of 'pupil voice' strategies (see Chapter 15), the use of the resulting data to inform your teaching should not cause any ethical difficulties.

However, if these strategies are not currently in use in your school, you should discuss any use of learning diaries or pupil evaluations with senior colleagues in order to gain their agreement, and that of the pupils and their parents, before introducing

Triangulation: used in a research context, this term refers to the use of more than one source of evidence to strengthen the findings of a research investigation.

them as part of your teaching. A simpler and more manageable strategy would be to ask pupils to evaluate their learning through the use of simple recording formats, at key points in the lesson series. Again, if you are a trainee teacher, you should check with your mentor that this approach is acceptable within the school. It may be also be the case that similar strategies are already in place as part of the whole-school approach to Assessment for Learning, for example the use of the 'traffic light' response by pupils, where they mark their work with red, amber or green dots to indicate how well they feel they understand a task or concept (see Chapter 10).

Questionnaires

Related to the strategy of lesson or topic evaluation is the 'attitude survey' or questionnaire focused on a particular aspect of the curriculum or a teaching method. Unless you are undertaking a piece of formal research as part of a recognised award, it is best to keep these short and simple if the main purpose is to inform or improve an aspect of teaching and learning for the development of your own professional practice. Effective questionnaire design can be quite a lengthy and challenging process, as is the analysis of results if you have a number of questions, or several 'open' questions. With younger pupils in particular you also need to be aware that they may try to provide 'correct' answers to your questions. The use of 'smiley faces' or cartoon pictures to be circled as response options is worth considering, as these forms of questionnaire are easy to analyse and quick to administer, requiring little or no writing in response. Judith Bell's well-known introduction to classroom investigation (see end of chapter) provides a good outline on the use of questionnaires in school-based research, along with a clear 'health warning' about the challenges of effective questionnaire construction.

Interviews

The use of individual or group interviews often appears as a method used in educational research published in journal articles, but this is not something that can be naturally integrated into your normal teaching activities in the same way as the methods we have discussed above. If you are undertaking a research investigation as part of your Initial Teacher Training course or for a further qualification, you may wish to interview teachers, or pupils, to gather their views about a particular aspect of teaching, or the curriculum or an educational development.

You will need to set time aside to plan for the use of interviews, not only to conduct the interviews themselves but to plan the questions you will ask and to obtain the necessary agreements from all concerned. If you intend to interview pupils this will be particularly important, and permisssion will need to be sought from senior staff in the school and in most cases from parents before you can begin your interviews. Ethical issues in relation to confidentiality and voluntary, informed participation are also extremely important and are further discussed below.

If you decide that interviews are the most appropriate method of obtaining the information you need, please remember that for both teachers and pupils this will be time they have agreed to give you outside normal classroom hours, so do make it clear how much time will be involved beforehand in order to give participants the opportunity to decide if they are able to work with you.

Relating the method to your focus

Hopkins (2002), quoted above, argues that your method of investigation needs to be carefully chosen to enable you to develop your hypothesis about learning on the basis of the evidence it produces. This means that you need to be sure that the method you have chosen will help you answer your focus question and that you have some ideas about the kind of evidence that would indicate the success (or otherwise) of your teaching and learning strategies.

THINKING IT THROUGH

What method(s) would be suitable for the following investigations (these are deliberately broad topics, which would need refining in relation to your specific school context or subject area)?

A. Pupils' responses to a range of different teaching approaches used during a given period.

B. The use of higher-order questioning in your own classroom teaching (questions that promote further thinking – not necessarily questions for more able pupils!).

C. Pupils' use of dialogue to support learning during group work.

D. The types of formative feedback that are most helpful in improving pupils' achievement in a given subject.

E. Pupils' response to the introduction of a new curriculum development or teaching approach.

Example for Investigation A

Methods	Questions for consideration
Analysis of pupils' work	Are there any patterns corresponding to the use of particular teaching approaches?
	Do these apply to the whole class or to groups of learners?
Your observation notes taken during lessons	Are there groups of learners who respond noticeably differently to different approaches?
	Do these match with patterns observed from pupils' work?

THINKING IT THROUGH: *CONTINUED*

Methods	Questions for consideration
Group observation conducted by a teaching assistant, using a focused schedule or questions, developed from previous information	What specific factors appear to influence these learners positively (or negatively) in relation to different approaches?
Video/audio recording	Time consuming to analyse and unlikely to provide useful information as this investigation extends over a number of lessons.
Pupil evaluations/ questionnaires	Useful to triangulate with your evidence from observation and analysis of pupils' work. However, will need careful design otherwise answers might provide only superficial information about pupils' preferences for teaching approaches
Interviews	Time consuming, with similar drawbacks to questionnaires

Can you develop similar tables for the other possible investigations? You should expect to find different methods being more effective in each case.

What counts as evidence?

The kinds of classroom-based investigations we have been discussing are intended to inform your own practice in relation to your pupils' learning. This means that the outcomes of your investigation may be relatively idiosyncratic; they may only apply to *these* pupils, in *this* school context, taught by *this* teacher. For many people, both within education and beyond, such results will not count as 'evidence' for professional change, as the particular events and personalities cannot be replicated elsewhere, as in more scientific types of investigation. However, this does not mean that you should not try to define evidence of achieving your own educational aims in undertaking your investigation. As the primary purpose of this *is* that of making a difference to learning in your own classrooom context, you need not feel apologetic about the nature of your evidence. However, schools and classrooms are highly complex environments, so that it can be very difficult (some would claim impossible) to ascribe a single cause to an educational outcome. You will therefore need to be cautious in drawing firm conclusions about your results, but based on knowledge of your learners and the evidence you have obtained, it should be possible to make some 'reasonable ' claims.

Evidence may be what Walsh and Hustler (2002) call 'hard' or 'soft'. Hard evidence is more measurable in nature, perhaps derived from systematic analysis of pupils' work or from the use of questionnaires; 'soft' evidence is less quantifiable, based on pupils' actions or their less formalised verbal responses, on your own notes and observations or on observations by others. Policy makers and some senior staff in schools tend to regard 'hard' evidence as being more significant precisely because it enables claims to be made about 'what works' in terms of improving achievement, attendance or behaviour, and it is important to remember that such improvements are an important part of the responsibilities of policy makers at both national and school level. However, being able to provide measurable evidence of some kinds of improvement in learning, such as attitudes to a subject or engagement with particular approaches to learning, is difficult, and probably beyond the scope of a teacher investigating within their own classroom setting. Here, evidence based on your notes and observations, pupils' comments and possibly observation by others will be important if you are seeking to change practice.

THINKING IT THROUGH

Now look back at the activity for relating the method(s) to the focus.

What types of evidence would be most helpful to inform each of these investigations?

For example, for Investigation A, evidence might take the form of:

- a summary of pupils' achievement matched with teaching approach;
- analysis of pupils' responses to a short questionnaire concerning their views about different teaching approaches and how they feel they help them learn;
- summary of observation notes of pupils' learning behaviours related to different teaching approaches.

The ethics of investigation

Any investigation into aspects of educational practice must respect the rights of all those involved. This means ensuring that participating in any research is *voluntary*, based on *informed consent*, and will not cause *harm or distress*. 'Informed consent' means that pupils or others taking part in your investigation should know what you are trying to find out and what they will be asked to do *before* they agree to participate. If you are intending to submit an account of your investigation to any outside organisation, such as a university or other awarding body, there will be specific requirements in terms of ethical conduct to which you should adhere. Some indicative reading on this topic is given below. For the purposes of this chapter, we are assuming that your investigation will be undertaken for your own information and possibly that of colleagues within your school, and the following points apply to this situation.

The ethical principles of classroom research are that *no actions that would not normally be part of your teaching* should be undertaken without the consent of those participating.

Even though it may be normal for you to involve pupils in group discussion, it is unlikely that this will normally involve video or tape recording and at the very least you should discuss the use of recording with a senior member of the school staff to ascertain whether parental agreement needs to be obtained. This will be particularly important if vidoe recording or photographs of pupils are to be involved, since many schools, particularly at primary level, have policies relating to child protection and photographic images of pupils. It is also important to obtain agreement from any adult working in the classroom who may also be involved in such a recording. Even where you have the agreement of senior staff, you should also make it clear to pupils that you will be the only audience for the recording, and that if they feel uncomfortable about being recorded they can let you know in confidence. If this should be the case, you should avoid recording pupils who are likely to feel unhappy about the process.

Similarly, with the use of questionnaires or interviews, you should explain to pupils why you are asking their opinions and you should attempt to make it clear that completing the questionnaire or participating in interviews is a voluntary activity. Given the nature of teacher–pupil relationships you will not be able to be sure that all your pupils fully appreciate their right to refuse, but you should do your best to avoid giving any impression that there is any expectation that pupils must provide the information you are requesting.

If you involve teachers or other adults in your investigation, through the use of interviews or questionnaires, you should aso make it clear that confidentiality will be maintained, and that you will do your best to ensure that neither the school or any individual will be identifiable in any written report. You should also make it clear who is likely to read your report once your investigation is completed.

Sharing your results

The Core Standards (C40) indicate that teachers should be prepared to share information about effective practice with colleagues where appropriate. Although we have been viewing the process of investigating learning as being primarily directed towards developing your own professional practice, there may also be opportunities for you to share some outcomes of your investigation with others, both colleagues in your own school and a wider audience.

Your school structures may provide you with formal or informal opportunities to talk with colleagues about what you have found out and how you undertook your investigation. Such opportunities could be through team meetings, staff meetings or department meetings, or through school training days. Through sharing your results, you may find other teachers who are also interested in working collaboratively with you on further investigations. You may also be able to share your results through local subject networks or local authority events, but you should gain agreement from your school in advance if any of the materials could be deemed to be 'sensitive'.

Most subject organisations run conferences where you can attend workshops or seminars to which you could contribute, and many also publish professional journals which welcome articles from teachers – the opportunities to share your results and to learn from the research of other teachers are considerable, if you want to take your own learning further.

SUMMARY

This chapter has discussed a number of ways in which you can collect information systematically as part of your normal classroom practice, in order to provide evidence to answer questions about learning and teaching. We have argued that undertaking this type of systematic investigation is an important dimension of professional practice. Increasing importance is being placed on the ways in which teachers contribute to bodies of professional knowledge through undertaking classroom investigation and sharing the outcomes with colleagues and through teacher networks. New developments aimed at further enhancing the professional status of teachers, such as the new Masters in Teaching and Learning programme, are also likely to promote the importance of classrooom investigation and the use of evidence to inform practice in the future.

TAKING YOUR PRACTICE FURTHER

There are a large number of helpful books focusing on classroom research, of which the list below is a small sample:

Bell, J. (2005) *Doing Your Research Project*, 4th edn. Maidenhead: Open University Press.

Cohen, L., Manion, L. and Morrison, K. (2007*) Research Methods in Education*, 6th edn. London: Routledge.

Durrant, J. and Holden, G. (2006) *Teachers Leading Change: Doing Research for School Improvement*. London: Paul Chapman.

This also contains ideas and suggestions about teacher research in the whole-school context.

Hopkins, D. (2002) *A Teacher's Guide to Classroom Research*. Maidenhead: Open University Press.

TAKING YOUR PRACTICE FURTHER *CONTINUED*

McNiff, J. with Whitehead, J. (2002) *Action Research: Principles and Practice*, 2nd edn. London: RoutledgeFalmer.

Newby, P. (2010) *Research Methods for Education*. Harlow: Longman.

Taber, K. (2007) *Classroom-based Research and Evidence-based Practice*, London: Sage.

If you want to find out more about the ethical issues involved in classroom research, Bell (2005), Durrant and Holden (2006), Hopkins (2002) and Taber (2007) above all have sections on research ethics.

Oliver, P. (2003) *The Student's Guide to Research Ethics*. Maidenhead: Open University Press.

This is a comprehensive text on the subject.

TAKING YOUR THINKING FURTHER

If you want to find out more about the development and principles of action research, there is a helpful introduction in Hopkins (2002) above.

An influential text in the past has been:

Elliot, J. (1991) *Action Research for Educational Change*. Buckingham: Open University Press.

Some interesting case studies of teachers' action research investigations are included in:

McNiff, J. with Whitehead, J. (2002) *Action Research: Principles and Practice*, 2nd edn. London: RoutledgeFalmer.

You might also find the following texts of interest:

Dadds, M. (1995) *Passionate Enquiry and School Development*. London: Falmer. This book uses a case study based around three action research projects undertaken by the same teacher, and examines the problems she faced and her feelings during the research investigations, as well as the details of the investigations themselves.

Durrant, J. and Holden, G. (2006) *Teachers Leading Change: Doing Research for School Improvement*. London: Paul Chapman.

This also contains ideas and suggestions about teacher research in the whole-school context.

Find out more

Useful websites

http://www.tlrp.org/pa/
This is the 'practitioner application' area of the Teaching and Learning Research programme. It contains a short 'stimulus' ideas on a substantial range of topics, starting with a practical question such as 'How do you ensure pupils understand what is expected of them?' Investigative activities are then suggested, with links to relevant research reports, articles and other materials.

http://www.standards.dfes.gov.uk/ntrp/
This is the home page of the National Teacher Research Panel. The publications contain research reports on a wide range of topics, all of which have been carried out by practising teachers in schools.

Research digest websites

These provide summaries of published research articles: gtce.org.uk: Research for Teachers (RfT)

The Research Informed Practice Site (TRIPS): **http://www.standards.dfes.gov.uk/research/**

Glossary

Action Research: as indicated in the chapter and suggested reading, there are a number of versions of 'action research'. The essential feature is that the researcher is actively involved in the process of progressive problem solving, rather than standing outside events in a 'traditional' researcher role.

Data collection: the systematic gathering of information/evidence to support your investigation.

Methodology: the overall approach taken to gathering and analysing data. This is an area about which a great deal has been written – Cohen *et al.* (2007, see above) would provide a good introduction to this topic.

Research method: the way in which data is collected. Some examples of research methods are given in this chapter. The list of useful texts provides more examples.

Systematic enquiry: a planned approach to investigating a question of interest to your professional practice, involving the selection of an appropriate research method, the collection of evidence or information relating to your focus question and an evaluation of your evidence leading to some form of conclusion and possibly a recommendation for future practice.

Triangulation: used in a research context, this term refers to the use of more than one source of evidence to strengthen the findings of a research investigation.

References

Bell, J. (2005) *Doing Your Research Project*, 4th edn. Maidenhead: Open University Press.

Elliot, J. (1991) *Action Research for Educational Change*. Buckingham: Open University Press.

Hopkins, D. (2002) *A Teacher's Guide to Classroom Research*. Maidenhead: Open University Press.

Hoyle, E. (1980) Professionalization and de-professionalization in education, in Hoyle, E. and Megarry, J. (eds) *World Yearbook of Education 1980: The Professional Development of Teachers*. London: Kogan Page.

Kemmis, S. and McTaggart, R. (1988) *The Action Research Planner*, 3rd edn. Victoria Deakin University.

McKernan, J. (1996) *Curriculum Action Research*, 2nd edn. London: Kogan Page.

McNamara, O. (ed.) (2002) *Becoming an Evidence Based Practitioner*. London: RoutledgeFalmer.

McNiff, J. with Whitehead, J. (2002) *Action Research: Principles and Practice*, 2nd edn. London: RoutledgeFalmer.

Walsh, M. and Hustler, D. (2002) Not only, but also . . . 'Hard' and 'soft' research stories, in McNamara, O. (ed.) *Becoming an Evidence Based Practitioner*. London, RoutledgeFalmer.

In this chapter you will:

- Explore what is meant by 'collaboration' in an education setting
- Consider recent policies and expectations that have implied the need for collaboration in schools
- Evaluate the layers of collaboration that are now considered necessary in the working lives of schools, teachers, assistants and pupils

The central aim of this chapter is to explore the complicated and integrated web of collaborations that are now expected, and even required, in the working life of a school. On the one hand, the very act of learning is considered by many as being dependent on social collaboration between peers and their teachers. On the other, it might be suggested that a vast number of policy initiatives since 1997 have impelled teachers to work within imposed structures which may result in 'clobberation' (Slater, 2004).

Collaboration is a central part of an exploration of classroom pedagogy, and while this chapter focuses on the wider school and teacher development issues, Chapter 15 is dedicated to a discussion on pupil voice and collaboration. In the context of this chapter, collaboration is taken to mean the mutual co-operation and working by various individuals, agencies and stakeholders involved in the education of pupils between the ages of 7 and 14.

Introduction

In the past 10 years, discourse and rhetoric around education have been dominated by terminology such as co-operation, collaboration, co-ordination (Frost, 2005), partnership, communities, networks, clusters and so on. Lorraine Slater, from the University of Calgary, suggests that this might accompany the increasing decentralisation of education policy and management away from central government to schools themselves (Slater, 2004). During this period the landscape of education policy in England has been dominated by two parallel and, some would argue, complementary strands: initiatives to support the remodelling of the school workforce and the policies surrounding the introduction of the *Every Child Matters* agenda. At their heart are the dual aims of improving working conditions for teachers and other personnel in schools and enhancing the education and life chances of young people. These policy initiatives will be discussed at greater length later in this chapter, but suffice it to say that in England the government see collaboration as central to these developments, with 'constructive collaboration' being listed by the Training and Development Agency (TDA) as one of the six core elements in the school remodelling process. Remodelling will be considered in detail later in the chapter. (**http://www.tda.gov.uk/remodelling/ managingchange/remodellingprocess.asp**)

What is 'collaboration?'

In an education setting there are a multitude of initiatives and activities being carried out at any one time, all of which might be viewed superficially as 'collaborative'. These might range from pupils working in groups on a shared task, teams of staff engaged in shared planning through to consultation meetings between teacher and parent. At their core, in order to be collaborative, Slater (2004) suggests they need to demonstrate certain common elements:

- common goals, joint work, and interdependence;
- parity of status;
- voluntary collaboration.

Consultation: often used synonymously with **participation**, but may imply a more passive level of involvement.

Interdependence: the process whereby, in this case, learning is mutually dependent on each other/ participant.

It would seem that central to joint working and interdependence is the sense that there is a shared interpretation and ownership of the common goals, but that the individual understands their own unique role in the collective endeavour. Jo Rose from the University of Exeter stresses the fact that the necessary negotiation of goals and defining of roles is time intensive (Rose, 2007). It is also important to make explicit the boundaries (Easen, Atkins and Dyson, 2000) in which the collaboration will sit, which includes time and resources constraints as well as shared goals. An illustration of collaborative working in this context might be the development of a healthy eating project in a secondary school. Teachers, school nurses and parents would be involved, each needing to know the aims of the project, understand what they were required to do and who was expected to provide which resources.

Andy Hargreaves, Professor of Education, provides some salutary messages in highlighting the importance of an external reference point in any collaborative activity. This might be a set of targets, policy initiative or mission statement. This avoids the danger of the venture becoming unchallenging, superficial and perpetuating ineffective practices.

Parity in collaborative relationships is a vital ingredient for effective collaboration (Slater, 2004). On the surface it might seem inappropriate that colleagues of different status and authority within an education setting are required to assume equality in the collaboration. However, in a situation where all participants understand their own and others' roles and feel they have a meaningful contribution to make, the power structures begin to shift. According to Anne Lieberman and Maureen Grolnick, scholars from Columbia University, the very act of 'learning to collaborate is about sharing power, knowledge and influence' (1997: 207).

Perhaps the most contentious aspect of collaboration is the need for participation to be voluntary. In the recent and current climate, education establishments of every kind are expected to collaborate within and across school boundaries. Andy Hargreaves warns of the dangerous and negative consequences of 'contrived collegiality'. He goes on to elaborate:

> contrived collegiality is collaboration imposed from above about what to plan or learn, with whom to plan or learn it, and where and when to undertake the planning and learning.
>
> *(2004: 130)*

Following the above scenario of a healthy school meals project, contrived collegiality might be where the menu plans and recipes are directed from a central source, with teachers, parents and school nurse having no say or ownership in how the aims of the project are made real for their children in this school.

OVER TO YOU

Reflect upon your most recent experience or employment in a school setting, and thinking only about yourself for now, list a range of activities *outside* taught lessons, where you were invited or expected to collaborate.

Who was involved in the activity? Parents? Teaching assistants? Senior teacher?

What was your role in the activity? What was the role of the other participants?

What were the aims of the activity?

Who owned the activity?

Was participation voluntary?

How did you influence the outcome of the activity?

Who benefitted from the activity?

Photo 14.1 Gerwine collaboration involves active listening, engagement and participation from all involved

Source: Pearson Education Ltd/ Ian Wedgewood

Collaboration in schools: who is involved?

In this section we intend to provide an overview of the 'big picture' of stakeholder collaborative involvement in the life of a school. The focus remains on teachers, other supporting services and parents. Pupil involvement in collaboration is vital and is given full attention in Chapter 15.

The current context is informed by the huge amount of government-initiated consultation and legislation leading up to 2004. The Children Act and the consequent publications *Every Child Matters: Change for Children* (DfES, 2003) and *Every Child Matters: Next Steps* (DfES, 2004) were an attempt to link educational achievement with child well-being and safety. In doing so, they stressed the centrality of engaging education, social services, health and child care providers in joint and collaborative approaches to working with children. The school was conceived of as the gateway to access the range of services for the child. The five key outcomes in this legislation are for the child to:

- be healthy;
- stay safe;
- enjoy and achieve;
- make a positive contribution; and
- achieve economic well-being.

The implications of the ECM agenda have been very significant for schools that are now required to facilitate the collaboration necessary for the health, social care and education professionals to work in a unified way. Out of this grew practices to support extended schools (see Chapter 3). Now known as the 'core offer', from 2010 all schools are expected to provide access to:

- a varied menu of activities, including study support, play, sport, recreation;
- child care from 8am to 6pm;
- parenting support;
- swift and easy access to specialist support services such as speech and language therapy;
- community access to school facilities. (**www.teachernet.gov.uk**)

Extended Services (extended schools): by 2010 all schools are expected to offer 'extended services' to pupils and the local community.

Importantly, the focus is on providing these services in partnership with local authorities and community-based groups. One might expect the core offer to look quite different in Key Stage 3 settings as opposed to Key Stage 2. The older pupils are likely to be housed in a large education establishment with many hundreds of learners and with more specialised sports and specialist facilities which might form the focus for the extended hours childcare and community involvement; the younger pupils might find themselves being offered these services in locations where the provision is clustered for many smaller primary schools and is therefore away from their own immediate school and community.

CASE STUDIES

Below are two case studies which illustrate the implementation of the 'core offer' (**www.teachernet.gov.uk/casestudies**). In reading them, reflect on

- the nature of the collaboration being modelled;
- the potential barriers to participation.

Case Study 1

Whitefield School is a specialist sports college which has introduced a number of extended services, including crèches, a breakfast club,

after-school activities, school counsellors, a nurse team, a weekly session from a youth worker and Citizens Advice sessions, a refugee service based on site, ESOL classes, ICT for parents, summer schools, a Somali parents' group, holiday sports activities and creative and drama activities.

Case Study 2

In North Solihull five primary schools are working in partnership to deliver a range of extended services across the four most deprived wards in the borough. The partnership has been developed using a hub-and-spoke model. Coleshill Heath Primary School is the hub, providing a full range of services. The school provides support and guidance to the four spokes: Hatchford Community Primary School, Bishop Wilson CE Primary School, Kingfisher Primary School and Yorkswood Primary School. A child and family worker has been appointed in each of the schools to help manage and develop the services. The head teachers of the each school meet regularly to discuss progress and developments and share good practice, as do other staff employed in the schools that cover various strands of extended services. The range of services and activities delivered across the area include: community learning spaces, UK Online centres, debt counselling, wrap-around childcare, breakfast clubs, smoking cessation classes, adult and community learning, family learning. The five schools in turn work closely with other nearby primary schools, forming a wider network of 16 schools which can access these services.

Remodelling the workforce

In order to realise the aims of the ECM agenda it has been necessary to engage in a major overhaul of the school workforce. In parallel with these developments various studies and reports (Ofsted, 1993 and 1995; the National Curriculum Council, 1993; Dearing, 1993) had identified the curriculum overcrowding in the primary phase, recruitment shortages and stress-related issues in the teaching workforce as a result of the introduction of the National Curriculum (1988). In 1998 the government set out the case for modernising the teaching profession (Green Paper: *Teachers: Meeting the Challenge of Change*, DfEE, 1998). The objectives of this paper centred on rewarding teachers more favourably and increasing flexibility in their working practices. These were embedded in a new set of standards and career progression stages.

In order to support the implementation of the necessary changes the government established a Workforce Agreement Monitoring Group (WAMG). This oversaw a phased reduction in teaching hours, introduction of leadership and management time, delegation of non-teaching tasks to other staff and planning and preparation time for all teachers. Interestingly, evidence reported by Hywel Thomas and colleagues from the University of Birmingham (2004) suggested that not all teachers made best use of their non-contact allocation. Their findings indicate that many teachers felt they would rather retain the pastoral elements of their jobs which are increasingly delegated to assistants. However, four years later, perhaps after the planning, preparation and assessment-time entitlement had become embedded, Professor Peter Blatchford and colleagues from the Institute of Education note that teachers reported an improvement in their work–life balance as a result of their non-contact allocation (Blatchford *et al.*, 2008).

The National Remodelling Team was set up to provide advice and guidance on how school leaders might creatively explore the workforce reforms in their schools. The implications for teachers have been significant. While they have been awarded an

Professional Standards: the current government requirements that all teachers need to meet in order to be recognised as qualified teachers in England.

increased salary, this is linked to performance. The research of Rosemary Webb and Graham Vulliamy from the University of Manchester highlighted the increasing need for teachers to be able to demonstrate new skills in co-operation, delegation and mentoring (Webb and Vulliamy, 2006). In 2007 this was recognised in the new framework of Professional Standards (TDA, 2007). This set out career stages and accompanying standards, including those for initial training. An important strand of these standards at all levels is the ability to work collaboratively. It is interesting to trace the attempt to demonstrate collaborative working in developmental stages. The TDA's Professional Standards are designed to provide a progression framework across an entire teaching career. At each stage of the Standards, teachers expect to be assessed on their ability to demonstrate team working and collaboration. Table 14.1 illustrates what is expected at each stage.

Table 14.1 The Professional Standards

Stage of Career	Professional Standards
Qualified Teacher Status	Q32 Work as a team member and identify opportunities for working with colleagues, sharing the development of effective practice with them. Q33 Ensure that colleagues working with them are appropriately involved in supporting learning and understand the roles they are expected to fulfil.
Core	C40 Work as a team member and identify opportunities with colleagues, managing their work where appropriate and sharing the development of effective practice with them. C41 Ensure that colleagues working together with them are appropriately involved in supporting learning and understand the roles they are expected to fulfil.
Post Threshold	P9 Promote collaboration and work effectively as a team member. P10 Contribute to the professional development of colleagues through coaching and mentoring, demonstrating effective practice, and providing advice and feedback.
Excellent Teacher	E13 Work closely with leadership teams, taking a leading role in developing, implementing and evaluating policies and practice that contribute to school improvement. E14 Contribute to the professional development of colleagues using a broad range of techniques and skills appropriate to their needs so that they demonstrate enhanced and effective practice. E15 Make well-founded appraisals of situations upon which they are asked to advise, applying high-level skills in classroom observation to evaluate and advise colleagues on their work and devising and implementing effective strategies to meet the learning needs of children and young people leading to improvements in pupil outcomes.
Advanced Skills Teacher	A2 Be part of or work closely with leadership teams, taking a leading role in developing, implementing and evaluating policies and practice in their own and other workplaces that contribute to school improvement. A3 Possess the analytical, interpersonal and organisational skills necessary to work effectively with staff and leadership teams beyond their own school.

Source: **www.tda.gov.uk/teachers/professionalstandards**

Qualified Teacher Status (QTS): a recognition that someone has met the first set of Professional Standards for Teaching in England and is able to start their Newly Qualified Teacher (NQT) year.

THINKING IT THROUGH

Reflecting on your own experiences in school, try to identify a piece of evidence or example of behaviours which demonstrate each of these standards. Looking back on Slater's indicators above, how far are you able to see if the collaboration was voluntary with a shared understanding of common goals?

For example, as a qualifying teacher, how are/were you able to demonstrate that the other adults understood and shared the same goals for the learners?

Mentoring and coaching

As a teacher in training or in the early stages of your career you will have worked with a more experienced colleague in school who acted as your mentor. They might have provided practical ideas and support as well as feedback on your teaching. Their role might have been variously conceived, and they may or may not have played a part in formal assessments of your progress. Webb and Vulliamy (2006) reported that the one of the outcomes of workforce reform and the revised employment conditions for teachers was the increased need for them to be able to deploy mentoring skills to support other colleagues. Mentoring and coaching have now become accepted and pivotal strategies to use for the professional development of school-based colleagues. Often used interchangeably, it is helpful to unpack the meanings of these two terms as there are subtle differences which may affect the extent to which the process might be seen as collaborative. The National College for School Leadership (NCSL) states that:

> Mentoring is more generally used to refer to a process whereby a more experienced individual seeks to assist someone less experienced, and coaching is used to refer to forms of assistance relating more specifically to an individual's job specific tasks, skills or capabilities.
>
> *(2003: 2)*

David Hargreaves from Roehampton University adds to this by suggesting that the coach is often a person in a position of authority, whereas the mentor is not. (Hargreaves, 2005). It is interesting to reflect on practices in schools for student or newly qualified teachers: how often is the person responsible for assessing performance against the Standards referred to as a 'mentor'? Their role is one that wields considerable authority in that they most often provide the summative judgements that will allow entry (or not) into the teaching profession.

The collaborative relationship between mentor and mentee, coach and coachee is at the heart of the development of the participant(s). Indeed, Kendall would go so far as to say that 'the relationships established . . . have a significant impact upon the success and performance of all involved' (2000: 167). David Hargreaves provides us with a list of terms which might describe the relationship between those engaged in a mentoring or coaching engagement:

- Makes suggestions
- Is often a role model
- Is non-judgemental
- Creates trust
- 'Big ears, small mouth'
- Challenges
- Asks questions
- Issues many challenges
- Shows empathy
- Avoids dependence
- Gives rapid feedback
- Gives advice
- Is a constructive critic
- Is usually on-the-job
- Is a sounding board
- Invites talk

(Hargreaves, 2005)

THINKING IT THROUGH

David Hargreaves challenges us to sort these terms and attribute them to the behaviour of either a coach or a mentor. Try engaging in this activity alone, then compare notes with a peer. How far are you able to agree? Which behaviours did you find most difficult to agree on? Is it possible to reflect on your experience of being mentored or coached and share some examples of these behaviours which you found:

a) constructive or destructive?
b) positive or negative?
c) collaborative or 'clobberative'?

Photo 14.2 Mentoring and coaching in schools requires professional and honest dialogue, where both parties are able to share expertise and experience in order to support teachers' professional development

Source: Pearson Education Ltd/ Ian Wedgewood.

The Centre for the Use of Research and Evidence in Education (CUREE, accessed 18 March 2009) adds to the discussion on the definitions of mentoring and coaching by providing a third term – co-coaching. This is used to refer to a process which 'is a structured, sustained process between two or more professional learners to enable them to embed new knowledge and skills from specialist sources in day-to-day practice' (**http://www.curee-paccts.com/mentoring-and-coaching**). In analysing the skills required for co-coaching, there would appear to be a more explicit need for reciprocity in the relationship, with participants actively seeking new knowledge rather than responding to ideas.

Demonstrating reciprocity (giving and taking ideas) is a key indicator of good collaborative mentoring. Among others, David Hargreaves (2005) notes that it is very possible for both mentor and mentee to adopt both roles in a professional learning context, with both parties gaining much. He goes on to argue that even in a non-reciprocal mentoring relationship, it is often the mentor who reports the greater gain. 'Helping others enriches the giver' (2005: 7).

An alternative way to look at the reciprocity and gain for the mentor might be to consider the kind of person who makes a good mentor. The image of a learning journey is useful here. In exploring the wisdom of the mentor in teacher education, Smith and Alred believe that a mentor 'is one who finds the world endlessly rich and surprising, and welcomes other people as fellow-learners rather than pupils or apprentices . . . continuing to travel rather than one who has arrived' (1993: 111).

> **Reciprocity:** the practice of responding to a positive action with another positive action, or indeed, a negative action in response to a negative action.

Learning mentors

Clearly there are many examples of where mentoring and coaching are seen as tools for **professional development** for teachers and head teachers, but increasingly the term is applied to an adult assistant working alongside pupils in the classroom. **Learning mentors** are in place to:

> provide support and guidance to children, young people and those engaged with them, by removing barriers to learning in order to promote effective participation, enhance individual learning, raise aspirations and achieve their potential
>
> *(The Functional Map at http://www.standards.dfes.gov.uk/learningmentors)*

They are seen as a vital strand in the repertoire of support to raise achievement and attendance in schools. Their role is unique in that it serves to bridge the academic and pastoral divide for pupils. The work of the learning mentor is divided into the following three areas:

- providing a complementary service that enhances existing provision in order to support learning, participation and the encouragement of social inclusion;
- developing and maintaining effective and supportive mentoring relationships with children, young people and those engaged with them;
- working within an extended range of networks and partnerships to broker support and learning opportunities, and improve the quality of services to children and young people.

(http://www.standards.dfes.gov.uk/learningmentors/)

> **Professional development:** the ongoing training, development and education that is available to a person working in a profession such as teaching.

> **Learning mentor:** a person working within a primary or secondary school to support pupils identified as being 'at risk' of academic failure.

Each of these areas requires collaboration and they are illustrated in the following case study, which outlines how a learning mentor has been deployed to support pupils through transition from primary to secondary school.

CASE STUDY

Katherine Fatherly started work as a Transition Learning Mentor (TLM) at Fairham School in Nottingham in November 2002. She works with Year 6 children – post-SATs – who have been identified for Learning Mentor support and who are likely to be coming to Fairham from its key feeder primaries participating in the Behaviour Improvement Programme (BIP). Many of the children she works with have behaviour problems, but a significant number have other difficulties which could make the transition to secondary school more difficult. Some are simply very shy, for example.

Katherine begins the process with letters to heads, parents and to the Year 6s themselves who have been identified as likely to benefit from her support. As part of her work, she then holds meetings with parents and makes presentations to Year 6s and to governors. She also holds after-school transition sessions, is beginning to work with Year 5s and organises for Year 7s to go back to their primary schools to talk in assemblies.

Using innovative and creative activities with the children – such as after-hours treasure hunts at the secondary school – Katherine is exceptionally committed and active with work that has proved powerful and effective. Through de-mystifying secondary school and easing the transition, she is able to minimise the risk that a potentially disruptive change of schools will create lasting problems for children already experiencing difficulties in school. The primary schools she deals with have been particularly positive about the role.

Source: **http://www.teachernet.gov.uk/ casestudies/casestudy.cfm?id=80**

OVER TO YOU

In the above case study, whose goals are being pursued? Consider the communication strategies that might be necessary to facilitate this project.

Exclusion: the practice of removing children temporarily or permanently from school, because they are unable to work with others in a safe manner.

SEN Register: this is a statutory responsibility on schools.

A survey of the early stages of deployment of learning mentors in secondary schools published in 2003 indicates a largely positive response from both pupils and teachers. In reporting for the National Foundation for Education Research, Lisa O'Donnell and Sarah Golden highlighted that Learning Mentors were more likely to be working with children who had a history of exclusion; were on the SEN register; were less motivated and less well behaved (2003: 35). Although early on in the development of the role in schools, O'Donnell and Golden had already detected a shift from targeted allocation to groups or individuals to more 'drop-in' sessions. In relation to collaborative working, it is perhaps of concern that this may hinder the fostering of the consistent relationships which are so important in a successful mentoring experience.

Multi-agency working

The ECM policy agenda referred to earlier has had the consequent effect that teachers are required to work with a range of interested professionals. Multi-agency working is described as:

> a range of different services which have some overlapping or shared interests and objectives, brought together to work collaboratively towards some common purposes.
>
> *(Wigfall and Moss, 2001: 71)*

In relation to the immediate education and care of the child, this may include:

- medical and health specialists such as the general practitioner, school nurse, physiotherapist, speech therapist, dietician;
- Education specialists such as psychologists, behaviour support services, education welfare officer, special needs advisers;
- Social services, police officers, counsellors, family liaison.

The Extended Schools Initiative was a government-funded project to support schools in extending their role at the heart of the community and promote the 'core offer'. This specifically aimed to broaden the range of individuals involved in working alongside teachers. These may include:

- health professionals, including specialist clinics;
- parenting experts;
- adult education;
- citizens' advice and general guidance;
- specialist coaches and teachers;
- social services;
- religious groups.

Collaboration is clearly at the heart of successful multi-agency working. Research for the NFER carried out by Mary Atkinson and colleagues identified a range of models in operation. It appears there is a spectrum of practices involved, from 'decision-making groups' who retained their distinct professional roles through to 'operational teams' who worked very closely, with a merging of professional roles and expertise sometimes evident (Atkinson *et al.*, 2002).

With the number and complexity of interested parties involved it is perhaps not surprising that a number of key issues emerge around expectations and understandings of one another's professional expertise. Rose (2007) highlights that these issues result from differing working practices, ideologies and priorities. These may be compounded by perceptions of status, different policy interpretations and even rivalry between agencies.

It is the case that, as with other aspects of the ECM agenda and the remodelled workforce, teachers and others working in schools need to be able to demonstrate a wider range of skills than might have traditionally been the case, or deploy their skills in different ways. These include communication skills, listening, negotiation and compromising. It is interesting to note the journey travelled for many education professionals – Atkinson *et al.* (2002) reported the emergence of a 'new and professional hybrid'. This person will have an understanding of the various agencies, including being aware of the cultures, language and structures which characterise each agency. The implications for teacher education and development are significant. Where teachers are being educated in a university setting it is now possible to see them working alongside social work, nurse and health professionals also in training.

Continuing Professional Development (CPD)

Today's CPD is very different from some of the 'in-service training' which was undertaken in the past. In previous models, individual teachers attended courses which were usually held off-site. Often courses lasted for one day, with little or no follow-up and little opportunity for those attending to disseminate what they had learned back in their schools, or to evaluate its effectiveness. Current views on effective CPD emphasise the value of a more sustained focus, the effect of collaboration and the importance of evaluating the impact of CPD on pupil learning (Cordingley *et al.*, 2003). Much evidence also exists to support the argument that involvement in effective CPD refreshes teachers and helps to retain them in the profession.

WORKING IN THE CLASSROOM

List the range of CPD activity which is available in school(s) with which you are familiar. Categorise these activities into informal/formal and individual/collaborative activities.

Schools are now increasingly likely to be part of 'learning communities' of various kinds. These will include teachers and other members of the school workforce, and may also involve members of other services, such as Local Authority Behaviour Support Services and National Strategy Consultants. University researchers may also work with individual schools or groups of schools to collaborate in different learning opportunities, which might involve recognised programmes of study such as Masters degree work and other school-based research investigations.

Many schools were part of the Networked Learning Communities initiative, which ran from 2002 to 2006. The project was supported by the National College for School Leadership (NCSL), the General Teaching Council for England (GTCE) and the Department for Education and Skills (DfES). Its purpose was to develop partnerships between schools in order to share knowledge, expertise and good practice. Many of the connections that were established between schools during this period have been sustained beyond the end of the formal initiative. ECM has also provided opportunities for groups of schools in local communities to work together with shared agendas, so that opportunities for learning within individual schools are increased.

Even where such wider networks do not exist, teachers can be involved in collaborative learning within a single school or subject department, on a sustained basis. Some forms of collaborative learning operate through peer mentoring or coaching activities, which are discussed in more detail in Chapter 15. Groups of teachers can also work together to investigate specific aspects of learning and teaching through small-scale research projects. More information about ways to investigate practice is provided in Chapter 13.

THINKING IT THROUGH

In training

Connections between other schools, groups of teachers, or members of the school workforce may not be obvious if you are following a teacher training programme, and spend a relatively limited time in one school. How does your own practice and understanding of educational issues benefit from discussions with trainees who have experience in different schools from yours? What might be the benefits of continuing similar discussions into your NQT year, and beyond?

Starting your career

List the learning communities of which you consider yourself to be a member. Do any of these involve people outside your immediate workplace? Are there opportunities for you to engage in learning with colleagues from other schools or professional contexts?

Investigating learning and teaching

Reflecting on the learning communities to which you belong, what factors contribute to a sustained impact on the quality of your own work in the classroom? What evidence is there to support your views?

Chapters 12 and 13 explore further aspects of researching your own practice and of learning collaboratively with others in your school.

RESEARCH BRIEFING

Philippa Cordingley and Julie Temperley are Director and Assistant Director of the Centre for the Use of Research and Evidence in Education (CUREE). Their work has included developing the National Framework for Mentoring and Coaching. In 2006 they published their findings from a systematic review of research on the impact of collaborative CPD on classroom teaching and learning. Aspects found to be effective were:

- emphasis on peer support rather than leadership by supervisors;
- use of outside 'experts' to support school-based activities;

●

RESEARCH BRIEFING: *CONTINUED*

- observation and shared interpretation (with some feedback) to support teachers implementing new strategies;
- scope for teachers to identify their own starting points and to refine school objectives to identify and specify the CPD focus;
- processes to structure, facilitate and encourage professional dialogue;
- processes for sustaining the CPD over time to enable teachers to embed new practices in their own classroom settings.

(Not all of the above aspects appeared in the 15 studies examined; Cordingley and Temperley, 2006.)

Through these processes teachers reportedly became more confident, more committed to collaborative working and more willing to try new approaches, and there were measurable examples of improvements in learners' motivation and achievement. The teachers also reported initial discomfort as their practice came under scrutiny, and it was important that this was recognised as part of the learning process (Cordingley *et al.*, 2003).

SUMMARY

The remodelled workforce is now, in theory, embedded, with teachers being trained to work alongside a range of other professional and support staff. The implications and outcomes of the ECM agenda are planned to be established in all schools by 2010. Slater takes our thinking further and confronts us with the actual and operational challenges that might present themselves in order for collaboration to be successful. She lists the following as essential ingredients in any collaborative venture which leads to sustained improvement;

- hard work;
- respect;
- time; and
- conflict.

It is perhaps alarming to note that we are encouraged to prepare for conflict! However, the skill set she encourages teachers to develop in order to manage this is one which is highly valued. This skill set includes:

- emotional competencies;
- communication;
- decision making/problem solving;
- conflict resolution; and
- team building.

(Slater, 2004)

SUMMARY *CONTINUED*

With this skill set in mind, it is pleasing to note the growing emphasis upon teacher well-being. The School Wellbeing Report (Teacher Support Network, accessed 19 March 2009) highlighted three key factors which, according to teachers, were the cause of most work-related stress. One of these was relationships with line managers and colleagues. The same report suggests that occupational well-being is financially expensive and neglected in both initial training and ongoing professional development (**www.teachersupport.info**). Increasingly, however, it would seem that school leaders are seeing the benefits of developing emotional literacy in staff teams (Lee, 2006). Leaders also seem to be promoting the social aspects of the relationships among their teachers and other professionals. It is very common now to find a 'Well-being noticeboard' in staffrooms, where colleagues share holiday photos, family celebrations, arrange social events and even set up massage appointments! It is to be celebrated that teachers and other adults are now being recognised as being equally entitled to nourishment for the cognitive, behavioural and emotional aspects of their person. This, according to Peter Salvoley (2002), is the true sign of a community where development can take place.

TAKING YOUR PRACTICE FURTHER

Take time to reflect on a school you know well. List the opportunities outside the classroom for you to develop the skills-set around emotional competencies, communication, decision making, problem solving, conflict resolution and team building. What were the factors that made these opportunities more or less successful for you?

TAKING YOUR THINKING FURTHER

Drawing on case study materials of multi-agency working available at **http://www.everychildmatters.gov.uk/resources-and-practice/EP00099/**, explore how the four different trailblazer authorities have developed good practice. Reflecting on selected examples, how far might a teacher need to draw upon the skills-set above in order to work in the best interest of the child?

Find out more

If you are interested in finding out more about the theories underpinning multi-agency working, you may wish to look at the report by Barron, I., Holmes, R., MacLure, M. and Runswick-Cole, K. (2007) 'Primary Schools and Other Agencies' (**http://www.primaryreview.org.uk/Downloads/Int_Reps/3.Children_lives_voices/Primary_Review_8-2_report_Primary_schools_other_agencies_071123.pdf**). While the focus is on the primary sector, the depth of discussion is rich enough to be very relevant for colleagues working in Key Stage 3 settings.

The following two texts will provide further material for reflection. The first text explores models of CPD for teachers in their early career and is a good introduction

to the excellent work of the Teaching and Learning Research Programme (**www.tlrp.org**).

McNally, J. (2008) *New Teachers as Learners: A Model of Early Professional Development.* **TRLP Research Briefing 56. Available at: http://www.tlrp.org/pub/documents/Mcnally56final.pdf**

This second text provides an excellent introduction and guide to multi-agency work as it affects the working lives of teachers.

Walker, G. (2008) *'Working Together for Children: A Critical Introduction to Multi-agency Working'.* **London: Continuum.**

Glossary

Consultation: often used synonymously with **participation**, but may imply a more passive level of involvement.

Exclusion: the practice of removing children temporarily or permanently from school, because they are unable to work with others in a safe manner.

Extended Services (extended schools): by 2010 all schools are expected to offer 'extended services' to pupils and the local community. These services can be offered by schools working together, rather than independently. The services depend on local demand, but typically involve extended opening hours for childcare, after-school clubs, sports and other facilities, such as ICT rooms available to the local community, parent support activities and access to specialist services such as speech therapy, youth workers, police, careers advice etc.

Interdependence: the process whereby, in this case, learning is mutually dependent on each other/participant.

Learning mentor: a person working within a primary or secondary school to support pupils identified as being 'at risk' of academic failure. They form a bridge

between pastoral and academic concerns. The learning mentor may be a qualified teacher or a member of support staff who has received specific training.

Participation: having some influence over decisions and actions which affect pupils' lives in school. Often used synonymously with **consultation**.

Professional development: the ongoing training, development and education that is available to a person working in a profession such as teaching.

Professional Standards: the current government requirements that all teachers need to meet in order to be recognised as qualified teachers in England.

Qualified Teacher Status (QTS): a recognition that someone has met the first set of Professional Standards for Teaching in England and is able to start their Newly Qualified Teacher (NQT) year.

Reciprocity: the practice of responding to a positive action with another positive action, or indeed, a negative action in response to a negative action.

SEN Register: this is a statutory responsibility on schools. They must keep a register of all children with Special Educational Needs. The criteria for inclusion on this register are governed by legislation.

References

Atkinson, M., Wilkin, A., Stott, A., Dohert, P. and Kinder, K. (2002) *Multi-Agency Working: A Detailed Study. Local Government Association Research report.* Slough: National Foundation for Educational Research.

Blatchford, P., Bassett, P., Brown, P., Martin, C., Russell, A., Webster, R. with Babayigit, S. and Heywood, N. (2008) *The Deployment and Impact of Support Staff in Schools and the Impact of the National Agreement (Strand 2, Wave 1, 2005/06).* DCSF Research Report 027. London: DCSF.

Cordingley, P., Bell, M., Rundell, B. and Evans, D. (2003) The impact of collaborative CPD on classroom teaching and learning, in *Research Evidence in Education Library.* London: EPPI-Centre, Social Science Research Unit, Institute of Education, University of London.

Cordingley, P. and Temperley, J. (2006) *Leading Continuing Professional Development in School Networks: Adding Value, Securing Impact.* Nottingham: NCSL.

CUREE (accessed 18 March 2009) *Mentoring and Coaching CPD Capacity Building Project. National Framework for mentoring and Coaching.* Available at: **http://www.curee-paccts.com/ mentoring-and-coaching**.

Dearing, R. (1993) *The National Curriculum and its Assessment, Final Report.* London: SCAA.

DfEE (1998) *Teachers: Meeting the Challenge of Change.* London: DfEE.

DfES (2003) *Every Child Matters: Change for Children.* Nottingham: DfES.

DfES (2004) *Every Child Matters: Next Steps.* Nottingham: DfES.

Easen, P., Atkins, M. and Dyson, A. (2000) Interprofessional collaboration and conceptualisations of practice, Children and Society, Vol. 14, No. 5: pp. 355–367.

Frost, D. (2005) *Building Capacity in the Teeth of the Performativity Juggernaut.* Paper presented within the symposium 'Leadership for Learning' at ICSEI 2005, the 18th International Congress for School Effectiveness and Improvement, Barcelona, 2–5 January.

Hargreaves, A. (2004) *Teaching in the Knowledge Society.* Maidenhead: Open University Press.

Hargreaves, D. (2005) *Personalising Learning – 5. Mentoring and Coaching, and Workforce Development.* London: Specialist Schools and Academies Trust. Available at: **www.ssat-inet.net**.

Kendall, S. (2000) Establishing and maintaining professional working relationships, in Herne, S., Jessel, J. and Griffiths, J. (eds) *Study to Teach.* London: Routledge: pp. 167–188.

Lee, K. (2006) *More than a Feeling. Developing the Emotionally Literate Secondary School.* Available at: **www.ncsl.org.uk**.

Lieberman, A. and Grolnick, M. (1997) Networks, reform and the professional development of teachers, in Hargreaves, A. (eds) *Rethinking Educational Change with Heart and Mind.* Alexandria, VA: Association for Supervision and Curriculum Development: pp. 192–215.

NCC (1993) *The National Curriculum at Key Stages 1 and 2: Advice to the Secretary of State for Education.* York: NCC.

NCSL (2003) *Mentoring and Coaching for New Leaders. Summary Report.* Available at: **www.ncsl.org.uk/literaturereviews**.

O'Donnell, L. and Golden, S. (2003) *Learning Mentors Strand – Survey Findings.* Excellence in Cities Report 19/2003. Available at: **www.nfer.ac.ukl/research/ documents/EIC/19-2003.doc**.

Ofsted (1993) *Curriculum Organisation and Classroom Practice in Primary Schools: A Follow-up Report.* London: HMSO.

Ofsted (1995) *The Annual Report of Her Majesty's Chief Inspector of schools, Part 1.* London: HMSO.

Rose, J. (2007) *Multi-Agency Collaboration: A New Theoretical Model.* Available at: **www.leeds.ac.uk/educol/documents/167930.htm**.

Salvoley, P. (2002) Emotional WHAT?: Definitions and history of emotional intelligence, in *EQ Today.* 2002–2003. Six Seconds. Available at: **www.eqtoday.com/02/emotional.php**.

Slater, L. (2004) Collaboration: a framework for school improvement. *International Electronic Journal For Leadership in Learning.* Available at: **http://www.ucalgary.ca/~iejll**.

Smith, R. and Alred, G. (1993) The impersonisation of wisdom, in McIntyre, D., Hagger, H. and Wilkin, M. (eds) *Mentoring*. London: Kogan Page.

TDA (2007) *Professional Standards for Teachers*. Available at: **www.tda.gov.uk/teachers/ professionalstandards**.

Teacher Support Network (accessed 19 March 2009) *School Wellbeing Report*. Available at: **www.teachersupport.info**.

Thomas, H., Butt, G., Fielding, J., Lance, A., Rayner, S., Rutherford, D., Potts, Powers, S., Selwood, I. and Szwed, C. (2004) *The Evaluation of the School Workforce Pathfinder Project, Research Report No: RR541*. London: DfES.

Webb, R. and Vulliamy, G. (2006) *Coming Full Circle? The Impact of New Labour's Education Policies on Primary School Teachers' Work. A First Report. Report Summary*. London: ATL.

Wigfall, V. and Moss, P. (2001) *More than the Sum of its Parts: A Study of a Multi-Agency Childcare Network*. London: National Children's Bureau.

15 Pupil Participation

In this chapter you will:

- Develop your understanding of why the active participation of pupils ('pupil voice') in all aspects of school life is important
- Critically examine the implications of active participation by pupils
- Consider the variety of ways in which active pupil participation ('pupil voice') can be encouraged
- Identify approaches that could be used within your own classroom context

Introduction

School council: a body consisting of pupil representatives (usually elected by their peers) and teachers. The most common method of consulting with pupils about aspects of school life.

Pupil voice: an umbrella term used to signify approaches to pupil participation and consultation – letting the 'pupil voice' be heard and valued.

The Education and Skills Act (DCSF, 2008a) requires school governing bodies to invite and consider the views of pupils concerning school issues, with due consideration for their age and understanding. In Wales it is now a legal requirement for all schools to have a school council, and further legislation is planned for England. The principle that pupils must be enabled to participate in decisions affecting their own education and the development of their school is sometimes referred to as 'pupil voice', and the importance of pupil voice activities has been increasing rapidly over the past few years. Involving pupils more actively in consultation about their experiences of school and their views on teaching and learning is claimed to increase engagement:

> Being consulted can help pupils feel that they are respected as individuals and as a body within the school. It can encourage them to feel that they belong, and that they are being treated in an adult way. Pupils who are at risk of disengaging may come back on board if they think that they matter to the school.
>
> *(MacBeath* et al., *2003: 1).*

It is claimed that increased engagement can, in turn, lead to improvements in behaviour, attendance and achievement (DCSF, 2008b).

The form(s) that pupil participation takes vary from school to school, and to some extent between Key Stages 2 and 3, but they include activities as diverse as:

- membership of school councils;
- pupil representation on school governing bodies;
- consultation on specific issues such as new school buildings, environmental impact or new staff appointments;
- involvement in the development of agreed class or school rules, behaviour policies and/or teaching and learning policies;
- lesson observations, in order to feed back information about the effectiveness of approaches to learning and teaching;
- peer support activities (e.g. peer mentoring, buddying schemes etc.).

At classroom level, as discussed in Chapter 10, the effective use of assessment for learning also enables pupils to participate actively in identifying success criteria for aspects of their work and in monitoring their own progress and agreeing future targets.

OVER TO YOU

Can you identify any examples from the list above from your own experience in school?

In training

Some forms of pupil participation may not be so evident during a relatively short period of school placement.

What evidence can you identify *without* asking direct questions of teaching colleagues? What does this suggest about the school ethos?

After talking to other teachers, are there other forms of pupil participation in operation which are less evident?

Starting your career

Undertake the same investigative activity to find out about the practice in your school.

List the ways in which you believe *you* encourage active pupil participation in your own teaching.

Investigating learning and teaching

Select one or two of the examples from the list above and investigate these further by undertaking web-searches and reading relevant literature.

What are the potential benefits for pupils and schools, and what might be possible barriers to successful implementation of your chosen examples? How do you think these examples relate to the principles of personalised learning?

Although not all teachers are positive about pupil voice activities, as we shall see, support for increasing levels of pupil participation is growing. For example, in March 2008, a *Times Educational Supplement* survey of 2,000 teachers found that three-quarters were in favour of involving pupils in drawing up teaching and learning policies. ('How do I rate my lesson?' *Times Educational Supplement*, 14 March 2008).

This chapter examines why pupil participation is being seen as increasingly important, and how it can be supported to enhance learning.

The growth of 'pupil voice' initiatives in schools

Ideas about increasing the level of pupil participation in schools have been promoted for over a decade, and have gathered momentum since the publication of *Every Child Matters* (DfES, 2004). Various policy and curriculum developments also contribute to this process, including:

- the Healthy Schools initiative, which promotes aspects of physical and emotional health in schools;
- the development of the Personal, Social and Health Education and Citizenship curriculum;
- the Social and Emotional Literacy programme (SEAL), referred to in Chapter 9;
- the most recent curriculum changes for Key Stage 3 and primary schools in relation to 'well-being' (see end of chapter for details of websites).

Beliefs about the importance of listening to pupils and enabling them to participate actively in decision making about issues that affect them can be categorised under the following broad headings:

- **Those relating to human rights issues**. The 1989 United Nations Convention on the rights of the Child (UNCRC), Article 12, establishes the rights of the child to have his/her views heard and respected: 'Parties shall assure to the child who is capable of forming his or her own views the right to express these views freely in all matters affecting the child, the views of the child being given due weight in accordance with the age and maturity of the child.'

- **Those relating to the need to develop pupils as future citizens**. The right to participation and consultation is also enshrined in the five outcomes of *Every Child Matters* (DfES, 2003) and the more recent *Children's Plan* (2007) which builds on *Every Child Matters*: 'Enjoying and Achieving' and 'Making a Positive Contribution'. In this context, children are recognised as citizens of the future, with both the need to have their views taken into consideration and also the need to develop an understanding of the responsibilities associated with these rights.

- **Those relating to the development of inclusive learning communities**. Pupils are both the key stakeholders in the education process and also experts in the experience of being educated. Thus we stand a better chance of improving education for all learners if we consult with them and learn from what they tell us. Jean Rudduck, one of the leading researchers into pupil participation in education, argues: 'Pupils have a lot to tell us about ways of strengthening their commitment to learning in school; they say they want: to be treated in more adult ways and to have more responsibility; to have choices and make decisions; more opportunities to talk about what helps and what hinders their learning' (Rudduck: **www.qca.org.uk/futures/**).

- **Those relating to aspects of school improvement**. It is argued (DCSF, 2008b) that increased pupil participation in aspects of school life contributes to higher levels of achievement and improvements in behaviour and attendance, as pupils feel more involved and less alienated from the school.

  > The Four Dwellings High School, Birmingham, has linked pupil participation to school improvement through its Teaching and Learning Discussion Groups. These are made up of twelve volunteers from each year group, and meet twice a term. The twelve pupils are randomly chosen by a teacher taking into account gender, ethnicity and ability, with representation for all the tutor groups. The work of the discussion groups, together with teachers, includes a review of the school's Improvement Plan, focusing on behaviour, feedback and assessment, professional development and extended schools. This has raised the profile and perceived importance of pupil participation in the school, particularly among teachers and governors. As a result, the school reports that pupils take greater responsibility for their learning and pupils feel increasingly that they are trusted and valued.
  >
  > *(Davies, Williams and Yamashita, 2006)*

- **Those relating to changing views of the child**. Traditionally, children and young people (at least up to the age of 14) were regarded as unable to take responsibility for decisions affecting their own lives. This has been referred to as an 'ideology of immaturity' (Grace, 1995: 202), meaning that a belief system had grown up around the idea that this responsibility could only be exercised when individuals were 'mature' enough. Such views are changing as evidence increasingly demonstrates that children, even of quite a young age, are able to express their views without the mediation of adults. Researchers now seek to understand events from the child's perspective, and are recognising that experience, rather than age, is a significant factor in children's abilities to express their points of view (Johnson, 2004: 8).

What do we mean by 'participation'?

So far in this chapter we have used the terms participation and consultation as if there is widely agreed understanding about what these terms mean in the school context. However, this is not necessarily the case.

Kirby *et al.* (2003a, 2003b) wrote a research report on young people's participation in a range of services for the government, and provided an associated handbook of strategies to increase engagement. They define 'participation' as 'having some influence over decisions and actions' as opposed to merely 'taking part' which could refer to a more passive level of involvement. Hart (1992) proposed a 'Ladder of Participation' against which organisations, including schools, could examine their own practice. This is widely used in both educational and community settings:

Participation: having some infuence over decisions and actions which affect pupils' lives in school. Often used synonoymously with **consultation**.

Consultation: often used synonymously with **participation,** but may imply a more passive level of involvement.

Roger Hart's Ladder of Participation

8) *Children/young people initiated, shared decisions with adults*	This happens when projects or programmes are initiated by children/young people and decision making is shared between them and adults. These projects empower children and young people while at the same time enabling them to access and learn from the life experience and expertise of adults.
7) *Children/young people initiated and directed*	This describes children/young people initiating and directing a project or programme. Adults are involved only in a supportive role.
6) *Adult-initiated, shared decisions with children/young people*	This occurs when projects or programmes are initiated by adults but the decision making is shared with children/young people.
5) *Consulted and informed*	This happens when children/young people give advice on projects or programmes designed and run by adults. The children/young people are informed about how their input will be used and the outcomes of the decisions made by the adults.
4) *Assigned but informed*	This is where children/young people are assigned a specific role and informed about how and why they are being involved.
3) *Tokenism*	This is when children/young people appear to be given a voice, but in fact have little or no choice about what they do or how they participate.
2) *Decoration*	This happens when children/young people are used to help or 'bolster' a cause in a relatively indirect way, although adults do not pretend that the cause is inspired by children/young people.
1) *Manipulation*	This happens when adults use children/young people to support causes and pretend that the causes are inspired by the children/young people.

Hart defines the first three 'rungs' of the ladder as *non-participation*, since the children or young people have no real choice or influence over decisions or actions at this level.

THINKING IT THROUGH

Go back to your previous list of 'pupil voice' examples. Where would you place each example on Hart's ladder?

Notice that Hart places 'children/young people initiated, shared decisions with adults' – rung 8, above 'children/young people initiated and directed' – rung 7. Why do you think this is? Do you agree with Hart here?

Not all those working in the field of children and young people's services do. Cutler (2003), for example, believes that all five of the upper rungs of the ladder can be equally participative, depending on the context.

Challenges to developing pupil participation

Implementing some of these forms of pupil participation in schools is likely to require a significant shift in both organisational terms and also in the ways teachers and pupils perceive their relationship with each other. Despite government endorsement of pupil voice as a means of developing skills for adult life and improving behaviour, attendance and achievement, there are vocal critics of the pupil voice movement.

For some, activities such as having pupils observing and commenting on lessons, or being consulted on aspects of running the school, undermines teachers' professional status and leads to poor behaviour as pupils lose respect for adults' judgement. They feel that the boundaries between the roles of teacher and pupil become eroded, with adverse consequences for all concerned ('Right to be Heard', *TES Magazine*, 23 January 2009).

For others, concerns centre on questions of pupils' maturity and the appropriateness of asking them to express opinions and be held responsible for the consequences:

I don't want to pretend that children are miniature adults, with similar reasoning skills. They aren't, and nor should they try to be. They inhabit a wide-eyed world of their own, one they don't fully understand, and they want rules, consistency and boundaries (even though most will test them occasionally). They want to feel that the adults around them are knowledgeable, wise and worth taking notice of. They don't want a questionnaire thrust in their face every five minutes.

(From an article by Mike Kent, Head Teacher, Comber Primary School,
Times Educational Supplement, 11 April 2008)

CONTROVERSY

Research evidence – or selective reporting?

In April 2008 the *Times Educational Supplement* (TES) reported research by the Eppe project, a government-funded longitudinal study of children's learning between the ages of 3 and 11 (**http://www.ioe.ac.uk/schools/ecpe/eppe**). The TES report appeared to suggest that listening to pupils' views increased the likelihood of hyperactive and anti-social behaviour.

> *Listening to pupils and giving them the opportunity to offer views on their education increases the likelihood that they will misbehave.*
>
> *Research carried out by the Effective Pre-school and Primary Education (Eppe) project reveals that children whose views were listened to in school were more likely to be hyperactive or antisocial.*
>
> *The researchers spoke to 1,160 pupils between the ages of 6 and 10, drawn from 125 primaries across England. They examined the ways in which school and teachers influenced the academic and behavioural development of these pupils.*
>
> *The report found that teaching quality significantly influenced pupils' academic progress but did not have a similar impact on behaviour. And methods traditionally believed to help improve behaviour did not necessarily have this effect. For example, many teachers expect that listening to and accommodating pupils' views will have a positive effect on their conduct.*
>
> *Instead the research found that children were more likely to be hyperactive and antisocial in schools where their views were listened to.*
>
> (*Times Educational Supplement*, 4 April 2008)

What did the research really say?

The researchers looked for statistical correlation between different factors observed in classrooms, and this kind of information is difficult to present in an accessible form within the pages of a newspaper. However, the findings were not as clear cut as the TES report suggests.

Pupils' progress in reading was actually better where they had *some* opportunities to organise activities for themselves and where their views were listened to and taken seriously (referred to as *pupil agency and voice*). Pupils in these classrooms also demonstrated better 'self-regulation': the ability to work more independently, to persevere and to take responsibility. However, where there were *high* levels of pupil autonomy, hyperactive and antisocial behaviour did increase. The researchers comment that there is a possibility that these schools were deliberately encouraging a higher level of pupil agency and voice in an attempt to engage disaffected pupils, but also suggest that 'beyond a certain point, children at this age may not respond well to high levels of autonomy because such strategies may adversely affect the disciplinary climate' (Sammons *et al.*, 2008).

While the TES article did quote this last sentence from the research report, this came quite far down in the article, after the text quoted above, which seemed to indicate a direct relationship between all forms of pupil voice activity and increased levels of poor behaviour.

OVER TO YOU

In training

This research took place in primary schools. How far do you believe primary school pupils' views should be listened to, and how much choice should they be given over organising their own learning? Is there a particular age when pupils should start to be consulted or should all pupils have some opportunity to comment on their learning from the Reception class onwards?

Alternatively, do you agree with the views of Mike Kent, reported above, that children should be treated as children and not be expected to make decisions about their own learning, or is the government right to encourage greater involvement?

If your experience has mainly been in Key Stage 3 – what are the implications of this research for 11–14 year olds? Do you think that a similar investigation would produce similar results?

Starting your career

Reflect on your personal list of pupil voice examples, and where you placed them on Hart's Ladder of Participation. What factors have influenced your decisions about the strategies you use?

Your concerns about behaviour? Your beliefs about the amount of autonomy pupils of a particular age can cope with? Your beliefs about how much autonomy pupils ought to have, compared with that of the teacher?

Investigating learning and teaching

The ways in which the educational and national press report educational research can have significant effects on how teachers and the general public view issues. Why might the TES have chosen to report the Eppe research project, above, in the way that they did?

Effective pupil consultation is also time consuming, and may divert attention from pressing concerns about covering the syllabus or preparing for tests. It becomes easy for such activities to be confined to the ends of terms and for consultation activities to have little or no lasting effect (McIntyre, Pedder and Rudduck, 2005).

Some forms of apparent pupil consultation may also exacerbate barriers to participation on the part of some pupils. Rudduck (**www.qcda.org.uk/futures/**) notes that

> there is the question of inclusion. In developing consultation, we have to ask, 'Whose voices are heard in the school?' Pupils are often able to tell us: 'I think they listen to some people, like the good ones'; 'If you're doing well they listen'.
>
> Consultation assumes a degree of social confidence and of linguistic competence and we have found that the more self-assured (often middle-class pupils) who talk the language of the school can tend to dominate conversations.

It thus becomes important for teachers to find ways to provide all learners with opportunities to participate in consultation about teaching and learning in the classroom, and issues that matter to them about their school. Some suggestions for strategies that do not rely on public speaking, or confidence in writing, are given in the next section.

Perhaps the greatest barriers to genuine pupil participation are those created by a lack of authenticity in adults' responses to pupils' views.

> Authenticity is about communicating a genuine interest in what pupils have to say: learning to listen, to offer feedback, to discuss lines of action, to explain why certain responses are not possible.
>
> *(Rudduck: www.qcda.org.uk/futures/)*

Some of these barriers are inadvertent. Teachers are often under pressure to deliver the curriculum or to meet particular outcomes, and this can make it hard for them to really listen to pupils' views. Other barriers relate to school culture or organisational factors which limit the topics pupils are permitted to comment upon. For example, 95% of schools now have a school council, but only 12% allow pupils to have a say on behaviour, or teaching and learning within the school (*Times Educational Supplement*, 14 March 2008). Teachers also tend to discount comments which they perceive as critical of current practice or that they consider to be inappropriately expressed (Johnson, 2004: 14).

Photo 15.1 Receiving feedback from pupils requires a genuine commitment to the principle of pupil participation, good listening skills and a willingness to accept sometimes less palatable truths!

Source: Pearson Education Ltd/Studio 8. Clark Wiseman

Developing a culture of participation

As we have seen, although not all members of the teaching profession respond positively to some pupil voice activities, these are being strongly promoted through a variety of policy initiatives. However, activities such as school councils and pupil feedback on teaching will only produce positive results if there is a genuine culture of listening and responding to pupils' feedback within the school. Forms of 'tokenism' can result in increased disaffection and lack of trust, rather than reduce them.

OVER TO YOU

What kind of learner are we hoping to develop?

It is worth while asking ourselves the question again, with a focus on pupil voice initiatives. Rudduck (**www.qcda.org.uk/futures/**) offers a simple diagram to summarise the possibilities (see Figure 15.1).

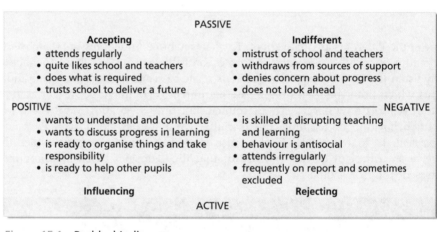

Figure 15.1   Rudduck's diagram

> *The 'positive-passive' pupil may be more compliant and easier to teach, but with the new emphasis on the school as a community, teachers are increasingly welcoming the 'positive-active' pupil. And looking to life beyond school, employers seem to be valuing similar qualities. . . .*

What do you think?

Have you encountered pupils who fit any of these general descriptions?

How far do you think that greater consultation and participation could make a difference to those on the negative side of the diagram?

In what ways could positive-passive pupils be encouraged to develop positive-active characteristics?

As with many other issues we have discussed in this book, effective and long-lasting pupil participation is a whole-school development area, which needs to be actively supported by the leadership of the school. This is not to say, however, that individual teachers' actions will have no effect on pupils' learning. It is also possible that your own values and beliefs about pupil participation, where they lead to recognised improvements in pupil learning, could be a catalyst for school change over time:

> individual teachers who are deeply committed to the principles and values of pupil voice are able to pioneer the work in their own classrooms. Once they have developed procedures for involving pupils in planning and commenting on aspects of teaching and leaning, and once they have sufficient evidence of the usefulness of what pupils have to say, they are often able to present the work to their governors, to their management team and to colleagues. In this way they and their pupils are the catalysts for school-wide change.
>
> *(McIntyre et al., 2005: 167)*

So how might this culture be developed? Mike Kent, quoted above, writes scathingly of presenting primary pupils with questionnaires about teaching and learning, and of course any approach can be counter-productive if it is inappropriate, over-used or does not seem to result in any visible change. The key rules for successful pupil participation in schools are those of *listening, managing appropriate expectations* and *responding*.

Listening to pupils' views and opinions can take a number of forms. Ruddock and Flutter (2004a, 2004b) and MacBeath *et al.* (2003) identify the main ways in which pupils are consulted directly:

- Through large-scale referenda where all pupils in a school or year group are canvassed via a questionnaire, or where their views are sought via pupil representatives at a forum or school council. These events will focus on specific issues.
- Through other writing activities such as learning logs, or suggestion boxes.
- Through a regular forum, such as the school council or circle time where pupils can raise issues.
- Through a special series of interviews which focus on the experience of particular groups of pupils (boys or girls, more or less able pupils etc.), exploring how they feel about their learning and whether things could be done to improve their experience.
- Involving pupils as researchers who undertake an enquiry designed by teachers and/or pupils, analyse the data and report back the results.

(Fielding and Bragg, 2003)

Inevitably there will be pupils whose age or experience makes it more difficult for them to be confident in a direct consultation process, or where the topic might make it more difficult for them to speak openly. Here 'prompted' or 'mediated' consultation (MacBeath *et al.*, 2003) would be more appropriate:

- starting discussion from examples of what other pupils have said about the topic;
- giving pupils a half-constructed sentence to complete;
- using visual means such as drawing, photographs or role play to help the discussion. Pupils are more likely to be able to talk about something they have created for themselves rather than to respond to questions which may be rather abstract.

It is also very important to take time to investigate shared understandings of key concepts between teachers and pupils. In one school, Year 8 pupils were asked to record what they had learnt in each lesson in a learning log. It was then noticed that many pupils only wrote down examples of acquiring new factual knowledge, and this led to subsequent discussion between teachers and pupils about broader definitions of learning. We thus need to try to ensure that our pupils understand the questions we are asking in the same sense that we will interpret their answers. Presenting pupils with a questionnaire or other evaluation activity without having undertaken some preparatory work around ideas about learning may not result in meaningful responses that will move our practice forward.

CASE STUDY

Prompted or mediated consultation

Some possible sentence starters

> I wish teachers would . . .
> I wish teachers wouldn't . . .
> I feel bored in lessons when . . .
> I feel frustrated in lessons when . . .
> I am pleased with myself in lessons when . . .
> What I really look forward to in lessons is . . .
>
> *Source*: based on ideas in MacBeath (2003).

Using photographs

In one secondary school, Year 7 pupils took photos of activities and ways of organising the classroom that helped them to learn. They were able to keep the cameras for several days but had to think, first, about what things they wanted to photograph and then were on the lookout, in their own classes and in others that they were allowed to observe, for the images they wanted to capture.

Photo 15.2 Involving pupils in active forms of evaluating and reporting back on their learning environment can result in improved motivation and engagement with learning

Source: Pearson Education Ltd/ Jules Selmes.

The photos indicated that pupils preferred classes which were more 'hands-on' (e.g. design and technology, ICT, science), and that they enjoyed working in groups and also in pairs with their learning mentors. It was apparent from the photographic record that they least liked lessons where they had just to sit and listen to teachers talking.

(MacBeath *et al.*, 2003: 39)

Using drawing

A primary teacher asked each child in her Year 3 class to draw pictures of the parts of the classroom that they felt helped them learn. She then identified features that were frequently included or omitted as part of an 'audit' of the room as a learning environment. As with the Year 8 pupils mentioned above, this activity also provided some unexpected insights into her pupils' conceptions of 'learning'!

Managing expectations of change, as a result of consultation with pupils, is also a very important element of successful pupil participation. This process has three main aspects: the first is the capacity to make changes on the basis of the consultation process, as well as a willingness to consider change.

This means that the issues on which pupils are consulted may need to be circumscribed in advance; for example, on a whole-school basis, we may consult on aspects of the school uniform policy, but not on whether to abolish the uniform completely. Within the classroom we can consult on many aspects of the teaching and learning experience, but we are not in a position to ignore unpopular areas of the subject curriculum.

The second aspect is to explain to pupils, in advance, that not all suggestions may be adopted, and the mechanisms by which decisions will be made. For example, will final decisions be made only by adults, or will there be further pupil participation?

The third aspect is to communicate with pupils not only which suggestions have been adopted, but also the reasons for not adopting others.

Responding to pupil consultation would seem on the surface to be straightforward, if the processes of listening and managing expectations have been employed appropriately. However, there may still be barriers to genuine responses to pupils' ideas. Making a genuine and sustained change to practice does require a commitment to learning from what our pupils tell us about ourselves as teachers, which is not always a comfortable experience.

RESEARCH SUMMARY

Pupil voice: comfortable and uncomfortable learnings for teachers

In a research study by McIntyre, Pedder and Rudduck (2005), pupils selected from six Year 8 classes were asked for their comments on teaching and learning in specific subjects. Their comments were then shared with the subject teachers (two each from English, Mathematics and Science).

How did the teachers respond?

The researchers found that the teachers were generally happy to accept pupils' comments where they were in line with teaching approaches which the teachers felt they already used, or where they identified areas for improvement which the teachers themselves had already accepted. The teachers were likely to reject suggestions on the grounds of practicality (availability of resources or the need to cover certain aspects of the curriculum), or because they felt they would not be appropriate for all learners. Where the suggestions related to teaching and learning approaches were not already in their existing repertoires, most teachers accepted these ideas and then went on to develop them further, often beyond the original suggestions made by the pupils.

What happened next?

Each teacher then decided on ideas they would try to implement in the last weeks of the summer term and here there were considerable differences between the outcomes.

Where the teacher tried to implement suggestions about greater pupil involvement in lessons too quickly, with insufficient opportunity for pupils to become used to taking more responsibility, this resulted in an unsuccessful lesson and some loss of enthusiasm by the teacher concerned.

Where the teacher did not consider the suggestions made by the pupils to have much value, few changes to practice were made, and these were not sustained the following year.

In two cases involving teachers new into the profession, the ideas were taken up quickly and enthusiastically, with good results, but the approach was not sustained into the following year. Although both had found the experience interesting, it had not changed their practice, and the pressures of curriculum delivery had taken precedence.

With two more experienced teachers, the changes appeared to be more long-lasting, despite their initial scepticism about some of the comments made by the pupils. Both felt they would continue to use greater consultation with their pupils, and that their teaching had benefited from the project. One teacher intended to involve other members of his department in similar activities.

What are the lessons?

This small project suggests that genuine pupil consultation on teaching and learning requires a belief on the teachers' part that pupils' views are worth listening to, and persistence in following suggestions through. 'Quick fix' responses were less successful, as pupils also need time to learn to take appropriate responsibility in more collaborative learning situations.

SUMMARY

The Primary National Strategy (DfES, 2005) identifies four overarching areas relating to pupil participation:

- having a voice and being listened to;
- being active participants in their own learning;
- collaborating with and supporting peers;
- engaging with the wider community.

OVER TO YOU

Looking back to the beginning of this chapter, which of the key beliefs underpinning the development of pupil participation are represented here?

This chapter has focused particularly on the first of these areas, but the remaining points have also been explored in Chapters 10, 11 and 14. These concepts of pupil participation move from that of the rights of the learner towards the learner's developing responsibilities towards others. 'Participation' is thus not solely participation in learning, or the life of the school, but participation in broader social contexts. This concept of participation is underpinned by the curriculum in Citizenship, Personal Social and Health Education (PSHE), and by voluntary programmes such as SEAL (Social and Emotional Aspects of Learning). In different, but related ways, these curriculum developments emphasise social responsibility, personal responsibility for healthy lifestyle and emotional responsibility, all of which contribute to social participation or active citizenship (for a further discussion of this term, see **www.teachernet.gov.uk/ teachingandlearning/library/active citizenship**).

This chapter has argued that pupil voice activities can make a powerful difference to learners' involvement with their own learning, and the life of the school. We would like to suggest that citizenship education in its broadest sense, including active involvement with the wider community, is more likely to be effective if pupils see themselves as having a genuine role to play within the school community.

Active citizenship: this term implies the direct participation of pupils in activities which develop their understanding of democratic processes, community involvement, and developing a sense of personal identity.

TAKING YOUR PRACTICE FURTHER

Download the poster 'Working Together' available at **www.dfes.gov.uk/ participationguidance**. This provides a detailed checklist for schools to audit effective approaches to pupil participation.

Identify aspects that you could put into practice in your own context.

> ### TAKING YOUR PRACTICE FURTHER *CONTINUED*
>
> If you are following an ITE course, discuss possible ways in which pupils could evaluate their learning in your lessons with your mentor or class teacher. Some ideas are given in this chapter, and more suggestions are provided in MacBeath *et al.* (2003).

> ### TAKING YOUR THINKING FURTHER
>
> As this chapter makes clear, devlping effective pupil participation mechanisms in schools is not easy. One barrier might be based in adults beliefs about children's capabilities.
>
> Educationalists and others argue that prevailing concepts of 'childhood' are socially constructed, and of relatively recent origin (James, Jenks and Prout, 1998). What do you think of this idea? Do you consider that there is an 'ideology of immaturity', which underestimates the potential of children and young people to understand issues and express their opinions?
>
> The following article discusses this, and other challenges to effectve pupil participation:
>
> Lodge, C. (2005) From hearing voices to engaging in dialogue: problematising student participation in school improvement, *Journal for Educational Change*, Vol. 6, No. 2: pp. 125–146.

Find out more

Teachers TV (**www.teachers.tv**) has several programmes with a focus on pupil voice:

Action! Teacher Video: Secondary Personalised Learning: student voice Video no. 4895.
Action! Teacher Video: Primary Pupil Voice Video no. 4887.
School Matters – Pupil Voice. Video no. 2773.
School Councils: Speak Out. Video no. 3479 – primary focus.
School Councils: Big School Democracy. Video no. 3480 – secondary focus.
School Councils: Starting Early. Video no. 3478 – focus on nursery and infant schools.
School Councils: Say Your Piece. Video no. 3481 – secondary pupils explain how their school council works.

www.ttrb.ac.uk has a number of reviews on articles and Teachers TV programmes with a pupil voice perspective.

The Research Informed Practice site (**http://www.standards.dfes.gov.uk/research/**) also has a themed area for research on pupil voice.

If you are interested in finding out more about the value of pupil voice activities, and ideas for implementation:

Cruddas, L. *Learning Mentors Supporting Student Voices*. A report written by Leora Cruddas on behalf of the Learning Mentor Strand Co-ordinator Task Group exploring student voice. Available at: http://www.standards.dfes.gov.uk/learningmentors/ downloads/studentvoices.pdf

Flutter, J. and Rudduck, J. (2004) *Consulting Pupils: What's in it for Schools?* London: Routledge-Falmer. MacBeath, J., Demetriou, H., Rudduck, J. and Myers, K. (2003) *Consulting Pupils – a Toolkit for Teachers.* Cambridge: Pearson.

If you are interested in the idea of pupils acting as researchers into learning and teaching in schools:

Fielding, M. and Bragg, S. (2003) *Students as Researchers: Making a Difference*, Cambridge: Pearson. Frost, R. and Rogers, J. *Every Child Matters: Empowering the Student Voice*. Available at: www.standards.dfes.gov.uk/ntrp.

This is a short research report outlining the process and outcomes of developing a group of secondary pupils as classroom researchers.

A similar project was carried out by Worrall and Naylor, also available at the National Teacher Research Panel website as above.

If you are interested in finding out more about the social construction of childhood:

James, A., Jenks, C. and Prout, A. (1998) *Theorizing Childhood*. New York: Teachers College Press.

Glossary

Active citizenship: this term implies the direct participation of pupils in activities which develop their understanding of democratic processes, community involvement, and developing a sense of personal identity.

Consultation: often used synonymously with **participation**, but may imply a more passive level of involvement.

Participation: having some infuence over decisions and actions which affect pupils' lives in school. Often used synonoymously with **consultation**.

Pupil voice: an umbrella term used to signify approaches to pupil participation and consultation – letting the 'pupil voice' be heard and valued.

School council: a body consisting of pupil representatives (usually elected by their peers) and teachers. The most common method of consulting with pupils about aspects of school life.

References

Cutler, D. (2003) *Standard! Organisational Standards and Young Peoples' Participation in Public Decision Making*. London: Carnegie Young Peoples Initiative.

Davies, L., Williams, C. and Yamashita, H. (2006) *Inspiring Schools: Case Studies for Change – Taking up the Challenge of Pupil Participation*. Available at: http://cypi.carnegieuktrust.org.uk/files/InspiringSchools_3.pdf.

DCSF (2007) *The Children's Plan*. London: DCSF.

DCSF (2008a) *Education and Skills Act*. London: HMSO.

DCSF (2008b) *Working Together: Listening to the Voices of Children and Young People*. Available at: www.teachernet.gov.uk/publications DCSF-00410-2008.

DfES (2004) *Every Child Matters: Change for Children*. Available at: www.teachernet.gov.uk/publications.

DfES (2005) Primary National Strategy: *Pupil Participation*. Ref: 17512005PD5-EN. London: DfES.

Fielding, M. and Bragg, S. (2003) *Students as Researchers: Making a Difference*. Harlow: Pearson.

Flutter, J. and Rudduck, J. (2004) *Consulting Pupils: What's in it for Schools?* London: Routledge-Falmer.

Grace, G. (1995) *School Leadership: Beyond Education Management*. London: Falmer.

Hart, R. (1992) *Children's Participation from Tokenism to Citizenship*. Innocenti Essays No. 4. Florence: UNICEF International Child Development Centre.

James, A., Jenks, C. and Prout, A. (1998) *Theorizing Childhood*. New York: Teachers College Press.

Johnson, K. (2004) *Childrens Voice: Pupil Leadership in Primary Schools*. Nottingham: NCSL.

Kirby, P., Lanyon, C., Cronin, K. and Sinclair, S. (2003a) *Building a Culture of Participation Research Report.* London: DfES.

Kirby, P., Lanyon, C., Cronin, K. and Sinclair, S. (2003b) *Building a Culture of Participation Handbook.* London: DfES.

MacBeath, J., Demetriou, H., Rudduck, J. and Myers, K. (2003*) Consulting Pupils – A Toolkit for Teachers.* Harlow: Pearson.

McIntyre, D., Pedder, D. and Rudduck, J. (2005) Pupil voice: comfortable and uncomfortable learnings for teachers, *Research Papers in Education*, Vol. 20, No. 2: pp. 149–186.

Rudduck, J. and Flutter, J. (2004a) *How to Improve Your School: Giving Pupils a Voice.* London: Continuum.

Rudduck, J. and Flutter, J. (2004b) *Involving Pupils, Improving Schools.* London: RoutledgeFalmer.

Sammons, P., Sylva, K., Melhuish, E., Siraj-Blatchford, I., Taggart, B., Barreau, S. and Grabbe, Y. (2008) *Effective Pre-school and Primary Education 3–11 Project (EPPE 3–11): The Influence of School and Teaching Quality on Children's Progress in Primary School.* Research Report no DCSF RR028. London: DCSF.

United Nations Convention on the Rights of the Child (1989) UN General Assembly Resolution 44/25.

Web references

Rudduck, J. *Pupil Voice is here to stay*! 'Think piece'. Available at: **www.qcda.org.uk/futures/**.

www.qcda.org.uk has an area devoted to Citizenship, with guidance on the curriculum in both primary and secondary schools. Links are provided to Personal Social and Health Education (PSHE) from these pages.

www.teachernet.gov.uk also has useful information on both Citizenship and PSHE with links to many resources.

The National Healthy Schools Programme (**www.healthyschools.gov.uk**) encompasses PSHE, healthy eating, physical exercise and emotional well-being.

The SEAL (Social and Emotional Aspects of Learning) website is available at **http://nationalstrategies.standards.dcsf.gov.uk/**.

Pearson Education Ltd/Ian Wedgewood

PART 4 Learning Futures

This final part of the book looks forward to how some of the themes considered earlier are likely to develop over the next few years, and also discusses the growing importance of preparing pupils for life as 'global citizens'. New technologies, a changing curriculum and new types of learning environment will mean that schools are likely to look very different from those you attended as a pupil yourself. This final part aims to prepare you for some of these changes.

16 Extending Partnerships

In this chapter you will have the opportunity to

- Understand what is meant by 'extended partnerships'
- Consider the range and nature of partnerships in which schools are involved
- Explore the potential benefits of extended partnerships for pupils' learning
- Begin to evaluate the potential impact of partnership working for the wider community

Introduction

It is an exciting time to be considering partnerships in schools; there is a strong movement emerging to encourage schools to work in exciting, creative and innovative ways with a range of partners such as community organisations, artists, drama groups or local businesses. The focus of this chapter will be on the partnerships which schools might wish to foster to enhance and enrich the learning experience for the pupils, with an emphasis upon the community-based partnerships which are seen as key to the enlivenment of the curriculum as well as central in the drive to support community cohesion. (Community cohesion is explored in detail later in this chapter.)

For schools, the recent history of 'working in partnership' follows a series of political undercurrents and initiatives. The 1988 Education Reform Act (ERA; DfE, 1988) marked the start of a period when schools were given more autonomy and control over their own governance. According to Geoff Whitty, an influential academic on education policy, this movement was underpinned by the Conservative government's view that local education authority control of schools lead to inefficient use of resources, and that self-management by schools would be more effective and respond to local need (Whitty, 1997). Alongside this was the explicit encouragement, through changes in the constitution of governing bodies, of more private sector and parental involvement in the running of schools. The election of the New Labour government in 1997, in many ways continued its commitment to the local partnerships that were already developing to support the management of schools. Maria Balarin and Hugh Lauder, writing for *The Primary Review*, note that New Labour were keen to support partnerships in schools which bridged the divide between public and private sector interests. The focus here is very much on school management and administration, with the assumption that using expertise and leadership skills from community and private companies would lead to enhanced school performance (Balarin and Lauder, 2008). The following case study serves to illustrate how one rural primary school tries to deploy and exploit the expertise available within the local community.

CASE STUDY

School governors

A rural school in Kent serves three parishes. It is a Church of England controlled school with a roll of 100 children from 4 to 11. The school has four full-time teachers, a non-teaching head teacher and four teaching assistants. The governing body numbers 12 members, each of whom has a remit or expertise. Five of the governors are elected from the parent body but also have other expertise to support the running of the school, including being pre-school manager; university teacher educator; chair of the parent association; and church warden. Two of the governors are elected parish councillors but are also on the village hall committee; council planning officer and recreation ground trust. Two co-opted members of the governing body have been elected because they are the local post-master and retired accountant. The Chair of Governors and vicar are both representative of the views of the local diocese, but also have business expertise and a community liaison brief.

WORKING IN THE CLASSROOM

Reflecting on the case study above, ask to see a list of governors for a school with which you are familiar. This information will be in the school prospectus and, in some cases, on the website. Try to map out the local interests and expertise reflected on the governing body. In what ways might this pool of expertise support the leadership and management of the school?

Policy context

DCSF:
Department for Children, Schools and Families: government department created in 2007, responsible for all matters affecting children and young people up to the age of 19, including child protection and education. Changes to government policy over the years have meant that there have been several renamed departments concerned with education.

Policies to give more autonomy to schools working in partnership with business and communities have been introduced in the past decade. These initiatives included Education Action Zones (EAZ), the Excellence in Cities (EiC) project and Specialist Schools and Academies Trust (**www.specialistschools.org.uk**). The EAZ and EiC projects were introduced with the explicit dual brief of raising educational achievement and promoting social inclusion in disadvantaged areas. The intention was to draw in additional private sector funding to support the integration of school, business and community facilities for the greater good of all pupils and the whole community. EAZs in particular were established following a bidding process by a partnership made up of schools, local authorities and businesses and other organisations. The success of these zones was varied, but worthy of celebration has been the setting up of some strong partnerships between schools and businesses. Ofsted (2003) note that the success in addressing disaffection has been greater than that in raising achievement. The EiCs project followed the EAZs and removed the need for schools to bid in partnership with other parties, but the project was designed to operate alongside other initiatives to support regeneration in areas of deprivation. The most notable success of the EiCs has been the establishment of the role of learning mentors to work with underachieving pupils. You can read more about these two initiatives in Oftsed (2003) 'Excellence in Cities and Education Action Zones: Management and Impact'.

The Specialist Schools and Academies Trust (SSAT) has as its aim 'to give practical support to the transformation of secondary education in England by building and enabling a world-class network of innovative, high-performing secondary schools in partnership with business and the wider community' (**http://www.specialistschools.org.uk**). This is an independent organisation grant funded by the Department for Children, Schools and Families (DCSF) to provide a programme of bespoke support to secondary schools applying to achieve 'specialist' status – this being a formal recognition of excellence in one or more curriculum areas. Once successful, the SSAT will facilitate ongoing networking opportunities and resource development. Key to the achievement of this recognition is the ability to demonstrate the engagement of business and community partners. To read more about Specialist School Status please go to **http://www.standards.dfes.gov.uk/specialistschools/**.

The policies and initiatives detailed above have been evaluated extensively (for example, see **http://www.nfer.ac.uk/research-areas/**) and while favourable aspects are noted in relation to pupil performance and engagement, the strengths seem to focus on the benefits of working in partnership with other schools, communities and organisations. One criticism sometimes noted is that the higher education sector has much to offer to these partnerships and has, in some cases, been marginalised. As Robin Alexander reports in his work for the Primary Review, extended school collaborations involving universities and colleges are the place where the 'most significant educational innovations have originated' (Primary Review, 2007, witness statements).

Partnerships and curriculum innovation

The previous section focused on partnerships which might support business and community involvement in the management and leadership of schools. However, some of the most exciting examples of partnership working are centred around curriculum innovation and development. It is significant that Alexander's Primary Review, in offering a series of aims for the curriculum, makes one of them 'celebrating culture and community'. This is realised in the way the curriculum content might be determined, with 30% being locally decided, managed and supported through the establishment of 'Community Curriculum Partnerships' (CCPs). These would be run in a similar way to those that currently exist for religious education – that is, through Standing Advisory Council for Religious Education (SACREs). (This is discussed further under Partnerships with Faith Communities below.) In addition, Alexander recommends that pupils have a voice in the CCPs through the vehicle of school councils.

THINKING IT THROUGH

Select a topic, theme or project you have planned and taught. Take your plans for this section of work and highlight how the community might have helped with:

- expertise, perhaps at the planning stage to enhance your subject knowledge in the local context;
- expertise, perhaps by working alongside you in the classroom;
- expertise, perhaps by working with pupils in the community;
- resources.

What impact do you think it might have had on the unit of work had you had one or more of the above? What are the potential practical issues with this kind of community-based involvement? What are the potential benefits for the community members?

The following section of this chapter explores each of the areas of 'expertise' listed in the box above and unpacks them further with reference to case study examples.

Enhancing subject knowledge in the local context

Many students and new teachers will be unfamiliar with the local area and communities in which they are teaching. Before turning to the community for curriculum expertise it will be important to become familiar with the context, issues and sensitivities that are influencing the pupils in the classroom. This can be achieved through careful research, discussion with colleagues and informal conversations with parents and colleagues who live in the immediate area. Local newspapers are an excellent source of information to help understand the issues that are pertinent.

Having identified the person or organisation you wish to approach, it will be important to consider the style and method of communication. As an ambassador for the teaching profession and for your local school, you would want to ensure that you invest the community with confidence in your role as a teacher. There is a fine line between demonstrating pedagogical expertise and confidence while proactively seeking subject and locality specific subject knowledge. The Institute of Community Cohesion is an organisation set up in 2005 to support community relations around race, diversity and multiculturalism. In offering advice on establishing community partnerships, they note that it is important to engage in 'myth busting'. For teachers seeking support for community-based curriculum subject knowledge, it will be essential to actively challenge one's own personal stereotypes and assumptions.

The following case study illustrates how a teacher uses the local community to support her context-specific subject knowledge. This in turn leads to opportunities for the pupils to work with members of that community.

CASE STUDY

A local history project

A newly qualified teacher, working with the Year 6 class in a small town primary school, was responsible for planning a local history project which focused on oral stories in the community and the Second World War. She was clear about the historical skills and curriculum requirements she needed to develop with her pupils, but needed to find out more about how the town was affected by the war. As well as asking parents to introduce her to older relatives, she also contacted local care homes and arranged to visit residents who might be able to provide the relevant knowledge. She was also able to arrange a meeting with the local history society and look at original documentation and resources which were subsequently made available to the pupils. The teacher was able to build up a good understanding of the local context, and from this was able to develop the project so that her pupils visited the care home to interview residents and write up their work in the form of a newspaper based on eye-witness accounts.

Photo 16.1 Giving pupils the opportunity to work alongside professional artists as part of the school curriculum can enhance creativity and imagination

Source: Pearson Education Ltd/Ian Wedgewood.

Community expertise in the classroom or learning setting

Traditionally it has been common to see outside visitors invited into the school to work with pupils – these might include a faith leader, employee from a local business or members of the community services like a fire or police officer. This most often has been managed through a 'guest appearance' model where pupils ask questions and then engage in a follow-up activity. The Arts and Education Interface (AEI) initiative provides an example of how far practice can be extended. This project was located in secondary schools in the southwest and sought to develop relationships between teachers, artists and pupils through a range of arts-based interventions. John Harland and colleagues, all arts education experts, were commissioned to evaluate the impact of this project and as a result suggested that working in this way might be termed a 'mutual learning triangle' (MLT) (Harland *et al.*, 2005). For teachers the benefits included enhanced knowledge and skills gained from the artists and more confidence in managing arts-based activities in the classroom. For pupils there were very significant benefits around enjoyment, sense of pride in their work, self-esteem, social skills and awareness of others. The artists themselves reported a sense of satisfaction and enjoyment, an increased awareness of pupils' capabilities and new skills around activity management. The reciprocity and mutual benefits for all involved are key to the success of the MLT, although it is essential for partners to be actively involved.

THINKING IT THROUGH

In order to have a more informed understanding of the Mutual Learning Triangle (MLT) in your own context, have informal discussions to gather the perceptions of a teacher, an 'expert/artist' and a group of pupils about their experience of working together on a project. How far do their views match those reported by John Harland *et al.*?

Creativity in partnership

A plethora of policy initiatives has grown around the area of creativity in education. Sparked by the White Paper 'Excellence in Schools' (DfEE, 1997) and the subsequent publication of 'All Our Futures' by the National Advisory Committee on Creative and Cultural Education (NACCCE) (DCMS, 1999), the government has lent its support to a number of innovative projects. At the heart of all the publications and projects is a view that creativity can only happen in partnership with the creative industries such as artists, potters, designers and musicians. NACCCE notes that partnerships are essential in unlocking the 'creative potential' of learners and the Department of Children, Media and Sport (DCMS) indicate that creativity thrives where 'successful partnerships are established with creative professionals to enrich the experiences of young people' (November, 2006: 4).

One high-profile project, now series of projects, which encapsulates these ideals is Creative Partnerships. Funded by various government and independent bodies, this organisation was set up to foster long-term partnerships between schools and creative professionals. While it describes itself as 'the Government's flagship creative learning programme' (**www.creative-partnerships.com**), it is generally seen by the academic and professional communities in education as being worthy of celebration. Significantly, independent research and Ofsted have both identified the positive impact on all involved, including pupils, parents, teachers, schools and the creative professionals. These multiple beneficiaries can be seen reflected in the aims of their work, which seeks to develop:

- the creativity of young people, raising their aspirations and achievements;
- the skills of teachers and their ability to work with creative practitioners;
- schools' approaches to culture, creativity and partnership working; and
- the skills, capacity and sustainability of the creative industries.

The following case study is taken from a long-term project based in Leicester. It is particularly helpful in illustrating the integration of an arts-based project into the wider life of the school outside the curriculum. As you read it, reflect on what kind of staff development or support you would need to be part of developing a project like this one.

CASE STUDY

Working with a design company

During the Reimagining Fullhurst project, Young Consultants worked together over a three-year period to transform particular aspects of school life. In one project, they wanted to target communication in school and designed a brief for the development of their ideas. Creative practitioners were asked to submit proposals for the project and the Young Consultants selected Innersmile, a Leicester-based design agency, specialising in producing communication material aimed at the youth market. Innersmile worked alongside an Art & Design teacher and a group of 15 Year 7, 8 and 9 students to develop an innovative guerrilla marking campaign to support the Young Consultants' safe school and positive behaviour agenda.

One example of the campaign was the installation of graphic artwork at the bottom of a set of stairs, the purpose of which was to emphasise the importance of safe behaviour on the corridors and stairwells. The campaign also targeted healthy eating and smoking. Innersmile also worked with students to redesign and re-launch the school newsletter. The students were given journalistic and editorial roles and made decisions about content, layout and branding.

Young Consultants used their skills in research, teamwork and planning. Through their involvement in selecting the creative practitioner for the project, students' confidence and ownership of the project were increased. Students involved in the project learnt about careers in design and journalism and were able to improve their creative skills across fields of graphic design, marketing and journalistic publishing.

Project themes and objectives

- Transforming the learning environment and communications
- To explore creative approaches to visual communication in school
- To engage the whole school body in positive behaviour and safety issues

WORKING IN THE CLASSROOM

How might you apply some of the aspects of this case study to working with children in a school or setting with which you are familiar?

Photo 16.2 Genuine and shared dialogue is essential in supporting deep learning rather than superficial encounters with members of faith communities

Source: Pearson Education Ltd/ Ian Wedgewood

Partnerships with faith communities

Working in partnership with faith communities (for example, the local church or a Muslim community centre) has been singled out for particular attention as it is an area which gives rise to a need for heightened sensitivity. The current government is very focused on strategies to develop community cohesion, and religious education (RE) is seen as having a key role to play. (Community cohesion will be explored in greater detail later in this chapter.) In addition, the development and management of partnerships in RE have been proposed as a model worthy of further consideration under proposals from Robin Alexander's 'Primary Review'.

RE is the only curriculum subject which remains under local control, and there is a requirement in law (The Butler Education Act, 1944; HMSO, 1944) that every local authority establish a Standing Advisory Council for Religious Education (SACRE) to oversee the teaching of RE in its schools. The membership of the SACRE is important here as it illustrates how there might be a structured approach to developing extended partnerships with local communities. By law, the SACRE must have representation from local faith organisations, professional/teaching organisations and political bodies. These groups must be comprised as follows;

Group A – representatives of different religious faiths and denominations in the area;
Group B – representatives of the Church of England;
Group C – representatives from the local teachers, including teaching unions and head teachers;
Group D – representatives of the local authority with a balance to reflect local political control.

The remit of the SACRE is focused around providing advice and guidance to the local authority and school governing bodies to ensure that collective worship and RE are provided in all schools. This includes overseeing the development and monitoring of the RE syllabus. The effectiveness of SACREs varies across the country and they are subject to Ofsted evaluation as part of the inspection of local authorities. It is interesting to consider whether they do promote effective partnerships with communities. In 1998, QCA placed 'promoting partnerships between schools and faith communities' and 'bringing people together and enhancing community harmony' as the top two indicators of a successful SACRE. Lynn Broadbent, a significant writer and RE teacher educator, is not convinced by such views and questions whether 'these encounters [with faith communities] will bring about changes in community relations' (Broadbent and Brown, 2002: 20). She is more of the opinion that structures such as SACREs could serve to develop individual personal relationships which might not be representative or inclusive of the views of whole faith community in question.

SACREs are sometimes seen as quite distant from the practicalities of curriculum delivery in schools, and it is at this interface that one might explore faith community partnerships in action. This interface is most often seen as visits to places of worship or encounters with people from the faith community. While these experiences are very valuable, for deep learning to occur it is important that the focus is on the development of the attitudes of respect, open-mindedness and understanding (Walters, 2007; available at: **www.re-net.ac.uk**). This will only happen through dialogue and engagement with religious communities, rather than superficial encounters.

Dialogue and encounter with religious traditions are also important as tools for challenging stereotypes about the sets of beliefs and practices as represented by the 'establishment' or popular media. The work of the Warwick Religious Education Research Unit (WRERU) is prominent in this area. Professor Robert Jackson, Director of the unit, is regarded as a pioneer in the use of ethnography in RE. He has developed a three-tier model to explore the religious traditions (Jackson, 1997). When the learner is introduced to people of faith, they are encouraged to view the experience by looking at:

- the individual believer and their faith (for example, how the family practise their faith);
- the group membership, such as denominational or ethnic expression of that faith (for example, this might be a Roman Catholic community in the Christian tradition or a part of New York's Jewish community);
- The umbrella tradition with which the individual or group identifies. (for example, this might be Islam or Christianity)

While Jackson and his colleagues are keen to point out that this model cannot be over-simplified, it does provide a rich matrix which may give the learner a deeper insight into the lives of believers which moves away from the stereotyping or 'boxing' of the world faiths. In terms of extending partnerships with faith communities which might enrich the learning experience for the pupils, it could be proposed that this matrix would serve teachers well when exploring, researching and establishing community links which are genuine and born out of a deeper understanding of the lives of the local population.

Qualifications and Curriculum Authority (QCA): the official body responsible for all aspects of curriculum development, and statutory assessment in England. It is sponsored by the Department for Children, Schools and Families (DCSF)

Ethnography: this is used to describe a way of researching and usually involves the researcher becoming part of the group or community they are studying. Ethnographic research usually involves studying the whole context rather than an isolated factor.

Faith community: this is used to refer to a group, society, congregation or gathering of people who subscribe to the same set of religious beliefs and practise together.

THINKING IT THROUGH

With reference to a religious community with which you are familiar or is located near your school, explore how far you can apply Jackson's three-tier model to your understanding of the faith. How far can you see the model being useful in trying to research and enhance your subject knowledge for teaching? In applying the model, were any stereotypes challenged or shattered?

Community cohesion

A cohesive community is characterised as one which shares a common vision, values diversity, shares a sense of belonging and proactively tackles inequality (Institute of Community Cohesion, 2008). As noted in Chapter 3, since 2007 it has been a requirement that all maintained schools promote community cohesion. A series of policy initiatives and strategies were developed in response to the terrorist activities in London in 2005, and while some of the early reports focused very strongly on Islamic extremism which promoted violence, the later publications are applicable across a broad spectrum of society. Analysis of the reports and recommendations from the various working parties and committees reveals that there is an inherent thread of 'partnerships' running through all aspects of these initiatives – these include examples of schools working with Muslim community organisations or Pakistani women's groups. The schools' potential to contribute to community cohesion is focused in three areas:

- teaching, learning and the curriculum;
- equity and excellence for all groups in society;
- engagement with and provision of extended services.

These areas have been explored in considerable depth elsewhere in this book; nonetheless, it is useful to revisit these areas in relation to their implications for partnerships. The following abridged case study explores each of these areas with the focus on the Citizenship programme as an example of one curriculum area.

Extended Services (extended schools): by 2010, all schools are expected to offer 'extended services' to pupils and the local community. These services can be offered by schools working together, rather than working independently.

CASE STUDY

The community guiding the curriculum

Salford City Academy is an inner city school located in Salford with just over 600 students. The Academy holds a sports specialism supported by Business and Enterprise and a new sixth form. The students are predominantly from working-class backgrounds; 6% of students are from ethnic backgrounds. In 2007 the school achieved significant improvements in results, with 62% of students receiving 5 A–C GCSEs.

The community is at the heart of Salford City Academy's Citizenship programme. Like all schools, issues in the community find their way into schools but the Citizenship programme at the Academy aims to pre-empt these issues and respond appropriately through its curriculum.

From the programme's inception it was important to establish strong community links. Initially this was achieved by establishing a Citizenship Steering Group.

Composed of students, members of the school and wider community, local councillors and business partners, the steering group's main terms of reference were:

- to give Citizenship (as a discrete subject) an identity within the school;
- to make sure Citizenship addresses the needs of Eccles' young people;
- to develop links with the local community;
- to develop a Citizenship ethos at SCA.

By being inclusive of the community in the planning of the Citizenship curriculum at the Academy it was hoped that the community would recognise the importance of developing a common community-driven vision and that positive relationships between its young people and the community would prevail.

One recent example of how the curriculum directly addresses the concerns raised by the Steering Group was the introduction of an active Citizenship Day to respond to the increase in antisocial behaviour on the housing estate and the subsequent installation of talking CCTV cameras. Prior to the day, students investigated antisocial behaviour in their community and the impact that such behaviour was having. This was built upon during the day by investigating how communities could respond, in particular through the use of CCTV cameras. Students visited CCTV camera control rooms and then

prepared themselves for a community debate in the afternoon. Several community guests were invited to the debate, including local councillors, companies responsible for the monitoring of the CCTV cameras, the Victims Support Service and the Community Police. Not only did the day provide active Citizenship opportunities for students but it also helped shape a shared vision and dialogue between local community members. As a result, students, the local council and the local police gained a deeper understanding of each other's perspectives.

Equity and Excellence

At Salford City Academy issues of equality are given an open forum within the Citizenship curriculum. School policies now reflect this, and while previously students may have been removed from the classroom for inadvertent discriminatory comments, they now remain in the classroom so that their peers can challenge and explore where these views may have come from. The conversation is not always an easy one; however, the use of a structured 'focused conversation' is a useful tool to allow this to take place in a sensitive manner.

The Citizenship programme at the Academy engages the local community in several ways: through the Steering Group and through involvement in active Citizenship days such as the Year 8 day on CCTV cameras discussed above.

Outside visitors are often invited into school to provide an input into classes. Examples include the fire service discussing the impact of antisocial behaviour, such as prank calls, on the service that they can provide to the community.

Students have engaged with a variety of community organisations and individuals through creating podcasts. This has included the local community police to report on antisocial behaviour and racism on the estate, the teenage pregnancy unit at the local hospital on the issue of teenage pregnancy and the planners of Media City currently being built in Salford to investigate how this may benefit young people in the area. Whatever the issue reported upon, students are interacting with the community, investigating different viewpoints and through this developing more positive relationships within the community – all of which support the community cohesion agenda.

OVER TO YOU

In reflecting on the above case study, it is clear to see the commitment to working in partnership with community groups. How far do you think it is the school's responsibility to be an agent in facilitating community cohesion?

Research and evaluation of community cohesion and partnership working have highlighted some significant challenges. A key issue seems to lie in the perception of what a school is for. Colleen Cummings and colleagues, writers on extended schools, note that schools working closely with communities remain very focused on the outcomes for individual learners, rather than seeing the overall benefits for groups within the community (Cummings, Dyson and Todd, 2004). One could argue that a testing and reporting system which is focused on individual pupils' examination results mitigates against engaging in community activities which might be seen to distract from the focus on academic attainment. Further, other research suggests that school managers, in reflecting public policy initiatives, seem to revert to a deficit model when engaging with communities and see their work as having to make up for personal and private inadequacies in their families (Dyson, Millword and Todd, 2002). Given these findings, it is questionable whether the dual role for schools in 'education' and 'community engagement and support' is achievable. David Halpin, a very influential educational theorist, does attempt to bridge this divide by noting the importance of education learners developing a vocabulary of hope. This, he suggests, will serve both individual and community (Halpin, 2003).

SUMMARY

In summary, this chapter has explored the potential for expanding the boundaries of 'working in extended partnerships' for teachers, schools and communities. It is clear that in recent political history, school is seen as a vehicle to address a range of social and community-based 'issues'. It is also possible to see that working with communities presents a vast array of energy, resources and expertise which can be utilised to enhance the learning experience for pupils.

SUMMARY *CONTINUED*

Whether the impact and benefits to communities is long term or sustainable is questionable. One message that is consistent throughout is that:

the key to developing partnerships seems to be a careful and sustained process of trust-building where the partners seek to understand each other's aims, priorities and working methods. (Cummings *et al.*, 2004: 5)

TAKING YOUR PRACTICE FURTHER

Building on some of the ideas in this chapter, consider ways in which you might engage with the local community in the planning, resourcing, teaching and evaluation stages of a project or theme you have undertaken or are working on. What practical strategies might you use to ensure that the partnerships with the community benefit all involved?

TAKING YOUR THINKING FURTHER

This chapter has begun to explore some of the issues around ownership, influence and power in extended partnerships involving schools. On the one hand, schools are encouraged to invest in community relations because it will reap rewards in terms of a shared understanding of the aims of education. On the other, schools are seen as a key vehicle through which to address the fragmentation and isolation experienced in many communities. In taking your thinking further, it is useful to evaluate the 'Seven Steps' to support Community Cohesion:

1. leadership and commitment;
2. developing a vision and values for cohesion;
3. programme planning and management;
4. engaging communities;
5. challenging and changing perceptions;
6. community cohesion and specialist areas;
7. ensuring sustainability of programmes. (available at **http://www.communities. gov.uk/archived/publications/communities/sevensteptool**)

While each of these 'steps' showcases projects, it is useful to look at the case studies around 'Engaging Communities' and reflect on the role suggested for schools throughout. How far might these projects subconsciously promote a 'deficit' model?

Find out more

If you are interested in finding out more about the debates around the benefits and challenges of partnership working, the following texts provide some discussion of the issues:

Charlton, H. (2007) *Building Creative Partnerships – a Handbook for Schools*. **London: The Arts Council.** This book provides an accessible guide to the practicalities and issues around establishing creative partnerships at the school level. It is drawn from an extensive database of case studies.

The Creative Partnerships website also provides a diverse range of research-based resources to explore aspects of creative partnerships at a more considered level (**http://www.creative-partnerships.com/research-resources/**).

If you wish to think further about extended partnerships within the context of the Every Child Matters Agenda, it would be useful to refer to

Middlewood, D. and Parker, R. (2009) *Leading and Managing Extended Schools: Ensuring Every Child Matters (Education Leadership for Social Justice)*. **London: Sage.**

The Institute for Community Cohesion (**http://www.cohesioninstitute.org.uk/**) is a key gateway into research and policy discussions; however, you may wish to challenge your thinking further by reading Flint's book which sets the issues into a much broader social and political context:

Flint, J. (2008) *Community Cohesion in Crisis? New Dimensions of Diversity and Difference*. **Bristol: Policy Press.**

Glossary

DCSF: Department for Children, Schools and Families: government department created in 2007, responsible for all matters affecting children and young people up to the age of 19, including child protection and education. Changes to government policy over the years have meant that there have been several renamed departments concerned with education. DCSF replaced the Department for Education and Skills (DfES), which existed between 2001 and 2007. Prior to 2001, education was part of the remit of the Department of Education and Employment (DfEE), which was in turn created in 1995.

Ethnography: this is used to describe a way of researching and usually involves the researcher becoming part of the group or community they are studying. Ethnographic research usually involves studying the whole context rather than an isolated factor.

Extended Services (extended schools): by 2010, all schools are expected to offer 'extended services' to pupils and the local community. These services can be

offered by schools working together, rather than independently. The services depend on local demand, but typically involve extended opening hours for childcare, after-school clubs, sports and other facilities, such as ICT rooms available to the local community, parent support activities and access to specialist services such as speech therapy, youth workers, police, careers advice etc.

Faith community: this is used to refer to a group, society, congregation or gathering of people who subscribe to the same set of religious beliefs and practise together.

Professional development: the ongoing training, development and education that is available to a person working in a profession such as teaching.

Qualifications and Curriculum Authority (QCA): the official body responsible for all aspects of curriculum development, and statutory assessment in England. It is sponsored by the Department for Children, Schools and Families (DCSF)

References

Balarin, M. and Lauder, H. (2008) *The Governance and Administration of English Primary Education*. Primary Review Research Survey 10/2. Cambridge: University of Cambridge Faculty of Education. Available at: **www.primaryreview.org.uk/Publications/Interimreports. html**.

Broadbent, L. and Brown, A. (eds) (2002) *Issues in Religious Education*. London: RoutledgeFalmer.

Cummings, C., Dyson, A. and Todd, L. (2004) *Evaluation of the Extended Schools Pathfinder Project*. London: DfES.

DCMS (1999) 'All our futures: Creativity, culture and education' by the National Advisory Committee on Creative and Cultural Education. Available at: **www.culture.gov.uk**.

DCMS (2006). *Government Response to Paul Roberts' Report on Nurturing Creativity in Young People*. Available at: **www.culture.gov.uk**.

DfE (1988) *The 1988 Education Reform Act*. London: HMSO.

DfEE (1997) *Excellence in Schools*. Available at: **www.teachernet.gov.uk/publications**.

Dyson, A., Millword, A. and Todd, L. (2002) *A study of 'Extended Schools Demonstration Projects'*. London: DfES.

Halpin, D. (2003) *Hope and Education*. London: RoutledgeFalmer.

Harland, J., Lord, P., Stott, A., Kinder, K., Lamont, E. and Ashworth, M. (2005) *The Arts-Education Interface: A Mutual Learning Triangle?* Slough: NFER.

HMSO (1944) *The Education Act*. London: HMSO.

Institute of Community Cohesion (2008) *Community Cohesion: Useful Links for Schools*. Available at: **www.cohesioninstitute.org.uk**.

Jackson, R. (1997) *Religious Education: An Interpretive Approach*. London: Hodder and Stoughton.

Oftsed (2003) *Excellence in Cities and Education Action Zones: Management and Impact*. Available at: **www.ofsted.gov.uk**.

Primary Review (2007) *Community Soundings: The Primary Review Regional Witness Sessions*. Cambridge: University of Cambridge Faculty of Education. Available at: **www.primaryreview.org.uk/Publications/ Interimreports.html**.

QCA (1998) *An Effective SACRE – Making a Difference*. Available at: **www.qcda.org.uk**

Walters, R. (2007) *Working with Faith Communities*. Available at: **www.re-net.ac.uk**

Whitty, G. (1997) Creating quasi-markets in education: a review of recent research on parental choice and school autonomy in three countries, *Review of Research in Education*, vol. 22: pp. 3–47.

17 Internationalising Learning: Global and Local

In this chapter you will:

- Reflect on the importance of developing pupils' views of themselves as 'global citizens'

- Develop your understanding of how the curriculum at Key Stages 2 and 3 can reflect the 'global dimension'

- Think about the meanings of 'global' and 'local' in the context of education, and how they are interconnected

- Consider ways in which schools as a whole can promote and develop an international dimension

- Reflect on the changing nature of society and Britain today, and the implications of this for developing some concepts of citizenship

What is your response to the following?

An international survey of the attitudes of over two thousand fourteen year-olds to issues of citizenship showed that students in England have relatively less positive attitudes towards immigrants than in some other countries. Although the majority of the young people surveyed upheld the rights of immigrants to speak their own language (62 percent), to have the same rights as everyone else (62 percent) and to vote in elections after living in a country for several years (61 percent), around one-third of all 14-year-olds disagreed with immigrants having such rights. These attitudes are likely to shape young people's interactions with peers from other ethnic groups, particularly those from migrant and refugee communities.

(DfES, 2002)

Should we be concerned?

Introduction

In the extract from the National Curriculum (England) *Values, Aims and Purposes* given overleaf an argument is made that education flourishes only if it adapts to changing social conditions. Arguably the most significant influence on social change in recent times is that of **globalisation** and its effects on societies around the world.

In 1988, the year of the **Education Reform Act** (ERA, 1998), the curriculum was developed with a key aim of ensuring economic competitiveness in a global market (Conroy, Hulme and Menter, 2008). Twenty years later, major revisions to the primary and Key Stage 3 curricula are giving considerably greater prominence to the issues of citizenship in a diverse community and to global interdependence, rather than simple competition, although this is still a factor. The nature of global citizenship and both local and global commitment to **sustainable development** are now high on the agenda. The findings of the citizenship survey briefly outlined above indicate that in 2002 a sizeable minority of 14 year olds in England held negative views of the rights of immigrants. Since 2002, the secondary curriculum has been intended to address this challenging social issue, among many others, through the introduction of Citizenship as a subject, which also become a non-statutory area of the Primary National Curriculum at the same time. The more recent arrival of the cross-curricular dimensions in the secondary National Curriculum (**www.curriculum.qcda.org.uk/key-stages-3-and-4/cross-curriculum-dimensions/**) has also sought to address issues of global citizenship, community cohesion and global awareness.

While there have been some significant shifts in emphasis within the changing curriculum, economic competitiveness is still very important. Policy makers are strongly influenced by the outcomes of international comparisons of pupil performance, and are also quick to look abroad and to 'borrow' ideas from other countries if it is felt these will improve pupil achievement. Changing patterns of global industrial development mean that Western societies are less and less involved in 'heavy' industry and more focused on a 'knowledge-based economy', with increased expectations for levels

Globalisation: this term is used in a variety of contexts: to indicate economic interdependency and the power exerted by some multinational corporations that no longer have strong links with any particular country, but see themselves as transcending national boundaries.

Education Reform Act: a major Act of Parliament passed in 1988, which established the National Curriculum and standardised national testing as statutory, amongst many other revisions to the governance of schooling, too numerous to discuss here.

Sustainable development: the need to avoid the further depletion of the world's resources.

National Strategies (Primary and Secondary): These are professional development programmes for primary and secondary teachers. They provide resources to support teaching, and suggested frameworks for the curriculum. They are widely used in schools, but are non-statutory.

of literacy, mathematical understanding and technical competence. These changing patterns have had a significant influence on the curriculum through the development of the National Strategies, and are continuing to do so in ongoing further reforms. Thus, while the current international strategy from the Department for Children, Schools and Families (DfES, 2004) has been supplemented by a range of later guidance documents for schools (DfES, 2005; QCA, 2007) which emphasise different aspects of global awareness, the importance of retaining economic strength is still a major theme. It could well be argued that this is a legitimate purpose for a national education system.

OVER TO YOU

In the first part of this book we asked you to reflect on your values and beliefs about teaching and education.

How far do you feel that education should serve the needs of the individual, and how far should it serve the needs of society?

Can these be separated? How do we decide what the needs of society are?

Alongside the need to remain competitive in a world where the balance of economic power is shifting towards fast-developing countries such as India and China runs the need to sustain and develop community stability, both locally and globally. Rapid technological development has meant that worldwide communication is almost instantaneous. Thanks to the internet and Web 2.0, technologies such as social networking and blogs, communication is also not always directly controlled by organisations such as media companies, or governments. Television news broadcasts present events as they are happening, or at least appear to do so. Social networking sites, developed by thousands of different interest groups, can offer further perspectives, but also include those dominated by political or religious ideologies. Mobile phones can send messages and images that enable groups of people to learn about events as they happen, or encourage people to congregate together within hours, for different purposes.

So although we now have access to much more information than any previous generation, it can be harder to make sense of it, and to know what we believe about national, global or local issues. Changes to the curriculum in primary schools and at Key Stage 3 reflect a desire on the part of government to provide a framework for understanding some of these issues that will strengthen a sense of community commitment both nationally and internationally. Although it is difficult to define community commitment exactly, it implies developing a sense of responsibility for other people both in our locality and elsewhere in the country, coupled with respect for cultural differences. This is seen as important for national stability in the face of extremist opinions expressed by groups from all parts of the political spectrum. It may be harder to create social divisions where there is a shared sense of community.

This sense of commitment also needs to extend to the environment. Despite wranglings over the extent of, and responsibility for, global warming, environmental issues are pressing for governments around the world. Particularly in Western, consumer-led societies such as the UK, there is a need to convince the population about taking individual actions that will, collectively, make a difference. One such message concerns reducing CO_2 emissions and lowering the collective 'carbon footprint'. The education system has a significant role to play in helping to deliver this message.

This chapter will consider some of the ways in which curriculum developments for pupils in Key Stages 2 and 3 are preparing them as future members of a global community. The main focus of the chapter will be that of the 'global dimension', which will be considered both discretely and also in relation to the other cross-curricular dimensions in the National Curriculum (England). We will consider what it means for a school to become 'internationalised', and we will also discuss some of the implications for learning and teaching of the current moves towards global citizenship.

> **Internationalisation:** an attitude of openness to learning from, and with, those from elsewhere in the world. This term may have different connotations in other contexts such as universities, where there is also an economic dimension.

The international strategy

The government's international strategy for education, skills and children's services in England and Wales was published in 2004 (DfES, 2004). *Putting the World into World-Class Education* is still a current policy and underpins later guidance on curriculum issues such as the 'global dimension' in education.

There are three key areas outlined for development in the international strategy, the first of which is to equip children and adults for life in a global society and economy. Many aspects of this area are addressed through the 'global dimension' of the curriculum, and it also includes developing modern language capabilities in pupils and increasing international recognition of qualifications. The 'global dimension' is characterised in terms of eight key concepts, which are outlined in the next section of this chapter, and is expected to permeate all areas of the National Curriculum for pupils aged 5–16.

The second key area is that of working with other nations 'to achieve their goals and ours' (DfES, 2004: 3), which includes learning from best practice in education from other countries, developing as part of a Europe-wide knowledge-based economy and sharing expertise and resources to improve worldwide education and children's services, particularly in Africa.

The third area is that of maintaining an education system which will be economically competitive in a global context; this area of the policy in mainly aimed at the higher education and training sectors.

The influence of evidence from other countries

Successive governments have viewed the school curriculum, and the education system in general, as the foundation of economic competitiveness in both European and world markets. Close attention is paid to international comparative data about pupils' achievement to monitor the performance of pupils in the countries of the UK against those of other countries, as we saw in Chapter 1.

The Programme for International Student Assessment (PISA) considers the educational performance of 15 year olds in 57 countries using a standardised set of tests. The 2006 results show the UK as a whole rated at number 10 for science, at 14 for reading and 22 for mathematics. Countries such as Canada, Hong Kong and Finland consistently out-perform the UK, and educational policy makers examine the possible reasons for their relative success very carefully.

It seems likely that cultural factors, rather than pedagogical or organisational factors, play a significant role in these differences (Alexander, 2000). These cultural factors are often based in different beliefs about the nature and purpose of education, so that, for example, greater emphasis is placed on social development of young children in Scandinavian countries than in the UK where there is a much greater academic emphasis. This means that 'borrowing' teaching approaches may not, in themselves, make the major differences to educational performance desired by some policy makers. Nevertheless, ideas from other Western countries have had a significant impact on current curriculum content and teaching approaches within the National Strategies since their initial introduction in 1998/9. The encouragement of 'interactive whole class teaching' as a recommended pedagogy in literacy and numeracy, for example, can be partly attributed to international studies of high-performing countries such as Japan and Singapore during the 1990s. This approach is now commonplace in schools, but at the time it was contrasted with teaching approaches where pupils often worked mainly in groups or as individuals, with relatively little whole-class input from the teacher.

Globalisation has resulted in an increasing standardisation of the curriculum across many countries, at least in terms of the names given to subject areas. However, the emphasis given to different subjects or areas of learning within the curricula of different countries, including the countries of the United Kingdom, varies considerably (Hall and Øzerk, 2008). Until recently, England lagged slightly behind many other countries in the past by not making modern languages, citizenship and global awareness a compulsory part of the primary curriculum.

Developing a global dimension in the curriculum

The global dimension and sustainable development is one of the seven cross-curricular themes which is part of the 'Big Picture' of the curriculum as the 'entire planned learning experience for a young person' (QCA, 2008). These are:

- Identity and cultural diversity
- Healthy lifestyles
- Community participation
- Enterprise
- Global dimension and sustainable development
- Technology and the media
- Creativity and critical thinking.

The themes are interrelated, so that, for example, the theme of identity and cultural diversity also has a close connection with that of the global dimension. All of the other remaining themes could be (and should be) similarly linked.

The global dimension is defined as a combination of different concepts:

- global citizenship;
- conflict resolution;
- diversity;
- human rights;
- interdependence;
- social justice;
- sustainable development;
- values and perceptions.

Each of these concepts could be defined separately, but they are also closely related to each other, and it is important to remember that the global dimension in education is not intended to be a set of 'subjects' or discretely taught areas of the curriculum, but is meant to permeate all subject areas and all aspects of school life. It is intended to develop an attitude of mind through the combination of these concepts, many of which are already present within the curriculum as the remainder of this chapter explores. As you read through the rest of the chapter you may wish to note down ideas about how you would define 'global citizenship' and how this relates to the other six concepts in the above list.

THINKING IT THROUGH

The following statements all provide arguments in favour of increasing a 'global dimension' in education. Which do you feel are the most significant for the educational contexts with which you are familiar? If you have the opportunity, these statements could be discussed with two or three other colleagues and arranged into a 'Diamond 9'.*

A. We are increasingly economically interdependent across the globe. Individual actions in the UK can have a impact on the lives of others elsewhere in the world.

B. One in four jobs involves communication with people from other countries. Pupils will need skills and understanding for inter-cultural communication.

C. We live in a diverse society within the UK. The international dimension is on our doorstep. We need to prepare pupils to live in this diverse society.

D. Technology and the media remove physical barriers to communication. We need to help pupils make sense of the range of information they have access to from across the world, and to recognise different perspectives.

E. When pupils and teachers from other countries arrive in UK schools they offer a significant resource for developing international understanding.

* This involves writing the statements, or their letters, on slips of paper and arranging them to create a diamond shape: most important at the top, then the next two choices side by side, followed by the next three choices, then two and finally the least important at the bottom.

THINKING IT THROUGH: *CONTINUED*

F. As citizens of the future, pupils need to develop understanding of concepts such as human rights and social justice in order to combat prejudice and racism both locally and in relation to other countries.

G. Pupils benefit from contacts with pupils and teachers from else where in the world, so that they can develop an understanding of the similarities and differences in cultures and education systems.

H. Environmental issues mean that pupils need to understand the principles of sustainable development and how actions in one country can affect the lives of others elsewhere in the world.

I. Being able to recognise and value similarities and differences between cultures (local and global) helps to develop a stronger sense of personal and cultural identity.

Do you think your responses to these statements depend on whether you are primarily concerned with pupils at Key Stage 2 or Key Stage 3, or are they driven mainly by your personal values and beliefs?

SEAL: Social and Emotional Aspects of Learning (see Chapter 9).

Resilience: the ability to accept being unsuccessful in a task, and to persist in attempting to master a skill or understanding. Can also include the idea of having strategies to support persistence, such as a willingness to try different approaches.

Planning to develop a global dimension asks teachers to consider how teaching in their particular lesson or subject area can contribute to fostering the attitudes, values and skills required for the future in a global society, and the expectation is that all subjects in the curriculum have some opportunities to contribute. These attitudes, values and skills include tolerance of the views of others, an awareness of different perspectives and challenging stereotypical assumptions. As such, they are not exclusively associated with the 'global dimension' or cross-curricular themes: inclusive teaching, in its broader sense, can also be seen as fostering these attitudes. Social and emotional learning (**SEAL**) also has a part to play in developing active listening skills and fostering an understanding of conflict resolution.

It can also be argued that the possession of 'learning skills' such as '**resilience**' and 'resourcefulness' (Claxton, 2002), or 'learning how to learn' makes a contribution to a pupil's ability to develop the qualities associated with the global dimension of the curriculum (see Chapters 8 and 10). This might suggest that 'good teaching' and a positive school ethos will support the development of these significant concepts in any case, but the implication of current curriculum thinking is that we should not assume that such connections will automatically be made. Various curriculum developments, such as the *Personal Learning and Thinking Skills* dimension of the National Curriculum in Key Stage 3 and 4, and SEAL, will contribute to the development of the concepts underpinning the global dimension, but are not a replacement for the deliberate inclusion of this dimension in the curriculum.

Guidance on *Developing the Global Dimension in the School Curriculum* (DfES, 2005) identifies the eight 'key concepts' from the international strategy (DfES, 2004) which should be developed through this curriculum dimension, which are listed on the following page.

This guidance is further supported by *The Global Dimension in Action: A Curriculum Guide for Schools* (QCA, 2007), which provides a number of case studies from primary and secondary schools, showing how aspects of the global dimension have been integrated into the curriculum. This integration can take a number of forms: through themed weeks, links with other schools elsewhere in the country, or elsewhere in the world, projects, assemblies, visits to school by outside speakers and pupil visits to other locations, as well as through making explicit links to curriculum content.

Photo 17.1
Expert outside speakers or facilitators can engage pupils in learning about different aspects of the global dimension: from talking about their visits to schools elsewhere in the world to leading discussion around issues of social justice
Source: Report Digital

CASE STUDIES

Pupils at Key Stage 2 can be encouraged to make *personal links* with global issues, through (literally)mapping international contact with families and friends, and indeed personal travel experience. Many schools and/or classrooms now display world maps with coloured pins or flags showing the different countries where pupils have connections. While there are obvious connotations for schools and classrooms with culturally diverse populations, there are many other opportunities for developing global awareness. This type of activity reinforces awareness of the effect of world travel on individuals, but also on other countries. Pupils might study which countries are most frequently visited for holiday purposes and discuss the effect of this on local economies. Even in less culturally diverse classrooms, there are likely to be friends and family members who live elsewhere in the world, pointing out that migration operates in two directions, and that employment opportunities can take people to many parts of the world.

Pupils in both Key Stages 2 and 3 can be helped to develop an understanding of *global interdependence* through finding out where the ingredients in school dinners come from, and investigating how these are produced and the pressures on producers in other countries. Direct contact with pupils from schools in other countries, via the internet, can substantially enrich this understanding. In one case study reported by QCA (2007) a similar investigation resulted in more FairTrade products being used by the school. In another case study an investigation of where chocolate comes from raised similar issues.

Values and perceptions are examined through linking projects with schools elsewhere in the world. Not all linking projects have involved schools from less developed countries, although many do. Teachers in the QCA (2007) case studies report benefits to pupils' awareness of different perspectives and cultural *diversity* from links with schools ranging from Japan, the Gambia and Poland. Where links are made with schools in countries such as the Gambia or rural India, negative stereotyping can sometimes be challenged. For example, in a recent exchange of e-mails and photographs between a rural primary school in Kent and another in southern India, the English pupils asked their Indian peers where they got their water from each day (expecting to hear about wells, rivers and water carrying) and were duly taken aback by the puzzled reply: 'From the tap'!

Key campaigns such as *Send My Friend to School* or *World Water Day* have also been used effectively by schools to engage pupils' interest and examine issues of *human rights* and *social justice*.

Details of these campaigns and organisations which support links between schools across the world are given at the end of this chapter.

Sustainable development

The theme of sustainable development is linked with that of the global dimension within the cross-curricular dimensions of the National Curriculum. This is because of the relationship between these two concepts: shifting our perspective towards that of sustainable development is a global issue, as well as a local one.

This chapter cannot explore the area of sustainable development in relation to education and the school curriculum in any detail. However, the education system is identified as key to government plans to increase public understanding of sustainability. As we noted in Chapter 4, pupils in the later years of Key Stage 2 and in Key

Stage 3 often become highly engaged with environmental concerns, and part of the role of education for sustainable development is to broaden awareness from relatively local topics, such as recycling and switching off lights, towards the impact of decisions about society today on the world of the future.

This is a relatively sophisticated concept for pupils in the 7–14 age range, who are moving towards the ability to see things in more abstract terms (see Chapter 4). However, in addition to the specific areas within the National Curriculum which currently consider sustainable development issues (Geography, Science, Design and Technology, and Citizenship), the DCSF identifies particular skills which will be needed by pupils in order to engage with some of the more challenging aspects of sustainable development:

- understanding the *connections* between our lives and the lives of others, at both a local and a global level;
- having opportunities to think through problems from a *range of viewpoints*;
- exploring issues and problems and developing the *confidence* to seek solutions;
- developing *key skills* such as listening, communication, teamwork, organisation and problem solving;
- understanding how classroom studies can be applied to *real-world challenges*. (www.teachernet.gov.uk/sustainableschools)

As we have seen, these skills and understanding also apply to the global dimension of the curriculum.

Photo 17.2
Many opportunities exist to support pupils in developing an understanding of issues of social justice and human rights across the world

Source: Report Digital/ Janina Struk

The National Framework offers eight 'doorways' through which schools can consider issues of sustainable development:

- Food and drink
- Energy and water
- Travel and traffic
- Purchasing and waste
- Buildings and grounds
- Inclusion and participation
- Local well-being
- Global dimension.

Each door way corresponds to a target which the government hopes to achieve by 2020. A downloadable poster is available at: **www.teachernet.gov.uk/sustainableschools/ framework**

WORKING IN THE CLASSROOM

Where can you see connections between the eight 'doorways' of the sustainable development dimension, and the global dimension?

Can you identify ways in which you could integrate aspects of the sustainable development framework into your teaching (other than in the curriculum areas already identified)?

How would you then make links to issues within the global dimension?

For example: a survey of items used in school dinners might raise questions about the use of local produce as opposed to imported foods in relation to the impact of transport on the environment. Additional questions might then arise as to the impact of producers elsewhere in the world if demand for these food items decreased (see *global interdependence* in the previous section).

Lessons from abroad: what can experience of education in other countries teach teachers?

It is noticeable that many of the case studies presented by QCA (2007) have been initiated following visits to other countries by teaching staff. These visits have enabled personal contacts to be made which have then supported pupil-to-pupil communication, and a clear appreciation of the issues facing schools elsewhere in the world which can be shared with pupils and colleagues in the UK through the use of video, photographs, and artefacts brought back by the teacher(s) involved in the visits. In an article written in 2006 for the National College of School Leadership on 'Going Global', Peter Greaves, a Primary Deputy Head, also sees this pattern in schools that had successfully gained the International School Award (ISA). This is a nationally recognised award with standards against which schools can measure their progress towards 'internationalisation'.

More and more opportunities are being provided for trainee teachers and those new to the profession to enjoy similar experiences. The development of the Modern Languages strand of the primary curriculum requires all primary trainees with a language specialism to spend at least four weeks teaching in a European school. While this experience is aimed primarily at developing language competence, it also provides an opportunity to make comparisons between different approaches to teaching and curriculum. These can be particularly noticeable in areas such as inclusive practice, which is interpreted differently in some other countries compared to the UK.

Most training institutions offer other opportunities to experience educational settings abroad, apart from those associated with primary Modern Languages, although these may be self-funded. University education departments also enter into partnership arrangements with institutions elsewhere in the world, which can mean that even if you are unable to travel you may have the opportunity to meet trainee teachers from abroad and to compare experiences in schools. You may also be studying alongside fellow trainees whose previous education has taken place elsewhere in the world and who will be able to make comparisons between their own education and the system they are entering in the UK.

These opportunities do not come to an end once you are in a teaching post: a number of organisations offer opportunities for teachers to undertake short visits to schools in Europe, and sometimes further afield. Many of these organisations also offer funding support. See, for example, the DCSF Teacher International Professional Development programme: **www.teachernet.gov.uk/professionaldevelopment/tipd**, also accessible at **www.britishcouncil.org/learning-tipd.htm**

Finally, there are opportunities presented by the media to examine different educational systems and to consider the implications of these approaches. Teachers' TV has a series of comparative education programmes looking at the ways in which different countries approach curriculum areas: 'How do they do it in . . .' – for example, teaching primary mathematics in Hungary, the topic of 'Empire' in India or sex education in Holland. There is also a thought-provoking programme following a Finnish primary teacher's response to the experience of a week's teaching placement in an inner city English primary school, which presents a different view of the English education system: Changing Teachers – Finland comes to England – Primary (Teachers' TV programme id 24015). This programme is also reviewed on **www.ttrb.ac.uk** article id 14497. This can be compared with the experience of four English secondary teachers on a visit to Kenya: Wider Horizons – Four go to Kenya (Teachers' TV programme id 4973), although it must be remembered that the cultural contexts of the two programmes are very different.

Teachers' TV also has a number of documentaries examining broader aspects of education elsewhere in the world, which are aimed at both teachers and pupils (search under International). However, in terms of the programmes aimed at both pupils and teachers, whether provided by Teachers' TV or other media, we need to ask ourselves some careful questions about the ways in which other cultures are presented. TV programmes have to be, by definition, 'watchable'. Thus they may present the more 'colourful' or unusual aspects of daily life elsewhere in the world as if it is the norm. For example, Teachers' TV has a series of 10-minute programmes about the different ways in which some children in India get to school. The main purpose of these programmes, aimed at secondary pupils, is to emphasise the importance of education to Indian pupils. Pupils are shown travelling to school by boat, to schools in monasteries, on mountaintops and in deserts and to a school located in a bus. While these insights are powerful in terms of demonstrating the diversity of educational provision in India (the series has won awards in this respect), much less emphasis is placed on 'ordinary' schools in villages, towns and cities across India, which are attended by the vast majority of pupils.

THINKING IT THROUGH

How can we address the tendency for such media images to present other cultures as 'picturesque', even where this is not the main intention?

In view of this, how far can television documentaries or resource packs support the global dimension and foster international understanding?

This is not to criticise some well-respected materials, such as the *Chembakolli* resources used in many primary schools, or those developed by Oxfam, but to encourage you to consider how the global dimension and international understanding could be developed further.

Internationalising schools

Although 'internationalisation' and the 'global dimension' have many points of similarity, they are not the same thing in practice. It would be possible for a school to be integrating many aspects of the global dimension into the curriculum without also fostering the links that characterise an 'internationalised' school. Conversely, many schools have been actively involved in developing links in Europe and beyond since well before the inclusion of the global dimension in the curriculum. Such schools are very well placed to maximise the benefits of their existing contacts to enrich the curriculum further as a result.

The Comenius programme, offered by the British Council, has facilitated links between schools across Europe for many years. As Europe has expanded as a political entity more countries have become involved and there are currently 31 involved in the Comenius programme. The programme supports school twinning arrangements within Europe, including funds for visits by head teachers and other teachers to establish the relationships. Examples of the ways in which such relationships have enriched the curriculum and challenged stereotypical assumptions can be found at **www.britishcouncil.org/comenius-case-studies**. Some of the most interesting examples come from schools in socially deprived areas or with significant numbers of ethnic minority pupils.

CASE STUDIES

Widening perspectives through contact with Europe

School 1: located in a former coal mining area with high unemployment and family difficulties:

> The Comenius project brought about an improved understanding of other cultures and especially about religious observances. This has contributed to tackling racism and xenophobia – particular problems in this community which has very little experience of ethnic minorities, but is currently experiencing an influx of central and eastern European workers.

School 2: located in an inner London Borough:

> About 80 per cent of pupils . . . are from a Muslim background. While most pupils come from caring families in a strong community, it is a fairly insular environment. Pupils do not normally think of themselves as Londoners, let alone Europeans. The project has done much to widen the horizons of all pupils – where they are in London, in Europe and in the world. Pupils have begun to appreciate that the world is a wider place than their own community.

> *Source: Extracts from Widening Participation Through Comenius, available at **www.britishcouncil.org/comenius-case-studies***

Some schools have taken the international aspects of their work sufficiently seriously to apply for the government's International School Award (ISA) and there are currently 1,000 schools with this status. This award is also managed by the British Council and to gain it the school has to demonstrate that an international ethos is embedded throughout the school, and impacts on a majority of the pupils in a direct way. This is a demanding requirement, along with a requirement for year-round international activity and collaborative curriculum projects in several subjects, and with a number of partner schools. Although not many schools have yet achieved this award, the stringent requirements provide an indication of how the government hopes schools will operate in the future.

In his article written for the National College of School Leadership on 'Going Global', referred to earlier in the chapter (Greaves, 2006), Peter Greaves notes that there are a series of stages through which schools that have gained ISA status have progressed, which he identifies as:

- the experience;
- the event;
- the evaluation;
- the expansion;
- the embedding;
- the embracing.

The process often started with the 'experience' of visiting schools elsewhere in the world by a staff member or members. These individuals often returned as 'enthusiasts', determined to increase the international dimension in their school. This was often kick-started by an 'event' such as an international day, or week. Events such as these are fairly common in schools, particularly in primary schools, but if the international dimension of the school stops there, it may not be much more than a 'food, festivals and fashion' approach, which does not engage seriously with the issues of internationalisation of the school, or the global dimension of the curriculum.

Schools need to discuss and agree on the value of internationalisation for the school in its own context (the evaluation stage) in order to sustain commitment to developing links, which can be slow in the early stages. In some parts of the country, this will be to extend pupils' experience of other cultures, whereas elsewhere it might be to enhance existing connections with a local multi-ethnic community and to build on the cultures of pupils already within the school. In the latter case, Greaves (2006) found that some schools enhanced their connections with the local community as parents and community organisations contributed to developing connections with schools in other countries.

Sustaining the international aspect of work means reviewing all areas of the curriculum – something that can only be done by groups of teachers, rather than lone 'enthusiasts' (the expansion stage). Such developments need not be large scale. Greaves (2006) provides an example of a topic on bridges and structures, where the examples chosen were taken from all over the world instead of just within the UK. Many curriculum areas already draw on resources from a range of cultures and countries as a regular part of classroom work, rather than as part of special events. Auditing lesson content and resources across the school can identify areas where perhaps some adjustments could be made and lead to a deeper 'embedding' of an international dimension in the curriculum as a whole:

> having a developed international perspective is not dependent on the big events and the passionate enthusiast, but rather is built by lots of small elements working together in such a way that everyone is involved and affected.
>
> *(Greaves, 2006: 13)*

CASE STUDY

The embracing stage

On walking into one local 'international' primary school, the visitor is confronted by a dazzling array of colours and designs. All around the entrance lobby, enhanced by its previous life as a chapel, are flags from around the world, each of them labelled and vibrant. World maps can be seen on the walls and there are photos of schoolchildren happy and smiling. These children are not just pupils from this school, however. There are also children, smartly dressed in their school uniform, standing outside their own school in India. The two schools are linked in both curriculum and purpose. A school with developed and established links with schools around the world is likely to be at this developed and ever-deepening stage of having embraced a global perspective in its curriculum. The links also provide a context for that direct contact that allows the embracing to take place at an individual level as well as whole-school level. (Greaves, 2006: 13)

Some primary schools are also adopting materials from the *International Primary Curriculum* (IPC) (see www.internationalprimarycurriculum.com). This material was originally developed for children of employees of the Shell petroleum company, to provide continuity if they moved countries. Now independent of Shell, the materials are organised in **cross-curricular** units, around topics such as 'Chocolate', 'Space' or 'Airports'. Pupils are encouraged to carry out their own research using the internet and links are made to **multiple intelligence** theory. Schools need to join the IPC as members to access the materials, but there are positive reports of its impact on pupils' interest and engagement and the philosophy is very much in line with current revisions to the primary National Curriculum.

Cross-curricular: approaches to teaching which seek to make links between different curriculum subjects. The National Curriculum currently has a set of stated cross-curriculum dimensions for Key Stage 3 (**qcda.org.uk**). This term is more commonly used in the first sense.

Multiple intelligence: a concept developed by Howard Gardner (1983). The idea that humans possess a number of discrete 'intelligences' such as linguistics intelligence, musical intelligence, spatial intelligence. Gardner first proposed seven intelligences, but later increased this number (see Chapter 9 for full reference).

OVER TO YOU

In training

On the basis of your observations or experience in school, how would you characterise the levels of internationalisation you have noticed?

- As 'food, festivals and fashion' as some multicultural approaches to the curriculum have been described? This might involve a day where pupils taste foods from another culture, find out about festivals and perhaps participate in a simulated event and/or dress up in items of national 'costume', but do not sustain their engagement beyond the event.

- Explored more deeply, but in only one or two areas of the curriculum, such as geography, citizenship or modern languages?

- Through contact with schools elsewhere in the world?

- Embedded across the curriculum and supported by regular contact with pupils and teachers from other countries?

Have you experience of a school where there is a designated member of staff responsible for international issues? How does this impact on life in the classroom?

In what ways, if at all, do you see this as distinct from the way the school is developing the 'global dimension' in the curriculum? You may wish to return to this question after reading the following sections.

Starting your career

How important do you feel it is to promote an international dimension to the work of the school?

How evident is the school's international dimension at present (see above)?

In what ways might you contribute to the development of an international dimension in your own teaching?

In what ways, if at all, do you see this as distinct from the way the school is developing the 'global dimension' in the curriculum? You may wish to return to this question after reading the following sections.

Investigating learning and teaching

What do pupils and/or teachers in schools with which you are familiar understand by terms such as 'global dimension' or 'global citizenship'?

How would you investigate this question, depending on the age of the pupils with whom you are concerned? If pupils or teachers are unfamiliar with these terms, how could you phrase your questions so that they make sense to the individuals concerned?

Chapter 13 provides some strategies for school-based investigation – which would be most appropriate in this instance?

Local to global – global to local

Developing the global dimension in the curriculum does not necessarily involve international partnerships, or only considering topics relating to other countries. Many of the key concepts can be explored and developed through engagement with local communities or with links with schools elsewhere in the UK and it is important to support pupils in making the links between the global and local environments in as many ways as possible.

As we have already discussed earlier in this book, in Chapter 3, schools have a duty to promote 'community cohesion', where there is a sense of belonging to a local community coupled with an appreciation of diversity and a commitment to providing similar opportunities for all its members. Thus, starting from the local environment creates a sound base from which to extend and examine pupils' understanding of global issues. How this aspect of the curriculum can be developed will, of course, depend on local circumstances and whether you are teaching within a primary or secondary context. However, the development of project-based or problem-based approaches to learning at Key Stage 3 in many secondary schools means that similar opportunities may be available in both key stages.

A local environment study could involve all or any of the following:

- An historical/geographical study of how and why the community developed: where did different population groups come from during earlier phases of the community's development, and where have people come from now, to emphasise the fact that migration is a normal aspect of life in industrialised countries (in the secondary phase this form of study is part of the Citizenship curriculum).
- Visits to local community facilities, places of worship, or events hosted by different cultural groups; visits to school by members of different cultural groups,

to talk with pupils and/or share examples of dance, music, art etc. from their own culture.

- Evaluation of the local environment in terms of how well it currently caters for the needs of the community; evaluation of environmental issues such as litter, graffiti, building use.
- Making links between the effects of weather conditions in local, national and international contexts, such as flooding or drought. How are the lives of people in the local area affected compared to those in other parts of the country and why? What happens in other parts of the world when these conditions occur?
- Contact with a school or schools elsewhere in the UK to exchange information about local communities and to engage in joint projects. These could be anything from environmental campaigns to shared story-writing or art-based projects.

However, there is a danger in assuming that learning projects such as the above will always run smoothly and that pupils will 'learn' tolerance, respect for diversity or environmental awareness as a result. Case studies such as those in documents from QCA, and from other sources such as Teachers TV, can inadvertently give the same impression, although they are undoubtedly helpful in generating ideas. Such learning experiences may also raise challenging or controversial issues in relation to stereotypical assumptions about race, class or regional prejudice within the UK, or questions around the causes of poverty, war and social injustice.

In secondary schools these questions are fundamental to parts of the Citizenship curriculum, and if you are a teacher of another subject perhaps you may feel they are less relevant to your teaching, but in practice these assumptions and questions can arise at any time and in any subject area, particularly where links are being made to aspects of the global dimension. In primary schools, although Citizenship is a non-statutory subject in the 1999 National Curriculum, class teachers may well find themselves facing some of these challenging or controversial topics in the course of work planned to include global awareness. In one of the case study primary schools identified by QCA (2007: 20) pupils began to consider questions such as '*Are poor people less happy?*' and '*How do people grow in countries where they haven't got much food?*' after an assembly focusing on 'What is poverty?' which had been led by a local Development Education Centre. (Such centres exist in some areas, but not all, specifically to promote awareness of issues relating to developing countries and development education.)

THINKING IT THROUGH

If you were asked similar questions by pupils in school – what would you do?

Some possible responses are given below, which are not mutually exclusive.

Select those which you feel would be appropriate to the age range of pupils with which you are most familiar.

Depending on your stage of training or experience in school, identify one or more actions you would take yourself in these circumstances.

Are there any actions you would *not* take, and if so, why?

THINKING IT THROUGH: *CONTINUED*

i.   Acknowledge the question or comment seriously, agree it should be discussed at a later time and make sure this happens as soon as possible.

ii. Respond to the question with your own opinion.

iii. Acknowledge the question or comment seriously and say you will ask if it can be discussed in another lesson (such as PSHE/Citizenship/ form time depending on school circumstances).

iv. Ask pupils how they think they could begin to investigate their question. What information would they need to find out and how could they find it?

v.   Acknowledge the question or comment, but say it isn't relevant to the lesson under study.

vi. Ask pupils for their opinions on the question within a structured context, i.e. people must be given the chance to express their views uninterrupted; pupils should give reasons why they hold a particular opinion; everyone should be allowed to speak; where disagreement occurs ideas should be challenged, not the individual pupils who hold them (Oxfam, 2006).

vii. Discuss the question with your mentor or another teacher to decide on an appropriate response e.g. an assembly, a corridor display or invitation to an outside speaker.

viii. Research the topic and look for suitable resources to support your teaching.

Some comments on responses ii and v: we anticipate that you felt you would *not* wish to respond in this way and that you have clear reasons why these responses would be inappropriate.

Giving pupils your own opinion in answer to a challenging or controversial issue could lead to accusations of bias, and might not offer a balanced view. The Education Act 1996 (HMSO, 1996) aims to ensure that pupils are not presented with one-sided arguments by their teachers.

In responding as in option v, you give the message that these questions and issues are not valued or significant. Although it *is* important not to be side-tracked from your planned teaching, it is also important to acknowledge such questions and to build on them in a visible way wherever possible.

What does it mean to be British?

When one university tutor recently asked a group of PGCE students this question, some of the answers were:

- eating fish and chips;
- drinking warm beer;
- being cold on the beach as a kid . . .

What answer would *you* have given to this question?

In 2006 the government asked Sir Keith Ajegbo, a former Head teacher, to review the state of diversity in schools, following the London bombings in 2005. One of the key findings concerned how White British pupils felt about their own identities:

> 'It makes no sense in our report to focus on minority ethnic pupils without trying to address and understand the issues for white pupils,' Ajegbo said. 'It is these white pupils whose attitudes are overwhelmingly important in creating community cohesion.'
>
> 'Nor is there any advantage in creating confidence in minority ethnic pupils if it leaves white pupils feeling disenfranchised and resentful. Many indigenous white pupils have negative perceptions of their own identity. White children in areas where the ethnic composition is mixed can often suffer labelling and discrimination. They can feel beleaguered and marginalised, finding their own identities under threat as much as minority ethnic children might not have theirs recognised.'
>
> The Guardian, *'Curriculum Review Diversity and Citizenship'* p. 30
> *publications.teachernet.gov.uk/eOrderingDownload/DfESDiversity&Citizenship.pdf*

One of the results of this report was the introduction of a new strand in the secondary Citizenship curriculum: 'Identity and diversity: Living Together in the UK', which aimed to consider this important issue for twenty-first-century Britain. Another is the development of a national programmme: *Who Do We Think We Are* (**www.wdwtwa.org.uk**). The website provides ideas for lessons for Key Stages 2 and 3 (for example, one series is based around the London 2012 Olympics) and leads up to a national week of activity around the key theme of national identity.

The report has stimulated national debate around the concept of community cohesion (discussed in Chapter 3) and 'Britishness'. Teachers' TV has a 45-minute documentary: 'The Big Debate – Britishness' where Krishnan Guru-Murthy interviews, among others, Sir Keith Ajegbo and right-wing writer and academic Douglas Murray (Teachers' TV programme id 29032).

RESEARCH BRIEFING: BRITISH VALUES AND THE TEACHER'S ROLE

In 2008 Teachers' TV also commissioned a poll of teachers via YouGov to find out their views about whether teaching 'British values' should be part of a teacher's role. The following information is taken from the press release following analysis of the results:

- 72% of respondents agreed that teaching British values was part of their role, and 21% saw it as a central part;
- 25% felt it was *not* part of the teacher's role;
- 46% felt that pupils should not be allowed to wear religious symbols in school.

RESEARCH BRIEFING: *CONTINUED*

The results of the poll showed some regional differences, with 81% of teachers in the south of England responding positively to the idea of promoting British values in their teaching, compared with 70% in the north of England.

What do these figures mean?

The press release from which this information was taken did not indicate the number of teachers who took part in this poll, so it is hard to know how representative these figures are. It is also not clear what the respondents meant by 'British values', which could mean very different things to different people. Although Alan Johnson, the Home Secretary at the time of the Ajegbo Report, identified respect for free speech and tolerance as British values, commentators rightly asked what made these values distinctively *British*.

However, the responses do seem to indicate a change in teachers' views. Andrew Bethell, Chief Executive of Teachers' TV, felt this represented a 'shift away from multiculturalism in schools. There seems to be an increasing feeling among teachers that simply embracing difference is no longer enough. Pupils need a sense of common identity and "Britishness" is a big part of this'.

OVER TO YOU

Do you think there are any uniquely '*British* values'?

Or do you think that there are values we need to share as a society in Britain, whether or not they are also shared by other societies elsewhere in the world?

If you had responded to this poll, where would you have placed yourself? With the 25% who felt it was not part of their role?

With the 21% who felt it was central to their role?

Somewhere in between?

As with a number of other areas we have discussed in this book, it is important for you to reflect on, and evaluate, your own beliefs about your own British identity – including whether you feel that you have one – and on your role as a teacher in terms of promoting Britishness with your pupils. For some pupils and their parents, and indeed for some teachers, this is a controversial area of debate. However, as with the issues raised in the previous section, we need to ask ourselves if we are genuinely helping our pupils develop their broader understanding of the world, if we avoid responding where questions arise.

SUMMARY

This chapter has considered the recent curriculum developments in Key Stage 3 in respect of the 'global dimension 'of education and also looked at how these are emerging in Key Stage 2. This development has been located within the area of economic competitiveness, but also of global interdependence and the necessity for pupils of the future to be more aware of themselves as part of this international network.

Developing the concept of global citizenship requires a recognition of some of the challenges involved, in terms of examining our own identities as British citizens (where this applies) and enabling our pupils to engage with other cultural perspectives on a meaningful level – both within and beyond the UK. This chapter has sought to explore some of these issues and to make some suggestions for practice.

Engaging with educational practices elsewhere in the world, actually or vicariously, can also contribute to our own professional development as teachers. We hope that you will take up some of the opportunities suggested in this chapter to find out about different approaches to schooling and to reflect on what this might teach us about our own systems and practices.

TAKING YOUR PRACTICE FURTHER

Select a sample of lessons you have taught, and examine them in the context of developing the global dimension. Did you take up opportunities to make links with any of the eight key concepts?

- Global citizenship
- Conflict resolution
- Diversity
- Human rights
- Interdependence
- Social justice
- Sustainable development
- Values and perceptions

TAKING YOUR THINKING FURTHER

How did you define the concept of 'global citizenship' as you read through this chapter?

What qualities do you feel are necessary for someone to possess in order to be seen as a global citizen?

What knowledge and understanding do we need to develop in pupils in the 7–14 age range to support their development as global citizens?

How does this differ (if at all) from the curriculum for Citizenship currently part of the National curriculum?

Many of the ideas discussed in this chapter are very topical, and still being explored through research and academic writing. For this reason we have made considerable use of Teachers' TV programmes as a resource, although it is important to emphasise that these are journalistic in approach, and represent particular points of view. Your own critical judgement will be needed to determine your opinions of the ideas within the programmes.

Having said this, here are two themes explored in this chapter that are also represented in Teacher's TV programmes, which may stimulate further thinking and research:

Mainly for secondary teachers

White Under-achievement – putting class into the classroom. This programme was made in 2006 before the Ajegbo report (DfES, 2007), id 5458.
Britishness: following the Ajegbo report a series of three programmes were made following six teenagers from diverse backgrounds through an outdoor activity programme in the Lake District. All three episodes are brought together into one longer video: *Brit Camp – the whole story*, id 29080.

- What issues are raised for your teaching after watching both the above programmes?

Mainly for primary teachers

Comparisons are made between the standards reached by pupils in Finland and England at the end of Key Stage 2. We have already referred to the programme where a Finnish primary teacher spends a week in an English inner city classroom. There are also further Teacher's TV programmes which examine the Finnish system, to try to determine why pupils achieve better results in international comparative tests. Search on **www.teacherstv finland**

- Are there lessons that the English (or UK) system could learn from Finland, or are there too many differences between the cultural composition of the population and attitudes to education for this to be possible?

What *can* we learn from other education systems? *Culture and Pedagogy: International Comparisons in Primary Educati*on was written by the prominent educational writer and researcher Robin Alexander, based on classroom observation in European, non-European, English and American classrooms. In this he argues that culture and approaches to teaching and learning are inextricably linked, so that there are questions as to how far we can really 'borrow' ideas from other countries.

Find out more

For information on international comparative data see the 'Find Out More' section in Chapter 1.

Two major guidance documents to support teachers and schools in developing the global dimension within the curriculum and in integrating it into the life of the school:

> *Developing the Global Dimension on the School Curriculum* (DfES, 2005) provides a rationale for the inclusion of this aspect of the curriculum and offers brief suggestions for activities.

> *The Global Dimension in Action: A Curriculum Guide for Schools* (QCA, 2007) provides a number of case studies and a comprehensive list of organisations which provide resources and links with schools and organisations overseas.

Both these documents can be downloaded from **www.globalgateway.org.uk** or **qcda.org.uk/**.

If you want to find out more about resources for global citizenship and internationalising schools:

> **www.actionaid.org.uk/schools** produces resources for both primary and secondary schools, including the chembakolli resource pack and website: **www.chembakolli.com**.

> The Global Gateway is provided by the DCSF and offers resources and also links to support twinning partnerships with other schools: **www.globalgateway.org**.

> Other opportunities to find school partners exist through **www.britishcouncil.org/globalschools**.

Oxfam education offers an extensive set of web-based resources:

> for 7–11 year olds, topic examples include children's rights, global trade and 'going bananas'

> for 11–14 year olds they include activities on world trade, dealing with disasters and human rights. There is also a downloadable guide to developing active citizenship with secondary pupils: *Get Global*. **www.oxfam.org.uk/education**.

If you want to find out more abut teaching controversial topics:

Oxfam (2006) *Global Citizenship Guides: Teaching Controversial Issues.* **Oxford: Oxfam.**
This is an excellent guide which also includes a detailed list of references to other helpful texts to support pupils' thinking.

If you want to find out more about the national campaigns mentioned in the chapter:

> *Send My Friend to School*: 75 million children in the world still do not receive an education. This campaign is supported by a number of organisations, including Voluntary Service Overseas and Christian Aid: **www.sendmyfriend.org**

> *World Water Day*: this takes place each year on 22 March, following the United Nations conference on Environment and Development in 1993. *Water for Life* is a 10-year initiative (2005–2015) focusing on clean water and sanitation: in 2005 there were 1.1 billion people around the world without adequate access to water and 2.4 billion without adequate sanitation.

www.globaldimension.org.uk provides information and ideas for teachers around World Water Day, as does *Christian Aid*. For photographs and recent information *see:*

www.guardian.co.uk/environment/gallery/2009/mar/20/gallery-water-projects-christian-aid?picture=344857753.

Glossary

Cross-curricular: approaches to teaching which seek to make links between different curriculum subjects. The National Curriculum currently has a set of stated cross-curriculum dimensions for Key Stage 3 (**qcda.org.uk**). This term is more commonly used in the first sense.

Education Reform Act: a major Act of Parliament passed in 1988, which established the National Curriculum and standardised national testing as statutory, amongst many other revisions to the governance of schooling, too numerous to discuss here.

Globalisation: this term is used in a variety of contexts: to indicate economic interdependency and the power exerted by some multinational corporations that no longer have strong inks with any particular country, but see themselves as transcending national boundaries; to indicate the ways in which technologies are enabling near-instantaneous communication across the world; to indicate the spread of cultural artefacts (such as film, music, fashion) beyond their original countries of origin to become 'global brands' – this last use of the term is closely related to the first two.

Internationalisation: an attitude of openness to learning from, and with, those from elsewhere in the world. This term may have different connotations in other contexts such as universities, where there is also an economic dimension.

Multiple intelligence: a concept developed by Howard Gardner (1983). The idea that humans possess a number of discrete 'intelligences' such as linguistics intelligence, musical intelligence, spatial intelligence. Gardner first proposed seven intelligences, but later increased this number (see Chapter 9 for full reference).

National Strategies (Primary and Secondary): These are professional development programmes for primary and secondary teachers. They provide resources to support teaching, and suggested frameworks for the curriculum. They are widely used in schools, but are non-statutory. See **www.nationalstrategies.standards.dcsf.gov.uk/**. A recent government announcement indicates that they will be phased out by 2011.

Resilience: the ability to accept being unsuccessful in a task, and to persist in attempting to master a skill or understanding. Can also include the idea of having strategies to support persistence, such as a willingness to try different approaches.

SEAL: Social and Emotional Aspects of Learning (see Chapter 9).

Sustainable development: the need to avoid the further depletion of the world's resources. This includes ecological issues such as the use of renewable energy or building materials, but also recognising the ecology of workplaces to improve work–life balance.

References

Alexander, R. (2000) *Culture and Pedagogy: International Comparisons in Primary Education*. Oxford: Blackwell.

Claxton, G. (2002) *Building Learning Power*. Bristol: TLO.

Conroy, J., Hulme, M. and Menter, I. (2008) *Primary Curriculum Futures* (Primary Review Research Survey 3/3), Cambridge: University of Cambridge Faculty of Education. ISBN 978-1-906478-19-3.

DfES (2002) *Minority Ethnic Attainment and Participation in Education and Training: The Evidence*. Research Report 375. Nottingham: DfES.

DfES (2004) *Putting the World into World Class Education*. Available at: **www.teachernet.gov.uk**.

DfES (2005) *Developing the Global Dimension in the School Curriculum*. Available at: **www.teachernet.gov.uk**.

DfES (2007) *Curriculum Review: Diversity and Citizenship (the Ajegbo repprt)*. Nottingham: DfES.

ERA (1988) *Education Reform Act*. London: HMSO.

Greaves, P. (2006) *Going Global: Leading and Developing an International Dimension in Primary Schools*. Available at: **www.ncsl.org.uk**.

Hall, K. and Øzerk, K. (2008) *Primary Curriculum and Assessment: England and Other Countries (Primary Review Research Survey 3/1)*. Cambridge: University of Cambridge Faculty of Education.

HMSO (1996) *Education Act 1996*. London: HMSO.

Oxfam (2006) *Global Citizenship Guides: Teaching Controversial Issues*. Oxford: Oxfam.

QCA (2007) *The Global Dimension in Action: A Curriculum Planning Guide for Schools*. Available at: **www.qcda.org.uk**.

QCA (2008) *The Big Picture*. Available at: **www.qcda.org.uk**.

In the chapter you will

- Reflect on the needs of learners in the twenty-first century and how these may be reflected in changing school environments
- Identify ways in which schools are already adapting to new developments in curriculum, organisation and technology
- Consider how the use of new technologies in education will impact on learning, teaching, and the concept of schooling
- Begin to consider how the role of the teacher will need to change in response to changes in learning environments

Pearson Education Ltd/Ian Wedgewood

What was school like for 7–14 year olds in 2000?

Perhaps you were one of these pupils yourself, or you know someone who was:

a) Did you/they access information from the internet at school?
b) Did you/they have a computer at home?
c) Did you/they have internet access at home?
d) Was there an Interactive White Board in your/their classroom?
e) Would you/they have known what a Virtual Learning Environment was?
f) Would you/they have known what video-conferencing was, or experienced it in school?
g) Would you/they have known what a 'chat room' was? Would you/they have had any experience of online social networking?

For many pupils in 2000, the answer to all the above questions would have been 'no'.
What would their answers be now?

In 2000 the National Literacy and Numeracy Strategies (later to be combined in the Primary National Strategy) had just been introduced. In many primary schools teachers were still adjusting to new teaching and learning approaches, and often to new forms of subject knowledge.

In 2000 a revised version of the National Curriculum was introduced.

There was no Key Stage 3 National Strategy.

What will schools be like for 7–14 year olds in 2020?

Perhaps you will be teaching in one of these schools yourself.

- Will pupils be attending school at the same time every day, as most of them do now?
- Will all pupils be attending lessons at the same time, as most of them do now?
- Will the curriculum still be based mainly around subjects, as it is now?
- Will teachers be based in classrooms?
- Will teachers still work solely or mainly in one school?
- Will teachers still mainly be involved in direct teaching of pupils?

How do you feel about some of these ideas?

Introduction

There is not going to be a particular moment when suddenly schools become 'future schools', but a more gradual shifting of perspective over the next decade. This chapter explores some of the possible changes to education and schooling that may occur, and indeed are already occurring. In the process, we will also review key ideas from many of the earlier chapters in this book to see how these may continue to develop in the future. Many of the developments discussed in this chapter are already happening in some schools, so that we can have some confidence that at least some of them will become more widespread, and may become a commonplace aspect of your own teaching career. The next chapter in this book focuses on how the role of the teacher is changing as the nature of schools and schooling changes to meet the perceived needs of twenty-first-century society.

THINKING IT THROUGH

If you have not already encountered this PowerPoint presentation, first created in 2007, watch *Shift Happens* on YouTube:
www.youtube.com/watch?v=QeoKQbT8BKs.

What are the implications of this information for education?

What do we think pupils will need to know?

Are we using what they know already, and are we prepared for what they might know in a few more years?

Photo 18.1 We do not know what kinds of employment opportunities will be developing over the next 10 years, but it is certain that they will require very different skills and personal qualities from those needed in many jobs in the past

Source: Pearson Education Ltd/digital stock

Visualising twenty-first-century education

In Chapter 1 it was noted that many countries are currently changing their curriculum to respond to the perceived needs of the twenty-first century. This is certainly the case in the UK as well as elsewhere in the world. In 2006 the Report of the Teaching and Learning in 2020 Review Group was published: *2020 Vision* (DfES, 2006). The review group was made up of a number of very prominent figures involved in education: the Chief Inspector of Schools at the time, and government advisers and consultants such as David Hargreaves, formerly head of QCA and now working with the Specialist Schools Trust, and Jim Rose who is regularly involved in reviews of education – most recently that of developing a new Primary National Curriculum.

The Review Group were asked to develop a vision of personalised learning for the year 2020: the year that children starting school in 2006 would enter higher education or employment. We have referred to personalised learning in a number of places in this book, particularly in Chapters 8 and 10, as this idea has been a central theme in government thinking since 2003, and has informed a number of policy developments. 'Pupil voice' initiatives, discussed in Chapter 15, are also an important aspect of personalisation. However, as you will see in this chapter, discussions about exactly how personalised learning might develop in the future are still very much ongoing.

The *2020 Vision* Review Group consulted widely in developing their report; they visited schools, referred to research and discussed ideas with various groups and organisations with an interest in education. They located their report in the context of predicted changes on a national and international level by 2020 which they term the 'drivers for change' (DfES, 2006: 9):

- Demographic change:
  - In 2002 there will be more people in England over the age of 65 than under the age of 16, although the primary school numbers may be expanding.
  - There will be greater ethnic diversity, particularly in some geographical areas.
- Social change:
  - Greater diversity of social attitudes and values.
  - More children with parents who have a university education.
  - Possibly less interest in party politics, but more interest in 'single issue' politics, such as environmental issues.

  Technological change:
  - Acceleration of technological developments.
  - Reducing costs for both internet services and personal devices, leading to very wide use of ICT across the population (see discussion later in this chapter).

  Economic change:
  - In 2006 the Report predicted a continuing rise in standards of living, although this has since slowed down. Nevertheless, the global knowledge economy will continue to dominate.
  - Higher skill levels will be required in the workplace and employees will need to be flexible and responsive to change. Working patterns will become more flexible.

Personalised learning personalisation: current policy developments towards enabling education to match the needs and interests of learners.

Pupil voice: a term used to identify a range of strategies utilised to gather pupils' views about all aspects of school life. See Chapter 15.

Demographic: the study of population, involving birth rates, age profiles and ethnicity.

Knowledge economy: a term used to identify the use of 'intangibles' such as knowledge, skills and innovative ideas in the 'information age' as resources to bring about economic advantages for countries.

Global dimension: one of the cross-curricular themes in the Key Stage 3 National Curriculum. See Chapter 17.

Transmission: a view of teaching and learning where information is given (transmitted) by the teacher to the pupils, as opposed to involving pupils more directly in their learning; often associated with behaviourist learning theory.

Environmental change:
- Increasing awareness of environmental issues will mean that individuals as well as organisations will need to be aware of their impact on the environment, and be expected to take personal responsibility.

The implications of many of these issues for education are discussed in other chapters in this book. Chapter 17 considers the importance of the '**global dimension**' of education in recognising economic interdependence across the world and developing education for sustainability. The concept of 'global citizenship' also supports pupils in learning to live in a socially and ethnically diverse society and helps to develop 'community cohesion' (also discussed in Chapters 3 and 16).

In order to promote the development of the so-called 'soft skills', such as teamwork or effective communication skills, that are likely to be valued by employers now and in the future, learning and teaching strategies will continue to need to move away from forms of **transmission** towards developing greater collaboration and independence in pupils.

Soft skills

'Soft skills' include: resilience, perseverance, teamwork, high levels of oral communication, independence, evaluation and problem solving skills, creativity, innovation and entrepreneurship, taking responsibility for one's own learning, being able to make informed choices, recognising the consequences of actions and understanding how to influence events (see Figure 18.1).

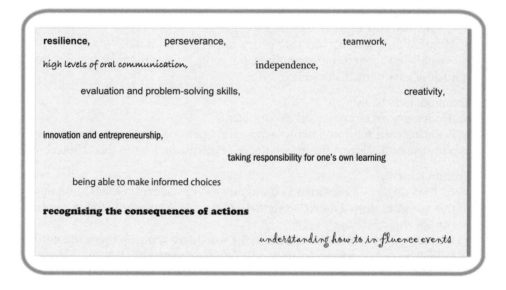

Figure 18.1
Soft skills

> ## OVER TO YOU
>
> How many of the 'drivers for change' are already influencing the curriculum, and other aspects of the education system in England and other nations within the UK?
>
> How far have we got towards developing learners with the 'soft skills' and qualities demanded by employers?
>
> Based on your experience or observation in schools, what examples of learning and teaching, or other aspects of school life, can you identify which have sought to foster the development of any of these skills and qualities? (We anticipate that you should be able to produce quite a long list!)
>
> Where do you think we might need to focus attention in the future?
>
> How might school structures or organisation have to change to facilitate this?

Many of these skills and qualities identified by *2020 Vision*, and how they might be developed, have been mentioned in previous chapters: **resilience**, perseverance, teamwork, talk, responsibility. One other important area is the group of skills and qualities which are clustered together in *2020 Vision*: 'being creative, inventive, enterprising and entrepreneurial' (DfES, 2006: 10). These skills are seen as being vital for the UK's place as a 'hub' of innovative and creative industries within the global marketplace, and education is seen as the place where such skills will be developed. *Innovation Nation* (DUIS, 2008) sets out a blueprint for developing the UK as the most innovative country in the world and calls for public services, including education, to adopt innovative practice at all levels. This includes developing innovative thinking in pupils, especially in the subjects of science, technology, engineering and mathematics (the so-called STEM subjects). Schools must become innovative environments, and teachers, innovative practitioners.

Resilience: the ability to accept being unsuccessful in a task, and to persist in attempting to master a skill or understanding. Can also include the idea of having strategies to support persistence, such as a willingness to try different approaches.

The revised 11–14 Key Stage 3 curriculum, introduced in 2008, reflects this trend through its emphasis on personal learning and thinking skills (PLTS) to be developed through all subjects:

- independent enquiry
- creative thinking
- reflective learning
- teamwork
- self-management
- effective participation

and on the cross-curricular themes, which are also referred to in Chapter 17 of this book.

Similarly, the 'Rose' Review of the Primary Curriculum also emphasises the development of learning skills and the attitudes and dispositions that foster a love of learning, alongside the promotion of creativity. These are to be developed within a curriculum which is focused around six subject-focused themes, replacing, but not eliminating, the previous 13 subjects (including those intended to become statutory in 2010) within the Primary National Curriculum.

Innovations Unit: a non-governmental organisation, associated with the DCSF, which supports and encourages innovation on education and disseminates examples of new practice.

All-through school: a school catering for both primary- and secondary-aged pupils.

Learning mentor: a person working within a primary or secondary school to support pupils identified as being 'at risk' of academic failure.

All these developments have implications for the organisation of the curriculum, for teaching and learning, and for learners and teachers: both as individuals and as members of learning communities. The rest of this chapter, and the one that follows, explores some of these developments in more depth

Rethinking the experience of the learner

The traditional story is that children are the recipients of an education delivered to them according to centrally devised standards. Many children feel education is something done to them. Something they must endure . . . An alternative is to paint children and parents as consumers, picking and choosing between different options in an education supermarket, much as one might buy a washing machine. But this only engages users in choosing between different options delivered to them. The point is to engage them far more in designing, producing and creating the learning they seek.

(Leadbeater, 2005)

This is an extract from a short publication, *The Shape of Things to Come*, which offers a deliberately challenging view of 'personalisation' extending well beyond ideas of addressing pupils' learning styles, the use of assessment for learning strategies and monitoring of individual achievement which are now often seen as synonymous with personalised learning. The author of this publication, Charles Leadbeater, is a consultant and government adviser, and his ideas are being actively promoted by the Innovations Unit and the DCSF. So how might the role of the learner change more radically in the future, and what are some schools already doing to facilitate this?

CASE STUDY

Jonathan's day in an (imaginary) personalised learning school

(Based on examples from real schools. and Leadbeater (2005: 9–10))

Jonathan attends an all-through school for pupils from 5–16 in an inner city area. He is now in his first term in Year 7. Today he is starting school at 10.30 as all the teachers in his year group have the time between 8.30 and 10.30 designated for planning and professional development time each week. However, Jonathan *has* been working on school tasks at

home this morning, using a wireless tablet PC provided by the school. He is part of a learning to learn group involved in a collaborative task and he has been finding out information on the internet, ready to contribute to his group's meeting later in the morning. Last night he e-mailed his homework to his teacher, using the school's electronic submission system.

On arrival at school, Jonathan has an appointment with his learning mentor (or 'learning guide' as envisaged by *2020 Vision* DfES, 2006: 21) to review his progress against his personal targets. In Years 5 and 6 he found it increasingly difficult to remain motivated in some areas of learning as his literacy level is below expectation for his age. He was allocated a learning mentor from the school's team of support staff, who worked with him to set small, short-term targets that enabled him to recognise his own progress. He also received support in some areas of literacy as part of a small group taught by a specialised literacy teaching assistant. His confidence has improved, but he still regularly meets the same learning mentor, who has stayed with him into Year 7. The targets that are set are now becoming longer term, and Jonathan and his parents will be involved in the decision as to when he no longer requires this level of support. His learning mentor congratulates him on the research he has done, and also quickly checks the science homework he sent in last night. Jonathan has been given a range of options as to how he presents his understanding of this science topic, and has chosen to use a mind-map, using software provided on his school PC.

Jonathan also reviews his weekly timetable with his learning mentor and reflects on how he feels he managed during the previous week. As he has found some subjects challenging in the past, his timetable has a mixture of shorter sessions of whole-class work and longer sessions of small-group learning and some one-to-one sessions. Not all these sessions are taught by qualified teachers as there are several grades of trained teaching assistant who work with pupils requiring more intensive support. The content of the sessions has been designed by the teaching teams for the different subjects, often working collaboratively to develop materials and activities linking curriculum areas and intended to develop skills in problem solving, evaluation, collaboration, and reflection on learning. Jonathan's timetable has been discussed and agreed with his parents who have been able to maintain their contact with the school as he progresses into Year 7 since key personnel have remained the same as in the primary department. At this stage of the year, Jonathan's Year 6 teacher regularly teaches the class in order to support transition into Key Stage 3.

Jonathan's learning mentor is very pleased with his progress. Together she and Jonathan agree on what will be entered into his personal e-profile in the school's intranet as a result of this meeting, and also what message will be texted to his parents, as they do not have a computer in the home apart from the one used by Jonathan.

Jonathan's experience is typical of that for all pupils in this school, in many ways. While not all of them will have such regular meetings with a learning mentor, all pupils do have a personal tutor, or 'learning guide', who sends regular reports home after meetings where pupils reflect on their learning and identify personal targets. Communication with parents is frequent, and utilises a range of communications technologies. Timetabling for all pupils is flexible in order to meet their needs: some work better in short concentrated sessions, while others need longer periods of time, or more sessions, in order to feel confidence in their understanding of a topic. In some subjects, students peer-tutor each other. At times, as pupils move up the school, they are expected to work independently at home, for some of the time during the day, using materials available online via the schools **Virtual Learning Environment** (VLE).

> **Virtual Learning Environment:** a software product providing shared resources and information, with communication through e-mail and discussion boards, which is internal to a school organisation, but accessible remotely via password.

WORKING IN THE CLASSROOM

Based on your experience or observations in schools so far, how many of the features of Jonathan's day already exist in schools now?

For example, teaching assistants already work in specialised capacities in many primary and secondary schools, including leading whole-class lessons.

Many secondary schools already have extensive and highly developed VLEs where pupils can access homework and other resources and e-mail their teachers for advice.

What other similarities with current practice can you find?

What are the significant differences between this imaginary pupil's experience and schools with which you are familiar?

Rethinking the school environment

2020 Vision argues that changes to the ways schools approach teaching and learning are central to developing a more personalised education system (DfES, 2006: 27). The government-funded programme of rebuilding or redesigning schools, known as *Building Schools for the Future* (BSF), is seen as highly important in this respect. BSF involves both redesigning learning spaces so that they are more flexible, and extending the use of technology to support learning within these redesigned schools. Initially this programme has focused on secondary schools, but it is intended that primary schools will also become involved later in the programme timescale. A small number of primary schools have already shared in some redesign experiences, including the development of all-through schools and participation in a pilot project to envisage 'future classrooms', referred to below. Teachers TV has a series of programmes which follow the progress of planning a new school under the BSF scheme which involves primary and secondary phases (**http://www.teachers.tv/wholeschoolissues** and search on Future School).

Following quite a long period of relative underinvestment in school buildings, the BSF programme is obviously welcome. However, it appears to be underpinned by a number of assumptions about how much redesigned schools can influence learning, which require some examination. There are claims, for example, that the physical layout of the school can have a direct influence on pupils' behaviour, and some suggestions that the right physical environment can actually raise achievement.

RESEARCH BRIEFING: CAN CHANGING SCHOOLS 'FROM A FORD TO A FERRARI' MAKE A DIFFERENCE?

A number of researchers have investigated the effects of physical environment on learning, but with no clear-cut results.

In a large research study into the effects of secondary schools on children, Rutter *et al.* (1979) found no direct relationship between the physical environment of the school and learning and behavioural outcomes. In fact they found that some schools obtained good outcomes despite unprepossessing premises. However, times may have changed since the date of this research. Evidence cited by Hallam (1996) indicates that there *is* a relationship between poor learning environments, behaviour and attendance, where inadequate buildings can cause health problems and lower student morale with consequently higher levels of absenteeism and poor behaviour.

However, it may not be the case that improving the environment automatically reverses this trend:

> *Research does show that student achievement lags in shabby school buildings . . . but it does not show that student performance rises when facilities go from the equivalent of a Ford to a Ferrari.*
>
> (Stricherz, 2000 cited in Woolner *et al.*, 2007: 50)

Nevertheless, it may well be the case that improving the overall environment, including lighting and ventilation as well as general attractiveness, does make a difference to pupils' sense of well-being. This in turn may have an effect on their motivation and engagement with learning, leading to improved attendance and possibly – attainment.

THINKING IT THROUGH

Based on your own experience as a learner, as well as your experience in schools, how do the facilities and general environment affect *you* as a learner?

Why might some schools in Rutter *et al.*'s research still have gained good outcomes in spite of less attractive buildings and facilities?

'Small schools' and 'all-through' schools

Another recent development in secondary education is that of the 'small school'. While this is not strictly part of the BSF programme, the principles of 'small schools' may well become part of school redesign in some areas and are worth considering

'Small schools': in this content the term refers to the subdivision of large secondary schools into smaller, vertically grouped units, each of which operates semi-independently.

here. Similarly, the development of 'all through' schools has been seen as another possible direction in which future schools might develop.

The 'small schools' development in secondary education has grown from similar initiatives in the USA where it was realised that the unavoidable aspects of impersonality in large schools was contributing to disaffection and low achievement. There are now a number of secondary schools in the UK that are divided into vertically grouped 'small schools' of around 300 pupils each. Each small school has its own 'head' and key members of staff, meaning that there is a stronger sense of identity and more opportunity for personalisation. Teachers' TV has a series of programmes looking at the small schools movement both in the USA and the UK, entitled 'Human Scale Schools' (see **www.teachers.tv** and search on human scale).

'All through' or 'all age schools' are exactly that: either purpose-built schools catering for pupils from 5 to 16+ or federations of schools that work closely together to provide a 'seamless' educational experience for pupils. Schools that have adopted an 'all through' approach argue that this reduces the difficulties associated with transition between Key Stages (particularly Key Stages 2 and 3) and enables increased personalisation. Relationships with parents can be sustained through the pupils' school lives and closer links can be built with the local community. Staff can be deployed more efficiently and effectively, for example by having phase leaders responsible from Years 5 to 8 and by having specialist teachers working with pupils in more Key Stages, and there is greater coherence in practice across the school so that expectations for learning and behaviour are established and maintained thus providing a consistent ethos. (See 'All Age Schooling' published by the Innovations Unit available at: **www.standards.dfes.gov.uk/innovation-unit/collaboration/allage**)

Pupil and teacher consultation for BSF

Part of the process of implementing BSF has involved consultation with teachers and pupils about the features of new school buildings. The amount of influence these consultations have had has varied from area to area, as each local authority involved has taken a slightly different approach to how the process is managed. Nevertheless, the principle of pupil consultation is regarded as an important aspect of BSF and marks another step in moves towards increased personalisation. In a detailed review of research evidence on the impact of environments on learning, Dr Pamela Woolner and colleagues from the University of Newcastle emphasise the importance of the 'active role of human beings' in creating an effective working environment:

> Externally imposed changes, regardless of their merit might be expected to have less of an effect than changes brought about through genuine consultation and an inclusive design process . . . It is important to focus on the meaning of schools in different communities and to look clearly both at what is intended by 'consultation' and what is delivered.
>
> (Woolner et al., 2007: 61)

Twelve local authorities have taken part in pilot projects to examine the potential of different ideas for new learning spaces, involving both primary and secondary schools (see 'Classroooms of the future' at **www.innovation-unit.co.uk/publications**). As part of the project, pupils were consulted about what they felt would make a good learning environment, and a selection of their suggestions are given below:

> lots of natural light and air;
> lots of space and flexibility;
> different zones for different work;
> be colourful, but not too bright;
> use new technology and new furniture, that can be easily moved or rearranged;
> lots of green things;
> use renewable energy.

Other consultations with pupils, especially in secondary schools, have emphasised the importance of creating social spaces, both inside and outside the main buildings, so that pupils are able to interact informally and move around freely, reducing a sense of crowding and perhaps improving behaviour.

Teachers' TV has a short programme showing how pupils are consulted during the development of a creative digital and performing arts specialist school in Birmingham (**http://www.teachers.tv/video/28378**).

The role of technology in future learning

Most of the funding allocated to schools under the BSF programme will be spent on the buildings, but there will also be investment in new technologies to support learning which has the potential to effect a significant change to the way the curriculum is conceived and 'delivered', and its organisation. It has become commonplace to talk about curriculum 'delivery', or to use terms such as 'curriculum packages'. Implicit in this use of language is the view of the learner as a recipient of the curriculum rather than a participant in its development. Even where the contents of the 'package' involve pupils in active learning, the decisions about what and how they should learn have already been made for them. The power of communications technologies means that out of school, many pupils now have much greater autonomy over what they learn, how they learn and with whom they learn than they do in school. Commentators on learning for the future emphasise the importance of recognising these changes and their implications for education:

> While children are experiencing a highly seductive media environment outside school, in school new technology use is restricted, perhaps even considered banal by children as failing to keep up with cutting edge developments. In short, schools struggle to keep up with the slick and professional presentations of the new media environment.
>
> *(Williamson and Payton, 2009: 33)*

In their recent handbook, *Curriculum and Teaching Innovation*, the educational think-tank Futurelab suggests that pupils need to develop an awareness of how new media operate, and how to evaluate their content and presentation, in the same way as with other popular media such as newspapers, magazines and advertisements. The writers

Media literacy: the ability to 'read' a range of communications media in order to recognise authorial intentions and to understand that these media are not neutral sources of information.

of the handbook argue that 'media literacy' needs to become a necessary element of the curriculum (Williamson and Payton, 2009: 34). This is equally true for teachers, however. As various new learning technologies are introduced over the next few years, it is important to remember that these are developed by international corporations who have their own vested interests in promoting their products as essential for education (Molnar, 2006).

Nevertheless, we cannot, and should not, ignore the potential of new technologies to change our relationships with knowledge, the curriculum and the nature of learning. As the Futurelab team have argued in another publication:

> If educators are to shape the future of education (and not have it shaped for them by external technical developments) it is crucial that we engage with developments in digital technologies at the earliest stages. We need to understand what may be emerging, explore its implications for education, and understand how best we might harness these changes. Without this early engagement we risk, as always, being the Cinderella sector of the technology world – constantly receiving the hand-me-downs from the business, defence and leisure industries and then trying to repurpose them for educational goals. Without this early engagement, we also risk designing educational practices and approaches that will be rendered obsolete and anachronistic in the context of new human–technological capabilities.
>
> *(Daanen and Facer, 2007: 4)*

New technologies mean that those involved with education need to ask the following questions about learning in the future:

- *When and where* will learning take place? With increasing access to the internet and the use of school VLEs, will the idea of the 'school day' need to change? Will pupils need to attend school every day in order to engage with learning?

- *What* will pupils learn, and *who with*? Will increasing personalisation mean that pupils will be able to construct their own curriculum from a broader range of options than can be offered within traditional school structures? Does this mean that pupils may be learning in groups (actual or virtual) with different ages and perhaps with pupils from different locations, according to interest?

- *How* will pupils learn? Can new technologies cater for a range of preferred learning styles and also different forms of assessment, enabling pupils to demonstrate their understanding through the medium that best enables them to do so?

Answers to these questions are likely to reshape the role of the teacher and their relationship with learners and learning.

The Teachers' TV programme 'School Matters – Tomorrow's Teacher, Tomorrow's School' (**http://www.teachers.tv/video/31224**) explores two schools, one in England and one in the USA, where these questions are being explored in practice.

The Teachers, TV programme 'School Matters – ICT: A vision of the future' (**http://www.teachers.tv/video/221**) focuses on a group of primary and secondary schools that are using ICT in innovative ways and involves the teachers in discussing the challenges and opportunities presented by moving towards increased digital learning and teaching.

Photo 18.2 Social networking or engaged in learning? Digital technologies may blur the distinctions between in-school and out-of-school learning

Source: Pearson Education Ltd Jules Selmes

New technologies in the near future

(Well within the teaching lifetime of today's trainees and NQTs!)

What might happen in the relatively near future in terms of how new technologies are developing and their impact on education? How will the education system deal with the questions that are raised?

Personal digital technologies have the potential to completely change the ways in which we receive information. We are already able to access the internet freely in many different locations using hand-held devices. These are likely to become smaller and smaller, possibly to be embedded in clothing or jewellery.

What are the implications for curriculum and assessment in these circumstances?

Will we be testing pupils' knowledge without digital assistance, or with it?

In an increasingly digitised world, what would be the value of assessing 'unassisted knowledge'?

Should be we assessing pupils' capabilities for accessing information and then applying it, rather than the independent possession of that knowledge?

What are the implications in terms of equity for all learners?

Integrated networks and increasingly sophisticated communications technologies mean that there will be less and less necessity for learners to be physically present in a particular location, such as a school building. We are already seeing examples of pupils learning online from home via schools' VLEs during parts of the normal school day, as well as in the evening. Forms of video conferencing and the development of video phones mean that discussions with other pupils and teachers or learning advisors will be able to take place at a distance. Computer simulation will mean that

Integrated network: a computer-based system bringing together a range of functions such as video conferencing and real-time collaborative writing or editing facilities as well as access to resources, communication and information internal to a school or other organisation.

activities which are currently 'hands-on' in subjects such as science and technology can be experienced virtually, with the potential for providing a much wider range of experience than would be possible using the school's limited resources.

What are the advantages and disadvantages of these developments?

Would the positive aspects of 24-hour access to education outweigh the benefits of physical face-to-face engagement with peers and teachers, or not?

As programmes become more sophisticated and can offer more and more solutions to problems in design or experimentation, will this expand pupils' understanding or potentially limit their creativity?

New technologies will enable users to obtain information that is currently available in printed form through other means. Instructions for completing a task could be available via audio or an animated diagram.

In an increasingly 'paperless' world, how will an emphasis on print-based literacy change?

Is there something special about how the brain processes written information that is important for cognition, or will the twenty-first century see the demise of the printed word? Learning to read literally changes the brain (Blakemore and Frith, 2005: 73). How will the brain change in response to the increasing use of new technologies that may not be dependent on traditional literacy?

(Based on ideas from Daanen and Facer, 2007: *2020 and Beyond*)

CONTROVERSY

Neuroscience or nostalgia?

Neuroscientist Baroness Susan Greenfield, Director of the Royal Institution, suggested in the House of Lords that the use of social networking sites along with other screen-based activities such as computer games *might* change children's brains, leading to shorter attention spans and increased recklessness in behaviour. These suggestions were picked up by the media and widely discussed. For example, the *Daily Mail* of 24 February 2009 carried an article headed: 'Social websites harm children's brains: Chilling warning to parents from top neuroscientist' (**www.dailymail.co.uk/news/article-1153583**).

The following day the issue was followed up by the BBC *Newsnight* programme featuring a short interview with Baroness Greenfield and a studio debate between Ben Goldman of the 'Bad Science' column in *The Guardian* newpaper and Dr Aric Sigman whose recent article claimed that social networking and similar activities were having adverse effects on people's social engagement with others in real life. The programme: 'Social websites; bad for kids' brains' is available at **http://news.bbc.co.uk/1/hi/programmes/newsnight/7909847.stm**

Similar arguments have been made by Sue Palmer in her well-known book *Toxic Childhood* (2006).

But what is the foundation for these claims? Is this media 'hype'? Are these visions of doom based on nostalgia, rather than on a recognition of a changing learning landscape?

Ben Goldman of **www.badscience.net** pointed out on the BBC *Newsnight* programme that neither Baroness Greenfield nor Dr Sigman has any scientific evidence to support these arguments. In her recent book *ID: The Quest for Meaning in the 21st Century* (2008), Susan Greenfield repeats the ideas outlined above, but also presents arguments to suggest that perhaps children's cognitive abilities might be changing for the better, rather than the worse. A survey by the think-tank Demos (Green and Hannon, 2007) suggests that children and young people are actually more competent at finding information and sharing it with others than previously. However, the boundaries between 'learner' and 'teacher' are becoming blurred as young people seek help from friends and even strangers via the internet, rather than more traditional sources such as school teachers and parents.

OVER TO YOU

Should we be concerned that children and young people are spending up to 6.5 hours per day using electronic media?

Will the screen replace the book – and what effect might this have on how people learn in the future?

Are the critics of social networking sites and computer games unable to let go of out-moded beliefs about social life and learning, or are some of their concerns justified?

Rethinking the curriculum and school organisation

. . . the design of the curriculum and the routines of the classroom are completely synergistic. To innovate in the arrangement and composition of the curriculum implies an innovation in practice.

(Williamson and Payton, 2009)

The imaginary school attended by 'Jonathan', described above, is assumed to have many of the design and organisational features which may be developing within redesigned schools. All of the following features are already in operation in some schools in the UK, although they are not yet widespread (see **www.innovation-unit.co.uk** and follow links to Next Practice):

- flexible hours for the school day;
- 24-hour internet access to learning resources;
- building design that does not provide 'hiding places' or long corridors so that some aspects of poor behaviour are minimised;
- all-age schools to reduce the issues associated with transition;
- 'stage not age' teaching groups;
- a variety of flexible learning spaces that can be rearranged for large or small groups;
- the presence of other extended services, such as health clinics and family advice centres, on site as an integrated part of design;
- the use of a wide range of digital resources, such as Personal Digital Assistants (PDAs), MPs players, digital cameras, video cameras and mobile phones, in addition to more established technologies such as Interactive White Boards and tablet PCs.

Recent developments in the curriculum for the 7–14 age range are beginning to have an impact on how we think about teaching and learning, and how we conceptualise the roles of the teacher and the learner. As we have seen, the impact of technology will accelerate this process.

- If we are developing a curriculum which fosters creativity and innovation, and which encourages the other 'soft skills' identified earlier in this chapter, there may be relatively little place for the traditional, whole-class transmission type of lesson. Certainly it will no longer be the default model of teaching.
- If we are changing the ways in which school organisation operates at secondary level, through offering pupils more choices about where and when they study, the idea that all learning happens through face-to-face contact with teachers is no longer appropriate.
- If we are intending to develop perseverance, problem-solving and team-working qualities in our primary pupils – which will be needed within the Key Stage 3 curriculum – we may need to ask ourselves whether our interventions are actually supporting learning, or whether they may be over-directing pupils towards our own predetermined outcomes.

All these issues will be difficult to confront. Both teachers and pupils carry strong images of what teaching and learning 'look like', based on past experience. Teachers will also be influenced by their experience of their initial training. The kinds of change indicated in this chapter are not yet taking place in many schools, or are confined only to certain subjects or times of the day, so that teachers *and* pupils may find themselves operating with a kind of 'split personality', moving between 'old' and 'new' ways of thinking and acting in learning contexts.

Consultation with pupils has not only focused on the physical environment of future schools, but also on the nature and organisation of the curriculum. We have already seen some examples of the ways in which 'pupil voice' is developing, in

Chapter 15, and these strategies will continue to expand. However, this raises some interesting and important questions for consideration in terms of what actions for the future are taken on the basis of consultation with pupils *and* teachers. On what basis are those of us currently involved with schools and schooling able to visualise what a school for the future might look like? What are pupils' existing assumptions about schools and teachers and how might these assumptions affect their views about what learning is, and how it might develop? This is not to say that pupils ought not to be consulted; their views about what makes for a more or less successful learning environment are very important. However, it will be important to recognise the factors that may be influencing their views. These might include the influences of the popular media, as well as their assumptions or preconceptions about schooling based on their current experience.

OVER TO YOU

Whose views should we be considering in developing school buildings and learning environments for the next 20+ years? How important are the ideas of each of the following?

- Secondary pupils of today, many of whom will leave schools within the next 5–7 years?
- Secondary pupils of tomorrow, currently in primary schools?
- Secondary teachers – many of whom will still be teaching in 20 years' time?
- Primary teachers who will be preparing pupils to learn in these new environments?
- Educational writers and researchers who have investigated the impact of different environments and technologies on learning?
- Architects and building designers who have expertise in understanding how space can be used to best advantage?
- Parents and other members of local communities who would also have access to school facilities?

For a provocative look at learning in the future, watch the edited version of Professor Stephen Heppell's 2006 Royal Society of Arts Lecture available on Teachers' TV. Professor Heppell has been described as 'Europe's leading online learning guru' and in this programme he argues for a rethink of the curriculum away from subject disciplines towards project-based learning, and for a corresponding revision of the nature of assessment: 'RSA Lectures – Stephen Heppell – Learning 2016' (**http://www.teachers.tv/video/4957**). This programme is also reviewed by TTRB, with an embedded 15-minute extract from the programme (**www.ttrb.ac.uk**, article id 14157).

THINKING IT THROUGH

In training

What is *your* vision of a classroom of the future? Draw up a list of the features you would like to see in your own classroom in five and then in 10 years' time and try to compare your ideas with those of other teachers or trainee teachers.

How far are you in agreement with each other?

Do your visions change depending on the age group or subject area with which you are most concerned?

How will your ideas impact on the curriculum and its organisation?

Starting your career

Undertake the activity above and, if possible, ask your pupils to do the same.

How far do you feel your ideas and theirs overlap (taking their age into consideration)?

Some researchers have found that pupils can be more innovative than their teachers in activities such as these (being 'innovative' is not necessarily equated with having fantasy-type ideas in this context).

Do you think that your pupils are more open-minded about possible learning futures, or are they having difficulty envisaging schooling as being any different from today?

If so, how might you encourage them to think more creatively about learning possibilities?

Investigating learning and teaching

Organisations like Futurelab and individual commentators such as Charles Leadbeater base their visions for the future of education on 'leading edge' examples of current practice, and on particular ideological beliefs about education.

How would you characterise the educational values and beliefs underpinning the following documents and where do you see similarities and differences between them?

Williamson B. and Payton S. (2009) *Curriculum and Teaching Innovation: Transforming Classroom Practice and Personalisation*. Futurelab. Available at: **www.futurelab.org.uk/handbooks**.

Leadbeater, C. (2008) *What's Next? 21 ideas for 21st Century Learning*. Innovation Unit. Available at: **www.innovation-unit.co.uk**.

SUMMARY

This chapter has examined some of the developments that are already taking place in response to the perceived needs of education in the twenty-first century. We have touched upon a wide range of possible changes to school organisation and pedagogy that would result from the increasing use of new technologies and rethinking the school as a learning space. It seems likely that the perception of school as a building or set of buildings may become obsolete well within the teaching lifetimes of those currently in training or in the early stages of their career. As a result, we have suggested that many aspects of the traditional teacher–pupil relationship will also need to change in the future. These ideas will be explored further in the following chapter.

Responding to the changes in education that seem likely to occur will be challenging, but also exciting. The twenty-first-century learner described in documents such as *2020 Vision* (DfES, 2006) will need to be flexible and responsive to change, able to communicate effectively and to work collaboratively with others, able to overcome difficulties and be willing to identify alternative solutions. The twenty-first-century teacher will require the same characteristics!

TAKING YOUR PRACTICE FURTHER

Although we cannot know exactly how learning environments may develop in different schools, can you identify actions you could be taking now to prepare yourself *and* your pupils for changes in the future?

For example, could you aim to extend your use of new technologies, or could you plan more activities aimed at supporting the development of pupils' 'soft skills'?

What additional support, if any, might you require, through coaching or other CPD?

TAKING YOUR THINKING FURTHER

This chapter has raised a number of questions to which we do not yet have clear answers in terms of how education will develop. Part of the answer will lie in the perceived purpose of education in the twenty-first century. How far is it to equip pupils for employment, how far it is aimed at developing them as individuals and how far can these be reconciled, if indeed they are different purposes?

TAKING YOUR THINKING FURTHER *CONTINUED*

Should the curriculum continue to focus on subjects, or should it focus more on skills?

In either case, who will make the decisions as to what is important?

If you have not already done so, read Williamson, B. and Payton, S. (2009) *Curriculum and Teaching Innovation: Transforming Classroom Practice and Personalisation*. Futurelab. Available at: **www.futurelab.org.uk/handbooks**

   This text provides a commentary on current educational policy and future education directions.

Find out more

If you want to find out more about influences on government policy on personalisation and schools for the future: *2020 Vision: The Report of the Teaching and Learning Review Group* (DfES, 2006) Available at: **www.teachernet.gov.uk/publications** set out a series of recommendations, many of which are already being implemented.

If you want to know more about what is already happening in some schools in the UK:

Leadbeater, C. (2008) *What's Next? 21 ideas for 21st century Learning*. **Innovation Unit. Available at: www.innovation-unit.co.uk.**
This draws on practice in some 'leading edge' schools.

Teachers' TV also has a number of programmes looking at different aspects of innovative practice. Look for programmes in the areas 'Tomorrow's Teacher' and 'School Matters' or search on 'futures'.

The Innovation Unit (**www.innovation-unit.co.uk**) is an organisation supporting innovation in schools and children's services. The area on their website entitled 'Next Practice in Education' provides up-to-date information on new developments. The Innovations Unit also has downloadable publications, on topics such as personalisation as well as innovative practice in schools.

If you want to find out more about how technology can support learning, there are again a number of Teachers' TV programmes which can be located by searching on 'ICT'.

You can access the full range of Futurelab on-line publications at **www.futurelab.org.uk**. Futurelab is a not-for-profit organisation that specialises in developing resources and practices to harness technology for learning in the twenty-first century. Futurelab publishes literature reviews, handbooks, discussion papers and a range of resources, as well as working on projects with schools and other educational organisations.

Glossary

All-through school: a school catering for both primary- and secondary-aged pupils.

Demographic: the study of population, involving birth rates, age profiles and ethnicity.

Global dimension: one of the cross-curricular themes in the Key Stage 3 National Curriculum. See Chapter 17.

Innovations Unit: a non-governmental organisation, associated with the DCSF, which supports and encourages innovation on education and disseminates examples of new practice.

Integrated network: a computer-based system bringing together a range of functions such as video conferencing and real-time collaborative writing or editing facilities as well as access to resources, communication and information internal to a school or other organisation.

Knowledge economy: a term used to identify the use of 'intangibles' such as knowledge, skills and innovative ideas in the 'information age' as resources to bring about economic advantages for countries. This is in contrast to economies based on the industrial production of 'tangible' products. For further information see **http://www.esrcsocietytoday.ac.uk/ ESRCInfoCentre/facts/index4.aspx**

Learning mentor: a person working within a primary or secondary school to support pupils identified as being 'at risk' of academic failure. They form a bridge between pastoral and academic concerns. The learning mentor may be a qualified teacher or a member of support staff who has received specific training.

Media literacy: the ability to 'read' a range of communications media in order to recognise authorial intentions and to understand that these media are not neutral sources of information.

Personalised learning: this is now a widely used term in a range of contexts. Broadly, it reflects current policy developments towards enabling education to match the needs and interests of learners more closely than in the past, through a number of initiatives, many of which are discussed in this book. See **www.ttrb.ac.uk**, article id 12406, for a commentary on the concept of 'personalised learning' with further links to other resources.

Pupil voice: a term used to identify a range of strategies utilised to gather pupils' views about all aspects of school life. See Chapter 15.

Resilience: the ability to accept being unsuccessful in a task, and to persist in attempting to master a skill or understanding. Can also include the idea of having strategies to support persistence, such as a willingness to try different approaches.

'Small schools': in this content the term refers to the subdivision of large secondary schools into smaller, vertically grouped units, each of which operates semi-independently.

Transmission: a view of teaching and learning where information is given (transmitted) by the teacher to the pupils, as opposed to involving pupils more directly in their learning; often associated with behaviourist learning theory.

Virtual Learning Environment: a software product providing shared resources and information, with communication through e-mail and discussion boards, which is internal to a school organisation, but accessible remotely via password. Different VLEs have varying facilities such as options for learners to create personal online portfolios, upload assignments etc.

References

Blakemore, S. and Frith, U. (2005) *The Learning Brain*. Oxford: Blackwell.

Daanen, H. and Facer, K. (2007) *2020 and Beyond: Future Scenarios for Education in an Age of New Technologies*. Futurelab. Available at: **www.futurelab.org.uk/publications**.

DfES (2006) *2020 Vision: The Report of the Teaching and Learning Review Group*. Available at: **www.teachernet.gov.uk/publications**.

DUIS: Department for Universities, Innovation and Skills (2008) *Innovation Nation*. London: The Stationery Office.

Green, H. and Hannon, C. (2007) *Their Space: Education for a Digital Generation*. London: Demos.

Greenfield, S. (2008) *ID: The Quest for Meaning in the 21st Century*. London: Hodder and Stoughton.

Hallam, S. (1996) *Improving School Attendance*. Oxford: Heinemann.

Leadbeater, C. (2005) *The Shape of Things to Come*. Innovation Unit. Available at: **www.innovation-unit.co.uk/publications**.

Leadbeater, C. (2008) *What's Next? 21 Ideas for 21st Century Learning*. Innovation Unit. Available at: **www.innovation-unit.co.uk**.

Molnar, A. (2006) The commercial transformation of public education, *Journal of Education Policy*, Vol. 21, No 5: pp. 621–640.

Palmer, S. (2006) *Toxic Childhood: How the Modern World is Damaging Our Children and What We Can Do About It*, London: Orion.

Rutter, M., Maughan, B., Mortimore, P. and Ouston, J. (1979) *Fifteen Thousand Hours: Secondary Schools and Their Effecds on Children*. London: Open Books.

Williamson, B. and Payton, S. (2009) *Curriculum and Teaching Innovation: Transforming Classroom Practice and Personalisation*. Futurelab. Available at: **www.futurelab.org.uk/handbooks**.

Woolner, P., Hall, E., Higgins, S. McCaughey, C. and Wall, K. (2007) A sound foundation? What we know abut the impact of environments on learning and the implications for Building Schools for the Future, *Oxford Review of Education*, Vol. 33, No. 1: pp. 47–70.

19 The Teacher for the Future: 'Floating in the Wind or Rooted to Flourish?'

Teaching [in the future] means being in a reinvented profession that does not just deliver value, but is driven by values.

(Andy Hargreaves, 2003: 51)

In this chapter you will be supported to:

- Consider the skills and aptitudes a teacher of the future might need
- Anticipate the impact of the predicted education changes for the role of the teacher
- Explore the underpinning values that might be needed in order for the teaching profession to meet the needs of a changing education landscape

Pearson Education Ltd/Ian Wedgewood

What did the teacher do in 2000?

Perhaps you were taught by a teacher as a 7–14 year old at about this time. Did s/he:

a) Demonstrate good subject knowledge in the content of your lessons?
b) Anticipate being a teacher for most of their professional lives?
c) Work closely with other professionals to support their teaching?
d) Usually teach you in a large group, in a classroom-based setting?

For most teachers in 2000, their role would have been largely restricted to working with large class groups with an emphasis upon developing a set of core knowledge and skills for pupils. The subject content was generally prescribed by the government in the form of a national curriculum. Teachers would generally plan in isolation or in small curriculum teams with little or no input from other experts.

- As you begin or establish your identity as a teacher of today, how would you answer the above questions in relation to your own practice?
- What will your working life look and feel like in 2020?
  - What skills will you need to work as a teacher?
  - What might your career pathway look like?
- Why do you want to be a teacher in 2020?

Introduction

Think-tank: is an organisation, often linked to government or policy units, which engages in research or consultation to inform policy development.

The previous chapter considered the shifting institution that is a school or educational setting. The focus was on organisational, curriculum and technological advances and future developments. This chapter takes these ideas forward by building on the themes of the whole book to explore the role of a teacher in the future. This chapter will consider the research and 'think-tank' evidence from a range of educationalists who are publishing ideas around what a teacher of the future may need, be able to do and what support they may require to be effective practitioners in the future. The core thread woven through this chapter is the centrality of community and values for the professional lives of teachers of the future.

OVER TO YOU

Reflect upon these predictions about society in 2020. As you read them, note down your reactions to the question 'what will this mean for me as a teacher in 2020?'

- Individuals living longer rethink how they balance education, leisure and work.
- Anxieties over social division and inter-cultural conflict mean increased emphasis on citizenship and collective identities.

- Income, care and support is passed down as well as up through the generations.
- Voluntary work is part of most people's lives, and younger workers are 'working to live' rather than living to work.
- Public services, such as health and education, are increasingly personalised, allowing individuals to customise or 'pick and mix' from state provision.
- The meaning of national identity and citizenship weakens as individuals move between countries more rapidly and for shorter periods of time.
- Identity boundaries – gender, group, generation, age, race, ability, health, capacity – continue to blur, with more opportunity to move between and explore different identities in online interactions.
- Hyper-personalised media technology means people can choose their own worlds, and ignore others.
- Fierce global competition for every job means people of all ages are moving between countries more rapidly and more frequently.
- Speed and access to learning rises exponentially – resourcefulness, aggregating and editing skills are now key to success.
- Stronger links between industry and education drive greater innovation.
- Major economic, environmental and social challenges become so significant that they are beyond communities. National and international collaboration is required.

Source: Selected from Be Prepared . . . Future Trends. Available at: **www.visionmapper.org.uk**

Personalised learning/ personalisation: this is now a widely used term in a range of contexts. Broadly, it reflects current policy developments towards enabling education to match the needs and interests of learners more closely than in the past, through a number of initiatives, many of which are discussed in this book. See **www.ttrb.ac.uk**, article id 12406, which gives a commentary on the concept of 'personalised learning' with further links to other resources.

Reading the list above you get an overwhelming sense of change and exponential developments. In relation to education one almost begins to question whether the role of the teacher of the future will be recognisable against what it is today. Chris White, a consultant teacher educator, poses the possibility that education will be 'released from the constraints of place and time' (White, 2005: 269). Mike Newby, a significant figure in the debates about teaching in the future, believes that education will be everywhere and no longer constrained in a building called a school at a certain time of the day (2005). For White and Newby, this is largely as a result of technological advances, an individualised curriculum provision and a need for a more diverse set of skills in the world of work. The implications for the work and practices of teachers are significant.

What will the teacher of 2020 actually be doing each day? The idea that a teacher would be based in one school for an extended period, regularly working with a class size of around 30 to deliver a fixed body of subject knowledge, is going to become 'curious and quaint' (ATL, 2005: 22). Instead, teachers are going to have deploy skills of negotiation and facilitation to guide their learners through the vast bank of curriculum content knowledge provided by experts all over the world and made available via technology. One might conceive of a teacher's working day as including:

- online tutorials with learners from a geographically diverse area;
- face-to-face sessions with small groups with a common interest or need;

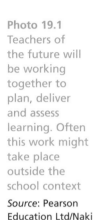

Photo 19.1
Teachers of
the future will
be working
together to
plan, deliver
and assess
learning. Often
this work might
take place
outside the
school context

Source: Pearson
Education Ltd/Naki
Kouyioumtzis

- planning the learning for groups of mixed age learners right through to adult learners;
- liaison with community representatives around shared learning activities;
- planning and teaching alongside community and other professionals online and face-to-face mixed age groups;
- electronic reading and marking of learners' work to provide individual electronic feedback and target setting;
- compiling learner profiles and discussing individual learning plans with parents; learners and other professionals;
- engaging in a distance-learning professional development programme with colleagues around the world.

These activities might be similarly managed from home or in a number of schools or community centres, and the hours spent working will be flexible during daytime and evening according to learner need.

In reflecting on this range of activities, it is clear that teachers of the future will need to develop a set of skills and knowledge base which might be quite different to those of today. Writing more than 10 years ago, John West-Burnham, a professor of educational leadership, began to predict the shifts that will need to be made in order to work as a teacher in the future. In many ways, 10 years on, one can see how these have already begun but also the changes that still need to happen. According to West-Burnham, teaching in the future may have:

- Less emphasis on age or subject-related teaching;
- Greater emphasis on the meta-cognitive aspects of learning;
- More time with individuals and small groups;

- Far more cooperative activity with qualified teachers leading teams of learning facilitators;
- ICT will be fundamental to all learning and teaching activities;
- A more sophisticated approach to personal and interpersonal effectiveness;
- The cognitive curriculum having higher status that the knowledge-based curriculum.

(1999: 23)

THINKING IT THROUGH

At this point it is perhaps useful to revisit the Teachers' TV programme referenced in the last chapter. In *School Matters – Tomorrow's Teacher, Tomorrow's School* (**http://www.teachers.tv/video/31224**) two schools are showcased. As you re-watch this programme, make a list of all the skills you feel might be required of teachers in these future schools. How far do you feel prepared to meet these requirements?

Teacher as networker

Deryn Harvey is a consultant on educational leadership and was featured in the above programme. She lists a number of essential roles that require specific skills. These include being a supporter, broker, negotiator and facilitator of learning. Mike Newby adds to this list by insisting that teachers will be 'portfolio professionals' who must be able to manage programmes deploying their understanding of children and learning to diagnose, demonstrate and guide learning. Key to these roles is an ability to work with effectiveness and confidence in a networked situation. In this context, one can interpret 'network' in a range of equally valid and relevant ways. Obviously, with the advances in technology teachers will be networked with colleagues, fellow professionals, learners and parents who might be working across a wide geographical area. One might conceive of a curriculum-based project which is taught online with a range of learners, 'subject' experts and learning mentors engaging with the topic of study. The role of the teacher in this network might be to channel the expertise so it is pitched at the right level for the learner, while at the same time advising the mentor as to how to support the learner's specific needs so they can access the learning.

A further conception of what this networked education community might look like is one where teachers work with a range of experts to support and enrich their teaching. This might be an online community around the world who provide guidance in teacher's assessment, diagnosis of special needs or pedagogical support. This could be, for example, a teacher uploading individual children's profiles and receiving guidance on how to make their provision more effective, or moderation of learners' work.

Alternatively, the network might be a vehicle by which the teacher is able to share their own area of expertise to support teachers and learners across a wide area. This could be an avenue for career progression much like the current 'Advanced Skills Teacher' who leads and supports fellow teachers. In an online network, the scope for advanced specialism and impact is that much greater (for more information about the roles of an Advanced Skills Teacher see **www.tda.gov.uk/teachers/professionalstandards/ downloads.aspx**).

The potential for visually linked networks is very powerful. Examples are already emerging of learners working together on projects across the world through video conferencing. Take this to teachers sharing their own practice with peers using similar media and exploring their own professional development through online coaching, and the possibilities become very exciting.

Clearly a teacher's ability to function in a network will be key in the future. Mike Newby, through the TDA Futures Project, has generated heated debate in the education sector. This influential 'think-tank' project group produced three scenarios about education in 2020 to stimulate thinking and planning for the future of teacher education. This group pick up the theme of networking in stating that education happens in networks around, for example, people's homes, hospitals and shopping centres. There is no set curriculum and the notion that subject knowledge is the sole domain of the teacher is nonsense. The implications of this scenario for the teaching workforce are quite shocking. The following extract from Newby's work summarises the possible state of the teaching profession in 2020.

CASE STUDY FROM THE FUTURE (2020)

Teachers grew dissatisfied with traditional employment conditions as others came to value their skills and pay more highly for them. Over the last 10 years or so, we've seen the rise of the *portfolio educator* (either multi-skilled or specialist) and nowadays freelance educators are in demand not only for children and teenagers but in adult education and workplace training too. *Learning coaches* work directly with learners of all ages to understand their skills and aspirations and help them identify the approaches best suited to their particular circumstances. In particular, they guide kids to become job-orientated. New *educational diagnosticians* have emerged as the elite of the educational professionals. The ability to assess, diagnose, design and then plan learning programmes is much valued and, of course, very well paid. Their direct contact with learners is, as you might expect, relatively brief (they have busy, often international, schedules) but even brief interventions can help others to ensure children and young people make progress. Rather than be tied to one employer, these portfolio educators are major players in the networked education market, offering surgeries, digital help-lines and home visits. Sometimes, you can see them giving teaching demonstrations and support to local *educare* teams, the people who you will find invited into people's homes and in the various social centres where learning takes place. The idea that these professionals would restrict themselves to work for years in one 'school' is simply absurd.

Source: Newby (2005: 257)

Teacher of the future: qualities and characteristics

In reflecting upon this view back from the future, one begins to consider the qualities required of the teaching professionals of the future. The past 15 years of teacher education have had a very strong focus on subject knowledge – the development of the teaching 'competences' and then 'standards' by the English government chart the perceived need for teachers to have advanced understanding of subject content. Although there has now been a move to include pedagogical subject knowledge (how to teach a subject, not only what to teach), it seems that the shift needs to be much more radical if teachers are to be equipped to work in schools of the future. It is better that teachers are prepared now to develop a set of attributes and characteristics to serve them in the rapidly changing educational landscape. Muriel Robinson, a senior teacher educator, notes that current entrants to teacher training might be considered 'risk averse' (2005: 263) whereas they really need to be able to manage rapid change. She makes a powerful argument that this aversion is linked to the educational experience of aspiring teachers, which has largely been dominated by a subject-compartmentalised national curriculum. It might be argued that teacher education which has served this subject-driven curriculum actually needs to focus on developing professionals who are forward-looking, reflexive, flexible and able to cope with uncertainty. The implications for teacher education are considerable.

It is an interesting exercise to review the current set of QTS standards against which all new and early career teachers are being educated and assessed. Table 19.1 is an attempt to map the changes that might be needed to better serve our new teachers:

Reflexive: is about being aware in the moment/present of what is impacting upon and influencing our actions and responses.

Qualified Teacher Status (QTS): a recognition that someone has met the first set of Professional Standards for Teaching in England and is able to start their Newly Qualified Teacher (NQT) year.

Table 19.1 Possible changes to QTS standards

Standards for new teachers, TDA, 2008.	How might these need to be applied in the future?
Attributes • Relationships with children and young people • Frameworks • Communicating and working with others • Personal professional development	• Working with varying ages from child to adult simultaneously • Working in many schools and settings in parallel • Confident communication with many professionals, learners and parents across a wide geographical area • Responding to rapid feedback from fellow professionals, online coaching and mentoring

Table 19.1 *Continued*

Knowledge and Understanding

- Teaching and learning
- Assessment and monitoring
- Subjects and curriculum
- Literacy, numeracy and ICT
- Achievement and diversity
- Health and well-being

- Adapting teaching and learning strategies to teach learners at a distance
- Deploying these strategies for simultaneous teaching of different ages
- Promoting strategies to guide learners through the developing subject knowledge available online
- Promoting high standards and inclusivity for all via virtual media

Skills

- Planning
- Teaching
- Assessment, monitoring and giving feedback
- Reviewing teaching and learning
- Learning environments
- Teamwork and collaboration

- Flexibility to teach in a range of settings with varying group sizes and locations
- Applying assessment data to the planning of individual learning programmes
- Reflecting on and evaluating learning alongside parents and other professionals
- Adapting planning and teaching to various learning environments
- Working with a complex network of fellow professionals

The General Teaching Council for England (GTCE) commissioned some research into stakeholder views about what skills might be required of teachers. Interestingly, as well as asking teachers themselves, Kathryn Riley, Professor of Education at the Institute of Education, also sought the views of parents, headteachers, support staff and pupils. The research aimed to identify the qualities of a good teacher and what they thought the profession of the future might demand of teachers' skills and attributes. The findings included the following qualities:

Resilience: the ability to accept being unsuccessful in a task, and to persist in attempting to master a skill or understanding. Can also include the idea of having strategies to support persistence, such as a willingness to try different approaches.

- Enthusiasm and energy
- Flexibility and adaptability
- Openness and an encouraging approach
- Sense of humour
- Creativity, imagination, divergent thinking
- An excitement for teaching
- Confidence and firmness
- **Resilience**, flexibility, innovation
- Emotional intelligence
- Willingness to recognise the role of other adults in developing children as learners.

(Riley, 2004: 24)

WORKING IN THE CLASSROOM

As you reflect on this list above from Riley *et al.*'s research, can you share, with a colleague or peer, examples of classroom or staffroom situations where you have demonstrated these qualities?

Photo 19.2
Teachers of the future will need to model openness, enthusiasm, excitement and flexibility

Source: Pearson Education Ltd/Phovoir. Imagestate

Teaching as a values-based profession

Teaching and learning increasingly will be about the stamina and resilience to cope with change. Jill Blackmore, an Australian education theorist, takes this forward by setting educational change within a trend towards a focus on society. Education, she says, must also be about 'developing a range of social and inter-personal capacities' (2000: 381) rather than a focus on conceptual knowledge. Robert Yinger, Professor of Education from the United States, explores the fact that we need to rethink what education is for. He argues that education must be 're-charted' so that it reflects society's values and goals, and teaching 're-framed' so that it supports moral purpose, responsibility and caring. Following on from this, he argues that learning must be 're-cast' to promote community and values-based engagement with the world

Social capital: 'Social capital refers to the institutions, relationships, and norms that shape the quality and quantity of a society's social interactions . . . it is the glue that holds them together' (World Bank, 1999).

(2005: 308–309). Consequently, it is obvious that teacher education needs to be more focused on developing these 'social capital' capacities in the next generation of teachers. Social capital, as opposed to intellectual capacity, is about forming values-based networks and relationships, contributing to and drawing from the community, co-operation and trust.

Andy Hargreaves is a significant education theorist and Professor of Education whose work in this area is seminal. In his writing on 'teaching in the knowledge society' he makes a strong case for an affective values-base for the teaching profession of the future. Successful teaching will be measured by the extent to which the teacher has established responsive, caring and inclusive relationships with the pupils. Teachers must be able to:

- Promote social and emotional learning, commitment and character
- Learn to relate differently to others, replacing strings of interactions with enduring bonds and relationships
- Develop cosmopolitan identity
- Commit to continuous professional and personal development
- Work and learn in collaborative groups
- Forge relationships with parents and communities
- Build emotional understanding
- Preserve continuity and security
- Establish basic trust in people.

(2003: 45)

'Community' as a value

In Chapter 2, we explored the importance of teachers reflecting on their own value systems and how these will influence curriculum, pedagogy and professional relationships. This same chapter also highlighted the impact of globalisation in challenging the teacher to encounter many more, sometimes competing values sets. The theme of 'community' has been explored throughout this book as being central in the development of learning. Oxford University's Elizabeth Frazer brings these themes together in proposing that 'community' might be termed a 'value' in its own right, rather than a context in which values can be realised (Frazer, 1999). Whereas traditionally we might conceive of a community as a setting in which people live out and practise their values, Frazer seems to be suggesting that 'community' is itself a core value. For teachers this raises sets of exciting possibilities, which simultaneously might also present contradictions and challenges.

While communities might be conceived of as having a place or geographical territory, be clustered to serve a particular interest or centred around an affiliation to a set of ideas or beliefs, the key similarity is the sense of identity that comes with membership.

THINKING IT THROUGH

The communities to which you belong will be many. As a teacher, adult, family member, friend and so on, you will be aware of what it feels like to belong to these communities. Think about social, neighbourhood, religious, society and virtual groupings. Take a few moments to list all these communities. Once you have done this, reflect on what it feels like to belong to each community. How do you know you are part of the community? How do others inside and outside understand your part in the community? This will give you a sense of the boundaries that define each community.

Are you able to list any values which are explicit to each community? How are these values made real in the way the members behave?

The boundaries surrounding communities are crucial for stability and sustainability. Members of the community understand the conventions, expectations and norms for that group, and they become known as 'members' by those within and outside the community in question. This gives members a reference point for their own personal identity. One might cite the example of a youth club. Individual members know where they meet, at what time, and the kinds of expectations in terms of behaviours, activities and conventions. The individual will then cite membership of that group as a part of who they are.

A sense of membership and belonging to a community is essential in cultivating a sense of personal identity, of knowing who we are and where we 'fit'. For teachers of the future it will be essential that they not only develop these reflective capacities in their young learners, but that as teachers they have a strong sense of their own identity and values. It is important that teachers have a sense of 'connectedness' with each other as professionals as well as with their learners. Writers such as the sociologist Graham Allan allude to the fact that awareness of the network around us provides the feeling of a safe and secure space to deal with demands and challenges as they arise (Allan, 1996). Throughout this book we have tried to highlight the massive pace of change ahead for schools and teachers. While exciting and stimulating, these changes will no doubt leave us feeling overwhelmed and threatened by the new pedagogies, technologies, curricula and working practices on the horizon. It will be increasingly important that pupils and teachers have a sense of their own identity in their various communities and networks if they are to thrive in this new world.

The implications are significant for teacher education – both initial training and continuing professional development. How far are we able to say that teacher education can and does prepare teachers for working in communities? Informal education expert Mark K. Smith, in drawing upon a range of research, crystallises the qualities needed for effective community working, and suggests that we need to focus on tolerance, reciprocity and trust (2001). Table 19.2 unpacks these qualities a little further.

Reciprocity:
is the practice
of responding to
a positive action
with another
positive action
or, indeed, a
negative action
in response to a
negative action.

Table 19.2 Qualities needed for effective community working	
Tolerance	• Openness • Curiosity • Respect • Willingness to listen and learn
Reciprocity	• Giving or doing something for someone without expecting an immediate payback • Confident that you will receive payback in the future • Mutual exchange
Trust	• Have faith or belief in someone • Confidence in someone

THINKING IT THROUGH

Imagine yourself in role as a teacher educator, university or school-based. You are charged with designing a new teacher education curriculum which will develop these essential qualities in the new generation of teachers. In a small group, plan a series of short activities or opportunities to develop, apply and demonstrate aspects of trust, reciprocity and tolerance.

Are there experiences or opportunities from your own training which are transferrable to this new curriculum?

SUMMARY

This chapter has traced the ideas around teaching being a relationship-based, networked and community-focused profession and sought to explore the attributes, skills and qualities that will be required of teachers of the future. The forecasts in this book have highlighted a future for schools which will be almost unrecognisable. On the one hand, individualised and tailored programmes of study where pupil voice is prominent might suggest that learning becomes a solitary activity, whereas it seems that the focus for the teacher will about creating and sustaining communities of learners. The work of Austrian-born Jewish philosopher Martin Buber is important in this discussion – he reminds us that we can only grow and develop in relation to others (Buber, 1958). An issue and a lasting question must be the role of policy makers – the current emphasis upon community cohesion serves to highlight the central steer and control in

SUMMARY *CONTINUED*

how agendas and directions are set. As Zygmunt Bauman, the famous Polish sociologist, has suggested, communities need to work collectively to take control (Bauman, 2001). It is debatable whether the trust, reciprocity and tolerance needed for effective communities can really be fully developed if outside agencies take away ownership and autonomy by prescribing the very substance of these learning relationships. The teacher of the future will need to be 'a courageous counterpoint' willing to stand up for their communities of learners and act as a stable force in a fast-changing world. Andy Hargreaves sums this up by saying that:

> *Teaching [will] require levels of skills and judgment far beyond those involved in merely delivering someone else's prescribed curriculum . . . Teaching cannot be a refuge for second choice careers, a low-level system of technical delivery . . . Teaching . . . should be a career of first choice, a job for grown-up intellectuals, a long-term commitment, a social mission, a job for life.*
>
> (2003: 51)

TAKING YOUR PRACTICE FURTHER

As well as providing support and guidance to access the latest research and thinking around teaching and learning for the 7–14 age range, this book has sought to highlight the skills and aptitudes that you will need to develop as teachers working with these young learners. A key skill will be the ability to reflect on your own practice and those factors influencing change around you and the texts suggested in Chapter 14 are the most helpful. In order to try to focus your thinking on what the future holds for you as a teacher in the next 20 years or so, you might find it useful to consider the current high-profile 'think-tank' reports such as *The Cambridge Review of Primary Education* (**http://www.primaryreview.org.uk/**) or the *Independent Review of Lifelong Learning* (**http://www.niace.org.uk/lifelonglearninginquiry**). Looking at these documents, and others that may be published, alongside materials from organisations that represent the teacher as a professional, will provide a considered reference point for you as the pace of change increases. The work of the General Teaching Councils (for England, **www.gtce.org.uk**; for Scotland, **www.gtcs.org.uk**; for Northern Ireland, **www.gtcni.org.uk**; and for Wales, **www.gtcw.org.uk**) is a key point of contact, as are some of the representative teaching unions. The Association of Teachers and Lecturers, for example, regularly commission accessible and thought-provoking research papers on matters affecting classroom practice (**www.atl.org.uk**)

TAKING YOUR THINKING FURTHER

The research base and future-gazing in teaching and education is growing. It will be important that you keep to date with these 'think-tanks' if your practice and thinking are to benefit. The work of the Initial Teacher Education (ITE) Futures project, now named 'Teaching 2020', draws together thinking in this area from across the academic and professional worlds. Their report is available at **www.publications.teachernet.gov.uk**. Influential research-based journals such as *Journal of Education for Teaching*, published by Routledge, and the United States based *Teaching and Teacher Education*, published by Elsevier, will provide you with access to the latest research. Of course, sources such as Teachers' TV (**www.teachers.tv**) often provide an accessible window into more in-depth and complicated discussions. The Teacher Training Resource Bank (TTRB) provides a peer-reviewed gateway to both professional and academic publications on teaching and learning. The service of an e-librarian is most helpful in guiding you to areas and topics of specific interest to you (**http://www.ttrb.ac.uk/ELibrarianHome.aspx**)

Find out more

In order to give you access to the latest thinking in educational research, and particularly in relation to the futures agenda, it is worth spending time keeping in touch with the national and international education research networks. These include:

- The British Education Research Association (**www.bera.ac.uk**);
- The European Education Research Association (**www.eera.eu**);
- The American Education Research Association (**www.aera.net**).

Each of these organisations provides an opportunity for networking, either at their large annual conference events or on online discussion boards. Each also hosts special interest groups for further networking around specialist curriculum or theme areas. All of these organisations publish a journal which commands considerable respect and credibility in education research.

The work of Andy Hargreaves is seminal in this area. He has published widely, but key texts would be *Teaching in the Knowledge Society* (2003) and his 2009 publication with David Shirley titled *The Fourth Way: The Inspiring Future for Educational Change*.

Glossary

Personalised learning/personalisation: This is now a widely used term in a range of contexts. Broadly, it reflects current policy developments towards enabling education to match the needs and interests of learners more closely than in the past, through a number of initiatives, many of which are discussed in this book. See **www.ttrb.ac.uk**, article id 12406, for a commentary on the concept of 'personalised learning' with further links to other resources.

Qualified Teacher Status (QTS): a recognition that someone has met the first set of Professional Standards for Teaching in England and is able to start their Newly Qualified Teacher (NQT) year.

Reciprocity: is the practice of responding to a positive action with another positive action or, indeed, a negative action in response to a negative action.

Reflexive: is about being aware in the moment/present of what is impacting upon and influencing our actions and responses.

Resilience: the ability to accept being unsuccessful in a task, and to persist in attempting to master a skill or understanding. Can also include the idea of having strategies to support persistence, such as a willingness to try different approaches.

Social capital: 'Social capital refers to the institutions, relationships, and norms that shape the quality and quantity of a society's social interactions . . . it is the glue that holds them together' (World Bank, 1999).

Think-tank: is an organisation, often linked to government or policy units, which engages in research or consultation to inform policy development.

References

Allan, G. (1996) *Kinship and Friendship in Modern Britain*. London: Oxford University Press.

ATL (2005) *A Learner's Curriculum: Towards a Curriculum for the Twenty-First Century*. Available at: **www.atl.org.uk**.

Bauman, Z. (2001) *Seeking Safety in an Insecure World*. Cambridge: Polity Press.

Be Prepared . . . Future Trends. Available at: **www.visionmapper.org.uk**.

Blackmore, J. (2000) A critique of neo liberal market policies in education, *Journal of Educational Change*, Vol. 1, No. 4: pp. 381–387.

Buber, M. (1958) *I and Thou*. Edinburgh: T & T Clark. Translation: R. Gregory.

Frazer, E. (1999) *The Problem of Communitarian Politics. Unity and Conflict*. Oxford: Oxford University Press.

Hargreaves, A. (2003) *Teaching in the Knowledge Society*. London: Oxford University Press.

Hargreaves, A. and Shirley, D. (2009) *The Fourth Way: The Inspiring Future for Educational Change*. London: Sage.

Newby, M. (2005) Some conclusions, *Journal of Education for Teaching: International Research and Pedagogy*, Vol. 31, No. 4: pp. 311–317.

Riley, K. (2004) *What Do You Think Makes a Good Teacher Now and in the 21st Century*? (Features. Redefining Professionalising: Teachers with Attitude) (online) Available at: **http://www.gtce.org.uk/news/cardsortexercise.asp** (14 October).

Robinson, M. (2005) Uncertainty and innovation, *Journal of Education for Teaching: International Research and Pedagogy*, Vol. 31, No. 4: pp. 263–264.

Smith, M. (2001) Community, in *The Encyclopaedia of Informal Education*. Available at: **www.infed.org/community.htm**.

TDA (2008) *Professional Standards for Qualified Teacher Status*. Available at: **http://www.tda.gov.uk/partners/ittstandards.aspx**.

West-Burnham, J. (1999) Teaching in the school of the future, *Learning and Teaching*, Vol. 2, No. 1: pp. 21–4.

White, C. (2005) The role of the teacher, *Journal of Education for Teaching: International Research and Pedagogy*, Vol. 31, No. 4: pp. 269–271.

Yinger, R. (2005) The promise of education, *Journal of Education for Teaching: International Research and Pedagogy*, Vol. 31, No. 4: pp. 307–310.

Glossary

Acceleration: the practice of 'speeding up' an individual pupil's academic development. Usually means moving a pupil into a year group higher than that for their chronological age for all or part of the curriculum, but can also mean providing individual work within their own classroom designed to meet learning objectives for older years.

Accountability: being publicly responsible for outcomes, including taking responsibility if pupils fail to perform as expected.

Acculturation: might be considered a change in the cultural behaviour and thinking of a person or group of people through contact with another culture. In this book this is conceived of as a two-way process.

Action research: as indicated in the chapter and suggested reading, there are a number of versions of 'action research'. The essential feature is that the researcher is actively involved in the process of progressive problem solving, rather than standing outside events in a 'traditional' researcher role.

Active citizenship: this term implies the direct participation of pupils in activities which develop their understanding of democratic processes, community involvement, and developing a sense of personal identity.

Affordances: opportunities that enable different forms of interaction, made available by particular technologies.

All-through school: a school catering for both primary- and secondary-aged pupils.

Assertive discipline: a term given to particular form of 'behaviour management' system first developed in the USA by Lee and Marlene Canter. Lee Canter was a psychiatric social worker. In this system the teacher takes control of the classroom using a discipline plan with clearly laid down rules, rewards and sanctions which must be followed by the pupils. It is based on **behaviourist** assumptions about learning and was highly authoritarian when first developed in the mid-1970s, although it has since been modified to a more co-operative approach.

Assimilation: is the process by which individuals or groups are absorbed into and adopt the culture of another society or group.

Behaviour for learning: patterns of behaviour likely to bring about successful learning.

Behaviourist: a theory of learning based on the idea that our behaviour is shaped by the feedback (or 'reinforcement') we receive. In school contexts this often takes the form of pupils being rewarded for successful learning (with ticks, stars, prizes etc.) or behaviour (merit points, prizes etc.) and the application of sanctions if behaviour is not satisfactory.

Child-centred pedagogy: an approach to teaching which focuses on the learning needs of the children in the class, rather than on following a pre-set curriculum with objectives determined by the teacher or adminstrators. It is closely linked, but not identical, to differentiation, which can also be employed in the context of a predetemrined curriculum.

Closed questions: questions for which there is a single right answer, or questions that are answerable by yes/no responses.

Cognitive acceleration: a teaching approach which claims to develop pupils' general thinking abilities, involving the social construction of knowledge and the development of meta-cognition. See: **http://www.kcl.ac.uk/schools/sspp/education/research/projects/cognitive.html**

Cognitive learning theory: a theory that seeks to explain how learners process information.

Constructivism: a view of learning that emphasises the active role of the learner in building understanding, and making sense of information from experience.

Consultation: often used synonymously with **participation**, but may imply a more passive level of involvement.

Core Standards: (see Professional Standards below). The Core Standards apply to all teachers and must be met by Newly Qualified Teachers (NQTs) by the end of their first year in teaching.

Corpus callosum: a mass of fibres located in the middle of the brain which connects the two hemispheres and allows communication between them.

Cross-curricular: approaches to teaching which seek to make links between different curriculum subjects. The National Curriculum currently has a set of stated cross-curriculum dimensions for Key Stage 3 (**www.qca.org.uk**). This term is more commonly used in the first sense.

Cumulation: evaluating and building on pupils' responses through careful listening so that pupils' answers are built into subsequent questions to create a 'chain' of coherent enquiry.

Curriculum enrichment: providing work within the normal classroom to extend the thinking of very able pupils, rather than 'moving the learner on' as with acceleration. Enrichment activities may also take place outside the regular curriculum: after school, at weekends or during the holiday period.

Data collection: the systematic gathering of information/evidence to support your investigation.

DCSF: Department for Children, Schools and Families: government department created in 2007, responsible for all matters affecting children and young people up to the age of 19, including child protection and education. Changes to government policy over the years have meant that there have been several renamed departments concerned with education. DCSF replaced the Department for Education and Skills (DfES), which existed between 2001 and 2007. Prior to 2001, education was part of the remit of the Department of Education and Employment (DfEE), which was in turn created in 1995.

Demographic: the study of population, involving birth rates, age profiles and ethnicity.

Dialogic teaching: a term coined by Robin Alexander to denote a particular approach to teaching through talk which operates to stimulate and extend pupils' thinking through the disciplined use of key strategies (see **www.robinalexander.org.uk/dialogicteaching**).

Didactic: teaching through direct instruction or demonstration, with little pupil involvement.

Differentiation/differentiated planning: the adjustment of the teaching process according to the learning needs of pupils. Differentiated planning is generally taken to mean the matching of work to the differing capabilities within the class, matched to an overall intended learning outcome. Differentiation may operate by varying the type of tasks set for different groups of pupils, by varying the resources provided, varying expectations of the outcome or providing higher levels of adult support.

Drill learning: the learning of facts through memorisation, reinforced by repetition. Sometimes also called rote learning.

Drill-and-skill: the learning of facts or simple skills through memorisation, reinforced by repetition.

Education Reform Act: a major Act of Parliament passed in 1988, which established the National Curriculum and standardised national testing as statutory, amongst many other revisions to the governance of schooling, too numerous to discuss here.

E-enabled: a measure of the ability of a school to make effective and strategic use of technology to improve learning. Judgements about a school's 'e-maturity' are made on the basis of the technical infrastructure and resources available, the confidence of staff to utilise technology effectively for both teaching and co-ordinating school activities and finally on how well technology engages the learners.

Ego-centrism: the assumption that other people view the world in the same way as yourself.

Emotional intelligence: a term made famous by Goleman (1996). Although definitions of the concept vary, it is generally taken to embrace both being self-aware about one's own emotions and likely reactions to different situations, and being able to respond appropriately towards others by being empathetic and displaying social skills.

Emotional literacy: similar to emotional intelligence, but preferred by some writers because the use of the term 'literacy' is felt to place greater emphasis on personal empowerment.

Enculturation: the gradual acceptance by a person or group of the standards and practices of another person or culture.

Enquiry-based approach: an approach to teaching which involves pupils in working together to solve problems rather than working under the teacher's direction. The teacher's role becomes that of a facilitator, rather than an instructor. General Teaching Council for England (GTCE).

Ethnography: this is used to describe a way of researching and usually involves the researcher becoming part of the group or community they are studying. Ethnographic research usually involves studying the whole context rather than an isolated factor.

Ethos: derived from Greek, meaning 'to be accustomed to', this has come to mean the distinctive character and fundamental values of a particular social grouping.

Exclusion: the practice of removing children temporarily or permanently from school, because they are unable to work with others in a safe manner.

Experiential learning: involves making meaning, or developing understanding, from direct experience, sometimes called 'learning by doing'.

Extended Services (extended schools): by 2010 all schools are expected to offer 'extended services' to pupils and the local community. These services can be offered by schools working together, rather than independently. The services depend on local demand, but typically involve extended opening hours for childcare, after-school clubs, sports and other facilities, such as ICT rooms available to the local community, parent support activities and access to specialist services such as speech therapy, youth workers, police, careers advice etc.

Extrinsic: in this case, external to the learner, as opposed to the internal satisfaction of doing good work or maintaining effective learning behaviour.

Faith community: this is used to refer to a group, society, congregation or gathering of people who subscribe to the same set of religious beliefs and practise together.

Family literacy: the use of structured literacy programmes shared by several members of the family. The intention is to raise the literacy levels of all family members through a focus on supporting the literacy development of one or more children.

Formative assessment: where the purpose is to help in decisions about how to advance learning and the judgement is about the next steps in learning and how to take them.

Gifted (and talented): there are no precise definitions of what it means to be academically gifted, but the term is broadly used to identify those pupils who demonstrate a significantly higher level of ability than most pupils of the same age. This ability could be displayed in one or more curriculum areas, or as physical or artistic talent. See **http://www.brookes.ac.uk/schools/education/rescon/ cpdgifted/docs/unit1/1-1-definitionsofabilityunit1.pdf** for a detailed discussion of this contested area.

Global dimension: one of the cross-curricular themes in the Key Stage 3 National Curriculum. See Chapter 17.

Globalisation: this term is used in a variety of contexts: to indicate economic interdependency and the power exerted by some multinational corporations that no longer have strong links with any particular country, but see themselves as transcending national boundaries; to indicate the ways in which technologies are enabling near-instantaneous communication across the world; to indicate the spread of cultural artefacts (such as film, music, fashion) beyond their original countries of origin to become 'global brands' – this last use of the term is closely reated to the first two.

GTCE: The General Teaching Council for England is the professional body for teaching in England. All trainee teachers are provisionally registered with the GTCE, and full registration is confirmed at the end of the induction year. The GTCE also provides a range of other services and resources for teachers, employers and parents. 'Our overall purpose is to work in the public interest to help improve standards of teaching and learning.'

Hidden curriculum: a term used to denote the way in which schooling 'socialises' pupils into certain behaviours that are not made explicit. Can be used in a critical sense to denote forms of social control.

Higher order: thinking or questions that involve deductive or inferential thinking, or that seek explanation or justification rather than repetition of known facts.

'High stakes' testing or assessment: where summative assessment is used for making decisions that affect the status or future of students, teachers or schools.

Ideology: a set of values, ideas and beliefs about the way things should be organised within a particular society or culture.

Induction: in education, the process by which the learner develops their own conceptual understanding by being supported to generalise, or recognise causal connections, or draw analogies with previous experience.

Innovations Unit: a non-governmental organisation, associated with the DCSF, which supports and encourages innovation on education and disseminates examples of new practice.

Integrated network: a computer-based system bringing together a range of functions such as video conferencing and real-time collaborative writing or editing facilities as well as access to resources, communication and information internal to a school or other organisation.

Interactive White Board (IWB): computer-linked classroom teaching aid that enables pupils and teacher to interact directly with material the screen while providing a large scale display visible to the whole class, thus increasing the potential for interactive learning. Can also be used to display pre-prepared materials.

Interdependence: the process whereby, in this case, learning is mutually dependent on each other/participant.

Internationalisation: an attitude of openness to learning from, and with, those from elsewhere in the world. This term may have different connotations in other contexts such as universities, where there is also an economic dimension.

Kinaesthetic: applied to education, this term means being actively involved in learning through doing, rather than by listening or watching.

Knowledge economy: this is a term used to identify the use of 'intangibles' such as knowledge, skills and innovative ideas in the 'information age' as resources to bring about economic advantages for countries. This is in contrast to economies based on the industrial production of 'tangible' products. For further information see **http://www.esrcsocietytoday.ac.uk/ESRCInfoCentre/facts/index4.aspx**

Learning mentor: a person working within a primary or secondary school to support pupils identified as being 'at risk' of academic failure. They form a bridge between pastoral and academic concerns. The learning mentor may be a qualified teacher or a member of support staff who has received specific training.

Learning platform: a software product which supports shared access to resources, communication and information internal to a school or other organisation (such as a local authority). **Virtual Learning Environments** (VLEs) or Course Management Systems are well-established examples of learning platforms.

Lesioned: deliberately cut. In this context the term refers to very rare brain operations on patients with severe epilepsy, where cutting through the **corpus callosum** alleviates the major symptoms.

Media literacy: the ability to 'read' a range of communications media in order to recognise authorial intentions and to understand that these media are not neutral sources of information.

Meta-cognition: being aware of how we think and behave in learning situations. Ultimately this implies active control over the process of thinking, for example: planning the way to approach a learning task, monitoring comprehension, and evaluating progress towards the completion of a task.

Methodology: the overall approach taken to gathering and analysing data. This is an area about which a great deal has been written.

Mind mapping: a term initially coined by Tony Buzan to describe visual representation of interlinked ideas. There are a number of software packages which enable 'mind maps' to be created, amended and linked to other electronic resources.

Multiple activity setting: a learning space in which different activities can be carried out simultaneously, such as practical work, group discussion and independent work.

Multiple intelligences: a concept developed by Howard Gardner (1983). The idea that humans possess a number of discrete 'intelligences' such as linguistic intelligence, musical intelligence, spatial intelligence. Gardner first proposed seven intelligences, but later increased this number (see Chapter 9 for full reference).

Multi-sensory resources: aids to learning that incorporate visual and auditory materials, and where appropriate opportunities for physical manipulation of items, such as mathematical equipment, or the use of aids for sequencing events to support writing.

National Strategies (Primary and Secondary): these are professional development programmes for primary and secondary teachers They provide resources to support teaching, and suggested frameworks for the curriculum. They are widely used in schools, but are non-statutory. See **www.nationalstrategies.standards.dcsf.gov.uk/**. A recent government announcement indicates that they will be phased out by 2011.

Neuron: a nerve cell in the brain that stores and transfers information. Neurons have long and short fibres through which connect to other cells takes place, across the **synapses**.

Ofsted: The Office for Standards in Education is the government department responsible for inspecting schools and local authorities. It publishes reports on a wide range of topics, using evidence from inspections.

Open questions: questions with more than one possible answer, or questions designed to encourage reflection and further thought.

Participation: having some infuence over decisions and actions which affect pupils' lives in school. Often used synonymously with **consultation**.

Personalised learning/personalisation: this is now a widely used term in a range of contexts. Broadly, it reflects current policy developments towards enabling education to match the needs and interests of learners more closely than in the past, through a number of initiatives, many of which are discussed in this book. See **www.ttrb.ac.uk**, article id 12406, for a commentary on the concept of 'personalised learning' with further links to other resources.

Probing questions: questions that encourage respondents to think more deeply or provide additional information or justification.

Professional development: the ongoing training, development and education that is available to a person working in a profession such as teaching.

Professional Standards for Teaching: the current government requirements that all teachers need to meet in order to be recognised as qualified teachers in England. They are organised in a progressive framework starting with those for **Qualified Teacher Status (QTS)** and moving on to the **Core Standards** by the end of the first year of teaching.

Provisionality: the concept that electronic text can be seen as a provisional, rather than permanent text form, unlike handwritten text which needs to be rewritten if changes are made; an **affordance** of word processing, and some other forms of software.

Proximal learning: learning involving others close by – paired or small-group-based learning.

Psychosocial: the combination of psychological and social factors affecting mental health or social and emotional development.

Pupil voice: a term used to identify a range of strategies utilised to gather pupils' views about all aspects of school life. See Chapter 15.

Qualifications and Curriculum Development Agency (QCDA): the official body responsible for all aspects of curriculum development, and statutory assessment in England. It is sponsored by the Department for Children, Schools and Families (DCSF).

Qualified Teacher Status (QTS): a recognition that someone has met the first set of Professional Standards for Teaching in England and is able to start their Newly Qualified Teacher (NQT) year.

Qualifying to Teach: the title of the current government standards for the award of Qualified Teacher Status in England.

Reciprocity: is the practice of responding to a positive action with another positive action or, indeed, a negative action in response to a negative action.

Reflexive: is about being aware in the moment/present of what is impacting upon and influencing our actions and responses.

Research method: the way in which data is collected. Some examples of research methods are given in Chapter 13. The list of useful texts provides more examples.

Resilience: the ability to accept being unsuccessful in a task, and to persist in attempting to master a skill or understanding. Can also include the idea of having strategies to support persistence, such as a willingness to try different approaches.

Scaffolding: the process whereby an adult or more experienced peer supports the learner to acquire new skills or understanding that are currently beyond their ability. Different techniques may be used, such as breaking the task down into smaller sections, questioning, cueing or modelling, but the important thing is that the pupil completes as much of the task as possible, and only receives support in those aspects that they cannot master at present. Once they have mastered the task or demonstrated the necessary understanding, the teacher or peer withdraws support, or 'removes the scaffolding'.

School councils: bodies established to provide a forum for pupil representatives to raise issues of concern, and to enable the school management to consult with pupils on issues directly affecting their learning, well-being and experience in school. See Chapter 15.

SEAL: Social and Emotional Aspects of Learning (see Chapter 9).

SEN Register: this is a statutory responsibility on schools. They must keep a register of all children with Special Educational Needs. The criteria for inclusion on this register are governed by legislation.

Self-concept: the set of beliefs about oneself, including attributes, roles, goals, interests, values and religious or political beliefs.

Self-efficacy: an individual's judgement of their ability to carry out a task or sustain behaviours that will lead to a certain outcome. Can relate to emotional issues such as anger as well as an individual's belief in their intellectual or physical capacities to undertake a task.

Self-esteem: how one feels about one's self-concept.

'Small schools': in this context the term refers to the subdivision of large secondary schools into smaller, vertically grouped units, each of which operates semi-independently.

Socialisation: a term used by sociologists to define the process of learning to live within one's particular culture. This process of inducting individuals into values and assumptions about social roles enables social and cultural continuity to be maintained, but can also result in the continuation of stereotypical views about gender, ethnicity etc.

Social capital: 'Social capital refers to the institutions, relationships, and norms that shape the quality and quantity of a society's social interactions . . . it is the glue that holds them together' (World Bank, 1999).

Social constructivism: the theory that learning is constructed through active participation with others within the contexts of the **socio-cultural group.**

Social justice: the belief that every individual should have the chances and opportunities to make the most of their lives and use their talents to the full.

Socio-cultural group: people with shared attitudes and values (culture) living within a particular society. The terms culture and society are often used interchangeably, but this combined term is used to indicate that larger social groups, whether nations or local communities, are composed of smaller groups of people with distinct attitudes and values. Thus one child's learning in terms of social constructivism may be very different from another's, even when they live in the same area.

Special Educational Needs (SEN): the legal definition is that a child has learning difficulties or disabilities that make it harder for them to learn than most children of the same age.

Standardised: criteria for success are established through an initial process of testing materials with large numbers of pupils in different schools and areas to arrive at agreement on levels of achievement (i.e. agreed standards).

Strategy learning: learning based in developing and understanding of problem-solving strategies, rather than memorisation (see **drill learning** above).

Summative assessment: where the purpose is to summarise the learning that has taken place in order to grade, certificate or record progress.

Sustainable development: the need to avoid the further depletion of the world's resources. This includes ecological issues such as the use of renewable energy or building materials, but also recognising the ecology of workplaces to improve the work-life balance.

Synapse: the tiny space between neurons. Chemical messages cross this gap between the fibres of different neurons and allow the neurons to form interconnected circuits.

Systematic enquiry: a planned approach to investigating a question of interest to your professional practice, involving the selection of an appropriate research method, the collection of evidence or information relating to your focus question and an evaluation of your evidence leading to some form of conclusion and possibly a recommendation for future practice.

Systematic review: an approach to examining a number of research articles or reports in order to evaluate the reliability of the evidence presented against a set of given criteria. Only research which meets the criteria is then discussed in the final review article. It has been argued that this approach sometimes excludes research that could offer valuable insights into difficult areas.

Think-tank: is an organisation, often linked to government or policy units, which engages in research or consultation to inform policy development.

Topic-based approach: a form of curriculum design where different subjects are linked by an overarching theme. Care is needed to avoid superficial connections being made between subjects.

Transmission: a view of teaching and learning where information is given (transmitted) by the teacher to the pupils, as opposed to involving pupils more directly in their learning; often associated with behaviourist learning theory.

Triangulation: used in a research context, this term refers to the use of more than one source of evidence to strengthen the findings of a research investigation.

VAK: the acronym used to refer to the theory that learners have preferred ways of receiving information through the senses: visual, auditory or kinaesthetic.

Virtual Learning Environment: a software product providing shared resources and information, with communication through e-mail and discussion boards, which is internal to a school organisation, but accessible remotely via password. Different VLEs have varying facilities, such as options for learners to create personal online portfolios, upload assignments etc.

Withdrawal: the practice of withdrawing pupils from classroom activities to provide additional support in relation to an identified need.

Zone of proximal development: this is generally described as the difference between what learners can do by themselves and what they can do with the help of a more knowledgeable adult or peer. See **scaffolding**, above. The ZPD is constantly changing as learners increase their understanding, so that ongoing assessment is an essential part of this process.

Appendix 1
Standards for the award of Qualified Teacher Status
Professional standards for qualified teacher status

1 Professional attributes

Relationships with children and young people

Q1 Have high expectations of children and young people including a commitment to ensuring that they can achieve their full educational potential and to establishing fair, respectful, trusting, supportive and constructive relationships with them.

Q2 Demonstrate the positive values, attitudes and behaviour they expect from children and young people.

Frameworks

Q3 (a) Be aware of the professional duties of teachers and the statutory framework within which they work.
(b) Be aware of the policies and practices of the workplace and share in collective responsibility for their implementation.

Communicating and working with others

Q4 Communicate effectively with children, young people, colleagues, parents and carers.

Q5 Recognise and respect the contribution that colleagues, parents and carers can make to the development and well-being of children and young people and to raising their levels of attainment.

Q6 Have a commitment to collaboration and co-operative working.

Personal professional development

Q7 (a) Reflect on and improve their practice, and take responsibility for identifying and meeting their developing professional needs
(b) Identify priorities for their early professional development in the context of induction.

Q8 Have a creative and constructively critical approach towards innovation, being prepared to adapt their practice where benefits and improvements are identified

Q9 Act upon advice and feedback and be open to coaching and mentoring.

2 Professional knowledge and understanding

Teaching and learning

Q10 Have a knowledge and understanding of a range of teaching, learning and behaviour management strategies and know how to use and adapt them, including how to personalise learning and provide opportunities for all learners to achieve their potential.

Assessment and monitoring

Q11 Know the assessment requirements and arrangements for the subjects/curriculum areas in the age ranges they are trained to teach, including those relating to public examinations and qualifications.

Q12 Know a range of approaches to assessment, including the importance of formative assessment.

Q13 Know how to use local and national statistical information to evaluate the effectiveness of their teaching, to monitor the progress of those they teach and to raise levels of attainment.

Subjects and Curriculum

Q14 Have a secure knowledge and understanding of their subjects/curriculum areas and related pedagogy to enable them to teach effectively across the age and ability range for which they are trained.

Q15 Know and understand the relevant statutory and non-statutory curricula, frameworks, including those provided through the National Strategies, for their subjects/curriculum areas, and other relevant initiatives applicable to the age and ability range for which they are trained.

Literacy, numeracy and ICT

Q16 Have passed the professional skills tests in numeracy, literacy and information and communication technology (ICT)

Q17 Know how to use skills in literacy, numeracy and ICT to support their teaching and wider professional activities.

Achievement and diversity

Q18 Understand how children and young people develop and that the progress and wellbeing of learners are affected by a range of developmental, social, religious, ethnic, cultural and linguistic influences.

Q19 Know how to make effective personalised provision for those they teach, including those for whom English is an additional language or who have special educational needs or disabilities, and how to take practical account of diversity and promote equality and inclusion in their teaching.

Q20 Know and understand the roles of colleagues with specific responsibilities, including those with responsibility for learners with special educational needs and disabilities and other individual learning needs.

Health and well-being

Q21 (a) Be aware of current legal requirements, national policies and guidance on the safeguarding and promotion of the well-being of children and young people.

   (b) Know how to identify and support children and young people whose progress, development or well-being is affected by changes or difficulties in their personal circumstances, and when to refer them to colleagues for specialist support.

3 Professional skills

Planning

Q22 Plan for progression across the age and ability range for which they are trained, designing effective learning sequences within lessons and across series of lessons and demonstrating secure subject/curriculum knowledge.

Q23 Design opportunities for learners to develop their literacy, numeracy and ICT skills.

Q24 Plan homework or other out-of-class work to sustain learners' progress and to extend and consolidate their learning.

Teaching

Q25 Teach lessons and sequences of lessons across the age and ability range for which they are trained in which they:
  - (a) use a range of teaching strategies and resources, including e-learning, taking practical account of diversity and promoting equality and inclusion;
  - (b) build on prior knowledge, develop concepts and processes, enable learners to apply new knowledge, understanding and skills and meet learning objectives;
  - (c) adapt their language to suit the learners they teach, introducing new ideas and concepts clearly, and using explanations, questions, discussions and plenaries effectively;
  - (d) manage the learning of individuals, groups and whole classes, modifying their teaching to suit the stage of the lesson.

Assessing, monitoring and giving feedback

Q26 (a) Make effective use of a range of assessment, monitoring and recording strategies.
  - (b) Assess the learning needs of those they teach in order to set challenging learning objectives.

Q27 Provide timely, accurate and constructive feedback on learners' attainment, progress and areas for development.

Q28 Support and guide learners to reflect on their learning, identify the progress they have made and identify their emerging learning needs.

Reviewing teaching and learning

Q29 Evaluate the impact of their teaching on the progress of all learners, and modify their planning and classroom practice where necessary.

Learning environment

Q30 Establish a purposeful and safe learning environment conducive to learning and identify opportunities for learners to learn in out of school contexts.

Q31 Establish a clear framework for classroom discipline to manage learners' behaviour constructively and promote their self-control and independence.

Team Working and Collaboration

Q32 Work as a team member and identify opportunities for working with colleagues, sharing the development of effective practice with them.

Q33 Ensure that colleagues working with them are appropriately involved in supporting learning and understand the roles they are expected to fulfil.

Chapters cross referenced to QTS Standards, where applicable.

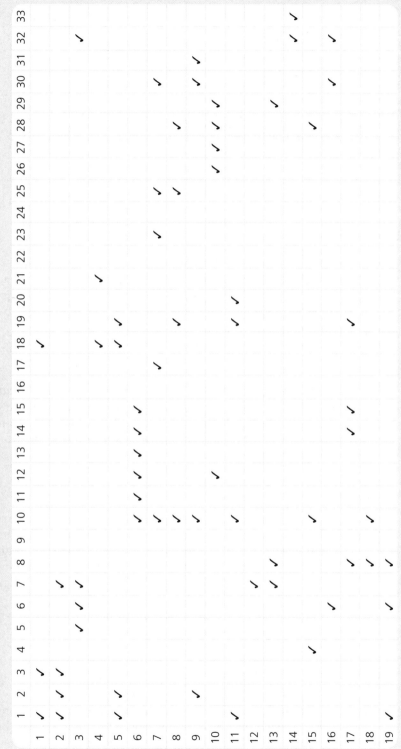

Teachers should meet the following core standards (C) at the end of the induction period and continue to meet them throughout their teaching career.

Professional attributes

Relationships with children and young people

C1. Have high expectations of children and young people including a commitment to ensuring that they can achieve their full educational potential and to establishing fair, respectful, trusting, supportive and constructive relationships with them.

C2. Hold positive values and attitudes and adopt high standards of behaviour in their professional role.

Frameworks

C3. Maintain an up-to-date knowledge and understanding of the professional duties of teachers and the statutory framework within which they work, and contribute to the development, implementation and evaluation of the policies and practice of their workplace, including those designed to promote equality of opportunity.

Communicating and working with others

C4. (a) Communicate effectively with children, young people and colleagues.
    (b) Communicate effectively with parents and carers, conveying timely and relevant information about attainment, objectives, progress and well-being.

C5. Recognise that communication is a two-way process and encourage parents and carers to participate in discussions about the progress, development and well-being of children and young people.

C6. Have a commitment to collaboration and co-operative working where appropriate.

Personal professional development

C7. Evaluate their performance and be committed to improving their practice through appropriate professional development.

C8. Have a creative and constructively critical approach towards innovation; being prepared to adapt their practice where benefits and improvements are identified.

C9. Act upon advice and feedback and be open to coaching and mentoring.

Professional knowledge and understanding

Teaching and learning

C10. Have a good, up-to-date working knowledge and understanding of a range of teaching, learning and behaviour management strategies and know how to use and adapt them, including how to personalise learning to provide opportunities for all learners to achieve their potential.

Assessment and monitoring

C11. Know the assessment requirements and arrangements for the subjects/curriculum areas they teach, including those relating to public examinations and qualifications.

C12. Know a range of approaches to assessment, including the importance of formative assessment.

C13. Know how to use local and national statistical information to evaluate the effectiveness of their teaching, to monitor the progress of those they teach and to raise levels of attainment.

C14. Know how to use reports and other sources of external information related to assessment in order to provide learners with accurate and constructive feedback on their strengths, weaknesses, attainment, progress and areas for development, including action plans for improvement.

Subjects and Curriculum

C15. Have a secure knowledge and understanding of their subjects/curriculum areas and related pedagogy including: the contribution that their subjects/curriculum areas can make to cross-curricular learning; and recent relevant developments.

C16. Know and understand the relevant statutory and non-statutory curricula and frameworks, including those provided through the National Strategies, for their subjects/curriculum areas and other relevant initiatives across the age and ability range they teach.

Literacy, numeracy and ICT

C17. Know how to use skills in literacy, numeracy and ICT to support their teaching and wider professional activities.

Achievement and diversity

C18. Understand how children and young people develop and how the progress, rate of development and well-being of learners are affected by a range of developmental, social, religious, ethnic, cultural and linguistic influences.

C19. Know how to make effective personalised provision for those they teach, including those for whom English is an additional language or who have special educational needs or disabilities, and how to take practical account of diversity and promote equality and inclusion in their teaching.

C20. Understand the roles of colleagues such as those having specific responsibilities for learners with special educational needs, disabilities and other individual learning needs, and the contributions they can make to the learning, development and well-being of children and young people.

C21. Know when to draw on the expertise of colleagues, such as those with responsibility for the safeguarding of children and young people and special educational needs and disabilities, and to refer to sources of information, advice and support from external agencies.

Health and well-being

C22. Know the current legal requirements, national policies and guidance on the safeguarding and promotion of the well-being of children and young people.

C23. Know the local arrangements concerning the safeguarding of children and young people.

C24. Know how to identify potential child abuse or neglect and follow safeguarding procedures.

C25. Know how to identify and support children and young people whose progress, development or well-being is affected by changes or difficulties in their personal circumstances, and when to refer them to colleagues for specialist support.

Professional skills

Planning

C26. Plan for progression across the age and ability range they teach, designing effective learning sequences within lessons and across series of lessons informed by secure subject/curriculum knowledge.

C27. Design opportunities for learners to develop their literacy, numeracy, ICT and thinking and learning skills appropriate within their phase and context.

C28. Plan, set and assess homework, other out-of-class assignments and coursework for examinations, where appropriate, to sustain learners' progress and to extend and consolidate their learning.

Teaching

C29. Teach challenging, well-organised lessons and sequences of lessons across the age and ability range they teach in which they:
(a) use an appropriate range of teaching strategies and resources, including e-learning, which meet learners' needs and take practical account of diversity and promote equality and inclusion
(b) build on the prior knowledge and attainment of those they teach in order that learners meet learning objectives and make sustained progress
(c) develop concepts and processes which enable learners to apply new knowledge, understanding and skills

(d) adapt their language to suit the learners they teach, introducing new ideas and concepts clearly, and using explanations, questions, discussions and plenaries effectively

(e) manage the learning of individuals, groups and whole classes effectively, modifying their teaching appropriately to suit the stage of the lesson and the needs of the learners.

C30. Teach engaging and motivating lessons informed by well-grounded expectations of learners and designed to raise levels of attainment.

Assessing, monitoring and giving feedback

C31. Make effective use of an appropriate range of observation, assessment, monitoring and recording strategies as a basis for setting challenging learning objectives and monitoring learners' progress and levels of attainment.

C32. Provide learners, colleagues, parents and carers with timely, accurate and constructive feedback on learners' attainment, progress and areas for development.

C33. Support and guide learners so that they can reflect on their learning, identify the progress they have made, set positive targets for improvement and become successful independent learners.

C34. Use assessment as part of their teaching to diagnose learners' needs, set realistic and challenging targets for improvement and plan future teaching.

Reviewing teaching and learning

C35. Review the effectiveness of their teaching and its impact on learners' progress, attainment and well-being, refining their approaches where necessary.

C36. Review the impact of the feedback provided to learners and guide learners on how to improve their attainment.

Learning environment

C37. (a) Establish a purposeful and safe learning environment which complies with current legal requirements, national policies and guidance on the safeguarding and well-being of children and young people so that learners feel secure and sufficiently confident to make an active contribution to learning and to the school.

(b) Make use of the local arrangements concerning the safeguarding of children and young people.

(c) Identify and use opportunities to personalise and extend learning through out-of-school contexts where possible making links between in-school learning and learning in out-of-school contexts.

C38. (a) Manage learners' behaviour constructively by establishing and maintaining a clear and positive framework for discipline, in line with the school's behaviour policy.

(b) Use a range of behaviour management techniques and strategies, adapting them as necessary to promote the self-control and independence of learners.

C39. Promote learners' self-control, independence and cooperation through developing their social, emotional and behavioural skills.

Team Working and Collaboration

C40. Work as a team member and identify opportunities for working with colleagues, managing their work where appropriate and sharing the development of effective practice with them.

C41. Ensure that colleagues working with them are appropriately involved in supporting learning and understand the roles they are expected to fulfil.

Chapters cross referenced to Core Professional Standards, where applicable.

Some Standards have been clustered, for ease of reference.

	1	2	3	4–6	7	8–9	10	11–14	15–16	17	18	19–21	22–28	29–30	31–34	35–36	37	38	39	40–41
1	✓		✓								✓									
2		✓	✓																	
3				✓	✓											✓	✓			✓
4										✓	✓									
5	✓	✓								✓	✓									
6								✓	✓											
7							✓		✓	✓			✓	✓			✓			
8							✓						✓		✓	✓				
9		✓					✓										✓	✓	✓	
10								✓							✓	✓				
11	✓						✓						✓		✓					
12				✓																
13					✓	✓											✓			
14																				✓
15						✓		✓							✓					
16									✓		✓						✓			
17					✓				✓	✓			✓							
18					✓	✓														
19	✓			✓	✓															

Index

Page numbers in bold refer to entries in the Glossaries